MULTNOMAH

Multnomah

THE TUMULTUOUS STORY OF
OREGON'S MOST POPULOUS COUNTY

Jewel Lansing & Fred Leeson

Oregon State University Press   Corvallis

ABOUT THE COVER:
All photos on the cover are duplicated in the text with explanatory captions and credits

The paper in this book meets the guidelines for permanence and durability of the
Committee on Production Guidelines for Book Longevity of the Council on Library
Resources and the minimum requirements of the American National Standard for
Permanence of Paper for Printed Library Materials Z39.48-1984.

Library of Congress Cataloging-in-Publication Data

Lansing, Jewel Beck.
    Multnomah : the tumultuous story of Oregon's most populous county / Jewel
Lansing and Fred Leeson.
      p. cm.
    Includes bibliographical references and index.
    ISBN 978-0-87071-665-2 (pbk. : alk. paper) — ISBN 978-0-87071-666-9 (e-book)
    1. Multnomah County (Or.)—History, Local. I. Leeson, Fred. II. Title.
F882.M9L36 2012
979.5'49--dc23
                                          2011052976

Oregon State University Press
121 The Valley Library
Corvallis OR 97331-4501
541-737-3166 • fax 541-737-3170
http://osupress.oregonstate.edu

CONTENTS

Preface vii

Acknowledgments ix

1 The Most Important Vote of the Century *(February 21, 1974)* 1

2 In the Beginning . . . *(1792–1854)* 9

3 The County's First Hanging; Early Elected Officials *(1855–1869)* 18

4 A Magnificent Courthouse, a Pauper Farm, and a Push for
   Consolidation *(1864–1880)* 25

5 Coxey's Army and Eight More Hangings *(1888–1903)* 33

6 The Progressive Era, a Crusading Sheriff, and the County Fair
   Begins *(1902–1914)* 42

7 D-Minus Report Card, the "King of Roads," and a New
   Courthouse *(1913–1922)* 54

8 County Hospital, the KKK, Kickback Scandals, and More
   Consolidation Proposals *(1909–1927)* 69

9 An Elegant Bridge, a Mighty Dam, Another Jail,
   and World War II *(1928-1945)* 81

10 Vanport Is Flooded, a Sheriff Is Recalled, and Sheriff Schrunk
   Is Put on Trial *(1946–1956)* 93

11 Parks, Roads, and Three Unrelated Tragedies *(1946–1960)* 103

12 Commissioners Feud, Delta Dome Is Rejected, and the First
   Woman Deputy Is Hired *(1962–1966)* 115

13 Home Rule Arrives, a Sheriff Is Fired, and Rocky Butte
   Prisoners Escape *(1966–1973)* 127

14 Freeways Revisited, City-County Consolidation Fails *(1970–1974)*. . . 136

15 The Don Clark Era, Charter Upended, Nursing Home Closed,
   Metro Created *(1975–1979)* 149

16 Employees Strike, PERS, Vote-by-Mail, and Rocky Butte Jail
   Closes *(1980–1982)* 161

17 The Laudable "Resolution A," City of Columbia Ridge Is
   Rejected, a Power Struggle at the Library, and More Charter
   Changes *(1983–1990)*...................................... 177

18 East County Discontent, the First All-Woman Board,
   and "Willamette County" *(1983–1990)*...................... 191

19 The Infamous Measure 5, Columbia Gorge Battles, and
   East County Efforts to Secede *(1990–2001)*.................. 208

20 From Pioneering Women to "Mean Girls," Plus a
   Controversial Sheriff *(2001–2009)*.......................... 221

21 Quo Vadis? *(2010)* 234

   APPENDIXES

A Multnomah County Timeline 245

B A Brief Property Tax Primer 250

C History of Multnomah County Home Rule Charter Changes....... 254

D Elected Multnomah County Officials: A Chronological List........ 263

E Elected Multnomah County Officials: An Alphabetical List........ 270

   Notes... 281

   Bibliography 309

   Index... 313

PREFACE

Multnomah covers the first 156 years of Multnomah County's existence and is the first such history ever written. The book is in many ways a companion volume to Jewel Lansing's *Portland: People, Politics, and Power, 1851-2001*, published in 2003, and to Fred Leeson's *Rose City Justice*, published in 1998. The research for both those books provided valuable background for our present work.

As Oregon's smallest county in geographic size and largest in population, Multnomah County has always faced problems related to an urban-rural divide in its relationship to the rest of the state, to the unincorporated portion of Multnomah County, and to the cities within its boundaries, especially Portland. Physically, the county stretches along fifty riverfront miles on the south bank of the Columbia River, from nearly sea level at Sauvie Island to towering mountaintops in the Columbia Gorge. The wide disparity between those elevations has been reflected in the political and financial fortunes of Multnomah County government, which, although it is often invisible, has attracted a goodly amount of public criticism along the way.

Public works projects have appeared on county commission agendas regularly throughout the past 160 years. Ranging from a network of roads and bridges in the county to the majestic Justice Center in downtown Portland, these undertakings have included the building of two courthouses; the Burnside, Sellwood, Ross Island, St. Johns, and Morrison bridges; the Inverness Jail; the oft-reviled Rocky Butte Jail; the old Multnomah County Corrections Facility, which was cutting-edge in its day; the Donald E. Long Juvenile Home; the Multnomah County Hospital (now a part of Oregon Health and Science University); Edgefield Manor; the Yeon Maintenance Shops; the magnificent Central Library in downtown Portland and eighteen neighborhood libraries; remodeling of the Multnomah County Building; the completed-but-not-yet-opened Wapato Jail; and construction of the west end of the incomparable Columbia River Highway.

A few words of caution about the book's contents: This book is primarily a political history of Multnomah County, not a comprehensive social one. Readers expecting to learn about Multnomah County jurisprudence or district attorney actions will find only brief mentions here. The Oregon judicial system and its elected officials are governed by state law and the Oregon Supreme Court, rather than by county charter. Judges and district attorneys are included in the text only when their activities overlap with other county government history. Additionally, a number of important county functions are touched on only lightly—aging services, animal control, assessments, bridges, probation and parole, juvenile justice, other social and health programs. All are worthy of further research.

The reader should also be aware that author Jewel Lansing served for eight years, from 1975 through 1982, as the elected Multnomah County auditor, and for four years, from 1983 through 1986, as the City of Portland auditor. In both those jurisdictions, she introduced performance auditing to help make government more efficient and accountable to its citizens.

For thirty-five years, author Fred Leeson was a reporter for Oregon's leading daily newspapers—at the former *Oregon Journal* from 1972 to 1982, and at the *Oregonian* from 1982 until his retirement in 2007—where he frequently covered local government issues. He currently teaches journalism at Concordia University in Portland.

As President Harry Truman famously said: "The only thing new in this world is the history that we don't know." We wrote this book to help fill that gap and to offer lessons for the future.

ACKNOWLEDGMENTS

This book would not be possible without the shared memories and documentation received from present and former county officials and staff. The result has been a collaborative effort, aided by dozens of present and former Multnomah County, City of Portland, and Metro employees as well as by private citizens who have followed the county's fortunes over the years.

Thanks to Gary Blackmer, Dick Feeney, Cay Kershner, Ken Upton, JoAnne Nordling, Dave Boyer, Kris Hudson, and Carolyn Kelly for reading and making suggestions regarding drafts of various portions of the book. Special thanks also to Terry Baxter, county archivist; Tom Linhares, Tax Supervision and Conservation Commission director; Steve Wright, sheriff's office "historian"; Agnes Sowle, former county counsel; Fred Neal, attorney; and Caroline Miller, former commissioner and organizer of a Multnomah County "old-timers" group that provided both moral support and valuable information. Annette Lansing managed the photographs and other images in this book, including the development of custom-designed Multnomah County maps.

Interviews conducted in the late 1990s and early 2000s by the former Portland Planning Director Ernie Bonner, who died in 2004, were helpful in gaining overall perspective regarding planning, development, and transportation issues of the 1970s. Bonner's completed interviews are now archived at the Portland State University library.

Much of the information about previous sheriffs came from the history room of the Multnomah County Sheriff's Office in the Hansen Building at Northeast 122nd and Glisan. Author Lansing visited there many times to pore over its treasure-trove of newspaper scrapbooks. *Oregonian* and *Oregon Journal* archives were especially helpful to author Leeson, who gained thorough familiarity with accessing old records over the many years he worked as a reporter for those daily newspapers.

Many people responded to queries and offered suggestions. Their input was invaluable. Such contacts included Ed Abrahamson, Rai Adgers, Tommy Albo, Lloyd Anderson, Pauline Anderson, Sally Anderson, Lori Arnett, Nathan Baker,

Bob Baldwin, Helen Barney, Earl Blumenauer, Deb Bogstad, Eileen Brady, Dennis Buchanan, MaryAnn Buchanan, Steve Buel, Kathy Busse, Doug Butler, Naomi Butler, Laurel Butman, Mark Campbell, Kenneth Carter, Mary Anne Cassin, Ron Cease, Don Clark, Shirley Clark, Arnold Cogan, Elaine Cogan, Tanya Collier, Easton Cross, Evie Crowell, Shawn Cunningham, Rena Cusma, Eloise Damrosch, Jim Desmond, Joe Devlaeminck, Clyde Doctor, Danny Dorand, Ralph Drewfs, Denise Duncan, Dan Ellis, Richard Engeman, Bill Failing, Delma Farrell, Bill Farver, Anne Kelly Feeney, Mary Fellows, Suzanne Flynn, Wayne George, LaVonne Griffin-Valade, Ross Hall, Jill Hanousek, Mindy Harris, Richard Harris, Mary Lou Hennrich, Tom Higgins, Larry Hilderbrand, Jack Hoffman, Brett Horner, Robert Hovden, Mike Howlett, Laurie Jack, Linda Jefferson, Deborah Kafoury, Gretchen Kafoury, Drummond Kahn, Pete Kasting, Sharron Kelley, Steve Kenney, Heather Kent, Carol Kinoshita, Carol Kirchner, Kevin Kitamura, Pam Knowles, Bud Kramer, Helen Lessick, Dick Levy, Diane Linn, Nichole Maher, Charles Merten, Hank Miggins, Norm Monroe, Sarah Mooney, Mark Moore, Sandi Hobbs Morey, Connie Morgan, Kathy Myers, Lisa Naito, Terry Naito, Julie Neburka, Billi Odegaard, Meghan Oldfield, Chet Orloff, Sharon Owen, Viki Ervin Paulk, Chris Payne, Karen Peterson, Dick Piland, Mike Pullen, Bill Radakovich, Ike Regenstreif, Capt. Monte Reiser, Barbara Roberts, Betty Roberts, Don Rocks, Eric Sample, Rhys Scholes, Mike Schrunk, Ethan Seltzer, Steve Shatter, Tom Sponsler, Jeanne Staehli, Barbara Stalions, Phil Stanford, Bev Stein, Becky Steward, Scott Stewart, Jim Strathman, Theresa Sullivan, Arthur Sulzberger, John Terry, Andy Thaler, John Thorpe, Rick Till, Felicia Trader, Dave Tyler, Bill Vandever, Dan Vizzini, Kathleen "Kip" Wadden, Dwight Wallace, Kateri Walsh, Dave Warren, Ted Wheeler, Gina Whitehill-Baziuk, Barbara Willer, Tuck Wilson, and Jeff Wohler.

We wish to acknowledge the able help of copy editor Steve Connell, cover designer David Drummond, and the entire OSU Press staff, especially Jo Alexander, Tom Booth, Mary Elizabeth Braun, and Micki Reaman, all of whom were a pleasure to work with.

Special thanks, also, to our spouses, Ron Lansing and Barbara Coleman, for their advice and support.

Our heartfelt thanks to all.

Jewel Lansing
Fred Leeson
Portland, Oregon, 2012

1
THE MOST IMPORTANT VOTE OF THE CENTURY
(February 21, 1974)

When four of the five Multnomah County commissioners strode into their sixth-floor Courthouse boardroom shortly after 9:30 a.m. on a winter morning in 1974, three of them knew they would soon be making front-page news. The matter before them was a land-use planning decision that had the potential to change the face of the region's highway system and initiate a new era of public transit that would ride on steel rails. As a result, the decision also was likely to change land-use patterns for residential neighborhoods and shopping malls across the eastern portion of the Portland region. For a local government that historically had been slow to provide amenities such as paved streets, sidewalks, sewers, water, parks, and fire protection to its growing population, the consequences of erasing a freeway from the region's planning maps and replacing it with an urban-oriented light rail transit system was a bold stroke indeed.

The drama of the morning was intensified by the fact that many citizens and public officials—including some county commissioners themselves—were questioning whether the Portland area even needed a county government anymore. These questions had been raised many times by business and government leaders since the founding of Multnomah County in 1854. Why have two local governments serving Portland, if one—presumably the City of Portland—could handle all matters by itself? Wouldn't a single government save taxpayers money by eliminating duplication? A special City-County Charter Commission had spent months studying these issues and had submitted a proposal to voters for a new, single government for Portland and Multnomah County. Voters would decide in May, just a few months later, whether to adopt the proposed new structure, which proponents said would cut costs and streamline local agencies.

The fact that in February 1974 the county board of commissioners stood willing to take a leading role in a public issue of deep consequence reflected a significant change in the often-sleepy county government. The decision would be made by an unusual triumvirate on the five-member board that already had wrested control of the county government from its aging chairman, M. James ("Mike") Gleason. Gleason had sat on the county board for longer than anyone in county history, but he was suffering serious health problems and didn't show up for the February 21 hearing when the Multnomah County Commission was in the process of transitioning from one political era to the next.[1]

The roll call that morning showed three commissioners—Don Clark, Mel Gordon, and Ben Padrow—in favor of rescinding the county's 1969 vote to construct a stretch of urban freeway between the Marquam Bridge in downtown Portland and Interstate 205, another new freeway that was already under construction five miles to the east, just outside the city's eastern boundary along 82nd Avenue. Commissioner Dan Mosee (pronounced Mo-ZAY) voted against the motion to rescind. Known commonly as the Mt. Hood Freeway, the planned Southeast Portland freeway would have run along the Powell Boulevard corridor. Fittingly, perhaps, Powell was one of the first county roads built when the young new county—Multnomah—was created 120 years earlier in 1854.

Portland had grown into a major West Coast city during the streetcar era from the 1890s to World War II, with early "suburban" yet dense neighborhoods such as Irvington, Northwest Portland, Laurelhurst, and Sellwood developing along urban streetcar lines and around clusters of neighborhood business districts. But growth in Multnomah County's political turf east of the East 82nd Avenue boundary came after the automobile had become the primary mode of transportation.

The mostly flat, developable land between East 82nd Avenue and the City of Gresham, often referred to as Mid-County, had grown quickly after World War II as a hodgepodge of commercial strips along major roads. Housing ranged from inexpensive small cottages to a few higher-income, mid-century suburban enclaves. Gleason, whose tenure on the board began in 1948, had succeeded as a road-builder, adding several major thoroughfares during his career. But city-type amenities were largely lacking. Water and fire protection were supplied by single-purpose districts managed by independently elected boards of directors.

Ambivalence about Multnomah County's future as an urban center dated back to the county's earliest days. Some pioneers hoped to establish a major American city, while others came primarily to take advantage of top-quality free land for farming. As a result, by the late twentieth century, when most of the unincorporated territory was finally annexed into the City of Portland, more

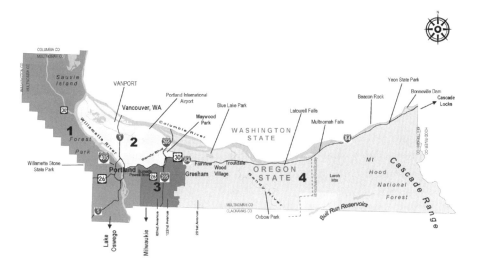

Multnomah County, 2010. shaded areas indicate the four county commission districts.

than 100,000 Mid-County residents faced health risks from septic tanks, unsafe pedestrian routes, poor street maintenance, and underdeveloped parks.[2]

From the time of its creation in 1854, Multnomah County has been dominated by Portland. That early dominance has led to complicated and sometimes strained relationships ever since. At the same time, Portland's presence created challenges unique to Multnomah County. Having a metropolitan city within its boundaries gave Multnomah the opportunity to serve as a transformational force locally, statewide, and sometimes even nationally.

"The County is one of the least understood of all areas of government," said a handbook published by the Multnomah County commissioners in 1961. Its lack of visibility is still an issue today, partly because Multnomah County government has no one central location—like city hall or the state capitol—with which to identify. The county courthouse belongs to judges and their courtrooms. Libraries are spread throughout the county. Most residents could not tell you where the county commissioners meet.

Throughout history, the functions of government have reflected societal attitudes about what government could and should do. For example, Multnomah County no longer hangs people, raids gambling houses, sponsors a county fair, provides hospital care, or runs an "old folks home." Nationwide initiatives that at one time seemed progressive and right-minded, such as building interstate highways to replace twisting roads and erecting dams to bring electricity to rural

America, later came to be regarded less favorably by subsequent generations of progressive citizens.

Major challenges to be faced by Multnomah County in the future—in addition to growth, planning, and zoning (or lack thereof)—would include responsibilities assigned to counties by the state constitution and state legislature (such as laws that pertain only to counties over 100,000 population), changes in county legal structure, relationships with other Oregon counties, relationships with Multnomah County cities, recurring jail-related challenges, and financial constraints imposed by diminished federal support and restrictive property tax measures. From the county's earliest days, caring for the indigent was a responsibility that would continually come to the forefront, though it usually went unnoticed by the public. The county would often play the role of "provider of last resort" with regard to health and social services.

The 1974 vote rescinding the county's support for the Mt. Hood Freeway indicated a dramatic new approach to thinking about the county's physical future. Momentum to scratch the freeway off a map of proposed regional freeways began in late 1973, when Oregon local governments learned about new federal legislation that would allow a region to "trade in" federal freeway construction dollars for public transit projects. In order for that to happen in the Portland metro area, there would have to be agreement to such a transfer between Portland, Multnomah County, and state highway officials. It would take another twelve years, and a seemingly endless succession of reports, studies, and public hearings, before the original freeway-funding transfer concept evolved into the opening of TriMet's MAX Blue Line, a light rail transit route between downtown Portland and Gresham.

As the years passed, the death of the Mt. Hood Freeway and construction of the light rail line became a key element in what was considered a praiseworthy six-year period as Portland's mayor for the young and forceful Neil Goldschmidt—long before revelations of sexual abuse of a teenager destroyed his reputation. It was the lesser-known Multnomah County government, however, powered by bright young assistants and the elected triumvirate of Don Clark, Mel Gordon, and Ben Padrow, that took the lead on the freeway issue. When the county took its vote in February 1974, the young mayor was struggling to find a third vote on the five-member city council to reach the same decision. Goldschmidt himself had not chosen a preferred transit option, and apparently had doubts that TriMet, the region's transit agency, had the managerial skill to build a major transit rail line.[3] It would take another six months of intense study and lobbying before the city council fell in line with the county's decision on the Mt. Hood Freeway.[4]

By early 1974, that suspense was missing at the county courthouse. The five-man commission revealed a clear three-to-two split. Mike Gleason and the fifth commissioner, Dan Mosee, reflected an older, laissez-faire approach to planning and government philosophy. It was apparent before the freeway vote that Mosee and Gleason would lose, even if Gleason had been present. Mosee was a populist who had built personal wealth as a successful used-appliance dealer and the owner of numerous run-down but low-rent houses in east county. Despite being a proven vote-getter at the polls, Mosee had few constructive results to show for his public service. That February morning, he demanded a public vote on the freeway, and he subsequently helped collect signatures in an attempt to put it on the ballot—a bid that was ultimately stymied in the courts.

If the county board's vote that day was not surprising, one of the motivating forces behind it surely was. Mel Gordon was a former auto battery and tire salesman, who served one term in the Oregon House of Representatives before being elected to the county commission in 1962 as a Republican. He pledged to bring more modern business practices to the county, where whispers—and occasionally louder claims—of cronyism sometimes arose. County government was a different creature when Gordon first arrived: the board then comprised only three members, and their powers were largely set by state laws, not their own legislative authority. Like Gleason, Gordon was a holdover from the period before the 1966 election, which established Multnomah County as a home-rule county, boosted the board's size to five members, and enhanced the county's legislative powers.

A decade after his first election, Gordon changed his registration to Democrat. The switch was motivated perhaps less by political philosophy than by a substantial Democratic edge in county-wide voter registrations. "Mel Gordon learned how to count," one Portland city council member said at the time.[5] Surprisingly perhaps, when Gordon resurfaced two decades later as a successful county government candidate in Clark County, Washington, he did so as a Republican.[6]

More significantly, Gordon, the businessman Republican turned Democrat, had begun to consider himself an environmentalist by 1974. He started showing interest in water quality and solid waste issues, for example. Portland's once-extensive private streetcar system had faded and died after World War II, but Gordon, with the help of Commissioner Don Clark and David Hupp, a young county assistant,[7] had seen how electric-powered transit was evolving in Europe into a system using bigger, faster trains known as light rail. With Clark prodding him in the background,[8] Gordon became one of the first to speak publicly about light rail as a possibility when Congress opened the door to trading highway funding for transit projects. With Clark and Ben Padrow, Gordon was the third vote for rejecting the Mt. Hood Freeway.

Since Padrow's arrival in 1971, the three commissioners had voted together on numerous matters, leaving Gleason and Mosee in the minority. Gleason was ostensibly the most powerful figure in the county, since the home rule charter gave him 100 percent of administrative authority as well as one of five votes as a legislator. But Gleason had been slowed since a heart attack in 1972,[9] and Clark had already announced plans to run for the chairman's seat in 1974—whether Gleason decided to run again or not. In the final months of Gleason's long tenure, the chairman appeared less often at the courthouse and had little voice in major decisions.

Clark, the heir apparent, was a former elected Multnomah County sheriff who had earned national attention in the mid-1960s by making college degrees mandatory for new deputy sheriffs. He had tried to win the top post in county government when voters approved a sweeping new home rule charter in 1966, but was beaten decisively by the veteran Gleason, who was then in better health and outmaneuvered Clark by winning major endorsements. Since the new charter eliminated an elected sheriff, Clark, then out of public office, taught as an adjunct in the urban studies program at Portland State University. Current ideas about land-use issues that he was exposed to at PSU reinforced his own ideas about urban freeways, which he'd experienced during a brief tenure as a prison guard in Southern California.[10] After winning a county commission seat in 1968, and later when he had succeeded Gleason as county chairman, Clark proved to be optimistic, intellectually curious, and gregarious by nature—and willing to swim against public opinion when he felt it was necessary.

Fifteen months before the final Mt. Hood Freeway vote, Clark had proposed and won support for a moratorium on buying up property for the Mt. Hood right-of-way.[11] State highway officials had planned to buy some 1,500 houses and 180 businesses to make way for the new highway. The moratorium was one signal that the freeway was not yet a done deal. But although retail gasoline prices in the county had almost tripled, to $1 per gallon, during the 1973 OPEC embargo, support for the new freeway remained high. A newspaper poll suggested that voters still favored the freeway by a 2 to 1 ratio.[12]

Padrow, the third member of the triumvirate, had been a speech professor at Portland State University. He first achieved widespread local acclaim in the mid-1960s as the coach of a Portland State College (as it was then known) team of students that retired undefeated after five victories in a national television quiz show called *College Bowl*. Many Portlanders sat transfixed in front of their black-and-white television sets as the young scholars from the little-known Portland institution brought glory to themselves and to their school—and to their coach, who made a brief bow and wave during each show. He then became master of ceremonies for *High-Q*, a local TV show featuring Portland-area high school students that followed a similar format. Padrow, who had been a speaking coach and backroom strategist on other politicians' campaigns, including Republican Bob Packwood's surprising 1968 U.S. Senate victory over Wayne Morse,[13] went out front himself in 1970 to win a seat on the Multnomah County Commission.

Short and stocky, with a lush head of hair, Padrow was sometimes an enigmatic commissioner. He could speak with elegance at any moment, but often chose to remain silent at unexpected times. He tried to humor Mosee but had little patience for his lack of intellectual depth. Padrow and Clark were good political friends before Padrow's election, so his voting pattern with Clark and Gordon came as no surprise. Just weeks before the freeway vote, Padrow had announced that he would not seek a second term on the county commission. He decided to return to Portland State University so that he would not lose vesting rights in his university pension.[14]

Meanwhile, Padrow was campaigning for a measure on the May 1974 ballot that called for the consolidation of the City of Portland and Multnomah County into a single local government. Consolidation was an idea that had been floated several times dating back to the earliest years of the county, but it had never seemed to generate political traction. Now a lengthy and detailed proposal by a public City-County Charter Commission was heading for a public vote. Padrow predicted a 55 percent vote in favor of consolidation.[15] He would be in for a surprise.

This was the context for the morning of February 21, 1974. The county commission was ready to reverse its long-standing attitude that roads and highways dictated land-use planning; an older generation of leadership was giving way to the next; and voters were about to decide whether, after 120 years, Multnomah County government should continue in its present form. Mel Gordon's resolution to rescind support for the Mt. Hood Freeway passed quickly, and Dan Mosee's motion to place that freeway decision on the ballot died without a second. The meeting finished in time for a significant account to make the front page of the *Oregon Journal*'s afternoon edition.[16] Still, the county government's deliberations were always of far less importance to local news outlets than those of the Portland City Council. On the morning of February 22, the *Oregonian* devoted only a few sentences to the county's decision. President Nixon's problems with the Watergate scandal were beginning to dominate the front pages.[17]

Public debate over whether the Mt. Hood Freeway should be built continued to be a major political issue in the Portland area for several more years—so much so that it was easy to forget that in this case, unlike so many others in the past and future, Multnomah County took the lead.

The dominance of the automobile had now been reduced with the adoption of a more balanced transit system that included light rail. This victory by neighborhood activists on freeway votes helped convince county and city planners of the value of protecting central city neighborhoods from the ravages of auto traffic and vehicular air pollution. The trend to preserve these vital neighborhoods continues unabated today.

2
IN THE BEGINNING . . .
(1792–1854)

The first Europeans to arrive on terrain that would later become Multnomah County had little immediate impact. Lt. William Broughton, a member of Capt. George Vancouver's naval expedition from Great Britain, was the first to touch down, in November 1792, on what later would be called Sauvie Island. Broughton engaged in peaceful trading with Native Americans on the island and quickly moved on. Arriving from the opposite direction, the expedition commissioned by President Thomas Jefferson and led by Meriwether Lewis and William Clark camped just across the Columbia River from the island on November 5, 1805. It was not a pleasant experience for Clark. "I [s]lept but verry little last night for the noise Kept [up] dureing the whole of the night by the Swans, Geese, white and & Grey Brant Ducks &c. on a Small Sand Island . . . . they were emensely noumerous, and their noise horid," he wrote in his journal.[1]

After wintering at Fort Clatsop near Astoria, Lewis and Clark's expedition passed by Sauvie Island again in late March 1806. Some members of the expedition ventured six miles upstream and hunted briefly below a bluff over the Willamette River. While their stay was brief, Lewis and Clark left behind one lasting memorial, the name "Multnomah." Lewis and Clark used the names "Mulknomans" and "Wapatos" for the Indians living in several villages on the large island at the juncture of the Willamette and Columbia rivers. They called the island Wapato, a reference to an edible bulb, the "Indian potato," that grows there.[2] Wapato Island—a 26,000-acre lowland—is today known as Sauvie Island (named for French-Canadian dairy farmer Laurent Sauvé, a Hudson's Bay employee who settled on the west side of the island in the early 1840s).[3]

Lewis and Clark estimated that eight hundred Multnomahs lived on Wapato Island. The tribe was part of the Lower Chinookan linguistic family, whose campsites occupied both sides of the Columbia from what is now The Dalles to the Pacific Ocean and along the Willamette River below the falls. The name

"Multnomah" was probably derived from the Indian word "nemathlonamaq," meaning downriver from the falls (at Oregon City).

The Multnomahs lived in cedar plank longhouses and lived by fishing and foraging for berries, the plentiful wapato, and other native plants. Native Americans had lived, hunted, and fished the Pacific Northwest for thousands of years before white settlers arrived but left little behind to mark their presence. Other tribes that occupied the 465-square-mile area that would later become Multnomah County included the Kalapuya, Clackamas, and Clowewalla.[4]

One Native American who befriended Lewis and Clark was known as Indian Chief John; he lived not on the island but near the mouth of the Sandy River. At that time, Broughton Bluff near Troutdale extended far out toward the Columbia River, with a deep overhang of rock. Chief John's tribe of fifty to sixty frequently took shelter there. One day when he and his bride were on a fishing trip up the Sandy River, a huge storm came up. When they returned home, they found the wind and rain had caused the bluff to collapse, wiping out everyone else in their tribe. In his last years, Chief John lived at the Multnomah County Poor Farm on the site of today's Washington Park Zoo. He was buried in a pauper's grave when he died in 1903 at the estimated age of 120.[5] Today's Indian John Island in the Sandy River is named in Chief John's honor. Under provisions of the National Wild and Scenic Rivers Act passed by Congress in October 1968, Multnomah County and the Department of Interior purchased Indian John Island in 1970.[6]

Relationships between Columbia River Indians and area pioneers were for the most part peaceful. The clearing along the Willamette River that later became Portland was a favorite stopping place for Indian canoes long before the first settler's log cabin appeared there.

Diseases introduced by early explorers and settlers decimated much of the Indian population, further erasing any impact they might have left on the land. The Native American population of Wapato Island and other nearby tribes had been virtually eradicated by malaria, smallpox, and the "cold sick" epidemics of 1829-44.[7] Merchant Nathaniel Wyeth described the high Indian death rate this way: "(A) mortality has carried off to a man (the island's) inhabitants and there is nothing to attest that they ever existed except their decaying houses, their graves and their unburied bones, of which they are in heaps."[8]

Though the original indigenous tribes of Multnomah County did not survive, the county and its largest city much later became magnets for Native Americans. Today, Native Americans are Multnomah County's hidden minority.

The Portland metropolitan area is home to the ninth-largest American Indian/ Alaska Native community in the United States.

In 1930, Native Americans comprised less than 0.5 percent of the 338,241 Multnomah County residents. By 2000, the total county population had merely doubled, while the number of reported Native Americans had increased eight hundred-fold—from 174 to 14,701.[9] The combined Native American and Alaska Native population of Multnomah County comprised 2.2 percent of the county's total population, more than twice the national average of 0.9 percent.[10] Data published by the Native American Youth and Family Center (NAYA) in 2009 suggested that Native Americans represented 28 percent of the homeless youth in Multnomah County but received less than 2 percent of government services.[11]

What brought so many Native Americans to Multnomah County? The federal Termination Act of 1954, the Relocation Act of 1956 (PL959), and federal Indian policies of the 1960s were all responsible. Against their will, Native Americans were forced to relocate by federal actions intended to assimilate American Indians into mainstream urban culture. Job training centers established in urban areas stipulated that participants could not return to their reservations. Even though Congress later reversed these policies by means of the Indian Self-Determination and Education Assistance Act of 1975, by then thousands of Native Americans had already moved to big cities, of which Portland was one.[12] Contrary to commonly held perceptions, far more Native Americans now live in Multnomah County than on any single Oregon reservation. In 2000, compared to Multnomah County's figure of 14,701, the Grand Ronde Tribes had the largest Oregon Native American reservation population with roughly 5,000 members.[13]

Back in the earliest days of white settlement, the impetus for the formation of an Oregon Provisional Government in 1843 was provided by disputes over how to divide up the property of those who had died. Counties harkened back to the shires of Anglo-Saxon England as the basic units of local government, so it was natural that the early settlers in the Oregon Country would pattern their government after organizational structures already used elsewhere in the United States. Counties were created to ensure that services were provided to all residents of a state, whether or not they lived in a city. The four original Oregon Country counties—Clackamas, Yamhill, Tuality (later Washington), and Champoeg (later Marion)—conducted state and national elections, assessed and collected taxes, built roads and bridges, tried court cases, enforced laws, recorded documents, and provided care for paupers, the infirm, and the insane. They functioned under provisional laws from 1843 until 1848, when Congress created the Oregon

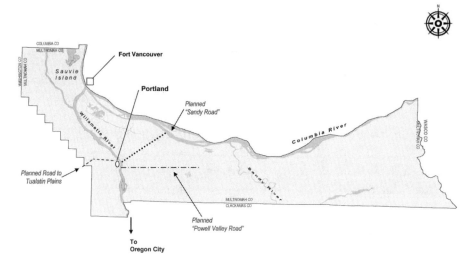

Multnomah County, Oregon Country, 1855. Oregon was not yet a state when Multnomah County was founded in December 1854. County Commissioners met quarterly to authorize new roads and ferries, levy property taxes (to be collected by the sheriff), provide courtroom space, and approve bills for payment.

Territory. This act brought land that would later become Multnomah County under United States law for the first time.

As settlers poured into the new region, drawn by reports of fertile earth, gentle weather, and free land, many came looking only for opportunities to farm. But others sensed that a major city would develop somewhere, bringing with it opportunities for land speculation and wealth. One early newcomer, Peter Burnett, thought it would be Linnton, a town site a few miles north of Portland which he named and tried to promote in 1845. Alas, steep terrain made access to the agriculture markets of Tuality County from Linnton difficult. Another early promoter, William W. Chapman, poked a pole to measure the Willamette River at various locations to determine accessible depths for sailing vessels. He bought a portion of a town site in 1849 and placed his bet on Portland. Others gambled on locations such as present-day St. Johns and West Linn.

The opinion of respected sea captain John Couch, articulated in 1840, was most influential in making Portland—the clearing on the Willamette River and its deep harbor—the winner of the competition: "To this point I can bring any ship that can get into the mouth of the Great Columbia River."[14] In December 1851, the Oregon Territorial Legislature approved a charter for the nascent city of Portland.[15]

The village soon surpassed Oregon City as the major settlement in the territory. Portland streets were bustling with lumberjacks, sailors, gold-seekers, and ambitious merchants by the time the Oregon Territorial Legislature bowed to the entreaties of Portland businessmen in 1854 and created a new county, with Portland as its county seat. Portlanders had complained that the day-long journey by horseback or wagon to the Washington County seat of Hillsboro was excessive. Approximately two thousand Portlanders lived west of the Willamette River, with another one thousand on the east side.

By 1854, new residents were arriving by ship and wagon train nearly every day. Oceangoing ships were bringing goods from all over the world to Portland, where cargo was being exchanged for sawdust, lumber, and farmers' produce from the fertile Tualatin Valley.

The editor of Portland's vocal weekly *Oregonian* newspaper (Thomas Dryer, a Whig) vigorously opposed the creation of a new county.[16] He argued that it would increase Democratic Party strength in the legislature (which it did, at least temporarily), because Washington County was one of the few jurisdictions in the territory that favored Whigs. "The sole purpose for a new county is to create more jobs for Democrats," Dryer fumed.[17] (At the time, Portland was in Washington County, which included parts of today's Multnomah, Columbia, and Clackamas counties. Washington County provided half the territorial votes against moving toward statehood.)[18]

In spite of Dryer's spirited protests, the territorial legislature created Multnomah County on December 22, 1854. *Oregonian* headlines blared "The Iniquity Fully Consummated" and "Destructionists Triumphant." Some four years later, on February 14, 1859, Oregon would become the thirty-third state in the Union.[19]

While Oregon and thirty other states were to honor George Washington by naming a county after him, and twenty-seven states, including Oregon, laid claim to a Jefferson County, only one county in the nation came into being with the name Multnomah. Multnomah County's 465 square miles covered an area roughly ten miles wide and fifty miles long, with the Columbia River as its northern boundary, its odd shape dictated by the gentle curve made by the Columbia on its way to the Pacific Ocean.[20] It was always Oregon's smallest county in size, and it would soon become the largest in population.

At the time of Multnomah County's creation, Marion County, the seat of territorial government, claimed a larger population than did Multnomah. In 1870, Multnomah wrested the title of "most populous" from Marion by a small margin—and has never let go of it. By 1950, Multnomah County would be home to nearly a third of Oregon's population. Clackamas County claimed 6 percent of the state's total, and Washington County, 4 percent. Some sixty years later, however, while growth still favors the metropolitan Portland region, Multnomah County's percentage today has dropped to 19 percent. Washington and Clackamas have mushroomed to 14 percent and 10 percent of the state's population, respectively, so that a total of 43 percent of Oregon's population lives in the tri-county area.[21]

Multnomah County boasted seven peaks over a thousand feet high. Five were in the Columbia Gorge: Larch Mountain—4,056 feet; Big Bend Mountain—4,034; Mt. Talapus—3,840; Pepper Mountain—2,137; Saint Peter's Dome—1,135. Two were within present-day Portland's city limits: Mt. Scott—1,083; and Council Crest—1,073 feet.[22] Much of the land in the far eastern part of the county where the tallest mountains were located—thirty miles from downtown Portland—was destined to become a federal wilderness area, encompassing a sizeable portion of the Bull Run watershed where Portland stored its water supply.

At the other end of the altitude scale, Wapato (Sauvie) Island—where the Willamette River joined the Columbia—was only five feet above sea level. While the new boundaries gave Multnomah County fifty riverfront miles along the Columbia, Washington and Clackamas counties were left with none.

The far northwest portion of the county contained the Willamette Stone, which marked the intersection of the north-south Willamette Meridian with the east-west Base Line; it was the starting point for all federal Pacific Northwest land surveys. In 1851, the territorial land office hammered a cedar post into the ground at that intersection. The wood later decayed and was replaced by a limestone obelisk that was vandalized in the 1980s. Today, a stainless-steel cap and an adjacent bronze plaque commemorate the historic spot, located in a wooded area at the end of a quarter-mile pedestrian trail off Portland's Skyline Boulevard.[23]

In December 1854, the territorial legislature named interim Multnomah County officials until an election could be held the following year. The interim commissioners chosen were Sauvie Island landowner James F. Bybee, hardware merchant George W. Vaughn, and east county resident John Emsley Scott. Also appointed were an interim sheriff, auditor, treasurer, and probate judge. The new county was entitled to one seat in the territorial House of Representatives and shared a Council (Senate) seat with Washington County.

The newly constituted Multnomah County board held its first meeting on January 17, 1855. At its second meeting, the commissioners rented the second floor of the Robinson Building on Front Avenue at $500 a year and requested sealed bids for benches and tables.[24] At the board's third meeting on January 29, with a full board present for the first time, George Vaughn was elected chairman.

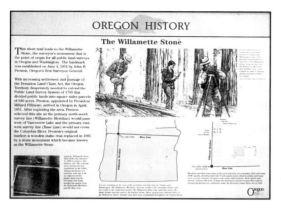

This contemporary photo of a sign at the trailhead to the Willamette Stone recounts the story behind the historic location. Established in July 1851, the Willamette Stone marked the point of origin for all Oregon Country public land surveys. A wooden post was driven into the ground in what would later become Northwest Multnomah County. Today, a ground-level monument is located at the end of a quarter-mile trail off N.W. Skyline Boulevard. (Jewel Lansing)

He was authorized to procure a county seal and instructed to include a ship in its design.

The early meetings reflected life in a small frontier city, where downtown buildings had not yet graduated from lumber to bricks. Not surprisingly, the board's first priorities centered on transportation in the form of roads and river ferries. Yet the need for social services also quickly became apparent. At their third meeting, the commissioners denied a request for compensation for keeping a Mrs. Kimberling, "an insane pauper," for twelve days at $7 per week. "There being no evidence produced of Mrs. Kimberling being entitled to receive compensation for her support as a pauper from the county . . . the bill . . . was laid over." This simple agenda item, while resulting in no payment by the county, was early acknowledgement that it was the county's responsibility to care for the poor. Two years before, the Portland City Council had refused to accept bills for expenditures made on behalf of a pauper, declaring that it was not a city responsibility and that the claimants should take their claims to Hillsboro, at that time still the county seat.[25]

The interim Multnomah County board did not meet again until nearly three months later, on April 2, when they devoted their time almost entirely to plans for building new roads. The first "viewing" was ordered for a planned route from Portland to the mouth of the Sandy River, which was based on an ancient Native American footpath from the Willamette River to the Sandy. Running diagonally to the street grid that would later be established in Northeast Portland, Sandy Boulevard, as it became known, would pose serious challenges for traffic engineers and motorists.[26] Three viewers—G. W. Brown, James Powell, and a Mr. Claggett—were appointed to meet with the county surveyor on "18 April, 1855 A.D." to examine the plans for the road.

The commissioners met on five days in April, in what would be a final wrapping-up of business for these interim officials. For every road approved, a petitioner had to furnish a $100 bond to cover costs in case the road was not finished. These early roads were the financial responsibility of the property owners within each road district, an "inefficient and impractical" system that contributed to the delay of development in outlying areas. A state road tax was enacted in 1889.[27]

Three more new roads—all on the east side of the Willamette River—were authorized during the final meetings of the interim county officials. County election procedures were approved. Ferry service from John Switzler's place to the Washington Territory on the north side of the Columbia River gained approval. Lewis Love was to pay $5 a year for a license to run the Switzler ferry. Passengers would pay fifty cents each, or one dollar for one person and a horse.

David Powell's petition to set the rate of ferriage across the Willamette River between the Stevens farm and Portland was granted. Rates were set at ten cents per passenger, twenty-five cents for one person and a horse, sixty-two cents for a wagon and a pair of animals, ten cents for each additional animal, and fifty cents for a horse and buggy.[28]

H. W. Clayton petitioned the board for payment of $23 for boarding Henry Marshall, "an insane man," at one dollar per day for twenty-three days. A citizen (name undecipherable) appeared to testify that he "knew said Marshall" and that Marshall had been residing in the county for twelve months. The board ordered payment of $15 to Clayton, approximately sixty-five cents a day.

During their short terms as interim officials, board members divided the county into eleven road districts to better assign responsibility for oversight of road-building. They also ordered compensation of $22.50 to Commissioner Bybee and $29 to Commissioner Scott for mileage and services, $12 to Sheriff William McMillan for attending four commission meetings, and $20 to auditor Shulbrick Norris for his clerk-of-the-board services.

Eleven officials were chosen at the county's first election in April 1855— three commissioners, an assessor, auditor, coroner, district attorney, school superintendent, sheriff, surveyor, and treasurer. The commissioners drew lots to determine which of them would serve the one-, two-, and three-year terms.[29] (Names of these elected officials can be found in Appendixes D and E.)

On July 2, 1855, the first day the newly elected board met, citizen John Caruthers asked the board to revoke the license granted two months earlier to Jacob Wheeler to operate a ferry across the Willamette River. A license had originally been granted to Wheeler by Clackamas County commissioners and was concurred in by the interim Multnomah County board. Now the new commissioners swore witnesses, took testimony, and placed evidence on file to review the merits of that decision. On the third day, the commissioners rescinded Jacob Wheeler's license, but included no explanation in the minutes to reveal why.

In other July business, the board directed the clerk to publish specifications and receive bids for a county jail. Hiram Smith once again presented his bill for boarding and furnishing clothing to Mrs. Kimberling, "an insane pauper." The board again declined to pay the bill, citing "lack of jurisdiction." (This apparently meant that no evidence was presented to show that Mrs. Kimberling had resided in the county for twelve months, as had been the case with a previous successful claimant.)

On September 17, at the board's fall quarterly meeting, the commissioners ordered a seven-mill tax levied on each dollar of assessed Multnomah County property value: five mills for general county purposes, one mill for territorial purposes, and one mill for school purposes—a total levy of $7 on each $1,000 of assessed valuation. These taxes were in addition to the eight and a half mills being levied by the City of Portland. (Note that this combined rate for Portland property owners was virtually the same as the 1.5 percent maximum rate imposed by Oregon Ballot Measure 5 passed in November 1990.)[30]

The December board meeting that marked the end of the county's first year was spent establishing and maintaining roads, ferries, and bridges. Powell Valley Road—today's well-traveled Powell Boulevard—was named for three early settlers who had claimed homesteads where the city of Gresham is today: James Powell, Jackson Powell, and Dr. J. P. Powell (who became a beloved family doctor for the area). None of these Powells was related to the owners of today's popular Powell's Books.[31]

In spite of all this attention to roads, the most critical thoroughfare of all—a roadway westward from Portland to the rich farmlands of the Tualatin Plains—was built not by Washington County or Multnomah County government but rather by a private corporation chartered by the territorial legislature. The Portland and Tualatin Plains Plank Road Company completed a toll road connecting Washington County farmlands with Portland's oceangoing ships in late 1856. *Oregonian* editor Harvey Scott later said that the plank road was "almost inaccessible" from Portland and was "most difficult of passage or travel when reached"; he nevertheless credited the Canyon Toll Road with providing a connection to the fertile Tualatin Plains, a long-sought goal that would reinforce Portland's recently acquired power and influence.[32]

3

THE COUNTY'S FIRST HANGING;
EARLY ELECTED OFFICIALS
(1855–1869)

The Oregon Constitution that took effect with statehood on February 14, 1859, was drafted by sixty elected delegates over a few weeks in 1857. Territorial voters approved it by a two-to-one margin in November 1857—7,195 to 3,215. Though amended several times in statewide elections, it remains the state's governing document after more than 150 years. The constitution required each county to elect three commissioners, one of whom would be designated by his peers to preside at meetings and to serve as a probate judge. The county judge and two elected commissioners comprised a "county court." These three men (it was always men, because women could not vote in Oregon until 1913) handled general county business while other elected county officials performed duties specified by state law.[1]

Criminal and civil cases were decided by traveling Oregon Supreme Court judges. The county judge presided over county board meetings and settled disputes regarding ownership of property after a person's death.[2] Prior to 1878, there was no requirement that county judges be lawyers.

Commissioners who held the title of county judge were appointed to that position by their fellow commissioners. Since there was no prohibition against voting for oneself, any commissioner who wanted the job had only to line up one other vote. The county judge achieved little of the name familiarity afforded the more-visible county sheriff.

One might assume that the creation of a new county government and election of its officials would allow for local control, but the county commissioners' powers were tightly restricted by the Oregon Constitution and the state legislature. From the time of its inception, Multnomah County's urban nature often generated problems different from those faced by counties with small towns and rural populations, but it was forced into the same mold as all other Oregon counties by state law. Exceptions and accommodations on the part of the state legislature were always difficult to obtain, because some legislators from other parts of the state had little sympathy for the "big city" needs of Multnomah County.[3]

Throughout Multnomah County's history, no county elected official has been more visible than the sheriff. Early sheriffs were usually better known and more popular than the county commissioners. The commissioners worked only part-time, while sheriffs had more time-consuming duties. In addition, the sheriff's job could prove to be lucrative, since sheriffs had wide discretion to charge fees for services such as feeding jail inmates, delivering court-related papers, and collecting taxes. The state legislature eventually eliminated discretionary fee schedules after indications of abuse in Multnomah County.[4] "With the single exception of kingship," says a 1968 National Sheriffs' Association brochure, "no secular dignity now known to English-speaking people is older. . . . It is the oldest law enforcement office known within the common-law system and has always been accorded a great dignity and high trust." Except for a sixteen-year period of appointed sheriffs (1967–1982), Multnomah County sheriffs were elected.

The Oregon Territorial Legislature that created Multnomah County named William McMillan as interim sheriff while he was also serving a one-year term as president of the Portland city council, a volunteer job.[5] After serving two terms as sheriff,[6] McMillan faced a challenge at the ballot box from an ambitious young man named Addison Starr, who had been elected Portland mayor in a hotly contested race only two months earlier.[7] In a "bitterly anti-Semitic editorial" regarding the sheriff's race, the weekly *Oregonian*'s Republican editor, Thomas Dryer, condemned Jewish support for William McMillan and endorsed Starr, even though the newspaper had previously praised McMillan as a man of "urbanity and natural desire to accommodate," and in spite of the fact that Starr was also a Democrat, albeit not part of the powerful Salem clique that controlled party politics at the time.[8] Starr ousted McMillan by a margin of 47 votes out of 891 cast.

The vitriol against Jews evidenced by Dryer's comments before and after the election reflected the intense political party fervor of the times. The week before the election the *Oregonian*'s headline blared: "PARTY AND POLITICAL TYRANNY." The *Oregonian* article, complete with italicized words, stated: "*Salemites ape* the *Israelites*, the *Danites*, and all other *ites* who have assumed to oppress, control, and govern the people by a system of tyrannical *humbuggery* unequaled by the petty Princes of Africa. . . ."[9]

The week following the election, Dryer wrote: "the Jews, or 'Israelites' as they call themselves . . . held several secret meetings to which a few gentile office seekers were admitted . . . [They] induced the whole Jewish population to center their entire opposition against Mr. Starr . . . . Our Israelitish friends (or rather enemies) were particularly boisterous in their efforts [to defeat] Starr. . . ."[10]

A week later, still another *Oregonian* editorial proclaimed that Democrats were winning elections "by fraud, bribery, and labor unknown heretofore in the political history of Oregon," and that two Portland Jewish firms had discontinued their *Oregonian* subscriptions. "Whether we shall be able to survive the shock or sustain ourselves after this great loss of patronage," Dryer sneered, "is a matter of deep and anxious solicitude with them, no doubt. . . ."

Newly elected Sheriff Addison "Ad" Starr bore a strong physical resemblance to Abraham Lincoln. Not only was Starr destined to be the only person to hold the offices of Multnomah County sheriff and Portland mayor at the same time, he also served in both those capacities in 1859, the year Oregon became a state.[11] Starr's volunteer mayoral position lasted only one year, while he served four full years as sheriff.

A native of New York State, 38-year-old Starr had lived in Oregon for eight years when he was elected sheriff. He and his three brothers had parlayed the gold they brought from California into several profitable enterprises, including a whiskey distillery, a tinsmith business, and a stove store. They also helped incorporate the oldest national bank on the Pacific Coast (the First National Bank of Portland, now Wells Fargo) and invested in a highly profitable Northwest navigation company.[12] Starr may have been motivated to seek the sheriff's office partly to demonstrate that his whiskey distillery business was no threat to community law and order.

Starr had been sheriff only six months when he was summoned to arrest a farmer named Danford Balch for shooting a man in broad daylight on the crowded Portland waterfront. Balch had hired Mortimer Stump to work on his farm, but he ordered Stump off the premises when the young man started courting Balch's 15-year-old daughter, Anna. So the young couple eloped. The newlyweds were staying northeast of Portland with Stump's family for a week when the entire Stump family, including Mortimer, Anna, and Mortimer's parents, made a trip to Portland to buy the basics that Anna and Mortimer would need to set up housekeeping.

On the afternoon of Thursday, November 18, 1858, the two fathers ran into each other at Starr's store and exchanged heated words. Balch rushed home for his double-barreled shotgun. As Anna and her new family boarded the Stark

Addison Starr served as the volunteer Portland mayor for a year during his four-year stint as Multnomah County sheriff (1858-1861). Twenty years later, Starr retired to California a wealthy man. His Portland business interests had included a distillery, a stove and tinsmith business, a navigation company, and the founding of First National Bank, the oldest national bank on the Pacific Coast. (Multnomah County Archives)

Street Ferry for their return trip home, Danford Balch shot and killed his new son-in-law, Mortimer Stump.[13]

Balch spent the winter awaiting trial in a flimsy rented building being used as a city jail.[14] He broke out of jail in early 1859 and hid near his farm in what is today's Forest Park for several months, fed by family and friends. [15] He was still hiding in July 1859 when Portland's new city marshal, James Lappeus, discovered his hideaway and arrested him. Balch was tried and found guilty in late August. On October 18, he was to be hanged.[16]

It was Starr's duty as sheriff to set the exact time of the hanging, to erect gallows, and, on the day of the hanging, to pull a wooden pin that would unlatch a trap door beneath the condemned man.[17] Starr built the gallows near the waterfront in an open area at Front and Salmon. The scaffolding had scarcely been completed before an enterprising individual erected wooden bleachers next to the gallows with intent to charge a fee for this prime view. The night before the hanging, however, other folks threw the bleachers into the river, thereby "spoiling a very mean speculation," according to author Eugene Snyder in *We Claimed This Land: Portland's Pioneer Settlers*. In his final statement before death, Balch confessed that he'd had two drinks on the day of the shooting and that he had been imbibing alcohol for several years.[18]

Balch's execution was the first of thirteen hangings conducted in Multnomah County before the Oregon Legislature ruled in 1903 that all future executions would occur in the privacy of the Oregon State Penitentiary. After Balch's hanging, subsequent Multnomah County executions occurred on the grounds of the first Multnomah County Courthouse, erected in 1864, under the purview of the current elected sheriff.[19]

Today a large commemorative stone marks the Danford Balch home site at Northwest 30th and Upshur in Lower Macleay Park, near the former site of the 1905 World's Fair Forestry Building. Balch Creek in Macleay Park bears the name of the hanged man.[20]

In March 1860, Sheriff Starr arrested Portland mayor Stephen McCormick and city marshal James Lappeus as they marched toward the Willamette River with a band of indignant citizens, intent on tearing down a waterfront warehouse that had been erected overnight in defiance of a city council order. (The underlying disagreement concerned public versus private ownership of land fronting on the Willamette River.) After a brief hearing, the county justice of the peace dismissed all charges against McCormick and Lappeus (charges brought by the city recorder, the mayor's political foe). Starr immediately released the mayor and marshal, and watched while the crew of irate Portlanders tore down the warehouse. "Although there was intense excitement" concerning the demolition, the *Oregonian* noted, "we are glad to chronicle the fact that there was no violence committed upon (any) person."[21]

Ironically, the man who built the illegal warehouse, George Vaughn, was a former county commissioner and the former Portland mayor whom Starr had defeated at the ballot box two years earlier. Vaughn argued that he owned the waterfront land and was entitled to use it as he pleased. For a time after the warehouse battle, the furious Vaughn took up residence across the Columbia River in Vancouver.[22] But although Vaughn lost this battle over the warehouse, he was to win the war. Unfortunately for the public, Federal Judge Matthew Deady ruled the following year that the Portland levee belonged to private landowners such as Vaughn, rather than to the citizenry.[23]

During Starr's final year as sheriff, he faced off against a would-be lynch mob infected with Civil War fever. The melee began when a Union officer, Captain G. W. Staples, was drinking with a fellow officer at a local hotel bar and lifted his glass in toast to the Union. "To hell with the Union," yelled a gambler named Ferd Patterson. Immediately the two officers went after Patterson, who ran out of the hotel into the street. Fire bells were rung. A great crowd collected around the Pioneer Hotel, on whose steps Patterson had taken refuge. Patterson yelled, "I will kill the first man to come up these stairs."

When Capt. Staples grabbed a rope and started upstairs, Patterson fired a shot in the air. But Staples kept coming, so Patterson shot to kill. Capt. Staples fell with a mortal wound in the stomach. Hundreds of people crowded around and threatened mob violence as a sheriff's deputy led Patterson to jail.

Sheriff Starr now appeared and drew his pistol. Threatening to kill the first man to touch Patterson, Starr kept the crowd at bay. The crowd eventually dispersed without further incident.[24] Although Patterson was acquitted by a trial jury in 1862, he was later shot dead in a barber's chair in Walla Walla, Washington. His assailant was a special policeman in Portland when Capt. Staples was killed.

The state of Oregon, barely six years old at the time, lost a proven leader when Addison Starr left for California in 1865, only three years after his tenure as sheriff ended. Starr took with him the fortune he had amassed in Portland.[25] At the time of his death in 1891, his *Oregonian* obituary focused on his role as a founder of First National Bank and failed to mention his trail-blazing years as sheriff.[26]

Starr's tenure as a county official overlapped with that of Philip A. Marquam, the most influential of early members of the county court. It was a miracle, perhaps, that Commissioner Marquam ever made it to Portland, given that he was shot through the neck with an arrow from a hostile Native American while prospecting for gold along the Sacramento River in 1850.[27] Marquam, a Maryland native who had come to the gold fields after studying law in Indiana, survived the attack and opened a law office in Fremont, California, the same year.

Marquam visited a brother who lived in Silverton, Oregon, in 1851 and decided to move to Portland. He first bought land in the Arleta neighborhood of what later would be called East Multnomah County, and subsequently purchased 298 acres in the West Hills that would become known as Marquam Hill. Marquam won the first of four consecutive two-year terms on the Multnomah County Court (1862-69), as the county commission was called in 1862, being the first person to serve as a commissioner for that long—a feat not matched until two decades later by H. S. Stone (1890-97). Likely as a result of his first land purchase, Marquam was a strong advocate for building county roads.

Besides practicing law and holding the part-time county commissioner's position, Marquam also became a prominent real estate developer. His most ambitious project was a ten-story office building and elegant 1,600-seat theater, which was constructed on Southwest Morrison Street between Sixth Avenue and Broadway. The Marquam Grand Opera House, as it was first known, was the tallest structure in Portland when it was completed in 1891. Alas, construction flaws led to the collapse of a central portion of the building on a late November night in 1912. Much of the rest of the building collapsed several hours later.

Remarkably, no lives were lost.[28] Philip Marquam had died five months earlier, at age eighty-nine.[29]

State highway officials named Portland's first freeway bridge across the Willamette River in Marquam's honor in 1966.[30] Portland's Marquam Nature Park also was named for the pioneer lawyer, businessman, and county official.[31]

Another prominent Oregon businessman who sat on the Multnomah County Commission in its early days was Henry W. Corbett. Between his two county commission terms (1864–65 and 1884–87), Corbett represented Oregon in the U.S. Senate from 1867 to 1873, in an era when U.S. senators were chosen by state senators, not by public election. After arriving in Portland in 1851 at age twenty-four, Corbett quickly became a successful dry goods and hardware merchant. He later branched into transportation, downtown Portland real estate investments, and banking, making him one of Portland's most influential businessmen as well as a leading political figure. The town of Corbett in the Columbia Gorge and Corbett Street in Southwest Portland are named after him.

Equally well known was former Portland mayor William S. Ladd, who served as a county commissioner from mid-1859 to mid-1860. Like Corbett, Ladd used a successful retail business in the 1850s as a springboard to greater wealth and influence in banking and real estate later in his career. As the owner of extensive real estate, both within Portland and in unincorporated Multnomah County, Ladd knew the importance of locating and constructing new roads, business which consumed a sizeable portion of county commission agendas. The part-time service by Corbett and Ladd on the county board proved mere footnotes in their prosperous careers. The Ladd Carriage House at 1330 Southwest Broadway, located across the street from his long-since demolished mansion, is the oldest surviving wood-framed building from Portland's early days. [32] Ladd was one of nineteen men who would serve on both the Multnomah County Commission and Portland City Council during those early days.[33] Moving back and forth between elective city office and elective county office was common practice. Other elected officials who did so included treasurers, district attorneys, surveyors, sheriffs, court clerks, assessors, coroners, auditors, and mayors.

4

A MAGNIFICENT COURTHOUSE, A PAUPER FARM, AND A PUSH FOR CONSOLIDATION
(1864–1880)

After ten years as a county—the first half as part of the Oregon Territory, the second as part of the State of Oregon—Multnomah County completed construction of Portland's first public building in 1864. Before the two-story courthouse opened for business in 1864, the city and county governments and federal agencies had all operated out of rented buildings. The new courthouse, designed by architects William W. Piper and Elwood Burton, included a basement jail and a quaint cupola on top that overlooked the young city.[1] Portland's population had climbed to approximately six thousand while the courthouse was under construction.[2]

The full city block on which the courthouse was built had been bought for $9,000 in 1862; the purchase price included a house and an orchard from which many old stumps had to be removed.[3] The block was bounded by Southwest Main and Salmon Streets between Fourth and Fifth Avenues, well away from the city center. The structure had a "wedding-cake" design with a cruciform footprint. The windowed dome reached a height of 106 feet.[4]

The building's opening was a proud moment for Portland and the county. The *Oregonian* virtually crowed that the "magnificent structure" was all the more impressive because its cost was entirely paid upon its completion. Lawns surrounded by wrought-iron fences enhanced the structure's regal exterior.[5] A likeness of Abraham Lincoln was carved into the large keystone over the front door. The total construction cost was $65,525, including delays caused by Civil War shortages.

At first, virtually all county business was conducted from offices in the courthouse, but space soon became a problem. A major wing was added to the Salmon Street side of the courthouse in 1885, and another wing was added to the Main Street side later. Smaller expansions and modifications also were made over the years, none of which alleviated the need for additional capacity for very long.[6] This courthouse was to have a working life of only forty-seven years before it was replaced by a larger building on the same block on which the courthouse still stands.

During the 1860s, in keeping with the county's responsibility to care for the indigent, county commissioners took major strides in providing medical services and work opportunities. The county signed a contract with a Portland physician, Dr. James S. Hawthorne, to treat patients at a small private hospital located at Southeast 12th Avenue and Hawthorne Boulevard.[7]

Dr. Hawthorne was a notable figure in East Portland. A native of Pennsylvania, he received his medical training in Louisville, Kentucky, and moved to Placer County, California, in 1850, perhaps attracted by the big gold strike of 1848. He practiced medicine and won election to two terms in the California State Assembly before arriving in Portland in 1859. He quickly opened a private hospital concentrating on neurology and what in his era was bluntly called "insanity."[8] In addition to managing his thriving medical practice, Dr. Hawthorne was a successful livestock breeder, and in 1878 formed the first of several companies that aimed to build Portland's first bridge across the Willamette River. He and his allies started construction in 1880 but were stymied by a court ruling that said the bridge would obstruct river traffic. (The bridge at Morrison Street was completed ultimately in 1887 by private owners as a toll bridge; in 1895 the City of Portland bought it for $150,000. A decade later, Portland sold the structure to Aberdeen, Washington, and built a new bridge.)[9] Both Hawthorne Boulevard and today's Hawthorne Bridge are named for Dr. Hawthorne.

The county's contract with Dr. Hawthorne was not enough to keep pace with the needs of a growing population, however. The county commissioners' answer was to set up a "poor farm," an establishment that would provide work, as well as room and board, for indigent residents. In 1868, the county paid $10 per acre for 202 acres on Portland's western fringe. Within a brief time, forty acres were fenced and put into cultivation, and some two hundred trees were producing fruit in its orchard. In 1876, the county shifted its medical services to the farm and ended its relationship with Dr. Hawthorne.[10] Thereafter, a county physician visited the farm twice a week. and as needed for emergencies. Access to the area was limited, however, to transportation by horse or horse-drawn carriage.

In response to criticism that the farm lacked facilities for women, a wing was soon built specifically to fill that need.[11] The farm's two buildings were shaped in an L and linked by a covered walkway. Surgical services were accommodated at Good Samaritan and St. Vincent Hospitals in Portland at a cost of $1 per day. A surgical room was added to the women's wing by 1906.[12]

Multnomah County's first home of its own was this two-story structure with basement and cupola, completed in 1864 on the block bounded by S.W. Salmon and Main Streets between Fourth and Fifth Avenues. The county's first jail was in the basement. The original building was expanded in 1885, then gradually demolished as a new courthouse was erected on the same block from 1912 to 1914. (Multnomah County Archives)

Meanwhile, public-spirited citizens and reformers began asking why the Portland area needed two governments—the city and Multnomah County. This theme would be repeated many times over the succeeding decades. The first call to consolidate Multnomah County and Portland governments came only fourteen years after the county was created. A petition calling for the state legislature to combine the two governments in order to cut down on "ruinous" taxes was circulated in 1868. "Your petitioners . . . being opposed to the heavy and ruinous taxation carried on by the support of a separate government of the city of Portland, and believing that a consolidation of the government of the city of Portland with that of the County of Multnomah, on an economical and judicious basis, would greatly reduce taxation, retrench expenses, and promote the general good of the community. We therefor pray your Honorable Body to pass such law . . ."[13]

Staunch support for consolidation came from the *Oregonian*, which cited San Francisco as the model to follow. Before the city and county governments of San Francisco consolidated in 1856, their combined expenditures totaled $8.6 million a year. After consolidation, the joint city-county government spent only $3.6 million per year, less than half as much. The article made a compelling case:

"Now if consolidation proved such a blessing to the tax-payers of San Francisco, may we not hope for a like result for Portland? There is one idea that seems to pervade every mind, and that is that our charter! our government! our financial affairs! are in horrible and disastrous condition . . . All are satisfied that it would be next to impossible to make the matter any worse. Hence nearly every man is signing the petition," the newspaper contended.[14]

The common-sense argument for consolidation, which has changed little in the ensuing years, was the same as that made for marriage: two should be able to live as cheaply as one. "It would certainly be cheaper to carry on one government than it is two," declared *Oregonian* editor T. J. Dryer. "We would then have no use of paying but one assessor; we now pay two. One Treasurer would safely keep all the money that would at any one time be in the Treasury. . . We have a court house ample and sufficient for a council chamber, city hall, etc., without ever interfering with the workings of the Circuit Court. Our city jail is now in a wretched condition. We have an ample and commodious county jail, which would save the expense of building a new one for the city."[15]

The article failed to note the many far-reaching changes that such consolidation would require. Counties were an arm of state government, as specified by the Oregon Constitution.[16] Only insiders would have known that Oregon counties were limited to $5,000 of debt by the state constitution,[17] while Portland's charter allowed ten times that much ($50,000), which could be increased whenever the state legislature met simply by amending Portland's charter.[18] In addition, the Oregon Constitution approved by Congress only nine years earlier would have to be amended in order for city and county to consolidate, and that would require a statewide vote of the people.[19] What is more, Multnomah County was basically rural: why would farmers want to pay for solving Portland's mud, crime, and harbor problems?

The five-foot-long consolidation petition (consisting of individual sheets glued end to end) was referred to Multnomah County members of the Oregon House of Representatives, where it died without being assigned a bill or resolution number.[20] If a consolidation proposal could not make it through even that first hurdle, the Oregon legislature, how could reformers expect to overcome statewide resistance to change? But although the procedure for combining the two governments was daunting, the idea of consolidation in some form would recur many more times in the following decades.

Around the same time as the first consolidation attempt, Portland was caught up in the anti-Chinese fever that was sweeping the West Coast. In August 1867,

Sheriff Joseph Stitzel arrested six Chinese for failure to pay a five-dollar poll tax levied by the Portland city council on every "Black, Chinese, Hawaiian, and Mulatto." The city ordinance stated that any foreigner who failed to pay the poll tax was to be arrested and forced to perform physical labor on the public streets at a rate of fifty cents a day. Fortunately, friends of the arrested men purchased their release before any prisoners were put to work on the streets.[21]

Tens of thousands of Chinese workers were recruited for railroad construction and other low-wage jobs during this period, and anti-Chinese sentiment continued. It culminated in the federal Chinese Exclusion Act of 1882, which closed the door to additional immigration by Chinese laborers. Persecution proved less severe in Oregon than in neighboring states, but even in Portland citizens opposed to the presence of Chinese immigrants tried as late as 1886 to seek removal of the city's approximately 4,000 Chinese residents.[22]

The 1870 election cycle raised another issue that would echo repeatedly down the decades: the fight against immorality. The fate of the newly elected sheriff, Cincinnati Bills, offers a curious twist. Bills was already a Portland city council member when he was elected sheriff in 1870. As a city official, he responded to citizen demands to curb prostitution by introducing an ordinance suppressing "bawdy houses." The irony was that Bills suffered from venereal disease, which he had contracted at one or more of these establishments. He died in office in December 1871, a year and a half after assuming his sheriff's duties. The diary of highly respected U.S. District Judge Matthew Deady often revealed truths that the newspapers were reluctant to report. "Bills," he wrote, "was naturally a good fellow, but the office of sheriff brought him in contact with vicious influences that he had not the stamina to resist. The newspapers and societies say that he died of inflammatory rheumatism, but I know that he died of a putrid fever which was brought on by the virus of clap getting into his blood and poisoning it, and his wife came pretty near dying from the same cause. . . ."[23]

The next sheriff, J. M. Caywood, served only one term before being turned out of office. During his short tenure, Caywood managed to amass "outrageous sums of money for diligent performance of his duties," in the *Oregonian*'s words. The sheriff was paid on a fee-for-service basis for delivering court papers and collecting taxes, among other duties. He was compensated for feeding prisoners at a daily meal rate, but he was allowed to spend as little as he wished on those meals.

When Caywood sought reelection in 1874, the *Oregonian* reported that he had received more than $30,000 in sheriff's fees in 1873 and would earn an estimated $40,000 in 1874. Those were staggering sums for the era; by comparison, reform sheriff candidate Edward J. Jeffery proposed an annual sheriff's salary of $3,000.[24]

Challenger Jeffery joined a "fusion" group of Republicans and Democrats on the 1874 ballot, all of whom were elected. Two years later, Jeffery was the only Democrat who won county office that year.[25] In its 1874 fall session, the Oregon legislature passed a law specifying a fee schedule for sheriffs in every county except Multnomah, leaving Jeffery's compensation to be decided by the county commission. Twenty years later, the state legislature specified an annual salary of $4,500 for the Multnomah County sheriff. In 1930, that amount was increased to $6,000.[26] Sheriff's compensation of $30,000 and $40,000 annually had clearly been out of line.

Two months after Jeffery's successor, Sheriff Ben Norden, took office, on the morning of August 20, 1878, three young men entered a Portland pawn shop with intent to rob.[27] One of them struck owner Walter O'Shea on the head with an iron bar, knocking him unconscious. The robbers immediately started stuffing a leather valise with gold watches, gold chains, silver watches, and silver coins. Suddenly one of the men looked up and spotted two young boys peering in the front window.

The robbers quickly fled. Meanwhile, the two boys raced to notify the city constable, who set out on foot after the robbers. One of the lawbreakers fired at the constable, who ducked behind a tree. Unfortunately, the bullet ricocheted off the tree and found another target—an inquisitive boy following close behind the constable. The community mourned the death of an innocent child and vowed to catch the thieves.

The three men were all captured within two months, charged with murder, and tried separately. One was sentenced to life imprisonment and died of consumption in prison four years later. In spite of pleas for mercy from opponents of capital punishment, the other two men were found guilty of first-degree murder and sentenced to hang.

Reporters from all over the world converged on Portland to observe the Archie Brown and James Johnson hangings. which took place in the courtyard of the county courthouse. Sheriff Norden erected a forty-foot-high stockade in the courtyard and allowed many government officials, official witnesses, and media representatives inside the enclosure. (The State of Oregon had recently required counties to build high fences around their gallows.)[28] On March 14, 1879, an estimated eight thousand people, including women and children, milled around outside the stockade in anticipation of the double hanging.[29]

*Reform sheriff candidate Edward J. Jeffery (1874-77)
advocated limiting the sheriff's salary to $3,000 a
year instead of the $30,000 in annual fees collected
by incumbent J. M. Caywood. In 1874, Jeffery joined
a "fusion" group of Democrats and Republicans who
made a complete sweep of county elected offices.*
(Multnomah County Archives)

On the day of his execution, Archie Brown held forth from the gallows
platform for more than half an hour. He ended his soliloquy with renditions of
two songs, "Trial by Jury" and "John Rogers." The first line of the latter song
implored, "Come all you kind-hearted Christians." In spite of Brown's heart-
tugging recitation and theatrics, the hangings proceeded without further delay.
Afterward, the bodies of Brown and Johnson were placed in black wooden coffins and displayed on the wooden sidewalk outside the stockade. Many viewers
placed wreaths and flowers inside the caskets.[30]

Just two years later, Norden presided over another hanging, which again
turned into an unsavory public spectacle. The unlucky prisoner this time was Ah
Lee, a Chinese immigrant convicted of retaliating against a Christian Chinese
who desecrated a house of worship attended by non-Christian Chinese. In his
final words from the gallows, Lee swore he did not commit the crime.[31]

Near chaos reigned in the boisterous and unruly crowd gathered near the
courthouse for his April 20, 1880, hanging. "Outside the stockade the crowd
overflowed the space available, pushing and shoving each other, climbing the
high fence, and crowding onto the balcony above the gallows," says author
Diane Goeres-Gardner in *Necktie Parties: Legal Executions in Oregon, 1851-
1905.*[32] "The mob had come to see a sideshow, and they saw it in their own
way, too, roughly, uncivilly and coarsely." The crowd was so rowdy that Sheriff
Norden found it difficult to carry out his hangman duties in a dignified manner.

In 1880, Sheriff Norden lost his reelection bid to a former unsuccessful sheriff candidate, Joseph Buchtel. Whether or not Norden's defeat at the polls had anything to do with the way he conducted his public hangings is not known, but the issue of executions as public spectacles in Multnomah County still had an ugly future.

5

COXEY'S ARMY AND EIGHT MORE HANGINGS

(1888–1903)

In the 1880s and 1890s, it was difficult to find anyone closer to being a "native" Portlander than Penumbra Kelly. He would serve eight years as a state representative and six high-profile years as county sheriff during turbulent times, winning the first of his three two-year terms as sheriff in 1888.

Born in 1845 in Kentucky as the son of an itinerant Methodist preacher, Kelly and his parents rode and walked the Oregon Trail via wagon train in 1848, when Kelly was a toddler. The family took a donation land claim east of the Willamette River in what would become Multnomah County and set about clearing land and creating a farm. Penumbra Kelly worked the family land and became interested in government and civic life. At age twenty-nine, he won the first of four terms in the Oregon House of Representatives, separated in 1876 by a single term on the Multnomah County Commission, which was then a part-time job. Starting in 1884, Kelly served three years as U.S. Marshal in Portland by appointment of President Chester Arthur, a job that largely involved the handling of federal court paperwork and overseeing custody of federal criminal defendants.

In his third term as sheriff, Kelly became the unwitting victim of a nationwide financial panic that started in the East and swept westward in 1893. At the time, many Portland businesses were going bankrupt. Several banks closed.[1] Kelly, like other Oregon sheriffs, was responsible for collecting property taxes, keeping this money safe, and delivering it, with interest, to the various local governments to whom it was owed. When Sheriff Kelly tried to withdraw school tax deposits from Oregon National Bank in 1893, bank president George Markle told him that the bank would have to close its doors forever if he did so. Markle assured Kelly and others that he would be able to raise the funds needed to keep the bank afloat. This proved untrue.

Penumbra Kelly served as Multnomah County sheriff for six years (1889-94), during a nationwide financial panic. In April of his last year in office, he led a posse to quell a contingent of "Coxey's Army" occupying the Gresham railroad station. However, when Kelly's posse arrived at the station, there was no disturbance to quell. (Multnomah County Archives)

Three men—a bank cashier, President Markle, and Sheriff Kelly—were subsequently indicted by a Multnomah County grand jury for misuse of $318,000 in public funds. Not only had Kelly failed to withdraw public funds entrusted to his care, he had deposited an additional $200,000 to help shore up Oregon National Bank. *Oregonian* editor Harvey Scott and a former Portland mayor, David Thompson, posted bail bonds for the indicted men. No court records were found to indicate how the case was resolved, according to historian E. Kimbark MacColl, who concluded that the charges were probably dropped.[2]

Sheriff Kelly had made a bad judgment call that resulted in heavy taxpayer losses. When the City of Portland sued the Oregon National Bank to recover deposited funds, no assets were left from which they could collect. Ironically, an 1893 Chicago publication described Kelly as a "man of quiet character and 'incorruptible integrity.'" Kelly had the misfortune to be unduly influenced by a powerful man in a highly volatile situation.[3]

In early 1894, Kelly faced another kind of fallout from nationwide hard times. A group of some fifty unemployed men arrived in Oregon by freight car and on foot from Northern California, intent on marching to Washington, D.C. Such jobless men had become known as "Coxey's Army," after an Ohio businessman named Jacob Coxey who organized a national movement to protest the widespread lack of jobs.[4]

Oregon's "regiment" of the "United States Industrial Army," as the movement was officially known, camped at the east end of Sullivan's Gulch, not far from the Columbia River, in April 1894. Acting Portland mayor Eugene Shelby and

Portland police chief Charles Hunt at first supplied rations to the men, but after a day or two dissent among city council members ended this largess. Oregonians at the group's previous train stops in Ashland, Roseburg, Cottage Grove, and Salem had provided food to the indigents; Portland citizens now did likewise.[5]

While the protesters were encamped at Sullivan's Gulch, five hundred more men joined their ranks. *Oregonian* editor Scott railed against these "tramps" and "beggars." However, the men were remarkably well-mannered and disciplined, and constituted no threat to the city. After the Union Pacific Railroad turned down pleas by protest leaders for eastbound transportation, the Coxeyites moved on to Troutdale, fifteen miles east, where they took control of a railroad station and a telegraph office.[6]

Three levels of government were soon involved in the encounter—city, county, and federal law enforcement officials. City Police Chief Hunt took charge of monitoring the situation while the protesters were camped in Portland. Railroad activity fell under the jurisdiction of federal courts and marshals, and both the Union Pacific and Great Northern railroad companies were in receivership. With the Coxeyites now in Troutdale, the federal marshal urged Multnomah County Sheriff Kelly to protect private property there. Hoping to avoid trouble, the Union Meat Company and merchants of Troutdale supplied meat, flour, and potatoes, and allowed the men to quarter in a livery stable and vacant houses. The men were reported as quiet and orderly.[7]

Sheriff Kelly telegraphed Governor Sylvester Pennoyer to request help from the state militia. Pennoyer fired back that it was Kelly's duty to quell any disturbance that might take place, and he was not to expect any state militia assistance unless and until a breach of peace actually occurred. Pennoyer was an irascible and intensely independent sort; U.S. District Judge Matthew Deady, an avid diarist, referred to him privately as "Sylpester Annoyer,"[8] a description with which Kelly likely would have agreed.

After being rejected by Pennoyer, Sheriff Kelly assembled a posse of five county sheriff's deputies, thirty Portland policemen, and eighteen federal deputies, all of whom rode east together by train. When the posse arrived in Troutdale, the railroad station was deserted and the jobless men were lined up in orderly fashion, as if to leave. This was an awkward situation. Troutdale leaders did not take kindly to Portland interference in their affairs, and Kelly's posse returned to Portland disgruntled that they had accomplished nothing.[9]

After a few days of back and forth maneuvering between the industrial army and the U.S. marshal, the Coxeyites seized a train in defiance of a federal injunction and headed eastward, accompanied by an engineer and conductor.

At the train stop in Arlington, 150 miles east of Portland, the insurgents' train was blocked between an eastbound train and a westbound one. Five hundred men were taken into custody and sent back to Portland (except for seventy or so who disappeared en route). A number of their leaders were confined in the Multnomah County jail; the rest of the men were housed in boxcars at the Albina freight yard.

At a court hearing on April 30, it became clear that the main offense committed by the industrial army was to insult the dignity of the court by disobeying a federal injunction. In the face of widespread public sympathy, some of the men were returned to California. Others faced no opposition from railroad officials when they rode boxcars eastward in small groups.

This 1894 incident foreshadowed the Bonus Army March of 1934, which began in Portland during the Great Depression. The goal of the Bonus Army was to force Congress to make bonus payments that had long been promised to World War I veterans. By then, the United States had seen decades of protests and encampments of the homeless, as well as the founding of the IWW (Industrial Workers of the World, whose members were known as "Wobblies").[10]

After Penumbra Kelly retired as sheriff, he continued to work as a deputy sheriff and later as a courtroom bailiff. Kelly's name was preserved for many years through the county-owned Penumbra Kelly Building at 4747 East Burnside Street. The building, which previously housed the county's data processing center and the Portland Police East Precinct headquarters, was sold to the City of Portland in 2011.[11]

Kelly's decision not to seek another term as sheriff in 1894 opened the door for the return of George Sears, who had held the position from 1884 to 1886 before deciding not to run again. Sears was a Vermont native who had moved to California as a teenager and ultimately found success as a store owner, timber owner, and cattleman. A serious drought in Santa Cruz, California, led Sears to Portland in 1871, where he bought a half interest in a grocery store and later added a livery stable. Only six years after his arrival in Portland, he was elected county assessor.

Sears's 1894 race for sheriff was more than a routine election. It was a contest between commitment to public service as embodied by Sears and the special interest politics of John W. Minto, who was later to serve as Portland police chief under Mayor George P. Frank. Historian E. Kimbark MacColl characterized Frank as a "man of few principles and extreme rascality."[12]

The *Oregonian* of June 4, 1894, reported the return of former sheriff George Sears as a candidate this way: "On the county ticket, the only close contest is that between Minto and Sears for sheriff, but not sufficiently so to cause any fear among the friends of the independent candidate. Mr. Sears was in and out of the courtroom during the day, watching the progress of the count, and had the satisfied air of one who had emerged a victor out of a closely contested struggle. The vote when the count closed last night was: Minto—4,186; Sears—4,800." The final tally gave Sears a comfortable margin of fourteen hundred votes.[13]

Sheriff Sears, unlike his opponent, was an "ardently public-spirited man," according to researcher John Gordon King.[14] Author J.W. Hayes says in his 1911 memoir, *Looking Backward at Portland*, "George C. Sears was probably the most successful politician we have had. It was never any trouble for him to be elected to any office to which he aspired and he never failed to give a good account of his stewardship."

In spite of his reputed popularity, however, Sears was soundly defeated for reelection in 1896 by a Scottish native named William Frazier.[15] The owner and operator of a Portland livery stable, Frazier would serve six years as sheriff. He hired his son, Charles Frazier, as one of his deputies,[16] along with the county's first black deputy sheriff, George M. Hardin, who had been hired by the Portland Police Bureau as its first black policeman thirteen years before.[17]

The final months of Sheriff William Frazier's tenure saw more public executions. The first was that of John Wade and B. H. Dalton, who admitted that they had murdered a near-stranger while seeking to rob him. The victim was a young bartender named James Barkley Morrow, who was walking home and offered no resistance when the two men held him up. When Wade reached to get Morrow's wallet out of his pocket, Dalton's gun went off, killing Morrow. Both Wade and Dalton confessed to the murder; the public was so incensed over their offense that officials feared a lynching and, for a time, boarded the felons in jails outside Portland.[18] Dalton and Wade were to experience speedy justice—they were hanged only 71 days after their crime.

For the January 31, 1902, double hanging, Sheriff Frazier issued 400 invitations to an enclosure built to hold no more than 250.[19] The dual hanging over which Frazier presided was the harbinger of a significant change in the way Oregon would handle its executions. George Chamberlain, who was the Multnomah County District Attorney when Wade and Dalton were tried and hanged, took office as Oregon's governor the following year. Chamberlain, a persistent force for reform and one of the state's most beloved public officials of the era, asked the legislature to end all county hangings. He signed a state law on February 16, 1903, that said, "all executions [shall] take place within the walls of the penitentiary [in Salem], out of hearing and out of sight of all except officials."[20]

Meanwhile, serious discussion about merging Multnomah County with Portland's municipal government occurred again near the end of the century at the urging of Portland mayor William Mason, a widely respected businessman who had served as president of the Portland Chamber of Commerce and had led the successful campaign to consolidate the cities of Albina, East Portland, and Portland in 1891.[21] In his January 1899 message to city council, Mason pointed to the county's annual tax levy of 5 to 6 mills being paid by city residents. Money now being paid for salaries and expenses of county government was spent with a "very small fraction" of that tax going for the maintenance and operation of bridges within the city. He argued: "If the county and city were consolidated under, say, the title of City and County of Portland, would not the saving of one set of officers be a great gain to the taxpayers of the county? This matter is worthy of thought."[22]

Mayor William Mason died less than three months later, on March 27, 1899, and his attempt at city and county government reform came to an abrupt halt. Perhaps if Mason had lived longer, city-county consolidation might have occurred, for Mason had the kind of power base and personal commitment that such an undertaking required. But for the time being, the issue died with Mason.[23]

A new city hall with spacious quarters had opened four years before, while the county courthouse was seriously overcrowded. County auditor W. H. Pope wrote this testy letter to the city in 1900: "County accommodations are now entirely inadequate. Considering that the County is required to perform much service for the city without compensation—in the collection of city taxes, the care of its boulevards and some of the streets, the maintenance of the criminal department of the Municipal Court, (the revenue from which in fines, costs, and forfeited bails all go into the City Treasury) . . . the Commissioners submit that the county is entitled to the use of necessary rooms . . . at a nominal rental, if indeed any charge, at all, should be made."[24] (If any such courtesy was extended to the county, it did not last long; city hall would soon be suffering its own space problems.)

Not only were the courtroom and office space on the top two floors of the courthouse inadequate; so was the courthouse basement jail. Courtroom space was virtually unmanageable. When three juries retired to deliberate at the same time, one jury met in the judge's chambers, another in the jury room, and the third in the attic.[25]

The county now built a second jail at Kelly Butte, a promontory located at Southeast 94th Avenue and Powell Boulevard (not to be confused with the future Rocky Butte Jail). Kelly Butte Jail housed up to seventy-five inmates in a stockade supervised by armed guards. Inmates worked in a quarry, grinding basalt rocks for use on county roads. The men earned twenty-five cents a day and were provided with three daily meals, shoes, socks, trousers, shirts, and a small weekly measure of tobacco. They also were granted up to ten days a month off their sentences for good behavior.[26] Occasionally, inmates were called to help fight forest fires, apparently without a significant risk that they might escape.[27] The Kelly Butte Jail would remain in existence for four decades, until the rock quarry played out.[28]

A strong advocate for a new county courthouse, prominent Portland trial lawyer Lionel Webster was elected to the county court in 1902. When Webster, a crusader for clean government, won office, the county was $700,000 in debt. Several elected officials were still being paid out of fees they collected rather than having fixed salaries. Webster hired accountants to examine the county books and sniff out opportunities for corruption. As reported by the *Oregon Journal*, "Revelations, frequently of a startling nature, followed in rapid succession. In some instances suits were instituted to recover amounts due that had been improperly taken or withheld from the county. The Webster administration ushered in a new day and set up a new standard for the administration of Multnomah County's business."[29]

Planning for a replacement courthouse was well advanced when Webster resigned from county government in 1910, although it would be several years before expanded quarters would actually be available.[30]

The last two hangings conducted in Multnomah County were performed by Sheriff William Storey, a controversial character who had previously served as president of the Portland city council. After considerable political maneuvering, Storey had managed to get himself named interim mayor when the incumbent, William Mason, died in office in 1899. Storey lost his bid to be elected as mayor at the next election, but two years later he parlayed the name familiarity he had gained on the city council into a two-year term as sheriff in June 1902. He was elected with only 34 percent of the vote over four opponents.[31]

A. L. Belding and George Smith were jailed at the same time. While incarcerated, they concocted a strategy for escape with help from Belding's mistress. Authorities learned of these plans, however, and quickly thwarted them.

Belding had shot and killed three people—his wife, his wife's lover, and his mother-in-law—and severely wounded his father-in-law, while his six-year-old son cowered in a bedroom upstairs. After the killings, Belding walked across the street to a saloon, telephoned the police to report his crime, and ordered drinks for himself and a friend.

Belding's crimes were so despicable that his lawyer pled the accused as not guilty by reason of insanity. However, Dr. Harry Lane, a future Portland mayor (1905-08) testified that he did not believe Belding was insane at the time of the murders. Lane's testimony helped secure a conviction. The gallows that had been erected for Wade and Dalton the year before had not been torn down, so Belding's sentence was carried out on March 27, 1903, inside the same "temporary" stockade.[32]

Sheriff Storey proposed selling invitations to the Belding execution for five dollars each, with proceeds to benefit the young son. The idea was quickly dropped when it met with strong public disfavor. Approximately 250 people witnessed the hanging. A sheriff's deputy cut the gallows rope into little pieces and threw them into the crowd as souvenirs.[33]

The thirteenth and final hanging conducted by Multnomah County was troublesome to modern observers because of the racial and gender aspects related to the crime. Thirty-year-old George Smith, a black man (he was referred to as "colored," the custom at the time), was convicted of killing his estranged white wife, Annie. Annie had been a prostitute prior to their marriage two years before. "Kansas" Potella, a broad-shouldered pimp who was harassing George Smith, convinced Annie to leave her husband and join the Potella brothel. After Annie warned George that Potella was "looking to kill him," George Smith bought a steamer ticket and went to Annie's room to persuade her to accompany him. During that visit Annie Smith was shot and killed.

Smith had previously served two years in the state penitentiary (from 1889 to 1891) for assault and robbery armed with a dangerous weapon. He also attacked with a knife a man who remarked on the fact that Smith, a colored man, was accompanying a white woman on the street.[34] Governor George Chamberlain cited Smith's previous record and "evidence that Smith had deliberately murdered his wife because her affections had been estranged" as his reasons for declining to commute Smith's sentence.

Sheriff Storey issued invitations to attend George Smith's execution "at 6:30 a.m. within the enclosure of the Jail Yard." The engraved invitations contained the following narrative in small print at the bottom: "George Smith (colored) murdered his white wife, Annie Smith, by shooting her through the breast on the 22nd of August 1902. He was tried, convicted and sentenced to be hanged on the 19th day of December 1902. He appealed this decision to the Supreme Court, where the opinion of the lower Court was affirmed. He was sentenced to be executed on Friday, June 5, 1903."

Once again, after Smith's body was cut down, a sheriff's deputy cut small pieces of rope and handed them out as mementoes of the county's last use of the gallows. Smith's execution occurred a month after the new state law went into effect mandating that executions be carried out at the state penitentiary, but the law specifically excluded warrants issued before May 1903. Because Annie Smith's death occurred in August 1902, George Smith was not afforded the end-of-life privacy provided by the new state law.

More than fifty hangings were conducted by Oregon counties between 1851 and 1905. In the following ten years, twenty-four prisoners would be hanged at the Oregon State Penitentiary in Salem. Oregon voters abolished the death penalty in 1914, but reinstated it in 1920. Sixteen more men were hanged between 1921 and 1931, after which lethal gas was utilized in carrying out executions.[35] At the end of the twentieth century, the death penalty had been part of Oregon law four times, had been voted out twice, and struck down once by the Supreme Court. Today, the death penalty is permitted in Oregon only in cases of aggravated murder.[36] Oregon executed only two people from 1967 until 2012.[37]

6

THE PROGRESSIVE ERA, A CRUSADING SHERIFF, AND THE COUNTY FAIR BEGINS

(1902–1914)

The first dozen years of the twentieth century brought startling political changes at every level of American government. Theodore Roosevelt, at the time the youngest man to serve as president, took office in 1901 following the assassination of William McKinley, bringing with him new, young minds who sought to break the stranglehold of business trusts on the national economy. In Oregon, a persistent Portland lawyer, William S. U'Ren, doggedly fought to install a series of laws aimed at giving the state's voters more power at the expense of entrenched and often corrupt political power brokers. The initiative, referendum, and recall processes championed by U'Ren, as well as a Corrupt Practices Act,[1] won national acclaim as the "Oregon System." In Portland, a new afternoon newspaper founded in 1902, the *Oregon Journal*, championed reformers and their causes and placed greater emphasis on local issues on its front page than the stodgier *Oregonian*, which backed the old-line political wheeler-dealers.

At city hall, a man who was a relic from the pioneer era won election as mayor in 1902, but even 79-year-old George H. Williams took a reformer's tack in the campaign. He ran on a platform of beautifying the city and cracking down on Portland's long-standing illegal gambling and prostitution businesses. Williams had been an often respected and sometimes despised figure, dating back to when he served as a judge of the Oregon Territory and a voting member of the 1857 Oregon Constitutional Convention.[2] Williams's argument at the convention that it was cheaper for farmers to hire labor than to provide lifetime care for slaves helped convince Oregonians to enter the Union as a free state.

Williams served as a U.S. senator from 1865 to 1871 and as U.S. Attorney General under President Ulysses S. Grant. In 1874, Grant nominated Williams to be Chief Justice of the U.S. Supreme Court, but Williams withdrew after the nomination resulted in political, personal, and professional attacks. His tenure as

Portland mayor generated his final controversy. Rather than trying to eliminate vice, Williams had set up a system under which illegal businesses made regular payments to city coffers to keep on operating.[3]

Portland was experiencing a "highly charged evangelical revival" at this time. A Presbyterian minister accused *Oregonian* editor Harvey Scott of helping to "fasten gambling and prostitution on the city of Portland." A young Baptist minister attacked Mayor Williams in sermons titled "The Mayor of Sodom," "Our City's Crimes and Criminals," and "What Shall It Profit a City to License Crime?"[4]

The real reformer proved to be a county official rather than a city one. The six candidates on the 1904 ballot for Multnomah County sheriff included reformer Tom Word and the incumbent sheriff, William Storey. Word won with more than a two-thousand vote edge over his nearest competitors, James Stott and Nathan Bird, both of whom received more votes than Storey.[5]

During his successful campaign, Word pledged to crack down on vice. Portland then had "five of the biggest gambling houses in the United States running wide open," in the words of *Portland Telegram* writer Dean Collins.[6] Word's supporters included the ministerial alliance and its member churches, the Municipal Club, and the owner of the Orpheum Theater, who wanted either a gambling license for his theater or for all other (illegal) gambling houses to be shut down.

Sheriff Word wasted little time in carrying out his campaign pledge. Just days after he was sworn in, Word arrested four of the city's major gamblers. Five days later, he closed all gambling houses in Portland, invading Portland Police Department territory to do so. His closures included the Orpheum Theater (whose owner had helped him get elected), all Chinese lotteries and fantan games, the Portland Club (where marked cards were discovered), and poker games that were operating freely everywhere in the city.[7]

Understandably, Word's actions precipitated a thunderous uproar. Some seven hundred people were put out of work when the gambling houses were shut down, and Portland city government lost $5,000 in monthly revenue. (The city was charging gambling houses hefty business license fees while city police looked the other way.) Almost immediately, recall petitions started circulating against Sheriff Word and District Attorney John Manning, who had issued the warrants carried out by Word.[8]

Undaunted, three days later Word closed a keno game at the Portland Club and raided a Chinese house that featured keno and blackjack. The *Oregonian* described the scenes that ensued as patrons scrambled to escape from the Chinese gambling establishment: "The door was broken down and the officers rushed into the room. As quickly as possible the lights were turned on and the deputies made a rush for the windows, through which Japs and Chinks were tumbling into the adjoining houses and to the ground."[9]

Thousands of out-of-town visitors were expected in Portland for the 1905 Lewis and Clark Centennial Exposition. Visible vice had to be curbed. Tom Word's part in this cleanup was described by reporter Dean Collins of the *Portland Telegram* as follows: "I'm responsible for Multnomah County," said Word, and inasmuch as Portland was in Multnomah County, he sent notice to the Chief of Police to clean up the gambling houses. The Chief responded by telling him to "go to Hell." He sent word to pool halls and gambling houses to close. He was told unanimously to go to Hell. After having sent three warnings, he gathered up his deputies and "moved upon the Bad Lands with wagons and axes." Portland rocked with excitement.

In the newspaper reporter's words: "[Mayor] George H. Williams . . . was horrified and outraged at Word's undignified methods and at Word's invasion of the Police duties of the city." Williams's resistance was dignified, Collins said, but in vain. "The axe campaign had captured the popular imagination."[10]

On January 4, 1905, Mayor Williams was formally indicted for malfeasance by a grand jury, which said that he had refused to perform the duties of his office by not cracking down on gambling.[11] Williams had failed "to direct the chief of police or some other officer to arrest the proprietors of a certain club for running a gambling house," the indictment said.[12] The charge was soon dismissed on motion of Multnomah County District Attorney John Manning, the same DA who had signed Sheriff Word's warrants for his gambling raids. The indictment might have been an example of a "runaway" grand jury, in which jurors sign an indictment not supported by the district attorney. But there also were insinuations that Multnomah county judges were beholden to the underworld machine that ran the gambling dens.[13]

Nevertheless, by the time the Lewis and Clark Centennial Exposition opened on June 1, 1905, a combination of efforts had transformed Portland's Fourth Street into a respectable place—Sheriff Word's crusade, the Portland Municipal Association, Mayor Williams's call for city beautification, and pressure from the public (partly brought to bear because more information was available daily through the new *Oregon Journal*).[14] Brothels relocated from downtown to less visible locations in Irvington and Portland Heights.[15]

The 1905 Lewis and Clark Centennial and American Pacific Exposition, as it was officially known, was held on former marshland near the Willamette

"There never was a better sheriff in any county, anywhere, a better or truer sheriff," said an Oregon Journal *editorial eulogizing Sheriff Tom Word (1904-6 and 1913-15) at the time of his death in 1929. "Those who knew him,"* the editorial continued, *"can easily wish that it could be spared some folks to live on forever."* (Oregon Historical Society, No. 018478)

River in northwest Portland. It was intended to bring new residents and businesses to the area, and it proved largely successful, drawing more than a million and a half visitors to Oregon from all over the world[16] and launching an era of unparalleled population growth in Multnomah County. County general election voters nearly quadrupled from 19,068 in 1904 to 73,658 in 1914. The 1905 World's Fair was the major reason for this rapid growth.

As a later Portland mayor, Dorothy McCullough Lee, would learn four decades later, cracking down on vice in Portland was not a surefire route to political success. Recall petitions against Word gained ten thousand signatures in the first months following his election. The effort soon died, however, partly because the county had no agreed-upon method for replacing a recalled official. Even so, widespread anger at Sheriff Word's bold crusade prompted his detractors to search for a strong opponent who could defeat Word at the ballot box.

When Word sought reelection in 1906, he was opposed by Robert Stevens, who was supported by business interests and endorsed by the *Oregonian*, while church groups and other reformers continued to back Word. Stevens defeated Word's reelection bid by a razor-thin margin—the closest ever in a county race. The difference was a mere five votes: 9,260 votes for Stevens to 9,255 votes for Word.[17]

Both sides claimed election irregularities. Word called for a recount. A federal judge from eastern Washington State was brought in to ensure impartiality.

The success of the Lewis and Clark Centennial Exhibition in 1905 prompted the Gresham Grange to initiate a Multnomah County Fair in 1907. This early photo shows the fair queen and her court. The fair survived more than sixty years in Gresham, but slowly faded after it moved to more urban locations.
(Multnomah County Archives)

Ballot boxes were locked in the county clerk's vault at night and on weekends, while men representing both candidates stood guard.

The *Oregonian* carried a daily tabulation of recount results. By June 22, Stevens's lead had increased to fifteen votes. The following day his margin dropped to eight. On June 27, the candidates were tied, with a third of the ballots yet to be counted. The end result was a 25-vote win for Stevens. Word did not appeal, but he would return.[18]

The freshly elected sheriff was frustrated to learn that the county commissioners had given themselves management authority over the new Kelly Butte Jail and its seventy-five prisoners, powers that Sheriff Stevens thought should belong to him. In February 1907, the state legislature sided with Stevens and passed a law specifying that custody and control of county prisoners would henceforth be the sheriff's responsibility in counties over 100,000 in population (read Multnomah County). The following year, a statewide referendum passed by a two-to-one margin, giving all Oregon sheriffs authority over county prisoners.[19]

Another law passed by the 1907 state legislature required Multnomah County to employ "discreet and capable women as matrons" when women prisoners were held in custody. Such matrons were to reside at the jail in comfortable quarters.[20] In 1908, the Portland Police Department hired its first woman police officer, Lola Green Baldwin, to head its new Women's Division. She was the first woman police officer in the United States and a lifetime crusader against vice.[21]

The success of the Lewis and Clark Centennial fair had another effect—it stimulated interest in ongoing local celebrations, including the Portland Rose Festival and the Multnomah County Fair. The first Multnomah County fair, held in east county from October 16 through October 19, 1907, was sponsored by the Gresham Grange. A large tent housed the main exhibits; a queen and her court were in attendance. The following year, the Grange Fair Board chose a fifty-five-acre site in the center of Gresham that would be home to the fair for the next sixty-two years. Shares of stock were sold for five dollars each to finance fair activities.[22]

Carnival booths and a racetrack enlivened the county fair from its inception. Over the years the duration of the fair grew from four days to a week, then to ten days. The timing was also changed, from mid-fall to late summer, the better to celebrate the county's agricultural bounty and boost attendance. The relentless urbanization of the county, especially east of Portland's city limits where farmers gradually accepted it as their fate that subdivisions grew more profits than crops, would eventually have a merciless impact on the annual celebration.

Though the years of 1904 through 1914 were a time of progressive election reform in Oregon, efforts to change county boundaries did not fare as well. A 1910 proposal for Multnomah County to annex part of Clackamas County was overwhelmingly defeated statewide, 81 percent to 19 percent. A similar measure for Multnomah County to annex part of Washington County was opposed even more strongly, by 83 percent of statewide voters.[23] The rest of the state did not want Multnomah County to have any more clout than it already had, and voters tended to vote "no" on measures that did not affect them personally.

Restlessness over county boundaries was not limited to the Portland area. State voters in 1910 also rejected changes that would have created new counties in parts of Lane and Douglas counties, as well as in Umatilla and Grant counties. Municipal lawyers in Seaside, St. Johns (then a separate city in North Portland), and Cottage Grove proposed an initiative in 1912 that would have permitted only qualified residents of affected cities and counties to vote on merging cities and creating new counties. New counties, under this proposal, would have to meet minimum standards regarding area, population, and assessed value. The idea made sense to editors of the *Oregonian*: "The only way now available to accomplish either of these two things is to initiate a measure and ask thousands of voters who know nothing about the merits of the plan to pass upon the issue." Still, voters rejected the initiative that would have increased local control by 57,000 to 40,000 votes.[24]

Another 1912 ballot measure would have created a new Cascade County in the eastern portion of Clackamas County, with Estacada as its county seat. That measure was defeated decisively, by 71,239 to 26,463 votes.[25]

"A perpetual hotbed for county division and separation movements" is how the *Oregon Voter* magazine described Clackamas County, with its secessionist fever. An east Clackamas County resident put the case this way, in asking to be annexed to Multnomah County (believe it or not!): "Division and Secession movements can never be eradicated in Clackamas County as long as the voting strength of its rural residents . . . is overwhelmingly in the minority as compared with the floating, non-taxpaying, labor vote of its county seat, Oregon City, with its monstrous mills and other industries."[26]

In words that would resonate with east Multnomah County dissidents ninety years later, a spokesperson for the secessionist cause said they were seeking relief from "county seat domination" and the right to own property in a county that would give them fair expenditure of their taxes. More than 90 percent of east Clackamas County residents favored annexation by Multnomah County, he said.[27]

Some political and business figures in Portland were also not ready to give up on city-county consolidation. The Portland Chamber of Commerce commissioned a study that recommended extending Portland's boundaries to be identical with those of Multnomah County, and eliminating all Multnomah County elective positions.[28] The scheme would have established differing taxation zones, based on the types of public services provided.[29] It would have required an amendment to the Oregon Constitution, however, to allow it to occur. The *Oregonian* favored the plan, describing it as a "simple grant of authority, the enactment of which can do no harm and may lead to economy in municipal and county government."[30] The Multnomah County Bar Association, on the other hand, criticized the plan as too loosely drawn and unlikely to achieve savings. The statewide vote occurred on a lengthy November 1914 ballot, in which measures that included Prohibition, elimination of the death penalty, and restrictions on the hours and work conditions of women attracted much heavier public attention. The consolidation plan was rejected by 103,194 votes to 77,392.[31]

The surprise at the 1912 ballot box was that, after a series of failed efforts, Oregon voters approved women's suffrage, albeit by less than a 4 percent margin.[32] Suffragist Abigail Scott Duniway, now seventy-eight and crippled with arthritis, wrote and signed the state's equal suffrage proclamation at the request

Suffragist Abigail Scott Duniway, champion of women's rights in Oregon, casts her first ballot in Multnomah County. (Oregon Historical Society, no. 4601a)

of Governor Oswald West. A few other states had already passed women's suffrage laws, but a federal mandate would not be adopted until 1920.

That 1913 election saw the first woman elected to public office in Oregon. The City of Troutdale in east Multnomah County chose Clara Larsson, who was one-quarter Indian, as its mayor. Larsson was a member of the Latourell family, for whom Latourell Falls in the Columbia Gorge was named, and the granddaughter of Joseph "Frenchy" Latourell, who went around Cape Horn as part of a whaler crew in 1859. Frenchy had married Grace Ough, the daughter of a respected local Indian chief, in a wedding witnessed by "White Headed Eagle" John McLoughlin of Fort Vancouver. The marriage helped maintain peace between white settlers and Indians in the early years of the Oregon Territory. Troutdale Mayor Larsson defeated her male rival, S. A. Edmunson, by five votes.[33]

At the end of Sheriff Stevens's first two-year term in 1908, former Sheriff Word challenged him to a return bout at the ballot box. Stevens was a popular figure and defeated Word by nearly 4,000 votes; he then won a third term against only token opposition two years later. Voters statewide had voted overwhelmingly to move all Oregon general elections from June to November, and this took effect in time for the 1910 general election.[34]

Without Word's zealous forays to close down gambling establishments, Portland's vice scene was again thriving. Concerned citizens now pressured the city council, which appointed a fifteen-member vice probe committee. The group reported back in January 1912 after a five-month investigation, finding: "On the west side alone there are more than 400 'immoral' places, by which [the committee] meant mainly brothels, but also hotels and rooming houses welcoming short-term guests. Many of these places are in the city's 'aristocratic section,' while between the court house, the police station and the river there is an average of three to every block. And somewhat disconcerting to 'a city of churches' is the quaint fact that 'a person might stand on the roof of one of the principal churches of the city and throw a stone into any one of fourteen immoral places, ten of which are wholly immoral!'"[35]

Few publications in the city's history attracted the degree of attention that was afforded to the famous 1912 vice report. A full page map, "with the street lines carefully erased, showed in variegated dots the relative location" of 431 of the 457 investigated apartment houses, hotels, rooming houses "and what not" that were "wholly given up to immorality."[36] An hour after the report was published, draftsmen in most of the architects' offices around town had reconstructed the streets on the map. Portland guffawed, and people gobbled up the reports as fast as they could lay hands on them.[37]

Owners of properties in which vice activities were conducted had profited by an outrageous 84 percent to 540 percent return on their investments. Venereal disease accounted for at least 25 percent of all diseases treated by city doctors, without counting any untreated cases or occurrences treated only with home remedies.[38]

The same year that the citizens' vice report was issued, Sheriff Stevens announced his retirement after six years in office, opening the way for Tom Word to again seek the office of sheriff. Word won the 1912 primary and faced off against Republican W. H. Fitzgerald in November.

The *Oregon Journal*, an afternoon daily with Democratic leanings founded ten years before by Pendleton newspaperman Charles S. "Sam" Jackson, was now a major force to be reckoned with in Multnomah County politics. Jackson strongly backed Tom Word.[39] The *Journal* reported that three Portland police officers—Detectives Snow and Colman and former Patrolman Charles Tennant—were forcing store owners to remove Tom Word's campaign signs and put up those of Fitzgerald.[40] The *Journal* also reported that rumors saying Tom Word would close all theaters and baseball games on Sundays if elected were false. Word was quoted as saying that the story was absolutely without truth.[41] He was elected by a comfortable 2,500-vote margin.

In fall 1913, another recall movement was launched to remove Word from office. "The recallers are against Tom Word because he wouldn't let the IWW

[Industrial Workers of the World, nicknamed the 'Wobblies'] gang run the town," declared a September *Oregon Journal* editorial. "What is the use of bringing on the expense of a vote . . . when there is no more chance for Portland to elect an IWW candidate than for the Willamette River to run up hill?"[42]

The Recall League countered by sponsoring a mass meeting attended by three hundred women on September 26, 1913. A representative of the Socialist Labor Party declared that men and women advocating for the strikers were "not only stopped but were dragged from their boxes and barrels, their clothes were torn and they were thrown into the patrol wagon and taken to jail." These alleged indignities were blamed on Sheriff Word.[43]

A new kind of labor-union protest—the eat-in—created additional headaches for city hall and the county courthouse. Forty Wobblies entered Meves Restaurant at S.W. Sixth Avenue and Washington Street, ordered bountiful meals, and attempted to leave without paying. They told the cashier that Portland Mayor Albee would foot the bill. A crowd of five hundred watched from the sidewalk as twenty police arrived to remove the well-fed Wobblies, who were then sentenced to jail. The experiment resulted in extensive publicity. Soon the Peerless Cafeteria and other restaurants were visited by Wobblies using the same political tactic.[44]

Petitions to recall Tom Word were still circulating in 1914, at the same time that Oregonians from all over the state were urging him to run for governor, a post soon to be vacated by Governor Oswald West. However, Word announced that he would instead seek reelection as sheriff. A *Journal* editorial proclaimed that Word's decision was "welcome news to tens of thousands of people in Portland. . . . [His record] will reelect him triumphantly and overwhelmingly . . . He has the reputation of being one of the most aggressive law enforcers that has ever filled the office."[45]

In spite of such optimism and acclaim, the Recall League continued to collect signatures. Word supporters argued that a recall vote would be an unnecessary expense because Word would be on the November ballot anyway. By mid-April, it became clear that no Oregon law provided a process by which a replacement candidate could be nominated or seated, so the recall effort collapsed.[46]

The final years of the new century's first decade brought changes in the county's dealings with indigent citizens and indigent medical patients, which had been consolidated since 1876 at the so-called "poor farm" or Paupers Farm, more formally Hillside Farm, off Southwest Canyon Road. By 1908, Portland's medical community and citizen activists criticized conditions at the farm as inadequate,

Faced with a growing need to provide medical treatment to indigent patients, in 1909 Multnomah County bought this once-elegant mansion at S.W. Second Avenue and Hooker Street and converted it to a hospital for sixty-five patients. The hospital rapidly filled and then became overcrowded as Portland experienced heavy growth in the early twentieth century. The Hooker Street mansion, which no longer exists, served patients until construction of a new hospital on the Marquam Hill campus of the University of Oregon Medical School. (Oregon Health Sciences University Archives)

antiquated, and inconvenient.[47] Some of those objections concerned the mingling of young and old with drug addicts, alcoholics, and a variety of indigent medical patients, including tuberculosis victims.[48] In the meantime, property values had changed significantly; land that the county bought for $10 per acre in 1868 now sold for $765 per acre.[49] The 202 acres on which the Paupers Farm was located were eventually acquired by the City of Portland for a golf course. Today it is the site of the popular Washington Park Zoo, off Canyon Road.[50]

In 1910, Dr. Ralph Matson, a deputy county physician, angered county commissioners by speaking out about medical conditions at the farm, including a lack of tubs for bathing, absence of toilets and sewers, and badly leaking roofs.[51] Matson was a 1902 graduate of the Oregon Medical School and would eventually become an international expert on lung diseases and tuberculosis. He studied and practiced in London, Paris, Berlin, and Vienna, and wrote medical articles in several languages. When he died in 1945 in his own sanitarium in Portland, the *Oregonian* lauded him for proving that tuberculosis could be treated just as well in Portland's climate as in Arizona or New Mexico.[52]

Despite their original anger at the negative publicity, county commissioners subsequently sold the Hillside Farm property and began assembling what would become a new "Multnomah County Poor Farm" on a site that would eventually expand to 345 acres, east of Portland on fertile land between Troutdale and Fairview. The big move would occur in November 1911, when 211 residents moved into a new three-story, red-brick edifice that would become known as the main lodge. A smaller, separate building then housed twenty tuberculosis patients.[53]

In a related move, county commissioners bought an elaborate four-story mansion at S.W. Second Avenue and Hooker Street in Portland for $50,000 in 1909. They invested another $38,000 to convert the once-elegant mansion into a 65-bed hospital for indigents. Once again, the county commissioners thought they were ahead of the curve; the new hospital was deemed "probably equal to that of any similar-sized community in the United States."[54] In just a few years, however, that picture would change.

7

D-MINUS REPORT CARD, THE "KING OF ROADS," AND A NEW COURTHOUSE

(1913–1922)

The Progressive Era of nationwide social activism and political reform included the formation of new citizen-powered groups aimed at improving the efficiency of state and local governments. One of the first and most notable private organizations of this type was the New York Bureau of Municipal Research, founded in 1907 and funded at the outset by major business figures such as Andrew Carnegie and John D. Rockefeller. Its staff combined social reformers as well as highly trained business experts, including accountants, engineers, statisticians, and administrators. The bureau hired out its personnel as consultants to cities and states around the nation, hoping to promote efficient and economical government. They were leaders in trying to bring the new field of "scientific management" to bear on government. Nearly a century later, scholars would find that "the bureau was utilizing reasonably sophisticated performance measurements in the early decades of the twentieth century."[1]

Eight years after the Lewis and Clark Exposition, the Taxpayers League of Portland commissioned the New York bureau to evaluate Multnomah County's organization and business methods. The results were released in a 54-page document in September 1913.[2] Four months earlier, the same experts had issued a scathing report itemizing inefficiencies and disorganization in Portland city government. The city was stuck in the dark ages, the experts said, "still managing its affairs in much the same manner" as it had in 1891 when the city was less than a quarter its present size. The New Yorkers' commentary, along with an earlier vice-committee report, paved the way for passage of a city charter amendment in May 1913 that revolutionized Portland's government. Only six elected officials—a mayor, four commissioners, and an auditor—would henceforth run the city, instead of the twenty elected officials whose task it had been previously.[3]

The Multnomah County survey by the New York professionals failed to engender the same degree of reforming zeal as the city report, because no change in county structure was at stake. And the county commissioners at the time— D. V. Hart, William Lightner, and Thomas J. Cleeton—thought the study was unnecessary. When the Taxpayers League asked the county to pay for the study, the county court refused. They noted that the state insurance commissioner had been given a $7,500 appropriation by the state legislature to install uniform accounting systems in all Oregon counties. "The court took the view that it would be duplication of effort and useless expense to employ the bureau," the *Oregonian* reported.[4] The Taxpayers League agreed to pay for the study.

The visiting experts combed through many departments of Multnomah County government. One idea the New York Bureau studied was that of combining services and administrative functions between local governments. City-county consolidation had been raised as a possibility since the county's first decade. No consolidations occurred as a result of this outside review in 1913, but the subject would continue to surface in the years ahead.

If one were to think of the final report as a report card, perhaps the overall grade would have been a D-minus. The bureau found a need for reform almost everywhere it looked, but many of the changes would require action by the Oregon legislature. The report cited both "commendable" and "defective" practices, albeit mostly the latter. Some highlights of their conclusions may be summarized as follows:

- Accounting. The elected auditor's methods and systems are inadequate to "secure accuracy, economy and protection of the county's interests," as required by state law. As far as the incumbent county auditor, S. B. Martin, is concerned, that law is almost a "dead letter." The survey included twelve pages of recommendations and added, "Notwithstanding the existence of the unbusinesslike and inefficient conditions enumerated in this report, both the county auditor and the state insurance commissioner, who has supervision over all county accounts in the state, have refused to approve our suggestions for correcting the defects."[5]

- Assessor. Only one deputy is responsible for assessing all 162,500 land parcels in the county, even though leading national authorities advise that 10,000 properties per year should be the maximum assigned to any one person. The assessor is elected, so every election year that brings to office a new assessor and triggers an almost complete changeover of personnel, resulting in the loss of valuable experience and expertise. In addition, Multnomah County land parcels are vastly undervalued. This keeps taxpayer complaints to a minimum but builds wide inequities between taxpayers into the system.

- Board of Relief. By statutory authority, the board of county commissioners sits as the county's Board of Relief to administer public charity work for both the county and city. The active work of the relief board is done by one man, the board clerk. Despite admonitions by national authorities that special training and experience is necessary to secure effective results, the present clerk appears content to drift along following the beaten path of routine charity relief and makes no effort to equip himself by reading publications relating to charity and social work. The current clerk was formerly in the liquor business in Portland, and prior to that was a detective in the police department.

- Bridges. All five Willamette River bridges (whose construction was paid for by the city) are now the county's responsibility by state statute and city-county agreement. Yet no qualified person has been hired to oversee bridge operation and maintenance. "Notwithstanding the fact that these bridges represent an investment of over $4.5 million dollars and the fact that the obstruction of a bridge at any time seriously affects the life of the city in its every phase, there has been no one in the county service competent to supervise them."

- Budgeting. The county board lacks adequate information from which to draw up an annual budget. Levies are based almost entirely on what was spent in the previous year. The board is informed as to how much cash is on hand, but there is no system for tracking unpaid bills and commitments that have been made. Other large cities and counties are now operating with detailed budgets. Multnomah County should do likewise.

- Civil service. Most county administrative officials are elected, and each is free to appoint any persons he may choose to place on the payroll. Appointments are used to settle political debts and to help keep these officials in office at election time. No examinations of any kind are utilized. The state legislature should establish a county civil service system, "pending consolidation of the county and city governments."[6] (It is clear that the New York Bureau envisioned that consolidation should and would occur, but it was an assumption that proved unwarranted.)

- Constable. The office of constable, which serves the district court, should be abolished and the constable's duties assumed by the sheriff.

- Construction of Assets. "Since the next generation of taxpayers will enjoy the benefit of a building (such as the new courthouse) fully as much as the present generation, it is manifestly unfair to impose the entire burden of payment on the present taxpayers." Permanent improvements should be constructed with the proceeds of long-term bonds. Last year, 34 percent of county expenditures were used for building the new county courthouse; in the preceding year 27 percent of all expenditures were used for this purpose. "To use the tax money of any particular year to construct a building having a life from 25 to 40 years is contrary to all principles of logic and sound finance." Fifty years later, County Chairman Mike Gleason, who grew up in Depression-era times, would still shun the use of bonding, thereby limiting the construction of needed facilities to "pay-as-you-go" projects.

- Coroner. If a person's circumstances of death afford reasonable grounds to suspect that death was by suicide or criminal means, a coroner's jury of six persons is convened to pass judgment concerning such deaths. In the first five months of 1913, over half of the coroner juries convened included jurors who had served more than once. One juror served eleven times, one served nine times, three served eight times. "The sense of justice is outraged at the idea of having verdicts on murder, personal injury and other important cases returned by 'professional' jurors whose condition of employment naturally makes them subservient to the coroner or deputy coroner."[7] The office of coroner should be abolished and provision made instead for preliminary investigation by medical inspectors and the judiciary of the county.

- County Clerk. Many indications of efficient management under the administration of the present incumbent, J. B. Coffey, were noted.[8]

- Poor Farm. Two years ago, the inmates of Multnomah County's poor farm west of Portland (later part of Washington Park) were moved to a newly purchased farm of 193 acres located 17 miles east of downtown Portland. There are between 250 to 350 persons at the farm at all times. Some of the people who live in the home are bedridden. There are nearly as many sick people on the farm as in the county hospital. No instruction has been given to present residents regarding fire drills.

- In nearby Troutdale, a village of about 500 people, there are four saloons. Inmates from the county farm frequently wander down to the village, beg money from sympathetic people, buy liquor, become intoxicated, stray away into the fields and onto the railroad tracks. The legislature should pass a law prohibiting sale of intoxicants to inmates of such institutions.

- The coffin makers should do their work somewhere other than in the large room where the old people congregate each day. The basement of the main building is equipped with seats as a lounging place. Here, each day, in full view of all those in the room, the carpenter is engaged in making coffins. This condition is not conducive to a cheerful frame of mind on the part of the inmates.[9]

- Hospital. There is a "crying need" for a new hospital building. The present county hospital, located in the West Hills south of downtown, is an old residence of frame construction. It is not only ill-adapted for use as a hospital but also a highly dangerous fire risk. The maximum number of patients last winter was 100, the policy being to place cots in the hallways as well as in the rooms to take care of all who come by. Annual reports have not been published and the superintendent does not know what has become of them. It is important that a comprehensive report of this institution be rendered at least annually. [10]

- Property tax collection. Taxpayers are compelled to stand in line and wait while their tax bills are prepared by hand. The county should buy a machine with which to prepare its tax bills. A typewriter or carbon process could provide four duplicate copies at one writing to allow better control and efficiency.

- Purchasing. The county wastes money because elected officials scatter their supply purchases here and there, "plainly evidencing an endeavor to keep political fences in repair against the next election time." The county should standardize its specifications for purchase of supplies, materials, and equipment and consider consolidating its purchasing with that of Portland.[11]

- Roads. "The proper construction and maintenance of the county's five-hundred miles of roads is undoubtedly the most important problem confronting present and future county administrations." During the study, road funds were being distributed largely as political patronage. A complete reorganization of the road function is needed. "The greatest asset a county can have is a network of well built and well kept roads."[12]

- Sheriff. The last state legislature changed the law so that sheriffs will no longer collect property taxes until after September first, when they become delinquent. The other two main functions of the sheriff are apprehending and housing criminals, and serving as an officer of the circuit court. Court documents are now served by both the sheriff and the constable. More efficient use of employees' time could be realized if all these documents were served by the sheriff. In his jail supervision capacity, the sheriff receives 12½ cents per meal for feeding county prisoners. Experience in other counties indicates that meals cost less when meals are paid for at actual cost rather than at a fixed price per day.[13]

• Treasurer. The present system used by the treasurer appears to be adequate.

Other functions and officials briefly reviewed by the New York team included the district court, juvenile court, detention home, superintendent of schools, surveyor, sealer of weights and measures, fruit inspector, veterinarian, and courthouse security and lighting. The visiting experts did not examine the district attorney's office, public library, or board of commissioners.[14]

The last eight pages of the survey reiterated recommendations and specified which of them would require action by the state legislature. Many of the operations mentioned in the report would later disappear from the county government's jurisdiction, including the armory, county farm, ferries, fruit inspector, indigent soldiers, sealer of weights and measures, superintendent of schools, and county veterinarian.

An underlying premise of hiring the New York Bureau was that public disclosure of poor management would encourage voters and public officials to make changes.[15] That did not happen promptly in Multnomah County's case, although many of the recommended changes would come to pass in subsequent years and decades. The city's newspapers, for reasons unknown today, largely ignored the county's 1913 report. Many weeks later, the *Oregon Journal* noted, almost in passing, that "the findings in county methods brought an agreement between independent elective officers to work cooperatively, and suggested the movement to combine the city and county governments."[16]

In spite of the disdainful and accusatory evaluation of the incumbent auditor, S. B. Martin, who came into office in 1911, he would go on to be reelected again and again, serving until 1924.[17] The Oregon legislature established a Multnomah County Civil Service Commission in 1929. The offices of constable and coroner, which the New York bureau recommended for elimination, remained as elected offices until the county's home rule charter eliminated those positions fifty-three years later.

Regarding budgeting, the state legislature established the Multnomah County Tax Supervising and Conservation Commission (TSCC), effective 1919,

to oversee the budgets of all Multnomah County local government taxing jurisdictions, including schools and utility districts.[18] The role of the new commission
was to ensure that local jurisdictions, often headed by part-time or unpaid local
officials, complied with state budget laws. The new commission was a step in the
direction of professionalism that the New York team would have encouraged.
Likewise, pressure would soon start mounting for a solution to overcrowding at
the antiquated county hospital, although the result would take another decade
to materialize in brick and mortar.

Though the 1913 report card by the New York experts created little public
ripple, it caused consternation internally. The results could not have been much
of a surprise to Rufus Holman, who became the county's new chairman in June
1913. Holman had been appointed to a vacancy on the county board by the
Oregon legislature.[19] The two holdover commissioners, William Lightner and
D. V. Hart, agreed that Holman should be chairman. As he took office, Holman
said that he hoped to install a "complete and competent accounting system" that
would help produce accurate annual budgets, introduce systematic purchasing
regulations, establish permanent road locations, and adopt modern maintenance
procedures.[20]

Speaking to a civic group in March 1914, Holman said: "I found county
business in a chaotic condition when I entered office nine months ago. Everything
was characterized by confusion and lack of system. The county farm, the road
department, the purchasing division, the detention home were irresponsibly
administered. To bring order out of chaos, and to install a beginning of responsible system has meant hard work, defiance of criticism and the securing of the
wisest counsel from public spirited men and women best fitted to give it."[21]
C. E. S. Wood, a prominent Portland lawyer, writer, free thinker, and political
reform advocate, introduced Holman at a public gathering as "one official, at
least, whom I believe to be in office solely for service he can render to the community."[22] Given Wood's outspoken criticism of other public officials, there was
little reason to question the sincerity of his remark about Holman.

Holman proved to be the dominant political force on the county board for
almost ten years. He also was one of the few county officials ever to advance to
higher office, first as state treasurer from 1931 to 1938, and then for a single
term in the U.S. Senate from 1938 to 1944. He was then defeated in the U.S.
Senate Republican primary by an aggressive young politician from Lane County,
Wayne Morse,[23] who would go on to earn the informal title "The Tiger of the
Senate."

By the end of Holman's career, *Time* magazine, often considered a conservative voice in national politics, dismissed Holman, then 66, as "a party hack, a reactionary, a labor baiter" who was out of step with the times. The magazine added: "Holman, big of girth, white of hair, loose of lip, distinguished himself in Congress mainly by his absence from roll-calls (he was absent when Congress declared war, and missed 148 out of 239 roll-calls in seven months of 1942). But he managed to be present enough to distinguish himself in the making of intemperate attacks. These he delivered in a grave, falsetto voice which the *Oregon Journal* liked to call 'a high tenor of protest.' The high spot of the campaign came when Holman answered accusations of anti-Semitism by saying: 'Now why would I be anti-Semitic? My own father was an Englishman. I have relatives in England.'"[24]

As a younger man, Holman was a progressive force in Multnomah County. A native Portlander, Holman trained to be a schoolteacher but gave up that profession after two years to explore business opportunities. He worked in farming and as a steamboat operator before starting a company in 1910 that produced paper boxes and record-keeping books. Even before taking office in 1913, he was involved with several prominent business leaders and good-roads advocate Samuel Hill to encourage construction of a Columbia River Highway, a challenging road running east from Portland along the south shore of the river to the city of The Dalles. The highway posed a difficult engineering challenge because of the steep basalt cliffs that edged the massive river.[25]

Samuel Hill, who by coincidence bore the same last name as Great Northern Railway magnate James Hill, married James Hill's daughter, Mary.[26] Samuel was a successful entrepreneur in his own right. He spent several years trying to convince Washington State officials to build a highway along the Columbia's north shore, but turned his efforts to Oregon and the south shore after failing in Washington State. In Portland, Hill mustered the support of several prominent business leaders and, perhaps surprisingly, the editors of both the *Oregonian* and the *Oregon Journal*. Knowing that he needed help from Multnomah County, Sam Hill helped Holman win his first full term on the county commission in 1914.[232]

Hill also secured the services of a pioneering highway engineer who had already established a reputation of prominence in the Pacific Northwest. Samuel Lancaster had designed some fifty miles of boulevards ringing Seattle for the 1909 Yukon-Pacific Exposition. He also had engineered seven-and-a-half miles of paved roads on Hill's expansive private holdings at his Maryhill ranch in Washington State, where he sought to prove that paved roads were a superior year-round alternative to rutted dirt roads. With Holman leading the initiative, Multnomah County contributed $75,000 to hire Lancaster as engineer and to start construction on the portion of a highway along the south shore of the Columbia in Multnomah County.[28] It was a bold project, requiring innovative bridges, tunnels through easily fracturing rock, and challenging curves. Lancaster wanted the daring highway to be more than an artery for commerce. "Deeply religious, his philosophy coincided with that of John Muir and other preservationists who revered the wildness of God's unspoiled work. It was widely believed by early-twentieth-century progressives that natural surroundings could help heal some of the ills of urban life," according to a National Register of Historic Places Registration Form.[29] Lancaster would later leave the county post over disputes about overruns.

Prominent businessmen stayed active in the Columbia River Highway project after work began. John B. Yeon, a well-known timber baron, became a voluntary "roadmaster" for the county. He and Amos Benson, son of another timber magnate, Simon Benson, oversaw some 2,200 workers who used picks and shovels in the difficult terrain.[30] Although the Multnomah County section of the road was largely finished by 1916, Holman fired Yeon as volunteer roadmaster early in 1918. Famed Portland architect Edgar Lazarus had designed a visitor center perched more than 700 feet above the Columbia River—Vista House, at Crown Point—with fabulous views both up and downstream. Alas, the $15,000 appropriated by county commissioners fell way short. The bill was $65,000 and the building was not yet outfitted with water and heating systems when Holman fired Yeon.

Ultimately, Multnomah County paid $1.5 million of the $11 million construction cost for the entire highway, which reached its terminus in The Dalles in 1922. The highway was a success from the start. It soon drew thousands of visitors from all over the country, who came to view the many wonders nature had carved in the sheer rock walls of the Gorge.[31] "An accomplishment equal to the first continental railroad, the Panama Canal and the Golden Gate Bridge," proclaimed a 1937 book by Harriet Salt, *Mighty Engineering Feats*. "The long and winding road possesses the best of all the highways in the world, glorified!" said the *Illustrated London News* of the Gorge Highway, "It is the king of roads." Others called it "the road that couldn't be built" because workers had to carve their way through sheer basalt cliffs. It was called "a poem in stone."[32]

The new highway also became the site of a simple yet powerful experiment in highway design. In 1918, a Multnomah County Sheriff's Uniform Patrol Unit

Construction of the Columbia
River Highway was a daring
engineering feat, especially in East
Multnomah County where the
Cascade Range meets the Columbia
River. The county's three-member
board of commissioners, headed
by Rufus Holman, played a major
role in winning political support
and financing for the innovative
highway, parts of which are now
a national historic monument.
(Portland City Club)

was formed to police the new Columbia River Highway.[33] One of the members of that patrol was sheriff's deputy Peter Rexford, who proposed painting a yellow stripe down the center of the road as a safety measure. The idea occurred to him while he was patrolling the highway in a heavy rainstorm. He broached the suggestion to his boss, Chief Deputy Sheriff Martin Pratt (later elected sheriff), who took the proposal to the county commissioners for funding. The commissioners declined to spend money on such an untested notion, so Pratt bought what paint he could afford out of his own pocket and had a yellow stripe painted down the middle of the Columbia River Highway from Crown Point to Multnomah Falls.

The innovation proved popular. Two years later, when the paint began to wear thin, Pratt repainted the lines at the highway's most dangerous curves. By 1926, both Multnomah County and the State of Oregon were painting a stripe down the middle of all their highways. The idea would eventually spread throughout the United States.[34] *A Chronological History of the Oregon Department of Transportation, 1899 to 1993* credits Pratt and Rexford with painting, on the highway east of Vista House, the first yellow line in the nation's history "as a means of preventing head-on crashes on dangerous curves."[35]

Great as the highway was, it proved no match for bigger, faster cars and trucks that soon wanted to drive at greater speeds. Major portions of the

Sheriff's deputy Pete Rexford conceived the idea of painting a yellow line down the middle of the Columbia River Highway to lessen the danger of head-on collisions. Rexford was part of a sheriff's motorcycle unit formed in 1922.
(Multnomah County Archives)

Columbia River Highway would be destroyed by construction of Interstate 80N (later named Interstate 84) in the 1950s. A few sections of the original highway remain in use today, most notably the section from Troutdale to Dodson/Warrendale and a section in Wasco County.[36] Ten miles of segments have been restored as bike paths and pedestrian hiking trails. The restored sections have been designated a Millennium Legacy Trail by the White House Millennium Council.[37]

Commissioner Rufus Holman was involved with another huge transportation project at the same time that the Columbia River Highway was being built. Ever since the 1905 Lewis and Clark Exposition, when horse buggies lined up by the hundreds waiting for a ferry to cross the Columbia River from Vancouver, Washington, to Oregon State, Clark County residents had clamored for a vehicular bridge. Multnomah County and Clark County voters approved bonds, leading to the start of construction of a Columbia River Interstate Bridge in 1917. Holman served as chairman of the Interstate Bridge Commission that chose the bridge engineering firm and supervised the project. The challenge frequently put him in the midst of controversy.

"Mr. Holman stood his ground valiantly in the face of newspaper and other criticism which for a time rendered him exceedingly unpopular, and by doing so he became largely responsible for the successful result," the *Oregon Voter* magazine noted five years after the bridge opened.[38] Multnomah County contributed $1.2 million and Clark County $500,000 to the project, both as a result of ballot measures. When completed, the bridge was more than 3,400 feet long. It included two lanes for vehicles, a sidewalk, and streetcar tracks. The bridge bonds were to be retired by a toll, which started at five cents when the bridge opened on Valentine's Day of 1917.[39]

The opening of this first interstate bridge over the Columbia River was a glorious event. Thousands of people perched at both ends of the bridge. Sam Hill, who had been pushing for the bridge as well as for the Columbia River Highway, made a brief speech. "Today is the day when Oregon reaches out her hand and takes back her child Washington, to whom she gave birth over fifty years ago," he said, referring back to the era when the area that became Washington State was part of the Oregon Territory. "I pronounce this bridge open as long as the world shall last."[40] Holman signaled for the cutting of a rope, and more than forty thousand people walked or rode across the new structure on its opening day.

The success of the new bridge was never questioned. After only five years, tolls had retired two-thirds of the bonded debt. "From a business standpoint, the Interstate Bridge has proven the best investment that Multnomah County has ever made," the *Oregon Voter* asserted.[41] The states of Oregon and Washington bought the bridge in 1929. In 1958, a second, parallel bridge was added to double the capacity, and the first bridge was rebuilt with a matching "hump" to let more river traffic pass below without having to raise the lift span.[42]

The start of Holman's tenure as a county commissioner had been quickly followed by the end of the notable career of anti-vice crusader Sheriff Tom Word. Word had returned to the sheriff's office for a second time in 1912, then was challenged in 1914 by Republican Thomas Hurlburt. The *Oregon Journal* remained loyal to Word; the *Oregonian* endorsed Hurlburt. A week before the election, Word addressed a huge crowd to answer the many charges that had been leveled against him. With reference to an *Oregonian* article published on behalf of his opponent, Word said the sense of the story seemed to be that, as sheriff, "Mr. Hurlburt would enforce the laws but would not interfere with the personal pleasures of the people."[43]

When the votes were counted, Thomas Hurlburt had beaten Tom Word by 171 votes. The first official tally was 34,290 votes for Hurlburt to 34,119 for Word. It was Word's fifth ballot appearance as a candidate for sheriff, the second time that he was involved in a razor-thin defeat, and the second time the election story did not end with the initial count. Both camps charged election fraud and illegal voting. Word filed a recount petition and posted a $2,000 bond, as required by a new state statute, to guarantee that he would pay all recount costs, including his opponent's attorney fees, if he lost.

A rancorous ballot recount followed. Additional charges of ballot fraud is-sued from both sides. The final result sustained the original results. Hurlburt won the election.

In five attempts, Word had lost three elections and won only two. In spite of those setbacks, he left office with his head held high. He had earned a special place in history as a legendary crusading sheriff.[44] For the next seven years, he continued to crack down on Oregon vice as a federal special agent. Then, in August 1925, Word received an abrupt telegram from the U.S. Department of Justice: "Go to Phoenix, Arizona, immediately, or send in your resignation at once."

Word did not want to go to Arizona. He wanted to stay in Oregon, where he had spent the last twenty-one years of his life. "The government will go far before it will find a more devoted or more able special agent," grumped an *Oregon Journal* editorial. "Multnomah County never had a better sheriff than Tom Word. He knew his duty and did it . . . He served in a time when it required brains and nerve to be a real sheriff. He had and used both. For nearly seven years Mr. Word has been equally effective as a special agent."[45]

Oregon Governor Pierce offered Word the job of warden at the state peni-tentiary in Salem. Word considered the offer but announced in September that the federal government had decided to allow him to stay on in Portland, and that he would not be accepting the position of state penitentiary warden.[46] When he died in 1929 at the age of 71, an *Oregon Journal* article said, "Tom Word was one of the best-loved peace officers in the state. When Word finished (his crusades), gambling in open establishments was a thing of the past." A *Journal* editorial said: "There never was a better sheriff in any county, anywhere, a better or truer sheriff . . . Those who knew him can easily wish that it could be spared some folks to live on forever."[47]

In 1914, soon after Holman took office and Word left as sheriff, the county's new courthouse, built on the foundations of its 1864 predecessor, was finally completed. The eight-story exterior was clad with limestone and classical Ionic columns, while the riveted steel inner structure, wrapped in concrete for fire protection, was one of the first of its kind in Portland. To avoid fire—the scourge of many cities in the nineteenth century—the only wood in the new courthouse was decorative trim, furnishings, and doors.[48]

The new courthouse sat on the same block as the old one; portions of the original building were demolished as the new one was erected in two L-shaped sections that ran flush to the sidewalks. It was designed by the Portland firm of William Whidden and Ion Lewis, two Boston-trained architects who between

This eight-story building, completed in 1914, is the second Multnomah County Courthouse at the same location. It was the seat of county government until 2000, when county administrative offices were moved to Portland's East Side. Today, the often-remodeled county courthouse is filled with courtrooms operated by the state court system. The building's poor condition is a major challenge facing contemporary county government. (Multnomah County Facilities Management)

1890 and 1910 designed several major Portland buildings, many of which still stand, including City Hall and the Arlington Club, as well as office buildings and residences.

At the time of the grand opening, the new courthouse was the largest on the West Coast and Portland's largest building. The $1.6 million structure boasted eight stories of courtrooms and office space, with wide, lustrous hallways of black and white marble. The interior featured four state-of-the-art elevators that drew curious crowds of sight-seers. An airy courtyard in the building's center helped overcome the lack of greenery around the exterior, as the new building extended out to the sidewalk on all four sides.

When first built, the courthouse contained eleven "elegant" circuit court-rooms, each two stories high, plus three smaller courtrooms for justice-of-the-peace hearings. Only six of the eleven two-story courtrooms were needed at the time, and the county commissioners congratulated themselves on their farsightedness, certain that they were providing enough additional courtrooms to fill future needs indefinitely. As has been the case with other county facilities throughout history, however, "indefinitely" was a considerably briefer time period than expected.

The interior courtyard in the middle of the courthouse furnished natural light for every office. This innocent-looking courtyard was the scene of a mini-scandal during 1918 Prohibition days. Some county employees who observed Sheriff Thomas Hurlburt using a courtyard drainpipe for disposing of confiscated alcohol considered this a waste of perfectly good spirits and decided to build a secret tap to capture the alcohol. The theft was eventually discovered, but not before a good deal of illegal alcohol had found its way from a courthouse drainpipe to eager consumers.[49]

Many people assume erroneously that the seventh and eighth floors of the courthouse were later additions because they are set back from the edge of the roof. In fact, the seventh and eighth floors were always part of the building; they were originally hidden from the street by a ten-foot-high parapet that was later removed, according to future sheriff and county chair Don Clark and other sources. Both the seventh and eighth floors served as a jail for many years, but after Rocky Butte Jail opened in 1941, half the seventh floor and all of the top floor housed other sheriff's functions, including a soundproofed interview room, dating back to an era when criminal defendants were not advised they had a right to remain silent, and some deputy sheriffs used extraordinary measures to obtain statements. The remaining half of the seventh floor served as a holding facility for prisoners whose court cases were being heard.[50]

The basic structure of the county courthouse that was completed in 1914 would last for at least a century. Though it now badly needs replacing or substantial renovation, the outlook as of 2012 holds no promise that this will happen in the near future. Financial constraints imposed by the infamous Measure 5, passed in 1990, would severely cripple Multnomah County and all other Oregon local governments. More will be said about Measure 5 later.

8

COUNTY HOSPITAL, THE KKK, KICKBACK SCANDALS, AND MORE CONSOLIDATION PROPOSALS
(1909–1927)

Multnomah County's 167 percent increase in population from 1900 to 1920,[1] fueled by the 1905 Lewis and Clark Centennial Exposition and a thriving economy, led to a correspondingly greater demand for indigent care at the four-story Victorian mansion at SW Second Avenue and Hooker Street that had been converted into a county hospital in 1909. It was designed to house 65 patients, but only four years later daily populations were running between 90 and 110.[2] Cots filled the hallways and some patients were hoisted up to the "roof garden," where canvas awnings provided weather protection.[3]

Perhaps prompted by criticism from the New York Bureau of Municipal Research in 1913, the grand juries that performed annual reviews of county facilities in 1914 and 1915[4] declared the converted mansion to be a firetrap and called for its closure. Emma Jones, a nurse who had trained at Cook County Hospital in Chicago and became hospital superintendent soon after her arrival in Portland, criticized the building for having no elevators, inadequate fire escapes, no heat during specified hours, only one telephone, and an apparently ineradicable rat infestation.[5]

Soon after the second grand jury report, County Chairman Rufus Holman proposed that the county board close the hospital immediately and pay for the treatment of indigent patients at other Portland hospitals. His motion was defeated two to one, though the board did call for the county physician to investigate the prices that other hospitals would charge for such services.[6] St. Vincent Hospital, then at its original site in northwest Portland, offered to take over indigent medical care at a cost of $8 per week per patient, with additional charges for drugs and surgery. The county declined, citing its current daily cost of 78 cents per patient.[7] Once the county decided to replace the old mansion, debate erupted over the new location. Holman, who had taken the lead on the

Columbia River Highway and the first Interstate Bridge, once again became the key figure. Dr. R. A. J. MacKenzie, dean of the Oregon Medical School, which had its roots in a two-room building in northwest Portland, encouraged Holman to consider the medical school's new site on Marquam Hill. Twenty acres of that steeply sloping site had been donated in 1917 by the Oregon-Washington Railway and Navigation Company.

Holman convinced county officials to build a new hospital on the medical school site. The agreement he negotiated with Dr. MacKenzie called for the medical school to provide a seven-acre site at no cost to the county, in return for which the county would build and maintain a hospital and allow medical students access to the patients. The medical school agreed to provide medical staff and to take responsibility for all care provided.[8]

The prolific architect Ellis Lawrence, who was based in Portland and Eugene, where he was dean of the University of Oregon architecture department, hoped to design the new county hospital. But as he wrote to an associate, "politics robbed us of the County Hospital, which went to Sutton and Whitney in spite of all the [university] Regents could do."[9] The decision could have been affected by Lawrence's opinion that the original acreage, given the steep terrain, was not big enough for the county hospital and the medical school; those worries were assuaged in 1924 when the wife of C. S. Jackson, publisher of the *Oregon Journal,* donated an adjacent 88 acres.

The firm of Albert Sutton and Harrison Whitney was eminently qualified to undertake the county project. In the medical field, their works in Portland included Emanuel Hospital, Good Samaritan Hospital, and the original Shriners' Hospital in northeast Portland, now demolished. Other notable surviving structures designed in their office include the Portland Masonic Temple, now a part of the Portland Art Museum, and the Weatherly Building, in its glory days the tallest building east of the Willamette River, both of which were also constructed in the early 1920s. As for Lawrence, he designed the first medical school building, now called MacKenzie Hall, and six other buildings on the hilly campus.

The Sutton and Whitney design for the new county hospital was in the shape of an H, and was originally intended to house up to five hundred patients. Because of high costs, only the first wing was completed in 1923. The original $500,000 cost estimated had ballooned to $1.25 million, reminiscent of Rufus Holman's experience with the Columbia River Highway. The new hospital earned glowing praise even before it opened. After a tour in 1922, Dr. Charles Mayo, a founder of the Mayo Clinic in Minnesota, one of the world's leading medical treatment and research institutions, called the new Multnomah County

Shown as it neared completion in 1923, the Multnomah County Hospital on Marquam Hill served indigent patients for fifty years. As a result of rising costs, the county convinced the Oregon legislature to let Oregon Health Sciences University take control in 1973. A surviving portion of the building, now called the Multnomah Pavilion, remains in active use on the now-crowded medical school campus. (Oregon Health Sciences University Archives)

Hospital "the finest hospital I have ever inspected and I expect it in coming years to set the model for many advances in medical work in other places."[10]

When the new hospital opened in late August 1923, eighty patients were transferred from the old mansion on Hooker Street. Nurse Emma Jones, who had spoken out about the unsafe conditions in the Hooker Street building, moved to the new hospital as well. She continued working at the county hospital until her retirement in 1944. Emma Jones Hall, a dormitory for nursing students on the Marquam Hill campus, is named in her honor.

The county hospital proved to be a successful collaboration with the medical school for fifty years. The second wing of the original plan was added in 1950, and an emergency room was added in 1964. Total capacity never exceeded three hundred, some two hundred below the original plan.

While the planning of the new county hospital was in its earliest stages, a new health threat arose from other ports on the West Coast, notably San Francisco, Seattle, and Tacoma. Outbreaks of venereal diseases, presumably from women who were pleasuring soldiers leaving for and returning from World War I, prompted local agencies to fear that Portland would soon face a public health threat from diseased women forced to leave those cities. (Newspapers of the day used gentler

Rufus Holman, the only elected county official eventually to serve in the U.S. Senate, was a progressive force instrumental in developing the Columbia River Highway, the Interstate Bridge, a new Multnomah County Hospital, and improved administrative practices during ten years on the county board. As a U.S. Senator, the older Holman's conservative views and poor attendance made him an easy target for aggressive candidate Wayne Morse, who defeated Holman after one term. (Oregon Historical Society, no. bb009004)

terms, using phrases such as "women of the underworld" whose "social diseases" posed a threat.) This led to a tense meeting involving County Chairman Holman, Portland Mayor George Baker, and members of the Oregon Social Hygiene Society in November 1917. The city had already agreed to allocate $25,000 to build a home for such women, but the Hygiene Society and Baker wanted the county to provide an immediate quarantine at Kelly Butte Jail. Sheriff Thomas Hurlburt, who was nearing the end of the first term of a tenure that would span seventeen years, said his jail lacked room for as many as fifty women.[11]

In a dust-up between the City of Portland and Multnomah County that was reminiscent of previous quarrels and foreshadowed future clashes, the Portland mayor and county chair staked out their medical territories. Mayor Baker said the city needed short-term help. Holman was reluctant. "In other words, you men ask the county to provide the funds and take responsibility which is the city's?" Holman asked. "We are not asking you to take responsibility that belongs to the city," said Baker, who stood up, waved to other city officials and added, "Come, let's go" as he left the room.[12] Within days, however, the county commissioners agreed to pay $10,000 to establish a temporary quarantine. "Immoral women who are arrested and found afflicted will either be placed in a quarantine station until they are cured or will be required to deposit a bond of $2,000 that they will observe strictly the rules and regulations prescribed by the city health officer," the *Portland Telegram* reported.[13] The newspaper added, "Enforcement of such a measure is considered a war effort."

The final months of Holman's ten-year tenure on the county board brought another dispute involving dollars and cents. This time the argument was whether the County Poor Farm near Troutdale was making or losing money. County auditor Sam Martin claimed net losses of $14,208 to $26,010 for the years 1917 to 1921, while Holman claimed annual profits of $7,500 during the same period. The matter came to the attention of a grand jury examining county facilities. U.G. Smith, farm foreman at the time, submitted reports showing an average annual profit of $7,092 during those four years, based on the wholesale value of milk and butter, hogs, poultry, potatoes, vegetables, and fruit grown and consumed at the farm or distributed to other county agencies. It turned out that auditor Martin had records of expenses paid but had not received documents about the value of goods produced.[14] Holman said the county's decision to turn over management of the farm, at his instigation, to the Oregon Agricultural College (now Oregon State University) was a key factor in keeping the farm profitable.

Holman's decade as the most powerful county official came to an end in 1922. Though he counted the Interstate Bridge, Columbia River Highway, and other managerial changes as reasons for seeking a new term, each of these projects had created political enemies. Even his supporters admitted displeasure with his "irritating voice and mannerisms."[15] He placed fourth in a field of ten commissioner candidates in the May primary, even falling 1,000 votes behind another former commissioner who had frequently been an opponent on county matters, William Lightner. That defeat ended Holman's career in local government, although he was to make two more attempts. He filed for election as a county commissioner in 1924, only to be narrowly beaten by Amadee Smith, an industrialist and real estate investor, by a count of 22,945 to 21,427. In 1928, Holman made a bid to become mayor of Portland, unsuccessfully challenging incumbent George Baker.

One of the biggest scandals in Multnomah County history captured Portland-area headlines soon after Holman's term expired. It would lead to the fastest housecleaning on the three-member commission in county history.

The top two vote-getters for county commission seats in the 1922 Republican primary, Dow V. Walker and John H. Rankin, respectively, each won seats in the November general election. They joined Charles Rudeen, who had been elected two years before. In 1924, all three would be accused of awarding "illegal, irregular, and accepted without competition" bids for building three bridges across the Willamette River. They were quickly swept from public office in the county's largest successful recall effort.[16]

In his landmark book *Growth of a City*, E. Kimbark MacColl says that Walker was recruited by the Ku Klux Klan to run against Rufus Holman, and that both Rankin and Walker were Klan-backed candidates.[17] MacColl described the most flamboyant commissioner of the three this way: "Dow V. Walker . . . had been a football star at Oregon State College early in the century. During and after his college years, he had played for the Multnomah Athletic Club which, like many similar athletic organizations, fielded competitive football teams in those days. Walker became so popular at the club that he was . . . [appointed] club manager in 1908. Walker was a big, jolly, "hail-fellow-well-met type" who energetically boosted the club membership from 800 to over 6,000 by the time he resigned in 1919."[18]

Walker later became associated with the prominent insurance firm of Jewett & Barton. In 1920, he managed the unsuccessful Oregon campaign of General Leonard Wood for the Republican presidential nomination. Historian MacColl says that Walker and Rankin were assisted in their county campaigns by the secretive Oregon branch of the Klan.

Because Portland and Oregon had few African-American residents at the time, the Klan's focus was religious and ethnic rather than racial. Its leader was Frederick L. Gifford, a former electric utility technician. "Mr. Gifford is an ideal-ist of the fanatical sort," wrote the editor of the *Oregon Voter* after landing an interview with Gifford, "who is determined to run Catholics out of public office and incidentally to damage the business and political influence of Jews and aliens."[19] Gifford said he was opposed to any groups that were not white, Christian, and American. The Klan's influence helped Governor Walter Pierce defeat incumbent Ben Olcott, and aided the passage of an artfully worded initia-tive aimed at eliminating parochial schools. A panel of the Ninth Circuit U.S. Court of Appeals held the school measure unconstitutional, and that ruling was affirmed by the U.S. Supreme Court in *Pierce v. Society of Sisters* in 1925.[20] By then, partly as a result of internal bickering, the Klan had declined as a political force.

The county bridge scandal had its genesis in 1922, when voters approved bond measures totaling $4,950,000 for replacing the old Burnside Bridge and constructing two new ones—the Ross Island and Sellwood bridges. The estimates allocated $3 million for Burnside, $1.6 million for Ross Island, and $350,000 for Sellwood. The existing Burnside Bridge, erected in 1894, was in such bad shape that it was closed during a severe flood in January 1923 for fear it might collapse. All three bridges were vitally needed to ease the area's growing transportation problems.[21]

CHIEF KLUXERS TELL LAW ENFORCEMENT OFFICERS JUST WHAT
MYSTIC ORGANIZATION PROPOSES TO DO IN CITY OF PORTLAND

To the surprise of assembled public officials, two Ku Klux Klan representatives swooped in from behind a curtain just as this news photo was snapped in 1921. Sheriff T. M. Hurlburt stood seventh from the left, next to a robed Klan figure. The photograph was considered a "frame-up" by the officials involved, but the Klan played a secretive and sometimes powerful role in local and state politics in the early 1920s. (Oregon Historical Society, no. 54338)

A consortium of three contractors submitted an unusual bid stipulating that their bids for all three bridges had to be accepted together or not at all. Another contractor bid only on the Burnside, but at a price that was $500,000 below the "all-or-nothing" bid. Moving with surprising speed, the three commissioners accepted the consortium's package as submitted on the same day they opened the bids, brushing aside the lower bid for the Burnside Bridge and without asking the district attorney whether or not such contract awards were legal.

The public reaction was quick and intense. Former Governor Oswald West, who had won the state's highest office as a reformer and earned a shining reputation for honesty in public service early in the century, said, "Those who are putting over the deal are working fast, and unless something is done at once the taxpayers of the county and city are going to get a wonderful trimming." Talk of recall was already in the air. "If the facts of the bridge deal ever come to light there will be no doubt as to the result of the recall movement," West said.[22]

Three days after the bid was opened and accepted, the *Portland Telegram* editorialized, "Public indignation over the awarding of the contract for the three trans-Willamette bridges this week is universal. No official act in the history of Multnomah County ever aroused more condemnation."[23] A Portland City Club report charged that by accepting this bid the county commissioners had "forfeited the confidence of the public."[24]

The commissioners stood by their speedy action. Chairman Rankin noted that no other bids were received for the Ross Island and Sellwood, so those bridges couldn't be erected unless the county took more time to issue a call for new bids. He said the package deal made sense in terms of the contractors sharing necessary equipment and acquiring concrete and steel. Rudeen said the city needed the bridges built quickly, especially the Burnside, whose closure had caused serious congestion problems during the flood of 1923. "The people have demanded action," Rudeen said. "They want bridges without further delay. And here we had bids, which, if accepted, would enable us to build the bridges within the overall budget."[25] The consortium bidders claimed to be able to complete the Burnside in 300 days, compared to 500 days proposed by the lower bidder. But critics noted that the Steel and Broadway bridges had each taken approximately two years to erect, throwing doubt on the shorter estimate.

Rumors spread that the bidding network involved kickbacks and trade-offs. "I'll award you this county contract if you buy your insurance from me" was said to be standard operating procedure. Commission seats at that time were only part-time, and most commissioners carried on their own business on the side. In fact, commissioners Rudeen and Walker had purchased eighteen residential lots near what would be the west end of the Ross Island Bridge before the bridge details were made public.[26] The lots would presumably appreciate in value rapidly once the new bridge was finished. Rumors circulated that Rudeen sought a $50,000 payment for hiring professional bridge engineers to win the design contract, valued in excess of $180,000, and that surety bonds for the projects would be purchased from Walker's insurance company.

The bridge controversy quickly took up a permanent place on the front page of Portland newspapers as allegations continued to fly. State Attorney General Isaac Van Winkle announced the start of a grand jury investigation on April 13, not even two weeks after the bids were opened.[27] A recall petition drive launched on April 9 reached 16,500 signatures nine days later and 26,075 signatures were turned in only thireen days after the drive began, assuring a recall election in the May primary.[28] The formal investigation, which took six weeks and involved more than sixty interviewees, may have been the most detailed to date in Oregon history.[29] The witnesses included all three commissioners, who testified without grants of immunity that they had done nothing wrong.

Ultimately, the grand jury issued two sets of indictments. In the first, issued only six days before the recall election, commissioners Dow Walker and Charles Rudeen were accused of soliciting and accepting a bribe of more than $10,000 from one of the professional engineers, Robert E. Kremers, and Kremers was accused of bribing Rudeen and Walker. A second indictment, which was handed down twelve days *after* all three commissioners had been recalled at the polls, accused the former commissioners of malfeasance for awarding a bid to the higher bidder. Five contractors were accused of submitting a collusive bid in the same indictment. Despite the lengthy investigation and weeks of public accusations, no charges were issued in connection with insurance-related dealings.

Of the three incumbents, only Rankin bothered to campaign during the brief recall campaign. He wasn't tainted with the bribery talk because he had voted against hiring Kremers as engineer. It helped, but not enough. In the final tally, 41,907 voters approved the recall of Rankin, versus 23,653 in favor of retaining him. The results were worse for Rudeen and Walker: more than 55,000 voters approved their dismissal, compared with fewer than 10,000 each to retain them.[30]

While the former commissioners awaited trial, the new county board members went to work dealing with the scandal's aftermath. Besides Amadee Smith, who had bested former commissioner Rufus Holman, the new panel comprised Erwin Taft, a flour mill export agent, and Grant Phegley, the retired co-owner of a clothing store. Their first official act was to abrogate the controversial bridge contract, acting on the advice of District Attorney Stanley Myers that they were on safe legal ground.[31]

The commission quickly hired Gustav Lindenthal, a well-known New York bridge engineer, to lead the three-bridge project. Lindenthal kept the same design that had been submitted by Kremers and his design partner, Ira Hedrick, for the Burnside Bridge, which opened in May 1926 at a cost of $3 million. Lindenthal redesigned the Sellwood and Ross Island bridges, which opened in December 1925 and December 1926, respectively. The Ross Island was completed for $1.9 million, but Lindenthal had to scrimp on the Sellwood because of budget constraints. It was built with only two lanes instead of four at a cost of $541,000. Given its narrowness, "the Sellwood was inadequate from the day it opened," Portland bridge historian Sharon Wood Wortman has noted.[32] It also proved less durable. As a result of cracks found in the concrete spans, in 2004 county officials reduced the maximum weight of vehicles permitted to cross the bridge from 32 tons to 10 tons, meaning that TriMet buses and large trucks could no longer use it.[33] By 2011, the county had developed plans for a new $290 million Sellwood Bridge, but struggled with a funding formula to pay for it.[34]

Former commissioners Dow Walker and Charles Rudeen faced separate jury trials in Multnomah County Circuit Court. Visiting judges were assigned to both cases to eliminate any suggestion of local political favoritism. Deputy District Attorney George Mowry contended that Kremers paid Rudeen $50,000 to win the design contract, and that as a result Kremers would receive 58 percent of the contract fees and Hedrick only 42 percent, although Hedrick was the more experienced bridge engineer. As the testimony unfolded, all the inferences about bribe money being sought involved Rudeen, not Walker. The trial judge took the matter out of the jury's hands at the end of the state's case. "There is nothing to connect Walker to the crime," said visiting Circuit Judge J. U. Campbell. "The facts in the case would tend to show that Rudeen offered the jobs for sale, but there is no evidence to show that Walker had any connection with this."[35]

Surprisingly, the same result occurred when Rudeen went on trial in October before another visiting judge, William Morrow. Morrow concluded after the state's case that there were no conclusive facts, only inferences. He said the state needed to prove that a corrupt agreement existed and that it was carried out. "There was no direct proof of either," he said, ending the case without need of evidence from the defense. The big county bridge scandal ended without a criminal conviction.

Conflicts of interest were inevitable in county dealings, said historian E. Kimbark MacColl. Kickbacks to county commissioners continued to occur over the years because most commission members were closely allied with real estate, insurance, or banking businesses.[36]

Soon after the bridge scandal trials, the 1925 state legislature took a run at trying to consolidate Portland and Multnomah County governments. It marked the fourth time that the consolidation issue had arisen in the county's 71-year history, and it came only eleven years after a previous unsuccessful proposal that would have allowed Portland to expand to fill the boundaries of Multnomah County. The legislature convened a Government Simplification Committee to study Portland's metropolitan government. The committee—chaired by Richard Montague,[37] a prominent Portland lawyer who had been involved in numerous progressive issues—studied possible merger scenarios for two years before proposing a state constitutional amendment that would enable city and county voters to adopt consolidated governments.

Before that proposal made it to the ballot, however, lengthy changes were proposed to the Portland city charter by a 25-member committee led by Mayor George Baker. The Portland charter amendment, titled "Simplify and Retain Commission Form of Government," provided for 50 percent increases in the mayor's and council members' salaries, as well as pensions for police, fire, and civil service employees, all to be paid for from a new property tax levy. "Taxes Go Up If Charter Is Adopted," warned a front-page *Oregon Journal* headline.[38] The measure was rejected by a 3 percent margin. The City Council resubmitted the amendment the following June (1927), only to have it rejected by Portland voters again, even more strongly this time, by a five-to-one margin.

Supporters of the Government Simplification Committee proposal to allow cities and counties to consolidate fought an onslaught of objections. In an impassioned, three-page response to counterarguments published in the *Voters' Pamphlet*, Richard Montague labeled existing local government structures "complex, ill-adjusted, expensive and inefficient." Arguments against the measure were ill-founded, he insisted: "The Grange declares flatly that the whole thing is a scheme by designing interests of Portland to bankrupt the farmers of Multnomah County by bringing them into the city and thereby increasing their tax burdens to the point of confiscation." That was untrue, Montague said, because "an intelligent consolidation system . . . most certainly would provide a zoning system by which taxes are graduated [based on whether] the property is urban or rural. . . . The charge that the consolidation would create bureaucratic control is sufficiently refuted by the fact that the entire bureaucratic force of county and city job-holders . . . is fighting tooth and nail against the amendment."[39]

The *Oregonian* added its editorial support. "This appeals to us as a real economy and efficiency measure, which does not increase taxes or bonds," the newspaper said.[40] Since the earliest days, rural county residents had feared that their tax dollars were being used to pay for services to city residents. Concerns voiced during the 1925 consolidation debate would surface fifty years later, when detailed analysis would conclude that the opposite was true, that city residents were paying for services available only to rural residents.

Voters were not persuaded that it was time for change. The June 1927 statewide measure drafted by the Government Simplification Committee to enable consolidation was defeated by 58 percent to 42 percent, with nearly 100,000 statewide voters casting ballots.[41] Portland-Multnomah County consolidation was again buried, this time for nearly half a century.

ST. JOHNS BRIDGE DEDICATION, PORTLAND, ORE., 718 ©Cross & Dimmitt

Construction started on the graceful St. Johns Bridge in North Portland just weeks before the stock market crash of 1929. The suspension bridge was finished two years later well below the original budget, making it a successful Multnomah County project. Decades later it was turned over to the Oregon Department of Transportation because it carries a state highway. (Oregon Historical Society, no. 26297)

9

AN ELEGANT BRIDGE, A MIGHTY DAM, ANOTHER JAIL, AND WORLD WAR II

(1928–1945)

The stock market crash of October 1929 was only a few weeks away when Multnomah County launched its last and arguably most elegant bridge project. Citizens in St. Johns had been lobbying for years for a bridge that would connect their community with Linnton on the west side of the Willamette and provide a faster, more direct route to downtown Portland. The last ferry operating in the Portland region still plied those Willamette River waters some five miles downstream from the city's center. Perhaps because of the bridge scandal of 1924, county commissioners appeared to be in no hurry to undertake another bridge project. But bridge proponents in St. Johns put together a vaudeville-style program that they presented to almost every school and grange in the county, outlining their need. In May 1928, county voters approved a $4.25 million bond measure to build a St. Johns bridge by 33,366 votes to 26,849.[1]

Seeking to avoid the kind of controversy that had beset the county on previous projects, county commissioners staged a national competition to select a bridge designer. The winner was David B. Steinman, a principal in the New York firm of Robinson & Steinman, who would design more than four hundred bridges over the course of his lengthy career.[2] Steinman submitted two proposals to Multnomah County. The commissioners settled on the less costly option, a graceful-looking suspension bridge with steel towers in the shape of gothic arches that would stand 400 feet high. The roadbed, some 200 feet above the water, would allow all watercraft to pass below without the need for opening or lifting any part of the bridge.

Still, there was one controversy to settle before construction could begin. Would the bridge hold three lanes for traffic, or four? Commissioner Fred German, no doubt concerned about overruns on other county projects, argued that three lanes and a 30-foot-wide bridge would save up to $750,000 and provide a buffer against unexpected contingencies. He also claimed that other Portland bridges were operating below maximum capacity, so there was no need to build an oversized bridge in St. Johns.[3]

Commissioner Clay Morse took the opposite view. He saw large, vacant parcels on both ends of the bridge as potential growth opportunities, and wondered how a three-lane bridge would manage if the county's population grew by another 100,000 beyond the current 350,000. He knew there would be political heat if the bridge turned out to be too narrow.[4] The Portland city planning commission and the Portland Realty Board supported four lanes. In the end, Morse's view for the wider bridge prevailed; the finished product boasted a 40-foot deck carrying four traffic lanes and two narrow sidewalks. Furthermore, the project was completed for roughly $1 million less than the original budget.

With the crash of the nation's economy, the St. Johns Bridge project provided hundreds of welcome jobs during its 21-month construction period. Some daring workers ate their lunch sandwiches at dizzying heights sitting on the massive suspension cables, which were composed of twisted steel strands, wrapped first in cedar to protect against moisture and then clad in a steel cover. There was talk that the new bridge would be painted with black and yellow stripes to warn airplanes using the Swan Island Municipal Airport just a couple miles to the south. But designer Steinman settled that issue when the impressive new bridge was nearing completion: he picked verde green instead, saying he was inspired by the hues of massive Forest Park, which rises sharply from the west end of the bridge.[5]

The grand opening on June 13, 1931, was a memorable day in St. Johns. The Portland Rose Festival rerouted its grand floral parade to celebrate the opening. Under overcast skies, the Rose Festival queen cut a giant ribbon and fire engines with blaring sirens raced from each end of the new bridge. Fireboats sprayed jets of water from 200 feet below. Some daring pilots celebrated the opening in a manner that lacked official approval. "Airplanes flew under the structure yesterday with ease," the Oregonian noted, "giving some indication of its height and reach, for under no other bridge in Portland could they fly."[6]

Steinman, who once said "A bridge is mathematics brought to life," put more than numbers into the St. Johns Bridge. He talked about selecting the Gothic arch motif as an attempt to add special beauty. Looking back on his career, Steinman said, "If you asked me which of the bridges I love best, I believe I would say the St. Johns Bridge. I put more of myself into that bridge than any other."[7] Multnomah County owned and maintained the St. Johns

Bridge until 1976, when it was deeded to the Oregon Department of Transportation because it serves U.S. Highway 30.[8]

A few months after the St. Johns Bridge opened, a different spectacle transfixed Portland area commuters crossing the Interstate Bridge between Portland, Oregon, and Vancouver, Washington. An amazing sight met their eyes in October 1931. An animal said to be thirty or forty feet long was swimming in the Columbia River Slough and spouting plumes of water.

A baby whale was just the thing to capture the public's attention in the middle of the Great Depression. Soon the whale, dubbed "Jim McCool's whale" after the *Oregonian* reporter who first broke the story, was making international news. Hundreds of spectators lined the riverbanks to catch a glimpse of the creature. After someone tried to shoot the animal, Governor Julius Meier forbade the use of firearms on the baby whale.

Edward and Joe Lessard, father and son, armed themselves with homemade harpoons and went hunting. After they killed the whale,

The carcass of a baby whale that was shot after it surfaced in the Columbia Slough in 1931 was suspended in the courtyard of the Multnomah County Courthouse while unusual legal proceedings unfolded, first in a criminal case against the shooter and later in a civil case over ownership of the embalmed remains. (The Oregonian)

the state sued them for violating Oregon's fish and game laws. The state also sought possession of the carcass. While the Lessards' trial was taking place, Sheriff Hurlburt, who was nearing the end of his long sheriff's career, hung the whale from scaffolding in the courthouse yard. Curious spectators came from far and wide to view the sight of an embalmed twelve-and-a-half-foot whale in the middle of downtown Portland.

Attorney Delmore Lessard obtained an acquittal for his father and brother on the grounds that fish and game laws did not apply.[9] Judge James W. Crawford ruled that the state had no restrictions on killing whales. In his legal opinion the judge said, "The legal considerations rendering these conclusions inescapable are not to be taken as any expression of personal approval of, or sympathy with, the act of the defendants in the unnecessary killing of Jim McCool's whale in the waters of the Oregon Slough."

Two years later the Oregon Supreme Court remanded Crawford's decision, proclaiming that the whale was a "royal fish," in legal terminology, while in coastal or inland waters. A different judge then awarded the embalmed carcass to the state.[10]

Sheriff Thomas Hurlburt died in December 1931 while serving in his seventeenth year as sheriff, the longest tenure to date in the county. As it turned out, his successor would hold the post for the next seventeen years. Hurlburt, who had defeated vice-hunting Sheriff Tom Word in 1914, had previously worked as an engineer for railway companies and served as county surveyor, Portland city engineer, and a U.S. Examiner of Surveys. He helped organize the Oregon State Sheriffs' Association and served as its first president, a position he held from 1916 until his death.

To complete the remaining year of Hurlburt's unexpired term (a state constitutional amendment had changed sheriffs' terms from two years to four years in 1920), county commissioners appointed Chief Deputy Martin Pratt.[11] Pratt, an expert on traffic safety, was a Portland native who had earned fame throughout the Northwest as a expert football tackle while still in high school. He was to steer the sheriff's office through the high-tension days of World War II and stand for election five times.[12]

Pratt brought a flair for innovation and showmanship to the sheriff's department. He ordered new deputies' uniforms featuring high-top boots and belted jackets, which strongly resembled those of the Royal Canadian Mounted Police. He organized an elite motorcycle corps that performed feats of daring to appreciative crowds throughout the West. Buicks that served as patrol cars were equipped with flasher lights and sirens, red and green lights, two-way radios, loudspeakers, Thompson submachine guns, and six other kinds of shooting irons and riot clubs.[13]

The start of Pratt's lengthy tenure as sheriff coincided with the beginning of Frank Shull's lengthy service as a county commissioner. The surprising fact about Shull, who would become the longest serving county commissioner at that time when he finally stepped down in 1954, is that he was already 61 when he took office in 1931. A successful businessman in flour milling and later as a grain exporter, Shull had served nine years on the Portland School Board before running for county office and proved to be one of the district's successful directors at the polls. He had been a small-college football, baseball, and track athlete in Indiana before heading to Portland in 1904 at the age of 35.[14]

At 58, Shull showed an interest in expanding his political activity beyond the school board when he announced himself a candidate for Oregon's Third District seat in Congress, following the death of the incumbent, Maurice Crumpacker. Shull had lobbied in Washington, D.C., on port-related matters just before his announcement. He was interested in deeper river channels for shipping and plans for the Columbia River dams.[15] His Congressional bid was unsuccessful, however.

Shull had served less than half his first county commission term when he announced that he would run for Portland mayor in 1932. It was a free ride politically, since he would still have his county seat if he lost.[16] Shull lost that race to Joseph Carson Jr., a cherubic-looking lawyer who had been practicing in Portland since 1919. Nevertheless, Shull's name remained golden in county politics. He won six terms before finally losing at the polls in 1954 at the age of 85. After his retirement, Shull remained active and athletic. He continued golfing into his late eighties—and shooting in his nineties—at Portland Golf Club. He died in 1960 at the age of 91.[17]

Along with Shull, Charles Bigelow was also elected to the county board in 1932. Bigelow, 55, was a former city council member with an extensive business background. During his lengthy tenure on the city council, he had overseen the transition from 250 horse-drawn wagons to a fleet of motorized vehicles to serve both the Fire Bureau and Street Maintenance Division. Bigelow was one of nineteen county commissioners in county history who also served on Portland City Council, mostly in the county's first fifty years.[18] Bigelow had served as a city council member for seventeen years in 1930 when a Citizens Recall League launched a signature collection drive against the entire city council. Although the league failed to collect enough signatures to place a recall on the ballot, Bigelow resigned in August and sat out the next two years before filing for the Multnomah County Commission.[19] When he died in office in January 1941, the *Oregonian*'s obituary said he was widely recognized as "the watchdog of the treasury."[20]

During the Great Depression, county government had no money available for capital projects except for minor, labor-intensive park improvements funded by the federal government. However, work on the biggest project ever to be undertaken within the county's boundaries started 40 miles east of Portland in 1934 with construction of the Bonneville Dam.

The mighty dam, an $81.8 million federal project, took more than three years to build. The project was part of President Franklin Roosevelt's Works Progress

Administration, a federal jobs program aimed at providing employment during the Great Depression. Some three thousand workers drawn from welfare rolls worked in continuous shifts for pay of 50 cents per hour to build the dam and associated roads.[21] Some said the dam was an example of government waste, the amount of electricity it would produce far in excess of what was needed.

Unlike most other dams at the time, Bonneville had nothing to do with irrigation. Its purpose was to generate electricity, put unemployed men to work, and control the devastating floods that ravaged the area after winters of heavy snow in the mountains. When fully equipped, the dam was expected to supply one-sixth of the total electrical power used in the United States.[22] President Roosevelt came to Oregon to dedicate Bonneville Dam on September 18, 1937, the same day that he dedicated Timberline Lodge on the southern slope of Mount Hood. Built by WPA craftsmen and artists, Timberline Lodge was to become a cherished National Historic Landmark.[23]

Even before the dam was finished, the contentious question of how much users of various classes of electricity should be charged led to impassioned lobbying in Oregon, Washington State, and Washington, D.C. Congress was considering a proposed Columbia Valley Authority (CVA) that would have the power to acquire privately owned public utilities.[24] The Bonneville Power Act passed by Congress in 1937 did not go that far, but was still "one of the most striking pieces of social legislation in the history of the United States," according to John Gunther's authoritative *Inside U.S.A.* published in 1951. The 1937 act specified that the Bonneville Power Administration (BPA) should "give preference and priority to public bodies and cooperatives."[25]

The Columbia Valley Authority was so controversial that a Portland City Club report on the subject of public versus private power was shelved as simply "too hot a potato" to handle.[26] Unlike other cities and counties in the region, Portland officials decided to stay out of the public power pool and let the Portland area continue to be served by private utility companies. It was a decision that would be debated several times in coming decades but never changed, resulting in higher electrical rates for those Oregon cities and counties that voted against formation of public utility districts (PUDs).[27]

The Bonneville Power Administration was created by Congress in 1937 to market power from several Columbia River dams, including Bonneville. In 1941, the BPA hired an itinerant folk singer to tour the dams and write songs about them. Woody Guthrie lived in an upstairs apartment in unincorporated Multnomah County just east of Portland for one month while a chauffeur took him on tours of the new dams. Guthrie wrote twenty-six songs in thirty days, including the iconic "Roll On Columbia," before packing up his guitar and hitchhiking out of Portland.[28] The rousing chorus went:

> *Roll on, Columbia, roll on,*
> *Roll on, Columbia, roll on,*
> *Your power is turning the darkness to dawn,*
> *So roll on, Columbia, roll on.*

Guthrie's songs literally sang the praises of the new dams and the power they generated. Knowing of his strong socialist political leanings, local BPA officials made it clear to Guthrie that they wanted him to write songs, not give speeches.[29] Bill Murlin, a former BPA employee who researched Guthrie's Portland visit and compiled a book of Guthrie's BPA songs, said it is unlikely that Guthrie could have been hired a decade later, when an anti-Communist mood had gripped national politics and federal agencies.[30] Guthrie likely had no idea of the damage the dam would cause Columbia River fish populations and the few remaining indigenous Native American cultures tied to Columbia River fishing.

Bonneville's much-needed electrical power was a major factor in attracting shipyards to Portland at the outbreak of World War II. After the war, then-president Harry Truman said that winning the war "would have been impossible" without the hydroelectric power provided by the Grand Coulee and Bonneville dams, both located on the Columbia River.[31]

One of the few on-the-job fatalities ever suffered by Multnomah County sheriff's deputies occurred on September 20, 1935, when a popular sheriff's deputy was murdered in a senseless daytime shooting in rural Multnomah County on the fringe of Southwest Portland. "Deputy Sheriff Shot to Death," the *Oregonian* front-page headline read. "A shotgun that roared twice on lonely Stephenson Road yesterday took the life of a Multnomah county deputy sheriff who had stepped out of his patrol car, apparently to challenge two men for out-of-season hunting. As the body of the deputy, Ernest Loll, 40, sagged to the gravel and dust of the road, the men fled in their own car . . ."

The two young poachers were soon apprehended. One of them, George Fiedler, was sentenced to fifteen years in the penitentiary and a $5,000 fine; the other, Ferdinand Weston, was convicted of second-degree murder and sentenced to life imprisonment. Ironically, the out-of-season pheasant the two men had shot would probably have brought them no more than a small fine.[32]

A monument was erected on Old Stevenson Road where the killing took place (near the corner of today's S.W. 35th and Arnold streets).[33] For many years, work-release inmates were transported to the scene every May to trim back the accumulated weeds and overhanging branches that border the monument. After the cleanup, sheriff's deputies conducted a brief ceremony and hung a wreath beside the concrete structure in commemoration of Deputy Loll's death.[34]

In the late 1930s, Sheriff Pratt warned county commissioners that the quarry adjoining Kelly Butte Jail in southeast Portland would be exhausted by 1940, and that a new supply of rock was needed to keep inmates busy. For the new county jail, commissioners chose the 54-acre Rocky Butte Quarry on the eastern slope of a volcanic cinder cone in northeast Portland. Construction started in January 1941 as a Works Progress Administration (WPA) project and included a two-story administration building and a pair of two-story dormitories for male inmates. Women inmates, the kitchen, dining room, and infirmary would be in a separate building. Built of hand-trimmed lava rock, the jail looked like a medieval fortress. The structures were designed to house as many as 400 inmates.[35] Multnomah County paid one-third of the construction cost ($93,000) and the WPA paid the remaining two-thirds ($181,000).[36]

County inmates quarried rock from Rocky Butte to build the jail. Thereafter, the county continued to blast rock from Rocky Butte until 1956, when commissioners halted the blasting in response to complaints by local residents and businesses about the noise generated by the process.

Once the new jail was finished, county officials planned to close one of the two floors of the courthouse jail downtown. The eighth floor would remain a temporary holding facility for inmates on trial, while the seventh floor would be remodeled to house county offices.[37]

Construction of the new jail was finished in late 1943, when county grand jurors inspecting county facilities found it mostly to their satisfaction, with one exception: "We do believe that the women's quarters in the new Rocky Butte Jail are too luxurious." The *Oregonian* sent one of its few female reporters to check it out. Phyllis Lauritz found the women's quarters to be spacious, clean, light, and "almost airy." "But," she added, "it's no suite at the Ritz." As far as Lauritz could tell, the grand jurors may have been offended by the new stove and refrigerator in the women's kitchen, because new appliances were not for sale to the public during World War II. Her conclusion? "Don't get hasty, girls. So far, the old axiom still holds true. Crime doesn't pay."[38]

Built from basalt carved from adjacent Rocky Butte, the Rocky Butte Jail was considered a model short-term penal institution when it opened in 1943. However, the jail had a long history of successful escapes and drew heavy criticism long before it was closed and demolished in the late 1980s. (Multnomah County Archives)

Ten prisoners escaped on a Saturday night before the jail construction was completed, the first in a long history of escapes from Rocky Butte Jail.[39]

Sheriff Pratt's responsibilities more than doubled during World War II after shipbuilder Edgar Kaiser built a huge housing complex next to the Columbia River for his workers. The development was named Vanport, a combination of VANcouver (across the Columbia in Washington State) and PORTland. New residents came to the metropolitan area from all over the country to fill the high-paying jobs that shipbuilding generated. Deep harbors, good port facilities, and cheap Bonneville Dam electricity had attracted Kaiser in the first place. Eventually, Vanport housed 42,000 men, women, and children. The largest war-time housing project in the United States, Vanport was, for a time, Oregon's second-largest city. The area was never incorporated, nor was the land annexed to Portland, so responsibility for law enforcement fell to Sheriff Pratt.

One of the Kaiser shipyards set a national record in September 1942 by assembling a Liberty ship in fourteen days.[40] In recognition of outstanding home-front efforts, the sheriff's wife, Birdie Pratt, was invited to smash a bottle of champagne against the bow of the tanker *S. S. Multnomah* to launch the ship on its maiden voyage.

A 1943 *Oregonian* photo shows Sheriff Pratt inspecting an 18-member Vanport patrol unit that was expected to double in size soon. Probably because 10 to 15 percent of Vanport residents were black, Pratt hired several African-American deputies to serve there.[41]

First Lady Eleanor Roosevelt found a receptive audience in Edgar Kaiser when she came to Portland to plead for child-care facilities. The Swan Island Child Care Center, built with U.S. Maritime Commission money and operated by Kaiser, became a national model, "a head-start program a quarter of a century

*During World War II, long-time
Sheriff Martin Pratt (1933-48)
was in charge of policing Oregon's
"second-largest city," the Vanport
housing project for shipbuilding
employees. Pratt's wife, Birdie
Pratt, was invited to christen the
tanker S. S. Multnomah. Martin
Pratt's nephew, Deputy Ard Pratt,
stands on Birdie's left.* (Oregon
Historical Society, no. 69454)

ahead of its time." Other shipyards across the nation later copied the Swan Island
Center in design and child-care methodology. In spite of all the laudatory national
attention it received, the center was closed permanently within two weeks of V-J
(Victory-in-Japan) Day.[42] On the other hand, the healthcare plan established for
Kaiser shipyard workers continued as Kaiser Permanente, today the largest not-
for-profit HMO (Health Maintenance Organization) in the nation.[43]

Some World War II activities that took place within the boundaries of
Multnomah County showed wariness on the part of the majority Caucasian
community when it came to accepting equality for racial minorities. Five
months after Pearl Harbor, in May 1942, approximately 3,500 area residents of
Japanese ancestry were rounded up and placed in a temporary assembly center
at the Pacific International Livestock Exposition Center (PI), a huge wooden
structure near the north Portland stockyards. An eight-foot-high barbed wire
fence was erected, together with searchlights and corner watchtowers, where
sentries cradled 30-caliber machine guns. All ethnic Japanese—both aliens and
American citizens of Japanese ancestry—were kept at the PI until September,
when they were transported to Camp Minidoka, an isolated internment center
in south-central Idaho.

Japanese immigrants had begun arriving in the Portland area as early as the
1880s. The first is believed to have been Miyo Iwakoshi, who settled in the Orient
area east of Portland with her Scottish-born husband, Andrew MacKinnon, in
1880, when she would have been 28 years old. Soon afterward, young Japanese
men started arriving in the Pacific Northwest in larger numbers, following the

passage of the federal Chinese Exclusion Act of 1882. The new arrivals found jobs on railroads, in lumber mills, and in factories. Many went to work on farms, hoping eventually to buy their own land. Fertile east Multnomah County soils were favored for vegetables and berries. Iwakoshi was a member of a Japanese Methodist church that sheltered and assisted new arrivals. She also hosted many immigrants in her own home while they were getting adjusted to their new lives. Iwakoshi, who earned the nickname "Empress of the West" for her efforts, died in 1931.[44]

By the time of her death, Japanese residents were finding themselves targets of the same types of discrimination as the Chinese had before them. The federal Immigration Act of 1924 and the companion Asian Exclusion Act of 1924 imposed tighter limits on new arrivals. Local laws were aimed at preventing land ownership by non-citizens.

Min Yasui of Portland was the only practicing Japanese-American lawyer in Oregon in 1942. He deliberately disobeyed a curfew law to test the constitutionality of President Roosevelt's February 1942 Executive Order 9066, which singled out ethnic Japanese for internment and other indignities. Min Yasui was held in Rocky Butte Jail in solitary confinement while awaiting trial in federal court.[45]

Yasui's first trial on June 12, 1942, required only a single day for arguments and testimony to be heard but took five months to be decided. While awaiting the court's verdict, Yasui lived behind barbed wire at the Portland Assembly Center from June to September, then was transported to Camp Minidoka with the rest of the Oregon detainees. In early November, he was brought back to Portland and Rocky Butte Jail to learn the outcome of his trial. Yasui was no longer an American citizen, the judge declared, basing this opinion largely on the fact that Yasui was previously employed by the Japanese consulate in Chicago. As an enemy alien, the judge said, Yasui had disobeyed curfew regulations. He was sentenced to a year in jail and a fine of $5,000.

Yasui was assigned the corner cell of Rocky Butte's isolation block while his case was appealed to the U.S. Supreme Court. Pleadings were heard on May 11, 1943, and the verdict was delivered on June 21. The high court ruled that, contrary to earlier decisions, Yasui was indeed a U.S. citizen. Since government had the right to restrict citizen activity during wartime, the guilty verdict stood because Yasui was guilty of violating a "legal" curfew law.

The case was sent back to the lower court for resentencing, where the monetary fine was revoked and jail time already served deemed sufficient punishment. On August 19, 1943, Min Yasui was escorted from Rocky Butte Jail back to Camp Minidoka in the Idaho desert.

West Coast Japanese detainees were notified on December 17, 1944, eight months before V-J Day, that they were free to return to their homes as of January 2, 1945.[46] In observance of Oregon's sesquicentennial in 2009, the Oregon Library Association recommended that all Oregonians read *Stubborn Twig*, a memorable book by Lauren Kessler describing the degrading treatment Oregon's Japanese-Americans received during and after World War II.[47]

Near the end of the twentieth century, members of Portland's Japanese-American community took another step to help the public understand the importance of the Bill of Rights and the inequities of World War II internment. Through the Oregon Nikkei Endowment, they raised funds to create the Japanese American Historical Plaza, located in Tom McCall Waterfront Park between the Burnside and Steel bridges in Portland. The plaza, completed in 1990,[48] featured the Bill of Rights along with poetic accounts of difficulties suffered during internment. The three leaders of the project had all been interned themselves as children or teenagers: William S. "Bill" Naito, a prominent businessman, for whom S.W. Naito Parkway is named; Robert Murase, the designer of the memorial; and Henry Sakamoto, president of Oregon Nikkei Endowment during the fund-drive.

On the twentieth anniversary of the memorial, Sakamoto said, "I tell students: be aware of what your government is doing. Because of what happened to us."[49]

10

VANPORT IS FLOODED, A SHERIFF IS RECALLED, AND SHERIFF SCHRUNK IS PUT ON TRIAL
(1946–1956)

The end of World War II brought with it an economic boom and exuberance of spirit unmatched in American history. Soldiers raced home from the war to marry their sweethearts and build homes—often with their own hands—on grassy plots in suburbs served entirely by automobiles rather than streetcars. Nothing seemed impossible, given a seemingly boundless economy and America's new prowess as a dominant world power.

Innovation came in many forms. Soon after the war ended, Sheriff Pratt set up an aero squadron of some thirty volunteer airplane pilots, modeled on a police air patrol that operated during the war. The squadron's peacetime goal was to assist during major disasters and local emergencies such as searching for lost persons in mountainous areas. The eleven planes used for these missions were donated by their owners. By 1950, the squad had flown twenty-one missions and donated 166 man hours.[1]

In 1946, the State Board of Higher Education opened a college extension center at Vanport, the temporary "city" on the Columbia River north of Portland built to house workers in the Kaiser shipyards during the war. Growing from this modest beginning at Vanport, Portland State University would be established nine years later in downtown Portland on the South Park Blocks. The federal G.I. Bill would lead to record enrollment at higher education facilities throughout the region.[2]

Nearly three years after the war ended, no decision had yet been made about the future of Vanport. A number of veterans had taken up residency there after the war, and half of the original residents had stayed on to call Vanport home. Because African-American veterans found it difficult to find alternative housing, the percentage of blacks residing in Vanport had increased to around 25 percent by 1948. By then, approximately 40 percent of Vanport residents were receiving some sort of rent relief.[3]

The future of Vanport had always been a divisive question. Portland Mayor Riley and Chester Moore, chairman of the Housing Authority of Portland (HAP), wanted Vanport demolished immediately and the land used for industrial development.[4] Others advocated converting the site to permanent low-cost housing. Shipbuilder Edgar Kaiser proposed building "several hundred permanent dwellings" there. Even as it faced an uncertain future, a new spirit of community had surfaced at Vanport after a series of ups and downs. The population had stabilized at about half the number who had lived there at its wartime peak.[5]

Then Mother Nature intervened. Spring 1948 had seen an unusually heavy snowpack. In mid-May, several days of rain and warm sunshine throughout the Columbia River watershed had combined to raise the water level of the Columbia River. The Army Corps of Engineers and HAP were monitoring the water level at Vanport closely, because the flood plain on which it was located was almost entirely surrounded by dikes and a railroad fill constructed in 1907.[6]

On the Friday preceding Memorial Day weekend, HAP notified the Corps that they had stockpiled 47,000 sacks of sand and an "almost unlimited" amount of baled straw, and that at least fifty men were available on a 24-hour basis. The river was running nearly 15 feet higher than the ground level at Vanport, with dikes keeping the water at bay. Telephone operators at Vanport administrative offices were placed on 24-hour duty and the sheriff's uniformed division started working around the clock in 12-hour shifts. (Because Vanport had never been incorporated, Sheriff Pratt continued the role he had played during the war as Vanport's de facto chief of police.)

HAP relied on the Corps of Engineers to advise if and when residents should be evacuated from their homes. At 4 a.m. on Sunday, May 30, a day that promised to be warm and clear, a notice was slipped under each Vanport door reassuring residents that Vanport was safe and that they would be given ample time to leave if it became necessary.[7]

Shortly after 4 p.m. that afternoon, Sheriff Pratt was headed for a special meeting on flood conditions when he received word that the first dike, as well as the Spokane, Portland, and Seattle Railroad fill, had broken.[8] A "wall of water 10 feet high" roared through a break in the dike on the Columbia River, "knocking down buildings like a bulldozer, crumbling some, and popping the walls out of others." Floodwaters quickly destroyed the entire unincorporated city. Most residents received a ten-minute warning to evacuate, which was far from ideal but allowed available Portland Traction Company buses to arrive at the scene,

this aerial view shows the devastation caused by the Vanport flood of 1948, which wiped out the homes of 18,000 residents living in World War II housing located in North Portland adjacent to the Columbia River. Although rumors suggested that hundreds, perhaps thousands, would be found dead, the official toll finally stood at fifteen confirmed dead, with another seven missing who were never found. (The Oregonian)

along with many taxis. Because there was only one exit, evacuation proceeded slowly, but without widespread panic.[9]

By the time Sheriff Pratt reached Vanport City after fighting his way through traffic, water was beginning to lap at the Denver Avenue fill. People were still being taken from the water. He immediately issued an emergency call for boats, and many arrived quickly. As the water continued to rise, children were tossed into the boats from upper floor windows. Soon boats were able to take people directly from roofs and upper floors.[10] The Multnomah County Health Department, Sheriff Pratt, and the American Red Cross all set up emergency headquarters near the Denver Avenue exit. (Denver Avenue itself was later to collapse.)

The following day, Memorial Day, President Harry Truman declared Vanport a disaster area and authorized use of surplus war property. The Oregon National Guard arrived to help patrol the area and keep out looters. Only the U.S. Coast Guard declined to get involved from the outset. A Coast Guard officer told Sheriff Pratt that regulations prohibited them from taking part in civilian police work.[11]

The Vanport flood was front-page news across the United States. A *Newsweek* article compared Vanport's tragedy to Pennsylvania's devastating Johnstown Flood of May 31, 1899.

Rumors flew that thousands of people had drowned at Vanport and that officials were keeping the news secret until after the Portland Rose Festival in early June, so that the festival could proceed as planned. Amazingly, Sheriff Pratt's estimate of twenty-five casualties turned out to be very close to the final total by the time data gathering was complete months later. Only fifteen deaths were ever recorded by the Multnomah County Coroner, while another ten people were reported missing and at least seven were never accounted for. An estimated eighteen thousand residents lost their homes.[12]

A major question arose after the flood: Why had Multnomah County Commissioners Frank Shull, Charles Bradley, and Tom West allowed a housing project for 40,000 people to be built with only one exit, even given wartime urgency? Finger-pointing between HAP and the Corps of Engineers and efforts to assign liability continued for years, but little was resolved. Criticism of the sheriff's office included an accusation that a deputy had shot at a beaver on the scene, when in fact he had shot at a rat. In general, Sheriff Pratt and his deputies received high praise for the role they played in rescue, anti-looting, and relocation efforts.[13]

No housing was ever rebuilt within the flood plain of Vanport, an area that was annexed to Portland in November 1960. The Blue Heron Golf Course, Expo Center, and the Portland International Raceway today occupy most of the area that was once Vanport City.[14]

Three months before the Vanport flood, a much publicized report critical of Portland police had shocked the citizenry. A retired Berkeley, California, police chief named August Vollmer lambasted the Portland Police Department as "overcostly, underproductive, poorly organized, inadequately supervised and underpaid." A month later, a Portland City Club study of law enforcement in Portland and Multnomah County declared that gambling, prostitution, bootlegging, and other forms of vice had been carried on openly and notoriously throughout the City of Portland for many years.[15]

Neither report contained anything negative about Martin Pratt's management of the Multnomah County sheriff's office; both documents laid the blame for police corruption squarely on Portland Mayor Earl Riley.

City Councilwoman Dorothy McCullough Lee, motivated by a notorious 1947 murder and evidence of rampant vice, was the only person willing to take on Riley in his May 1948 reelection bid. Lee pledged to clean up city government and strictly enforce the law. To general surprise she was elected Portland mayor in a landslide, without the need for a runoff election in the fall.[16] The

The only Multnomah County sheriff ever recalled from office, Marion "Mike" Elliott, won his election with the help of gambling bosses. During his campaign, he lied about his military service and education. He created havoc within the sheriff's office for ten months in 1949 before being recalled. (Multnomah County Archives)

Portland area's continuing concern over gambling and prostitution would generate front page headlines for the next decade, often with surprising results, and sometimes in ways that would expose a tension-filled relationship between the City of Portland Police Department and the Multnomah County Sheriff.

Sheriff Pratt was now running for reelection to a sixth term as sheriff. He skated through the primary with no opposition, but the fall election was a different matter. This time Pratt faced a strong challenge from one of his deputies, Democrat Marion Leroy "Mike" Elliott.

Elliott was a 200-pound extrovert and demagogue who marketed himself as a World War II veteran. (Ironically, Pratt had once been described as "200 pounds of iron-hard muscle in the Multnomah Athletic Club football team at the turn of the century.") Elliott promised a vigorous anti-crime crusade, called for a reduced budget, and pledged to use smaller county cars. The final November 1948 tally was 90,091 votes for Elliott to 89,270 for Pratt; Pratt was defeated by a margin of 821 votes.[17]

Gambling bosses had been Mike Elliott's main contributors. The vice industry feared that Mayor Dorothy Lee would force them out of the city limits and into unincorporated Multnomah County, where Sheriff Pratt was in control. And although Pratt was not known as a strict law enforcer, says historian E. Kimbark MacColl, "the gamblers and their Chicago bosses could ill afford to take any risks."[18]

Sheriff Elliott quickly grabbed headlines in early 1949 by raiding taverns and confiscating unlicensed pinball machines. He fired key employees and turned the sheriff's office upside down. He praised Mayor Lee's efforts in the city, linking her crackdown with his actions in a "Dual Drive on Vice."[19]

Soon, however, *Oregonian* police reporter Wallace Turner acted on a tip and discovered Sheriff Elliott vacationing in Nevada with "a couple of hookers."[20] Once Elliott's past record was scrutinized, reporters found that Elliott had lied about both his military service and his education. Not only had Elliott received a bad conduct discharge from the Marine Corps before World War II even started, he had never attended the University of Michigan as claimed. A recall effort against Elliott was supported by both daily newspapers.[21]

Sheriff Mike Elliott was recalled on October 21, 1949, less than ten months after he took the oath of office. Multnomah County commissioners appointed Portland Fire Captain Terry Schrunk to serve as sheriff until voters could choose a full-term sheriff the following year.[22] Unfortunately for Mayor Lee, Elliott had associated himself so successfully with her in the public's mind that some of his bad press rubbed off on her, contributing to her defeat at the polls by a Portland pharmacist, Fred Peterson, three years later. But another key reason for Lee's loss was that her crackdown wasn't limited to taverns and after-hours joints. Many of Portland's private clubs also relied on gambling profits to balance their budgets, and Mayor Lee went after well-heeled gamblers as well, which eroded her political support.[23]

Around this time, the Soviet Union's development of atomic weapons had heated up the so-called Cold War, and Americans were becoming concerned about the threat of nuclear war. Sheriff Schrunk, as the county's primary civil defense coordinator, sought to alleviate Portlanders' fears by assuring them that, despite rumors to the contrary, the city would not have to be permanently evacuated in the case of a nuclear explosion. "Portland is not by any means the most important target of the Pacific coast," he said. "Seattle, San Francisco . . . Hanford . . . Grand Coulee Dam . . . Bonneville . . . and Los Angeles are considered more important."[24]

Schrunk had been in office only nine months when he had to stand for election. And who should he find challenging him in the Democratic primary but Mike Elliott, who must have misunderstood the voters' recall message. Schrunk handily defeated Elliott, then faced little-known Republican nominee John Keegan in the fall. A month before the general election, the *Oregonian* enthusiastically endorsed Schrunk: "When Sheriff Terry Schrunk was appointed a year ago . . . the sheriff's office was a 'shambles' created by the cops-and-robbers antics of his recalled predecessor . . . [Schrunk] has reestablished the self-respect of his 221 employees, some of whom, a year ago, hesitated to admit that they worked for the sheriff's office . . . He doesn't claim to have eliminated all the gambling and prostitution in Multnomah County, but he is making progress . . . His record to date speaks for itself."[25] In his first election victory, Schrunk won 80 percent of the votes cast, "the highest vote in Multnomah county history for an opposed candidate," according to the *Oregonian*.[26]

Four years after Schrunk's first decisive victory as sheriff, the fall 1954 election again brought glowing editorial endorsements for Schrunk from both daily newspapers. He was praised for his efficient running of the county tax collection department, for making Rocky Butte Jail the best in the nation, for his smoothly operating uniform division, for his civil defense work, for his introduction of incentive pay and annual police training schools, for his youth and safety programs, and for establishing a volunteer deputy sheriffs' reserve. He was reelected sheriff over Republican Kelly Deaderick with 78 percent of the vote.[27]

Schrunk, whom author Phil Stanford has characterized as "personable" and a "hard-drinking . . . sort of guy who was perhaps a little naïve,"[28] was proving to be one of Multnomah County's most popular sheriffs ever. His editorial endorsements noted that Schrunk had already turned down recruiters who wanted him to run for higher office.

In 1954, former sheriff Martin Pratt died at the age of 73 after an unsuccessful campaign to unseat newly appointed Gene Rossman from the Multnomah County commission. After his death, Pratt was hailed as an outstanding sheriff. He had essentially been "king of the county," according to a retrospective article in the *Gresham Outlook*. "When the sheriff called the commissioners, they came to see him. He had a lot of power . . . If he wanted something, he went out and got it. The county had the money at that time and he got it."[29] Pratt's *Oregonian* obituary commented: "Multnomah County residents can consider themselves fortunate that men such as Martin T. Pratt have been willing to . . . accept the modest pay and the hard knocks that go with public jobs."[30]

On the other side of the ledger, the sheriff's office grapevine circulated rumors that Pratt had used inmates to build the beach house enjoyed by his family at the coast, as well as using inmate labor for maintenance chores, cooking, and cleaning. Don Clark, who would serve as a deputy under both Terry Schrunk and Francis Lambert before becoming sheriff himself, said that Pratt was known as a "bagman" for the Republican Party.[31]

Meanwhile, growth in both county administrative staff and the court system put pressure on the 36-year old Multnomah County Courthouse. The majesty of the building was notably diminished when the central courtyard was filled in with bricks and mortar, replaced with a three-floor interior addition composed of hallways, storage rooms, and offices with no outside windows. Other renovations soon narrowed the width of courthouse hallways to provide more usable space by extending office walls into what had been corridor space. All but four of the eleven double-story courtrooms were sliced in half horizontally to add more useable square footage, sacrificing architectural grandeur. As part of that process, many exterior windows were filled in with glass bricks and metal panels, dramatically damaging the architectural design of Whidden and Lewis. A few decades later the county, under new leadership, would remove the glass bricks in an effort to restore architectural integrity to the exterior facade.

Schrunk had been sheriff for nearly six years when he filed as a candidate for Portland mayor. But soon thereafter, the Portland political landscape was shaken by a newspaper exposé. Two *Oregonian* reporters, flushed with success after uncovering an Indian land fraud, launched a series of articles in April 1956 about possible Portland-area bribery and police payoffs. They were investigating alleged attempts by the International Brotherhood of Teamsters to take over and expand vice operations. In a copyrighted series, Wallace Turner and William Lambert laid out allegations against the Teamsters, who were supporting Sheriff Terry Schrunk over incumbent Portland Mayor Fred Peterson in the upcoming mayoral election.[32]

During grand jury presentations that summer, an employee of a Teamsters official "unexpectedly fingered Terry Schrunk as a bribe recipient."[33] Witnesses said Sheriff Schrunk had picked up an envelope containing $500 in bribe money from Clifford O. Bennett, a gambling operator, at the 8212 Club in north Portland.[34] The incident allegedly took place by an outdoor fountain during a late-night raid in September 1955. Schrunk vehemently denied any such bribe-taking.[35]

Throughout the summer and fall, the *Oregonian* printed new charges of vice activities and competition between racketeers to dominate Portland's vice scene. In August, District Attorney William Langley was arraigned on the basis of a state grand jury indictment for "willfully neglecting" to prosecute after he had visited, for twenty minutes, a charity function benefiting the Junior Chamber of Commerce at which gambling had occurred.[36]

A Multnomah County jury convicted Langley on a neglect-of-duties charge. Judge Frank Lonergan declared the DA's position vacant and fined Langley $100. During the trial, Lonergan allowed cameras in the courtroom, giving Langley grounds for appeal to the Oregon Supreme Court. Although Langley

Fire Captain Terry Schrunk (1949-56) was appointed sheriff after Mike Elliott's 1949 recall. The following year, Schrunk received 80 percent of the votes cast for sheriff, "the highest in Multnomah county history for an opposed candidate," the Oregonian *said. Sheriff Schrunk later overcame allegations of accepting bribery and went on to serve as Portland mayor for sixteen years.* (Oregon Historical Society, no. 74592)

lost that appeal, the Oregon State Bar failed to find any cause for disbarment or other sanctions, and Langley returned to private practice. During his arraignment, Langley made clear how he felt about cameras. "If you take one more shot I'll smash that thing," he warned a newspaper photographer in the courthouse hallway. The photographer snapped the shutter again and Langley, true to his word, jerked the camera from the photographer's hands and broke it.[37]

The mayoral contest between Mayor Peterson and Sheriff Schrunk grew more heated as summer turned to fall. September headlines blared: "Mayor, Sheriff Hurl Charges Following Raid"; and "Interference in Law Enforcement, Political Trickery Allegations Made." Portland's mayoral candidates were at each other's throats, the newspaper said, as charges of "politics" were hurled back and forth in the aftermath to a Tuesday night raid by deputy sheriffs on a gambling and drinking establishment. Schrunk accused the city police department of "destroying our chances" to raid a "fairly sizable" poker game just outside the city. Peterson accused Schrunk of "vicious" political trickery. Peterson also said Schrunk was "passing up brothels" in Multnomah County to stage a sensational raid in the city. Schrunk responded that the Keystone Club raid was initiated by the District Attorney's office, and that he knew nothing about the planned raid in advance.[38] Once again, a dispute over county authority versus city jurisdiction touched on a familiar local government battleground.

In the 1956 fall election, Schrunk trounced Peterson by nearly 40,000 votes to be elected Portland mayor. The following June he went on trial in Multnomah

County Circuit Court on a charge of perjury. Schrunk testified in his own defense, declaring: "So help me God, there was no package picked up. There was no bribe offered or accepted."[39] His defense lawyers draped the courtroom with butcher paper listing reasons why the state's case didn't make sense. Jurors acquitted Schrunk after deliberating an hour and fifty minutes. Then they lined up to shake the new mayor's hand as they left the courtroom. Like the big Multnomah County bridge trials of 1924, the alleged scandal against Schrunk ended without a conviction against the primary defendant.

Terry Schrunk would go on to tie the record for length of service as Portland mayor with George Baker, both of whom held the job for four terms, sixteen years each in total. As mayor, Schrunk "came to be regarded by many would-be candidates as virtually unbeatable," said the *Oregon Journal*.[40] Throughout the rest of his long public career, there were no public allegations of wrongdoing against Schrunk.

Citizens living in Portland at the time still argue the merits of the bribery case against Terry Schrunk. "*Nobody* in the sheriff's office believed the charges, regardless of whether or not they supported Schrunk politically," said former sheriff and county executive Don Clark, a deputy sheriff at the time. "Everyone at the sheriff's office was convinced it was a frame-up"—an argument made at trial by Schrunk's defense team.[41]

11
PARKS, ROADS, AND THREE UNRELATED TRAGEDIES
(1946–1960)

The same 1948 electoral cycle that saw the surprise election of Dorothy McCullough Lee as Portland mayor and elevated Mike Elliott to the sheriff's seat (at least temporarily) brought M. James "Mike" Gleason, then 38, onto the three-member board of county commissioners. The soft-spoken Gleason would sit on the county board for a record twenty-eight years, setting a mark that will never be broken, assuming that county voters continue to support limiting commissioners to two four-year terms as mandated by a charter amendment adopted by voters in May 1982.

A child of the Great Depression, Mike Gleason had worked in his parents' small grocery store, driven a taxi, and worked as an electrician before entering politics. He was a progressive force early in his career, helping the county establish a parks system, building new roads, supporting land-use planning, and speaking out on environmental issues long before environmental protection became a political hot-button. Yet by the end of his career Gleason came to represent the "old school" of county government. "He found himself out-of-step at the end," said his successor as county chairman, Donald Clark.[1]

The early postwar years marked Multnomah County's first ventures into ownership of public parks. The first, Woods Park, in a section of southwest Portland that had not yet been annexed to the city, began in 1946 as a gift from Mrs. Hosea Woods in the form of a deed transfer of 161 lots to two southwest Portland community organizations for the purpose of establishing and maintaining a playground. County commissioners placed a special recreational levy on the ballot to provide funds for such improvements, but the measure failed.

In 1950, the county assessor sent a $300 property tax bill to the two community organizations, informing them that they were no longer eligible for a tax exemption because they had not improved their wooded 22 acres. The clubs asked the county commissioners to assume ownership of the entire area, which they agreed to do. The deed to Multnomah County specified that the land would be used solely for park purposes unless and until a majority of county voters decreed otherwise.[2] Known today as the Woods Memorial Natural Area, the 35-acre park consists chiefly of steep and wooded terrain and draws comparatively few visitors. The county deeded it to the City of Portland in 1988 as part of a broad agreement dividing responsibility for various types of services between the city and county.

Before Multnomah County owned any parks, however, the county had assisted in an effort to clean up areas designated as future recreation sites. During spring and summer 1933, Depression-era projects sponsored by Portland and Multnomah County put thousands of unemployed men to work at a time when no federal government relief programs had yet begun. Nearly eighteen thousand men competed for the jobs; four thousand were hired to pave roads in Portland's Washington and Mt. Tabor parks, clear land and plant specimen trees in Hoyt Arboretum, drain the swampy area of Eastmoreland Park, and clean up the "jungle" between the highway and the river at Benson Park along the Columbia.

The lucky men who landed jobs were paid in the form of scrip, which they exchanged for stamps at the county treasurer's office. Most local merchants accepted the stamps as payment for goods. When the redemption fund ran out of money before all the issued scrip had been redeemed, a special session of the state legislature convened to authorize the sale of additional city bonds.[3]

The most dramatic public park creation in Multnomah County history came as a silver lining to the Great Depression—the establishment of 4,200-acre Forest Park. A citizens group called the Committee of Fifty pressured Portland City Council to dedicate hundreds of acres in the West Hills as a municipal forest park, 1,100 acres of which was owned by Multnomah County as a result of Depression-era property tax foreclosures. The area was considered worthless by many because its slopes were too steep to permit large-scale development.

Additional gifts of land and city property-tax foreclosures brought the total size of Forest Park to 4,200 acres by the time it was formally dedicated on September 25, 1948.[4] The overcoming of legal hurdles by the city council and Multnomah County Commissioners Frank Shull, Tom West, and Alan Brown was a far-sighted, priceless gift to future generations. The new park also represented a triumph for citizen involvement, for it was the groundwork laid by the Committee of Fifty that convinced the city council that a hodgepodge of parcels of land, with different owners, could be made into a unified whole. A fifty-mile network of trails was later added within Forest Park.[5]

An informal history and guide to Portland written thirty years after Forest Park's founding described the accomplishment this way: "Forest Park . . . stretches for seven miles along the flanks of the Tualatin Mountains, the largest wilderness park within the confines of an American city. This park . . . [is] rich with a variety of trees—hemlock, spruce, and alder, dogwood, willows, pine and fir. There is also much wildlife—bobcats, beaver, grouse and quail, flocks of mourning doves and on occasion elk and deer."[6] Today, small parts of Forest Park remain in unincorporated Multnomah County, although the park continues to be managed by the City of Portland.

Proposals for new roads and the maintenance of existing ones constituted a major part of the business that came before the county commission in the post-World War II era. While city streets were the responsibility of the various cities, it was up to the county to build and maintain arterials as well as roads to remote parts of the county.[7] The supremacy of the automobile over streetcars was unquestioned during the postwar boom, and neighborhoods built around the automobile looked a lot different from those built earlier around Portland streetcars. Residential lots grew larger with the advent of the auto, while sidewalks were often deemed an unnecessary expense, and stores in commercial developments along major streets needed big parking lots.

The east county road grid constructed during Gleason's early days as a commissioner included four-lane highways that started on the county side of the city/county line—east-west for Halsey, Stark, Division, and Holgate; and at the Columbia River or Clackamas County line for north-south 82nd, 102nd, 122nd, and 182nd Avenues. These streets were built in one- or two-mile segments in accordance with section lines established by the federal General Land Office (GLO) in the 1850s.[8] Many county roads were built through the middle of vacant fields, leading to the construction of tract houses for which there was no existing infrastructure.[9] Roads beckoned the population to follow, presumably blind to improvements that would subsequently be needed—sewers, sidewalks, schools, street lighting, city-quality streets. It would have been much cheaper to install sewers, for example, at the same time that new roads were being built, rather than having to tear up the asphalt to put in sewers years later.[10] The haphazard nature of development in what was called east county would prove a major stumbling block after the land was annexed to Portland and the city began providing urban services in the 1980s.

An urge to start managing growth in the rapidly populating east county area began to surface. In the early 1950s, county voters authorized

commissioners to adopt planning and zoning regulations "to put an end to
chaotic building conditions and indiscriminate use of land, unsafe buildings,
junk yards established next to fine homes, overcrowded residential lots, and
health hazards created by improper sewage disposal," says a 1961 county
handbook.[11] Residents of the four cities in Multnomah County (Portland,
Gresham, Troutdale, and Wood Village) voted for the measure, but a majority of voters most affected by zoning laws—those living in unincorporated
Multnomah County—did not.[12]

Land-rich farmers interested in real estate profits were the strongest opponents of zoning, while residents of new neighborhoods saw zoning as a means
to protect the value of their homes. Most homeowners welcomed the stability
of knowing what could and could not be built next door. "There was little question in the early 1950s that the need for zoning was greatest in the unincorporated sections of Multnomah County," historian Carl Abbott notes in *Portland:
Planning, Politics, and Growth*.[13]

In 1953, county commissioners Mike Gleason, Jack Bain, and Al Brown established a permanent planning commission and hired Lloyd Anderson as the
county's first planning director, with Bob Baldwin as his assistant. Before zoning could be imposed on landowners, painstaking staff work and extensive
public hearings were required. By 1959, the county's official Comprehensive
Plan for development patterns, zoning, and subdivision regulations was implemented. Throughout the process, Gleason remained a staunch supporter of
planning and zoning.[14] However, the clock was ticking during the years of
meetings and delays. During the decade from 1950 to 1960, Portland's population held almost exactly steady at approximately 370,000, while growth east
of the city boundary, mostly in the unincorporated Multnomah County, rose
from 471,000 to 522,000. In the decade before that, the county's non-Portland
population had soared by 100,000, with almost all of those people moving
into neighborhoods where no provision had been made for basic urban-style
services.[15]

One of the biggest-ever bonanzas for Multnomah County government came
in May 1956, when voters approved a generous new tax base. The increase was
hefty enough for the board to launch a "genuine" park system. Commissioners
Jack Bain and Mike Gleason enthusiastically embarked on plans to buy Blue
Lake Park, then a private resort, and fourteen smaller parcels, most of which
were near schools on the east side of the Willamette River. Commissioner Al
Brown acquiesced to the proposal "with reservations."[16]

The board immediately began budgeting $190,000 to $200,000 a year for park purposes (equal to $1.5 million a year in 2009 dollars). By July 1, 1958, $600,000 was available for buying park land.[17]

The owner of Blue Lake Park in east Multnomah County had offered it for sale to the county seven years earlier, when the commission had no funds available. So the owner, N. B. Welsh, decided to convert the park and adjacent land into a $1 million golf course, country club, and high-end residential district. When state agencies rejected his proposal, Welsh posted the property for sale at $350,000.[18]

In January 1958, the commissioners directed staff to obtain independent appraisals and proceed with the purchase of Blue Lake Park.[19] Five months later, the deal was at an impasse. Multnomah County offered $240,000; Welsh continued to hold out for $110,000 more.[20]

Blue Lake Park had been a public resort for swimming, boating, and picnicking for thirty-three years. It consisted of 35 acres and 2,900 feet of frontage on a small lake twelve miles northeast of downtown Portland. Luxury home sites occupied the opposite side of the lake. The idea of buying Blue Lake Park for free public use had been "in the wind" for some time. A January 6, 1958, *Oregon Journal* editorial said: "There has been some feeling that the state's development of the magnificent Rooster Rock Park on the Columbia River had reduced the need for Blue Lake Park, but the throngs which have crowded Rooster Rock indicate further developments are required to reduce the pressure" for more public parks and swimming areas.[21]

Concerned citizens worried that the park would be subdivided into home sites if the impasse over the purchase price continued. The lake should stay open

Multnomah County purchased a long-standing private resort at Blue Lake in 1960, establishing the first major county park. The county also purchased numerous small park sites but for the most part could not afford to develop them. Today, Blue Lake Park continues to be a popular venue for swimming and picnicking, but jurisdiction has been transferred to the Metro regional government. (Multnomah County Facilities Management)

to the public, commissioners agreed, but they could not ignore the value placed on the site by independent appraisers. Two years later, in 1960, the owner compromised and agreed to sell the property for $255,000.[22]

Blue Lake Park had 600 picnic tables, with wood and electric stoves for cooking. Softball, baseball, and horseshoes were available, along with swings and slides for the children. Rowboats could be rented for fishing and touring the lake. In the first year the county operated Blue Lake Park, 210,000 people visited the park, 81,000 of whom swam in the lake.[23] The county would later buy more land to expand the park. In 1996, the park would be turned over to Metro, the tri-county regional government.[24]

The county board next approved the purchase of thirty-one more sites for park purposes, the majority of which were adjacent to public schools. Several decades later, after much of the unincorporated area had been annexed by the City of Portland, a planning report criticized many of those small parks for poor access, limited street frontages and visibility, inadequate facilities, and "unusual configurations, which limits their ability to adequately meet needs."[25] Even so, the land had been preserved for future improvements when and if political will and resources allowed.

Bridges over the Willamette River were vital links—the life-blood, so to speak, of east-west commerce. County and city officials joined the public for a grand celebration on May 24, 1958, with marching bands, a 21-aerial bomb salute, swooping F-102 jets overhead, and fireboats shooting pillars of water skyward. The occasion was the opening of the new $12.5 million Morrison Bridge—the third to bear that name in roughly the same location and the first to be built without streetcar tracks; the automobile had become the undisputed transportation champion.[26]

The seventy-one years that had passed since the erection of the first, wooden-trussed Morrison Bridge had seen tremendous growth and change in Portland—and in American society as a whole. The first bridge was erected by the private Portland Bridge Company, and bridge users had to pay a five-cent toll. Outrage over the tolls ultimately led to purchase by the City of Portland, which replaced the wooden bridge with a steel one in 1905. In 1913, the Oregon Legislature turned over control of Willamette River bridges to Multnomah County.[27]

The need to replace the bridge had been obvious since the late 1920s, but the Depression and World War II delayed serious discussion. The structure, a swing-span rather than a lift bridge, had gears that sometimes refused to work in hot weather, and ships colliding with the open spans occasionally caused the bridge to be closed for repairs. In 1944, county voters approved $4 million in bonds for new road construction, but the county chairman at the time, Frank Shull, said it wasn't close to being enough to pay for a new bridge, and the county declined to pursue it.[28] By late 1948, the estimated cost of a new bridge had risen to $11 million.

In 1954, county voters approved $12 million in bonds for the new Morrison Bridge. It was designed by an international engineering firm, Svendrup & Parcel, whose work focused on building airports and missile-launching facilities as well as bridges. So perhaps it was no surprise that the two operations rooms on the south side of the modernistic new six-lane bridge looked much like airport control towers.[29] The county had hoped to sell the old steel-truss bridge for as much as $60,000, after county roadmaster Paul Northrup said it could be barged to some other location.[30] There were no takers, however, so the old bridge was dismantled for salvage soon after the new adjacent bridge opened. Amid the pomp of the opening ceremony, Mrs. Jack Bain, wife of the county chairman, snipped the ribbon. Commissioner Al Brown joked about how politicians liked to make promises. "Today we don't come with empty hands," he said. "We bring a beautiful new bridge."[31]

During the three-year period from 1958 to 1960, three major tragedies stunned the citizenry and stretched sheriff's office law enforcement and detective personnel resources to their limits.

Shortly after midnight on July 5, 1958, a huge explosion racked the Signal Fireworks and Specialty Company at S.E. 84th Avenue and Powell Boulevard. Twenty tons of fireworks shattered windows throughout a 200-block area. A four-year-old girl was killed as she slept in her home directly behind the warehouse, and a further twenty-six people were injured. Property damage was estimated at half a million dollars.

Three days after the blast, firemen from Rural Fire District No. 10 were still cleaning up debris while sheriff's deputies began removing street barricades. The rubble continued to smolder six days after the conflagration started.[32]

"Fireworks Blast Admitted; Mental Hospital Patient Confesses Accidental Blaze," read a September 3 *Oregon Journal* headline. Richard Wagner, a 20-year-old Oregon State Hospital patient on leave to spend the Fourth of July with his parents in nearby Milwaukie, admitted that he had slipped away from home around midnight, broken into the warehouse, lit a cigarette, and accidentally set his coat on fire. The warehouse exploded like a gigantic firecracker.

Psychiatrists at the state hospital estimated Wagner's intellect as that of a nine-year-old. Wagner told authorities he once lived near the fireworks warehouse and that he broke in through a rear window hoping to find money.[33]

A second holiday tragedy jolted the Portland metropolitan area five months later when a family of five failed to return home after a Christmas-tree-cutting expedition on December 7, 1958. Kenneth and Barbara Martin, aged 54 and 48, and their three daughters, aged 14, 13, and 11, had vanished. Kenneth Martin was an experienced hiker and camper, a careful and methodical driver who kept his car in mint condition. Their nine-passenger Ford station wagon, off-white with red trim, should have been easy to spot and remember.[34]

Sheriff's deputies first searched Larch Mountain, a winter wonderland of Christmas greenery, then launched an exhaustive, county-wide search. A nationwide missing persons report was filed and a $1,000 reward offered for information regarding the family's whereabouts. The search was called off officially ten days later. Deputy Sheriff Ard Pratt said he was reasonably convinced that the family was not in Multnomah County. Pratt, the nephew of former Sheriff Martin Pratt, headed up the sheriff's law enforcement division. He said the sheriff's office had covered the county by jeep, plane, helicopter, and on foot; if the family was in the county, they must be under water in the Columbia or Sandy rivers.

Clark County, Washington, and Hood River County, Oregon, each conducted its own search. By the end of December, the Martins' 28-year-old son accepted the probability that his family was dead. By January, most officials were convinced that the family had met with foul play.[35]

In May 1959, five months after their disappearance, the bodies of the two youngest Martin girls were recovered from the Columbia River downstream from Cascade Locks, some 35 miles east of Portland.[36]

Nine years later, in December 1967, the *Oregonian* interviewed five key individuals who were still trying to solve the riddle of the Martin family disappearance. Those interviewed included a retired Multnomah County deputy, the Hood River County sheriff, The Dalles Chief of Police, an Oregon state police officer, and a behavioral consultant who had taken up his own search (as did many individuals and groups, including the Trails Club and the church to which the Martins belonged). Four of the five individuals interviewed were convinced that the missing Martin family members and automobile were entombed in a deep trench in the Columbia River below a bluff outside The Dalles. The Hood River Sheriff conjectured that the car would someday be found near Cascade Locks.

Neither jurisdiction had the money or resources needed to conduct a professional river-bottom search. Skin divers attempted it, unsuccessfully, but their efforts were called off after one diver nearly died. Further compounding the mystery, an automatic hand gun with one shell fired was found at Cascade Locks. "Many Feel Sure Martins Victims of Crime," the *Oregonian* December 17 headline read.

The case has never been solved, although the possibility of reopening the case emerged in 2009. Sheriff Bob Skipper swore in eight retired sheriff's investigators to "take another run at homicides that had hit a dead end or been suspended for lack of evidence." The new volunteer cadre agreed to meet twice a week to reexamine cold

$1000 RENARD
(One Thousand Dors)

For Information Leading to the !hereabouts of the

MISSING MARTN FAMILY

On December 7, 1958 at 2:00 p.m. the KENNETH MARTIN family left for home at 1715 N. E 56th Avenue in Portland, Oregon. They have never returned, and all law enforcement agencies this area have been unable to find them, or any clue as to their whereabouts They were driving a 1954 Ford 4-door stan wagon, cream color with small red trim—

MOTOR # U4LX13241

OREGON LICENSE # 1G 7156

THE FAMILY CONSISTS OF THE FOLLOWING:

#1—The husband E. KENNETH MARTIN—54 years (white), 5' 10" 200 lbs Gray crew cut hair, blue eyes, wears glasses.

#2—The wife BARBARA JEAN MARTIN—48 years (white) 5' 8" or 10" 180 lbs Dark brown hair, blue eyes, round face.

THE CHILDREN:

#1—BARBARA MARTIN—14 years, 5' 5" 120 lbs. Blue eyes, medium complexion

#2—VIRGINIA MARTIN—13 years, 5' 3" 110 lbs. Wears glasses, dark frames, medium complexion.

#3—SUSAN MARGARET MARTIN—11 years, 5' 1", 100 lbs., hazel eyes, light complexion.

Any information on above family will be deeply appreciated by Multnomah County Sheriff Francis Lambert, Portland, Oregon

DECEMBER 26, 1958

With local developments in the Martin family mystery at a standstill, Multnomah County sheriff's office hopes nationwide circulation of this missing persons bulletin may turn up some lead in the family's disappearance. Deputies are mailing 6,000 bulletins throughout the United States.

Advertisement from the December 26, 1958, issue of Portland Reporter. (Multnomah County Archives)

cases, keeping in mind new technology, such as DNA evidence and underwater sounding, that might help solve a case.[37]

Another shocking Multnomah County crime saddened the nation near the end of Lambert's first term as sheriff. The notorious Peyton-Allan murders became the most spine-chilling murder case in Oregon history. And because the crime occurred in unincorporated Multnomah County, responsibility for investigating the case fell to the sheriff's office rather than the Portland Police Bureau.

On Thanksgiving weekend of 1960, 19-year-old Larry Peyton's mutilated body was found in the seven-mile-long city wilderness area of Forest Park. Peyton's 1949 Ford automobile was parked in a lovers' lane; his body was in the front seat. His 19-year-old sweetheart was missing.[38]

College students Larry Peyton and Beverly Allan had met in summer 1959 while working at Crater Lake Lodge in south central Oregon, where Peyton's father was a partner in the company that operated the lodge. Peyton, who had earlier attended high school in the Washington County suburb of Beaverton, was now a sophomore at Portland State University. Beverly Allan, who grew up in Washington's Puget Sound area, was a sophomore at Washington State

from the front page of the
Oregon Journal, *Monday, November 28, 1960.*

University in Pullman, Washington. She had spent Thanksgiving Day with her parents in Port Townsend. Peyton drove up to meet her in Olympia on Saturday and brought her back to Portland. She was described by fellow students as "studious," "pretty," and "popular."[39]

The teenagers ate an early dinner on Saturday at the home of Peyton's parents, where Larry was living. They left around nine o'clock to check out the new Lloyd Center Mall that was receiving nationwide publicity. When the teenagers failed to return home by Sunday afternoon, Peyton's mother and father reported them missing.

That evening, two Multnomah County sheriff's deputies patrolling Forest Park discovered a gruesome scene off N.W. Cornell Road. Larry Peyton's bloody body had been stabbed twenty-three times and his skull fractured. A bullet hole had pierced the front windshield. Beverly Allan's purse lay on the passenger seat, and her glasses were on the ground outside, one lens shattered.[40]

Six weeks later, Beverly Allan's partially nude body was discovered under an elderberry bush alongside busy Sunset Highway 40 miles west of Portland, one mile west of a tunnel on the route to Seaside. The autopsy report showed she had been raped repeatedly before being strangled.[41]

Neither Peyton nor Allan had any known enemies. The crime was especially disturbing because the public could relate so closely to the victims. "If this could happen to such a nice young couple," people thought, "it could happen to me or my family."

The Peyton-Allan investigation and subsequent trials were arguably the most extensively reported murder case in Multnomah County history. Detective Earl Son of the Multnomah County Sheriff's Office made the solution of the crime his life's work, and in doing so his name became a household word. Lawyer Phil Margolin launched his writing career as a best-selling mystery writer in 1978 with *Heartstone*, a fictionalized version of the Peyton-Allan case. Margolin's book highlighted the controversial use of hypnosis, by means of which the 17-year-old star prosecution witness (Nikki Essex in real life) recalled her damning testimony.

Peyton and Allan were seen cruising Broadway in downtown Portland on Saturday evening. What happened after that was the subject of rumor and conjecture. Nikki Essex testified that she saw the couple at a West Burnside Street Denny's Restaurant, prior to a drag race on S.W. 18th Avenue between the car in which she was riding and Larry Peyton's Ford.

No bullet wound was found on Peyton's body, or inside the car. Investigators concluded that the shot that pierced the windshield was fired from inside the vehicle, probably by the murderer, because Peyton's parents said the young man owned no gun. (However, a fellow Portland State student later told writer Phil Stanford that Peyton had told him two weeks before the murder that he was keeping a gun in his car.)[42]

By the time the Peyton-Allan murderers were brought to trial, nearly eight years after the crime, Sheriff Lambert had long since retired, Sheriff Clark had made solving the case a priority during his four-year tenure, and James Holzman was now the sheriff. The case had been exhaustively investigated by Earl Son and his fellow detective, Jack Elliott. Son and Elliott "interviewed 2,292 persons, checked out 424 cars, gathered 275 pieces of physical evidence, and coordinated information from 117 police agencies," according to an *Oregon Journal* story after Son's death in December 1981.[43] At various points in the ensuing trials, defense attorneys posed this rhetorical question to Essex and other witnesses: "Isn't it true that Detective Son refreshed your memory or planted those stories in your mind?"[44]

Three men were indicted by a grand jury for the murders of Peyton and Allan. The cases were prosecuted in 1968 and 1969 by Deputy District Attorney Des Connall (later elected District Attorney).

The first man tried, Edward Jorgensen, was a 36-year-old automobile mechanic and the father of five children. He was convicted of first-degree murder for the death of Beverly Allan and second-degree murder for the death of Larry Peyton, and sentenced to life imprisonment plus 25 years. His younger brother,

Carl Jorgensen, 28 years old at the time of his trial, was acquitted. Ex-convict Robert Brom, a former door-to-door salesman, was convicted and sentenced to life plus 25 years. Edward Jorgensen was said to have told chief prosecutor Des Connall at the conclusion of his trial, "I'm not guilty and you know it."[45]

In 1971, Edward Jorgensen and Robert Brom unsuccessfully petitioned then-governor Tom McCall for pardons, arguing that new information had come to light showing that the murders were committed by a gang that was "robbing and terrorizing" young couples in the West Hills. No proof of this allegation was found. In 1973, less than five years after his trial, Jorgensen was granted parole. Four years later, Brom was paroled on condition that he move to Hawaii, where friends had secured him a job.[46]

In April 2002, Multnomah County D.A. Michael Schrunk reopened the case to investigate allegations by "a long-time snitch" that Jack Rowlands, a fellow Rocky Butte Jail inmate, had confessed to Beverly Allan's murder. When no evidence was produced to support the allegations, the file was quickly closed again.[47]

The Peyton-Allan Files, a 2010 book by Phil Stanford, flatly states that the three men charged with the crime—Eddie Jorgensen, Carl Jorgensen, and Bob Brom—"simply didn't do it."[48] From the vantage point of half a century, Stanford declared that the fact of their innocence was the only thing one could say with confidence about this controversial, complicated, heartbreaking chapter in Multnomah County's history.

12

COMMISSIONERS FEUD, DELTA DOME IS REJECTED, AND THE FIRST WOMAN DEPUTY IS HIRED
(1962–1966)

U.S. involvement in the Vietnam War was escalating, the Beatles would soon make their American debut, and Oregon's Columbus Day Storm had not yet devastated the state as Multnomah County government stood on the cusp of momentous changes. Before it was over, "old" blood was purged from the three-man commission, a startling new government structure brought modern administration to the forefront, and county voters elected a young leader brimming with new ideas.

The starting point may have been January 1962, when 75-year-old Albert L. "Al" Brown, holder of various elective offices since 1939, suffered the last in a series of strokes and heart attacks. Brown had been elected to the county commission in 1951, after serving as the elected county clerk from 1945 to 1950 and before that as county auditor from 1939 to 1944. As auditor, Brown reportedly discovered a profitable way to enhance his salary. He would sort through a pile of outgoing checks until he found a vendor who sold something he could use. Brown would pick up the phone and say to the vendor, "I've got a check for you here that you can pick up anytime." Then he would pause and casually say something like, "Yes, two steaks would be fine. Your check will be waiting in my office." Once, Brown insisted that a businessman who brought him a case of twelve fifths of whisky exchange it for a case of twenty-four pints that would yield twelve full quarts. In spite of such transactions, Brown left only a small estate when he died, apparently satisfied to settle for the relatively minor creature comforts obtained through petty bribe-taking.[1]

As commissioner, Brown seldom agreed with his two cohorts, Mike Gleason and Jack Bain, but he never appeared to hold grudges and often sat silently for long stretches. Finally, at the end of one hearing, Gleason and Bain sat determinedly silent, waiting for Brown to speak. After a prolonged pause, Chairman

Gleason asked Brown if he would like to make a statement. After a lengthy pause, Brown responded: "The time has come, the Walrus said, to speak of many things: of shoes and ships and sealing wax, of cabbages and kings." Gleason never asked him again.

Brown, who served eleven years on the commission, was a politician of the old school, who handed out matchbooks with the words, "Vote for Al Brown." It was said that sometimes he would attend the funerals of total strangers, just to introduce himself and hand out complimentary matchbooks.[2]

Brown seemed especially mystified by land-use cases. He had worked in real estate early in his career, but that was before the era of zoning codes and public land-use appeals and litigation. Multnomah County didn't have to wait long to see litigation after adopting its zoning code in 1959. In 1960, the owners of a vacant plot of newly zoned residential land at S.W. 35th and Taylors Ferry Road sued the county—unsuccessfully—after county commissioners denied their request to turn it into a luxury trailer park.[3]

In 1964, with the moral support and an amicus statement from Multnomah County planners, citizens on both sides of the Multnomah–Washington County line challenged a three-to-two Washington County Commission vote (in which they had overruled their own planning commission) to rezone four and a half acres between S.W. Multnomah Boulevard and Garden Home Road from residential to industrial. The zone change would have allowed the Schwager-Wood Company to build an electrical equipment factory on land abutting Multnomah County that was zoned residential on both sides of the line. Washington County Chair Clayton Nyberg told visitors, "I am the zoning law in Washington County"—a boast that was firmly deflated when the Oregon Supreme Court, in the landmark case *Smith vs. Washington County*, ruled unanimously in 1965 that the Washington County Commission had acted "capriciously and arbitrarily" in allowing the factory. It was the most egregious case of spot zoning they had ever seen, the court said.[4] The site is today home to a Mormon church at 6605 S.W. Garden Home Road.

In what proved to be his eighth and final year on the county board, Chairman Jack Bain proposed construction of a new minimum-security jail to be located at the County Poor Farm near Troutdale. A new jail would help overcrowding at Rocky Butte Jail (which was only twenty years old), Bain said, and would separate lesser offenders with better chances of rehabilitation from the more violent, serious offenders held at Rocky Butte. Progressive penal ideas recognized that nonviolent offenders needed opportunities to learn new skills, rather than just being locked up twenty-four hours a day.

The proposed design unveiled by Bain—eight single-story wings radiating from a circular hub, like spokes on a wheel—would house 220 to 270 inmates under the watchful eyes of a single guard in the control hub. The model was similar to one county commissioners had visited in Alameda, California. "They call theirs an honor camp, but we'll call this a rehabilitation camp," Bain said.[5]

The jail plan drew opposition from residents in Troutdale, Fairview, and Gresham who feared it would damage the property values of nearby homes. They also worried about a public safety risk from escaping inmates. As a *Journal* editorial noted, however, "In a county as small as this, it would be difficult to find a site which would not be near either present or future home developments."[6] As for threats from escapees, the newspaper reasoned that any fleeing inmates would likely want to get as far away from the jail as possible.

Nevertheless, jail opponents tried to stop the case in court. They presented seven reasons why they felt the project should be halted, including negative impact on property values, threat to safety, nuisance, and waste of public money. A judge dismissed the case, ruling that the county had not been capricious or arbitrary in carrying out its planning duties.[7] Construction began soon thereafter and took less than one year to complete at a cost of $253,000—which would stand out as exemplary in light of later jail construction difficulties.

The new Multnomah County Correctional Institute (MCCI) was located on 72 acres adjacent to the county "poor" farm. Unlike the medieval-looking Rocky Butte, the new jail looked more like a college dormitory, with its single-story wings radiating from the central control room.

The building was finished in September 1963, although the new sheriff, Don Clark, was unable to muster county funding for jail staff until December 1963, after which the first inmates started arriving. Clark hoped to provide the low-security inmates with job training, work programs, and group therapy, to reestablish ties with their families, and, where possible, to provide support after their release. Many of the inmates were to receive job training in culinary arts, landscaping, and gardening, as well as work on the county farm. The medium-security jail remained in operation until 2001, and then sporadically on an as-needed, partial basis until 2006 when it finally closed and the property was listed for sale.[8] As early as 1989, county officials had said renovating the 1960s-era jail to meet modern standards would be too expensive.[9]

After Al Brown's death early in 1962, Mike Gleason found himself with two new board members the following January. Larry Aylsworth, who was appointed by the commission to replace Brown, lost in the May primary. And Jack Bain, the chairman and a commission member for eight years, was caught up in a

Before the era of term limits imposed by voters, M. James Gleason held a seat on the board of commissioners longer than anyone, from 1948 until his retirement at the end of 1974. He became the first county chairman under the Home Rule charter adopted in 1967, a title he held until his retirement. Gleason worked as an electrician before entering politics. (Multnomah County Archives)

controversy over county purchasing that knocked him off the board in November. Bain was accused in the newspapers of making some purchases without putting them out for public bidding—a practice that had surfaced many times in county history. An extensive study by the New York Bureau of Municipal Research in 1913 had detected sloppy purchasing practices, and controversies had arisen periodically ever since. Bain finished third in a race in which the top two candidates, David Eccles and Mel Gordon, both Republicans, won seats on the commission.

Since Gleason was a Democrat, fireworks were expected. As it turned out, the two Republicans were often at odds with each other, and Republican Eccles and Democrat Gleason frequently teamed up against Gordon. "It's been an open secret for some time that Mel Gordon and his two fellow commissioners weren't getting along very well," noted an editorial in the December 19, 1963, *Gresham Outlook*. "Rightly or wrongly, much of the difficulties stem from the widely-held belief that Gordon is 'running for another office.' Gordon gets into the headlines quite regularly and he's widely said by Democrats to be aiming at either [Congresswoman] Edith Green or [Mayor] Terry Schrunk. Meanwhile, the exchanges between Gordon, Eccles and Gleason are sparking interest in county government. As long as personal recriminations aren't involved, we don't care if the commissioners do feud."

The relationships between the board members remained much the same the following year. "The funniest show in town isn't on television," proclaimed another *Gresham Outlook* editorial. "It's at the county courthouse, where a teapot tempest has developed over chairmanship of the board of county commissioners

. . . Democrat Mike Gleason is the new chairman . . . put there by the vote of Republican Dave Eccles. The third board member, Republican Mel Gordon, had served as chairman last year. Eccles' action in supporting Gleason has raised all sorts of hackles in Republican ranks . . . For our money, it's all nonsense . . . We think all hands should get back to work and forget such petty issues."[10]

One of the "petty issues" was Gordon's request that Yvonne Laurine, executive secretary to Gleason in his capacity as chairman of the board, be assigned to Gordon as his personal staff. Gleason said it was the first time in his fifteen years on the board that any commissioner had asked for a personal secretary and that he would vote against the proposal. Gordon retorted that it was unfortunate for the commission to start the new year with a disagreement, although that was the way it had ended the old year.[11]

Gordon's feuding with his fellow commissioners was to continue for the next eleven years, even after a new home rule charter took effect in 1967, until Eccles was defeated at the polls in November 1972 and Gleason retired in 1974.

Gleason was near the apex of his political career and still in good health when he was elected president of the National Association of County Officials in 1962. He used that position to lobby for stronger federal controls on industrial stream pollution during testimony before a Congressional subcommittee in Seattle in 1963. Gleason said the Columbia and Willamette rivers suffered from pulp industry waste, and that Portland ranked second to Los Angeles on the West Coast for smog. He urged additional research into industrial and domestic pollution.[12]

Meanwhile, Gleason continued to pursue his interest in county parks. After negotiations with the state government, the county purchased historic Bybee-Howell House on Sauvie Island in 1962, with the understanding that it would be managed by the Oregon Historical Society.[13] The island had been the original stopping off point for the first Europeans who set foot in what would later become Multnomah County, and well over a century later it would have another claim to fame, after a hardy game bird known as the ringneck pheasant was introduced to North America on Sauvie Island in 1881. Seventeen such birds were sent to Oregon from China by Owen Denny, a former Portland police court judge then serving as U.S. consul in Shanghai. The pheasants were released on Sauvie Island, followed by two further shipments from China. Thereafter, the birds rapidly multiplied and spread across the continent.[14]

(Starting in the late 1920s, an enterprising businessman named George W. Weatherly raised a flock of a thousand pheasants as domesticated game birds on two acres near Multnomah Village. In 1931, Weatherly purchased a thousand acres east of Troutdale and was soon raising 20,000 pheasants a year for sale to restaurants and dining tables as far east as St. Louis and throughout the west. Weatherly also was the owner of a successful ice-cream manufacturing company.)[15]

Commissioners Mike Gleason, David Eccles, and Mel Gordon now launched a four-year program to turn a wilderness area in east Multnomah County into a people's park to be known as Oxbow. The 816-acre Sandy River waterfront property was jointly owned by Multnomah County (312 acres), the Bureau of Land Management (280 acres), and the Oregon State Game Commission (223 acres). Multnomah County assumed primary responsibility for converting the wooded site into a park and for its subsequent operation and management.

For four years, starting in 1964, the county hired 200 high school boys for ten weeks each summer to build paved roadways, parking areas, picnic tables, picnic shelters, overnight trailer and tent camp sites, and miles of hiking trails at Oxbow Park. The summer work crews received $5 a day plus transportation to and from the site, with compensation as high as $10.50 per day for junior foremen supervised by adults.[16] Oxbow Park opened to the public in August 1967.

"Oxbow Park is one of the most outstanding wilderness-type county parks to be found anywhere in the nation," proclaimed the 1968 edition of *Your Multnomah County Government: A Handbook*. "Natural forest settings and the picturesque Sandy River flowing through the area make for ideal outdoor activities for family and youth group outings."[17]

While summer work was underway at Oxbow, talk of an indoor, year-round sports facility gained momentum. In May 1964, a measure on the county ballot would have authorized the building of Delta Dome stadium as a home for big-league athletic events. It was to be built in Delta Park, part of the land flooded in the vicious Vanport flood of 1948. Unlike the steel and concrete Astrodome that had recently been completed in Houston, Texas, the Delta Dome would have utilized Pacific Northwest timber and laminated wood beams. Backers argued that such a facility would make a professional football franchise probable, a baseball franchise possible, and the 1972 Olympics "a plum to go after." The sale of $25 million in bonds would be paid off in twenty-five years with proceeds from stadium events. County voters rejected the measure by a 5 percent margin.

That November, a slightly altered proposal, extending the payoff period to thirty years, was again on the ballot. A group called "Volunteers for Delta Dome Covered Stadium" proclaimed that building the stadium would create an economic shot in the arm, take the county "out of its conservative not-looking-ahead role," and bring in money and jobs. This time the proposal failed by 10 percent.[18]

Commissioner Mel Gordon now commissioned a poll to test the mood of the electorate. The result: 59 percent of county voters queried in May 1965 favored building a stadium for big professional sports events and appearances by personalities such as the Reverend Billy Graham. When asked whether they favored the purchase and enlargement of Multnomah Stadium, a privately owned stadium near downtown that opened in 1926, the same voters said "no" by an overwhelming 67 percent. "As an aside," an *Oregon Journal* editorial opined, "Gordon's idea of taking a poll at public expense is a new twist . . . for local government. It's not a bad idea, so long as the cost is kept low (Gordon said this one cost the taxpayers about $100) and the answers are taken only as one indication of public sentiment among many, and not allowed to dictate public decisions. It would be better, though, if any future polls were authorized and composed by all three county commissioners, and not just one of them."[19]

Changed attitudes regarding penal institutions were also reflected in the commissioners' decision in 1946 to seek out a college-educated couple to upgrade the image—and the reality—of the county farm. They persuaded Clarence and Ruth Ownbey—he a well-liked high school principal, she a registered nurse—to take on the job. Under the Ownbeys' management, the "poor house" near Troutdale became known as a home and "inmates" were thereafter referred to as residents. Male residents received a small wage for farm work, which they were allowed to spend as they pleased.

During the Ownbeys' tenure, a woman made famous nationally by the popular ballad "Frankie and Johnny" was welcomed to the farm in 1950. Frankie Baker's story was already legend: it began in St. Louis, Missouri, in October 1899 when her 17-year-old sweetheart "done her wrong" by taking up with another woman. Baker, then a 22-year-old dancer, shot and killed him. She was arrested, tried, and acquitted on grounds of self-defense. Baker told other county farm residents that the song had invaded her privacy and that several details, such as the kind of gun used, were wrong. Baker was moved later to the Eastern Oregon State Hospital in Pendleton, where she died in 1952.[20]

Not all farm residents were penniless. After the death of a farm "guest" named Gust Erickson, Clarence Ownbey found "at least two hundred" 50-cent coins sewed into the linings of his clothes. Erickson was jailed for drunkenness forty-five times before being sent flat broke "or so they thought" to the farm. Ownbey later conjectured that the old man stashed the coins away while employed by a parking lot that charged vehicles fifty cents to park.[21]

When the Ownbeys retired in 1964 after seventeen years, the name of the institution they had managed was officially changed to Edgefield Manor. Commissioner Eccles said the name change was made specifically "to get away from the poor farm connotation."[22] The same year, the old tuberculosis hospital on the grounds, renamed Edgefield Lodge, became a treatment facility for emotionally disturbed and mentally retarded children. The Edgefield complex by then also included the Multnomah County Correctional Institution (MCCI)—a minimum security jail—and would later contain the county animal control shelter.[23]

The 1960s also brought important changes to the Multnomah County Fair. In 1949, citing mismanagement of fair funds, the county commissioners had terminated the Fair Association's lease in Gresham and taken over its operation. By 1961, the fair was in its fifty-fifth year as a successful endeavor, with more than 170,000 visitors (compared to 90,000 in 1950).

Fair displays ranged from exhibits by schoolchildren to highly skilled adult entries. The fair premium book listed potential entry categories for cattle, ponies, swine, sheep, goats, poultry, rabbits, agriculture, flowers, hobbies, needlecraft, canned foods, baking, art, and photography. The fair was the highlight of the year for thousands of 4-H and Future Farmers of America (FFA) members who pored over the 100-page premium book published every April to decide what to raise, plant, or prepare for that year's fair. Horse racing and stage show acts competed for cash prizes; commercial display booths and concessions continued to be part of the mix.

Harbingers of problems to come were quietly noted in the 1961 edition of *Your Multnomah County Government*, the handbook published by the Board of County Commissioners. The fair location was interfering with Gresham street extensions, the handbook said, and parking space was inadequate. There was no room to expand. Past efforts to obtain a new and larger site had encountered legal obstacles.[24]

The county's search for new fairgrounds, as well as for a year-round event facility, eventually brought the county together with the Pacific International Livestock Exposition (commonly referred to as the "PI") and its buildings and grounds. The county purchased the PI's north Portland site near the Columbia River in 1965, thereby providing metropolitan-area residents with facilities for trade shows, entertainment events, convention sites, and a future home for the Multnomah County Fair. The Portland Meadows racetrack was located nearby. The PI, founded in 1910 to promote the cattle industry, signed a lease with the county to continue using the facility for its annual livestock show.

Commissioner Don Clark donned bib overalls and a straw hat for the Multnomah County Fair after it moved to the site of the Pacific International Livestock Exhibition. But Clark— his white shirt and tie belying the rural look—was no farmer, and the dwindling rural roots of Oregon's most urban county spelled gradual doom for the county fair. (Sandi Hobbs Morey)

In the late 1960s, on a split vote by the county commissioners, the long-time Gresham county fairgrounds were sold to make way for a shopping center. A July 26, 1969, column by popular *Oregon Journal* columnist Doug Baker was headlined, "Heigh-Ho To Gresham Fair For Lingering Last Visit."

> Sure, they'll move it over to the Pacific International complex next year and they'll beef it up with new capital investment . . . But it won't be the Gresham fair and you can't tell me it will keep that slight rural flavor . . . Heck, yes, you can move all the smells—the stable aroma of the cow barn and the pungent smell of the chicken exhibits and the perfume of the floral bouquets and the slightly stale smell of the ladies' handicrafts.
>
> What you can't move is the ambience. . . . Take the Multnomah County Fair out of Gresham and you don't recreate it somewhere else. True, you'll have a fair, of a sort—but it won't be the Multnomah County Fair . . . I'll miss that rather hilarious little five-furlong dirt race track with its quaint grandstand which was built, nobody knows why, facing into the setting sun.[25]

In its new 1970 location at the PI site, the fair never equaled its previous glory. The fair's decline was partly a result of its isolated location and partly because agriculture continued to decline in importance throughout the metropolitan area. Many of the fertile vegetable and berry fields in Multnomah County east of Portland were being sold for housing developments. The fair was to continue at the Expo Center until 1993, but the heydays of the 1950s and 1960s Multnomah County Fairs were over.

In the early 1960s, dramatic changes were occurring in the sheriff's office, where Francis Lambert announced his intention to retire in 1962 after six years as the county's chief law enforcement officer. County commissioners had initially appointed then-county treasurer Lambert to complete Mayor Terry Schrunk's unfinished term. Lambert's prior credentials also included being a real estate broker and First National Bank assistant vice-president.[26] The words "Sheriff Francis Lambert, Tax Collector" had appeared on all property tax statements and return envelopes.

Lambert was credited with establishing the first permanent water patrol unit in 1958 and hiring the county's first woman deputy sheriff, Polly Dow, in 1961. But he faced repeated challenges from the police union, which contended that his promotions violated Civil Service regulations by not using qualifying tests, or that if he did employ tests, he didn't select the officers with the highest scores. Lambert cited fatigue with lawsuits as his main reason for not seeking another term in 1962.

Twenty-nine candidates filed to succeed Lambert. The last candidate to throw his hat in the ring, Donald E. "Don" Clark, did so fifteen minutes before the March 9 filing deadline. Clark, who had served as a deputy sheriff under both Terry Schrunk and Francis Lambert, won the Democratic primary in part because he earned the enthusiastic endorsements of both daily newspapers. In the fall 1962 contest, Democrat Clark faced off against Republican Eugene W. Ferguson, who received the *Oregonian*'s general election endorsement. In a close race, Clark was elected by 1,001 votes out of 189,901 cast, a margin of less than 1 percent, which amounted to less than one vote per precinct at that time.[27]

Clark embarked on his new political career with characteristic gusto. The former schoolteacher put his deputies to work enforcing state laws such as the one that required owners of old junked car lots to erect site-obscuring fences. Clark enlisted the support of Governor Mark Hatfield to stop the Oregon State Highway Commission from installing metal guard rails to replace picturesque stone guard rails along the Columbia River Highway. That Clark-Hatfield collaboration was to be the first of several times that the two men would join forces on historic preservation issues and other matters of public concern.[28]

In an early indication of Don Clark's future focus, he gave speeches about the need to preserve Oregon and to tidy up the countryside—things that he believed in but that "didn't really have a whole lot to do with being sheriff," Clark later acknowledged. A woman listening to one of his election speeches told Clark's uncle, Phil Lang: "I'm not going to vote for that man, I think he's a Communist."

"What makes you think he's a Communist?" Lang asked.

The woman replied, "Because he said that there are many places in Portland where we should tear down the buildings and plant trees."[29]

At the time Clark assumed control over the sheriff's office, fourteen different department heads, bureau heads, and leaders of sections were reporting directly to the sheriff. Clark believed that the existing chain of command led to "little kingdoms" in which "petty jealousies" were bred, so he went about changing that. Lewis and Clark College student John Gordon King, who wrote his 1965 thesis on the history of the Multnomah County sheriff's office, concluded that Sheriff Clark "was quite successful in establishing a chain of command which has increased communication and cooperation . . . to a degree never before known in this section of county government."[30]

Clark's most publicized action as sheriff was to require that all future candidates for deputy should have a college degree. Clark was the first Multnomah County sheriff to hold a college degree. While this effort to upgrade the image and quality of law enforcement personnel was controversial at first, it became widely accepted and served as a national model. (The requirement was later dropped for corrections deputies, because then-sheriff James Holzman said it was too hard to attract qualified candidates to staff county jails. The requirement was still in place as of 2012 for law enforcement deputies who performed patrol and detective duties.) In 1966, Clark persuaded the Multnomah County Commission to make his sheriff's deputies the best paid sheriff's uniformed officers in the state.[31]

Sheriff Clark's term ended at the end of 1966. He would be the last elected sheriff for the next sixteen years, because a new county home rule charter effective January 1, 1967, made the position of sheriff appointive.[32] Clark would also be the last Multnomah County sheriff to serve as tax collector, because the new charter specified that property taxes would henceforth be collected by trained county employees who would report to the county chair.[33]

In January 1966, the U.S. President's Crime Commission issued a report titled "The Challenge of Crime in a Free Society," which contained specific recommendations for improving the nation's criminal justice systems. Sheriff

Clark had served as an advisor to the commission on police and corrections matters and was working hard to bring about implementation of the report's recommendations regarding court reform, establishment of 911 emergency call systems, and the creation of detoxification centers that would free up jail and hospital space by providing an alternative to jailing intoxicated vagrants. The report also recommended that all police officers have college degrees, in line with the program that had been established in Multnomah County under Sheriff Clark.[34]

13

HOME RULE ARRIVES, A SHERIFF IS FIRED, AND ROCKY BUTTE PRISONERS ESCAPE
(1966–1973)

A proposed new charter on the May 1966 ballot put forward sweeping changes in county governance; it would give the board broader powers to legislate its own new programs, much like city council, rather than limiting commissioners to carrying out state legislative mandates. The number of commissioners would be expanded from three to five, one of whom would be designated as chairman by the voters; all officials would be elected county-wide. The chairman would hold all administrative authority, exercise the power of the gavel in presiding over commission sessions, and cast one of the five commission votes.

The new charter would eliminate numerous elected positions—sheriff, constable, surveyor, treasurer, assessor, county clerk, and district court clerk—with the aim of turning over those duties to trained professionals who would report to the county chairman. The district attorney and county judges were elected officials whose positions were governed by state law, rather than the county, so they were not affected by home-rule charter provisions.

Commissioner Mel Gordon had spearheaded the drive for home rule. Two years earlier, he had convinced his fellow commissioners to appoint an eleven-member committee to draft a Multnomah County charter for referral to the voters. Statewide voters had approved a constitutional amendment allowing counties to adopt home-rule charters six years before, and three Oregon counties had already adopted home rule—Lane and Washington in 1962, followed by Hood River in 1964. Commissioner Mike Gleason, who liked things the way they were, was lukewarm about the idea at first but eventually went along.[1]

Lloyd Anderson, who was at that time the manager of local engineering firm CH2M, chaired the charter drafting committee. Other members were George Birnie; William Brunner; Mrs. Arnold (Mary) Damskov, an active member of League of Women Voters; Sylvia Nemer Davidson; Neva Elliott, a lawyer; John

Elorriaga, president of U.S. National Bank; Alden Krieg; John Sonderen; and Stanley Swan. Brunner served as vice-chair and Elliott as secretary.

The wording of the charter was drafted by Orval Edder, an attorney employed by the League of Oregon Cities and the Oregon Bureau of Municipal Research. Edder's language was based on substantive decisions made by the appointed charter commission members. He copied the ballot title from the Washington County home rule measure passed four years before.[2]

County Commission Chairman Mike Gleason wanted to give the county board authority to create special districts, but charter commission member George Birnie, who represented several water and sewer taxing districts, opposed granting that authority. Birnie's position won out by a contentious five-to-four charter commission vote.

An early draft of the charter eliminated the office of auditor as an elected official, but after the incumbent auditor, former Teamsters' dock worker Jack O'Donnell, threatened to publicly oppose the charter and encourage his union friends to do likewise, the auditor's position was left an elective one. (Concerning O'Donnell's qualifications for the job, Commissioner Eccles once joked during an off-the-record commission meeting, "Jack O'Donnell doesn't know the difference between an audit and a ham on rye." The comment got quoted in a daily newspaper by a cub reporter.)

Voters approved the Multnomah County home rule charter by a narrow majority. "It was a surprise to almost everyone that the measure passed," said Charter Commission Chair Anderson. "Most county officials were apathetic about the issue and those opposed did little to fight the measure."[3]

Probably the major reason the county charter passed with so little debate was that the public's attention was focused on a highly controversial "strong mayor" form of government proposal for Portland on the same ballot. Also, words used to describe the two measures undoubtedly affected their outcomes. "Home rule" sounded folksy and friendly, whereas "strong mayor" conjured up visions of power-hungry politicians. The Portland measure was rejected by 68,158 votes to 41,848,[4] while the county home rule charter "slipped in under the radar," so to speak, with 71,771 yes votes to 64,331 no.[5]

Immediately after the May 1966 election, all the county officials whose elected positions were abolished by the new charter—with the exception of Sheriff Clark—circulated a petition to have the vote rescinded. The petitioners obtained enough signatures to put the measure on the November general election ballot before the charter went into effect.

Charter Commission Chair Anderson and other supporters hired attorney Jack Beatty to challenge the repeal petition in court, on the grounds that it had a misleading ballot title. That court challenge failed. Stan Terry—"a local gadfly," in Anderson's words—hired attorney George Joseph to oppose the repeal on the grounds that the petitioners' names were not counted within the time limit set by law.

The second court case was not heard until after the election. In the meantime, the measure to repeal was approved by the voters on the November 1966 ballot. When the court subsequently sustained Terry's argument, that rendered the November repeal vote null and void. The charter therefore went into effect as originally planned, on January 1, 1967. "We never figured out why Terry took the matter to court," Lloyd Anderson later said. "One credible rumor had it that he had bet that the measure would pass and was protecting his bet."

The diametrically opposed results of the Portland measure and the county's were especially ironic because the new county government model was as close to a "strong mayor" form of government as it was possible for an Oregon local government to enact.[6] In the years ahead, city voters would continue to resist major overhauls of city government, while various county charter changes—some better thought-out than others; some purely trial and error—generally passed. Did voters care more about city government and less about the county? Did they see county government as a better place for experimentation? Whether voters saw the county government glass as half full or half empty, it turned out that they were very willing to change the county charter virtually every time a new proposal was placed on the ballot, while at the same time refusing to repeal two or three very restrictive charter provisions.

Confusion upon confusion characterized the fall 1966 election. County candidates had to file for office not knowing whether or not the new charter would survive repeal. A complete roster of candidates for both possibilities appeared on the printed ballot; one set to be validated, the other to become a historical oddity. Sheriff Don Clark was a candidate for two different offices—county chair, if the charter stood; county sheriff if the charter was repealed.

When the new charter prevailed, Gleason was elected chairman with 55.5 percent of the vote over Clark's 44.5 percent. (Clark, who was no longer sheriff, started teaching part-time at Portland State University, still keeping county government in his sights.) There were twenty-two candidates for the four available commission seats. The election was a winner-take-all competition, with Democrats and Republicans alike thrown into the same pool.

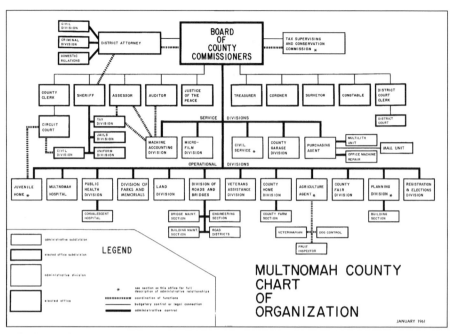

Before home rule (1966).

Four Republicans filed, thirteen Democrats, and five candidates who called themselves nonpartisan. Perhaps needless to say, this numerical difference gave Republican candidates a strong advantage. Incumbent Republicans David Eccles and Mel Gordon were the top two vote-getters, racking up 12.7 percent and 11.9 percent respectively. Democrat (and former board member) Larry Aylsworth was the third-highest vote-getter with 8.5 percent of the vote, and Republican Dan Mosee came in fourth, filling the final available seat on the commission. (Mosee also had the advantage of appearing on the ballot as a candidate for state representative.) Former state legislator Alice Corbett came within 870 votes of besting Mosee[7] and would win a seat eight years later. No woman had yet served on the Multnomah County board.

The five-member commission now consisted of Chairman Gleason, a Democrat; three Republican commissioners, David Eccles, Mel Gordon, and Dan Mosee; and Democrat Larry Aylsworth. Gleason was no longer beholden to his fellow commissioners for the title of chairman; the voters had bestowed that honor on him directly. His eighteen years of experience on the commission gave him a solid understanding of how to conduct efficient board meetings and how to get things done. County staffers, to whom Gleason gave strong support, considered him fair and objective.[8] On the personal side, the new

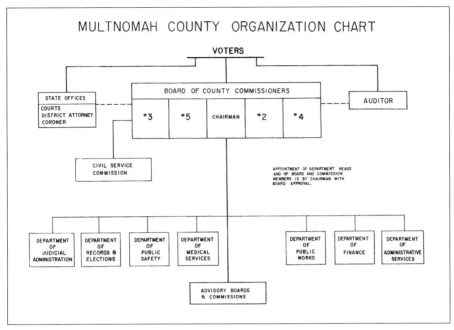

after home rule (1967).

chairman drank a minimum of 20 cups of coffee a day and smoked 4 packs of Camel cigarettes, smoking them right down to the nub.[9]

The county's new home rule charter was widely touted as a "triumph for local government," and allowed its leaders greater freedom from the strictures of the legislature and the state's statutory framework. In addition, the new charter made Multnomah County the first major county west of the Mississippi to elect its chief executive. After six months of trial, Chairman Gleason declared that home rule was a tremendous improvement over the old form of government. Commissioner Larry Aylsworth called it "the greatest thing that ever happened to Multnomah County government."[10] The following day, however, Gleason's fellow commissioners complained that Chairman Gleason was unwilling to share the "duties burden" of commission power with his colleagues on the board.

A week later another *Oregonian* headline said, "Triumph, Tragedy, or In Between?" County commissioners were embroiled in a struggle to define their roles, the story said. Commissioner Mel Gordon stated that he liked Gleason personally, but that Gleason was "inclined to procrastinate" and was "a poor leader." Commissioner David Eccles pointed out that there was no agreement about what fell under the purview of Chairman Gleason as an administrative matter and what did not. Commissioner Aylsworth sometimes acted as an arbitrator but also categorized Gleason as a "dictator."[11]

All in all, the six-month report card for home rule claimed that the new form of government had done more than anything else in the past hundred years to grease the creaking wheels of Multnomah County government machinery. Charter Commission Chair Lloyd Anderson said the transition to home rule had been rapid and orderly, and that home rule was on its way to streamlining county services. Union leaders had no complaints about employees being discharged or improperly relocated.[12]

The relationship between Gleason and three of the other commissioners remained prickly. (Mosee usually voted with Gleason.) In September 1967, an *Oregonian* editorial pinpointed the basic cause of commissioners' unhappiness: they no longer shared equally in board powers. "It hurts their pride to find themselves demoted to inferior, almost impotent, status while their one-time colleague exercises nearly all the enhanced powers of the new home rule government. Furthermore, they are apprehensive [that taxpayers will] wake up to the realization they have on the payroll four $18,000-a-year commissioners who really serve very little useful purpose when they are teamed with a self-sufficient county chairman . . . To his credit, Mr. Gleason has kept his temper under this barrage of criticism, some of it quite intemperate. His unfailing reply to his critics is the advice to go and read the home rule charter."[13]

In one of his first acts as the duly-elected county chair, Mike Gleason appointed Byron H. "Barney" Shields, a recently retired, thirty-year veteran of the Portland police, as interim sheriff. Shields was a popular choice.[14] Gleason then convened a blue ribbon search committee to recruit a permanent sheriff.

The nationwide sheriff search brought James C. Holzman from Chicago to Oregon. Holzman had strong professional qualifications: he had advanced rapidly through the Chicago Police Department in the fourteen years he served there. His resume included service as a patrolman and detective, graduating to the positions of commander and acting deputy chief in command of four districts. Holzman declared himself a champion of First Amendment rights and said he would maintain an open-door policy.[15]

Holzman's honeymoon with Multnomah County was short-lived. By the end of his first four months in office, an *Oregonian* editorial said it was "disillusioning" to have Holzman adopt "what almost could be called a hick cop attitude" toward Multnomah County's unique requirement that new recruits have a college degree. This policy reversal was especially galling, the editorial said, after Holzman had arrived with such dazzling credentials that it was natural for the public to think of him as a super-sheriff, ready to lead "an already fine department" to even higher levels of law enforcement excellence.[16]

For the next two years, Rocky Butte Jail escapes made regular headlines while Holzman's relationship with the board of county commissioners soured.[17] Holzman was fired on February 4, 1970, after only two and a half years as sheriff. During the ten days before his departure, nine more prisoners escaped from Rocky Butte Jail, an institution now nicknamed "the Sieve." Five inmates were still at large on the day of Holzman's dismissal. His stormy career had made him the most unpopular sheriff ever to occupy Multnomah County's top cop position. He arrived as an outsider and never succeeded in shedding that identity. His challenge to the local "sacred cow" of mandatory college degrees for deputies was probably also a factor in his demise.

In an interview with the *Oregon Journal* two weeks after his dismissal, the 39-year-old Holzman charged that he was fired partly because he refused to issue deputy sheriff ID credentials to friends of County Chair Mike Gleason.[18] Holzman's claim of nepotism was never investigated, although newspaper accounts listed several current or former county employees who had ties to Gleason by blood or marriage.

Holzman later said that the "manner and reasons given" for his discharge had destroyed him professionally. "I've had no job offers," he said, "and after what has been done to me professionally, it seems unlikely I ever will be able to obtain another job in the police field."[19] Ten years after the end of his controversial Oregon career, James Holzman was found dead from a self-inflicted gunshot wound in Prescott, Arizona. At the time of his death, Holzman had remarried his former wife and had retired after three years as a faculty member at an Arizona community college.

Sheriff Ed Martin told the *Oregon Journal* that in spite of Holzman's troubled tenure in Multnomah County, Holzman had an excellent reputation nationally. He cited a *Time* magazine story about corruption in Chicago, in which a tavern owner said he had made payments to police officers every month for twenty-three years except for the nine months that "an officer named Holzman was on the beat."[20] Former Sheriff Don Clark opined that Holzman was simply "out of place" in Multnomah County. "He was somebody from a big city police department with a history of corruption and he never fit into a small agency of excellence," Clark said.[21]

In 1969, against the wishes of Chairman Gleason, a majority of the board voted to shut down Edgefield Farm in east Multnomah County because it was no longer paying its own way. Over the years, younger residents had either grown old or moved on. By the late 1960s, the farm was effectively a retirement home more than a working farm. Buildings in the Edgefield complex were not affected by this closure, although the future of Edgefield Manor nursing home was under discussion. The farm's dairy herd was sold off at auction and the land leased to nearby farmers. Critics taunted, "Only the government could take a 300-acre farm with free labor and no taxes and lose money."[22]

Meanwhile, former Sheriff Don Clark was biding his time, awaiting an opportunity to return to county government. He took his chance in 1969 by challenging incumbent Dan Mosee for his commission seat. Clark was younger, more progressive, and better known; Mosee, a used-appliance-store owner and landlord of numerous small, low-rent houses, ran a single-handed, low-budget campaign with his black and orange lawn signs that in their own small way became unofficial landmarks. Clark defeated Mosee; Mosee then took a page from Clark's book and would soon return to the board.

The county commission dynamic changed noticeably with Clark's victory. He came onto the board with a clear understanding of the kind of behind-the-scenes negotiations required to gain the three votes necessary to pass county ordinances. Even though Gleason and his staff continued to "run things," Clark and the three other board members—Mel Gordon, Larry Aylsworth, and David Eccles—carved out more meaningful roles for themselves and were able to over-ride Gleason's vote on many budget and personnel matters. (After Dan Mosee subsequently defeated Aylsworth at the ballot box, the anti-Gleason majority group was reduced to three.)

The Clark, Gordon, and Eccles triumvirate of 1969-72—and a similar block of three after Democrat Ben Padrow defeated Republican Eccles late in 1972[23]— decided that the way to counterbalance the county chairman's dominance was to become more expert on the issues, understanding that knowledge is power. They agreed between them to take responsibility for acquiring expertise on issues such as transportation, housing, urban growth, land-use planning, waste disposal, and urban development. (Clark would later utilize this informal organizational structure when he became county chairman. He assigned the commissioners liaison roles to various county departments and asked for their help in providing oversight over county programs and responsibilities.)[24]

As part of the strategy adopted by the Clark-Gordon-Eccles triumvirate, Mel Gordon became Multnomah County's representative to CRAG, the Columbia Region Association of Governments, and announced his intention to focus on transportation-related issues. (CRAG was the successor organization to a thirty-eight-member Metropolitan Study Commission (MSC) appointed by the state legislators from Multnomah, Washington, Clackamas, and Columbia counties in 1963 to study governmental structures in their four counties.[25]) CRAG was created in 1966 in response to federal government pressure on local governments to do more joint planning in order to be eligible for federal highway, housing, and urban development grants. Elected local government officials representing 90 percent of Portland metropolitan area residents made up CRAG's governing body.[26]

The second member of the triumvirate, Commissioner David Eccles, played a key role in establishing another new regional government for Multnomah, Washington, and Clackamas counties in 1970, an organization charged primarily with overseeing solid waste disposal.[27] The City of Portland fought the legislative bill creating MSD (Metropolitan Service District), because city council feared MSD might try to take over the city's water supply, but Multnomah County voters solidly backed the formation of MSD in the May 1970 election, overcoming its defeat in both Clackamas and Washington counties.[28] MSD was administered by an executive director and governed by seven directors, all elected officials from cities and counties in the region.[29]

Keeping track of all these alphabet-soup-titled entities was hard enough for government observers, let alone ordinary citizens faced with trying to understand the difference between MSC, MSD, CRAG, and MPC, the Metropolitan Planning Commission on which Mike Gleason had earlier served.[30] The situation was further complicated in 1969 when the legislature created the Metropolitan Area Local Government Boundary Commission, a new state agency with power to review and arbitrate annexations, consolidations, and other changes in local government boundaries.[31] See chapter 15 regarding another new governmental agency that would soon supersede all of the above-listed ones.

For his part, Commissioner Don Clark opted to monitor health care, human services, and comprehensive land-use planning—issues that would later provide solid background for choices and decisions he would make during his tenure as county chairman.[32]

14

FREEWAYS REVISITED, CITY-COUNTY CONSOLIDATION FAILS

(1970–1974)

By 1970, rising costs at the Multnomah County Hospital were threatening a cooperative venture between the county and the University of Oregon Medical School that had worked successfully since the new county hospital opened in 1923. The original agreement called for Multnomah County to maintain the building and allow the medical students access to indigent patients in the furtherance of their training; the medical school would provide the staff. In the meantime, the annual county subsidy had grown from $1.4 million to $3.5 million between 1967 and 1970. "This is a trend we cannot afford to allow to continue," Commissioner Mel Gordon told state officials.[1]

The county hospital admitted 9,000 patients in the period 1970-71. Many of them arrived as medical emergencies, so it was not always possible to determine how many were Multnomah County residents. One study suggested as many as 10 percent lived elsewhere, which put Multnomah County at risk of becoming the hospital of last resort for all residents of the metropolitan area. To control costs, the county reduced the number of beds available from 254 to 186. Any further cuts would threaten the medical school's ability to train its students, said Dr. J. David Bristow, chairman of the Department of Medicine.[2] County records indicated that 20 of the 24 beds in the hospital's psychiatric unit were used almost exclusively for teaching medical students.

At the county's urging, Governor Tom McCall authorized a detailed study examining the best course of action. In its 1973 session, the Oregon Legislature approved the merger of the County Hospital into the Medical School Hospital, and medical school officials combined the Multnomah County Hospital, Medical School Hospital, and related outpatient clinics into what became known as University Hospital.[3] The following year, this all became the University of Oregon Health Sciences Center, independent of the University of Oregon. Its name was later changed to Oregon Health Science University and then to Oregon Health and Sciences University. Some parts of the old county hospital were eventually demolished, but one wing, now called the Multnomah Pavilion, remains in active service today, even though county government no longer contributes any financial support to the institution.

On the other side of the Willamette River, the private Portland Adventist Hospital announced plans in 1971 to build a new hospital on 46 acres of the 247-acre Glendoveer Golf Course in unincorporated east county, a move that would require a zone change or a nonconforming use designation by the county board. Commissioners Don Clark, Mel Gordon, and Ben Padrow denied the hospital's land-use request. Gordon saw this as a chance to preserve the acreage as a golf course, open space, and recreation area. Tired of seeing concrete poured for highways, he asked the Oregon Legislature for a loan to help buy Glendoveer. After lengthy negotiations, a $3 million sale of the property to the county was consummated in September 1974. This would be the last parks acquisition Multnomah County would make. The county was to own and operate the 36-hole Glendoveer Golf Course profitably until it was transferred to Metro regional government in 1994.

While vacationing in Mexico in April 1972, Multnomah County Chairman M. James Gleason suffered a stroke. It was probably clear at that moment that Gleason, with two and a half years left in his term, had waged his last campaign. The county board was plainly in transition: although Gleason remained the most powerful man in the county in terms of title, he could seldom muster three votes when he really wanted them. The power bloc of Clark, Gordon, and Padrow clearly held the majority.

Though he was only 61 at the time of his stroke, Gleason returned to his chairmanship job a grayer, old-looking man. He remained fully capable mentally, but spoke slowly and kept his words to a minimum at board meetings. A sign that Gleason was no longer thinking long-term was his appointment of Bard Purcell as sheriff in 1972, following the controversy over James Holzman. Purcell was a former schoolteacher with more than thirty years of Portland Police Bureau experience, but he clearly was not intended as a long-term appointment. Purcell would head up the sheriff's office from 1972 until early 1974, during a period of relative calm; he then resigned during Gleason's last year in office so that the incoming chairman could appoint his own person without political fallout.[4]

Gleason's administration took a major hit in December 1972 when one of the county's top bureaucrats, Loren "Bud" Kramer, announced that he was

Loren "Bud" Kramer was a high-ranking administrator under Chairman M. James Gleason. Kramer quit near the end of Gleason's long tenure only to surface quickly as chief assistant to the board of commissioners. A three-member majority on the board, comprising Commissioners Mel Gordon, Don Clark, and Ben Padrow, consistently outvoted Gleason in Gleason's final years as chairman. (Multnomah County Archives)

leaving his post as Director of Administrative Services because he felt Gleason was squeezing him out in a new reorganization scheme. The following day, Kramer announced he had accepted the position of chief assistant to the board of commissioners, casting his lot with the Clark-Gordon-Padrow alliance—an unmistakable sign that Kramer recognized where the real power lay. A good deal of credit for Gleason's reputation for "getting things done" belonged to Kramer, whom Gleason had hired away from the Association of Oregon Counties in 1961. In his role as Director of Administrative Services, Kramer was arguably the most powerful nonelected official in county history.

Kramer was instrumental in hiring the first female member of the county insiders' power circle, Rena Cusma.[5] A former staff member to Congresswoman Edith Green (as was Kramer), Cusma initiated the practice of adding a 10 percent evaluation factor to all federal grant applications, at the urging of Green and her staff.[6] This practice generated extra money that the anti-Gleason commissioners were quick to identify as a source of funds for hiring analysts and Portland State University faculty members to propose forward-looking agendas for Multnomah County. In an era in which federal grant money flowed freely, the county made sure it got its share.

With former sheriff Terry Schrunk in the Portland mayor's seat and former sheriff Don Clark in a county commission leadership role, joint law enforcement and incarceration planning moved forward. Schrunk and Clark, along with City Commissioner Neil Goldschmidt and state judicial system officials, reached an agreement in the early 1970s that all city municipal judges should be moved from Portland City Hall to the Multnomah County Courthouse and reclassified as district court judges. The county would remodel its holding facility on the top floors of the courthouse to accommodate those arrested by both county sheriff's deputies and city police, which in turn would allow the city to close its overcrowded city jail at S.W. Second Avenue and Oak Street in downtown Portland, an institution regularly criticized by county grand juries.[7]

A key factor in the successful implementation of these moves was the establishment of a sobering-up place for substance abusers, a safe and humane alternative to jail or a hospital emergency ward. The county's Hooper Detox Center, where inebriates were housed long enough to sober up and were then given the opportunity to join a long-term detoxification program, opened in 1973. The site was named for David P. Hooper, "the last chronic street inebriate who died in the old county jail." At first the Hooper Detox Center was operated by the county human services department; several years after its opening, responsibility for running it was shifted to the not-for-profit Central City Concern.[8] In its first thirty-five years of operation, more than 100,000 different inebriates passed through the center's doors. But many of the patients were "regulars," and the Hooper staff estimated they had dealt with roughly half a million separate bookings.[9]

Home rule had been in effect in Multnomah County for only four years when the state legislature, at the request of the Multnomah County Commission, established a citizen city-county charter commission to draft a consolidated Portland-Multnomah County charter for submission to the voters.[10] It would be the most serious attempt at combining the two governments since a failed effort in 1927, and the proposed charter was completed in time to be placed on the May 1974 ballot.

Polls showed that voters favored city-county consolidation in principle, so when "nobody really stepped forward to pick up the ball" to push for passage, Portland Mayor Neil Goldschmidt threw himself and his volunteer resources solidly into the fray. The mayor's support turned out to be both a blessing and a curse; once his energized volunteers hit the streets to solicit votes for the cause, many people saw consolidation as a Goldschmidt power grab.[11]

The specifics of the Portland-Multnomah County charter doomed it to failure. The consolidated city-county was to be governed by a legislative body of eleven council members, plus a strong mayor with veto power who would not sit on the council. Eight council members would be elected by districts and three more elected at-large, with seven council members' votes required to override a mayoral veto.[12] The measure was touted as a money-saving proposition, but many observers predicted no savings at all, since there would be no reduction in the number of elected officials.

The name of the new entity, "Portland-Multnomah," came in for heavy ridicule. Under the capital-letter headline "17-LETTER HYPHENATED NAME," a *Voters' Pamphlet* argument against the measure said: "The proposed official name change, to Portland-Multnomah, is not only long, cumbersome and costly, but displays the lack of decision and agreement among those appointed to draw up the charter."

Opponents of consolidation distributed a four-page, color tabloid featuring a cartoon character wearing dark glasses and a lapel rose, smoking a big cigar, with paper money sticking out of his pockets in every direction—money obviously stolen from gullible taxpayers. In the eyes of some, the cartoon figure was intended to be Goldschmidt. The tabloid warned of high tax bills, a sales tax without a vote of the people, ward politics, and a "mayor so powerful that not even council" could require him to justify his actions.[13]

Special interests found flaws in the proposed charter, too. Portland police officers strenuously objected to a uniform benefit plan for all sworn law enforcement officers, because they would lose the generous pension and disability provisions contained in the existing city charter. Other unions also joined City Commissioner Frank Ivancie, the Portland Chamber of Commerce, Multnomah County Labor Council, and many businesses to oppose the measure.[14]

Voters buried the 1974 "good government" proposal by 71 percent to 29 percent. The *Oregon Journal* summarized the results: "The five smaller cities . . . [could] opt out if they wished . . . The demand to stay out ranged from 95 percent in Wood Village to 83.6 percent in Maywood Park. In Gresham, largest of the cities, it was 91.2 percent. The experience of consolidation in the country indicates that it fails unless proposed during a crisis or outrageous scandal in local government. There was none such here, and there will be no consolidation."[15]

Prior to the May 1974 vote, anticipating passage of the city-county consolidation measure, county administrator Loren "Bud" Kramer negotiated with his city counterpart to combine or co-locate several functions, including telephone systems, purchasing, printing, a computer mainframe, and customized budgeting and financial software. These joint efforts could have saved money had they stayed together, but after the consolidation measure failed, city and county bureaus soon went their own ways.[16]

One such undertaking was a computerized accounting system designed to serve both entities. A massive IBM mainframe located in the county's Penumbra Kelly Building in northeast Portland constituted the hardware, while two national firms custom-designed the software.[17] The computer started processing transactions for the online Financial Management System (FMS) on July 1, 1973, well before consolidation ballots were cast. Unfortunately, the two software systems built by different vendors did not communicate with each other well. Near-panic resulted. The county avoided most of the problem by keeping two sets of financial records—one by hand and one by computer—while the changeover was in process. The city did not keep back-up records.[18] Two or three years later, in an emphatic repudiation of voluntary consolidation by both city and county employees, the city and county navigated back to their own separate computer systems.

Also in 1974, Kramer persuaded auditor Jack O'Donnell, who had served as the county's elected auditor for twenty-four years, not to seek reelection. Kramer accomplished this by first moving O'Donnell and his staff to windowless office space in the center of the courthouse, then holding out the promise of an office window and private bathroom as an inducement to O'Donnell if he would agree to retire in December. Not only did the carrot work; O'Donnell also acquiesced to Kramer's demand that he hire a certified public accountant to upgrade the work quality of O'Donnell's bean-counting staff. O'Donnell agreed to keep his decision not to seek reelection a secret until a qualified professional could be recruited to run.[19]

No issue had more long-term impact on county residents during the 1970s than decisions over the location of new freeways—decisions in which Multnomah County government would play a lead role. The 1956 Federal-Aid Highway Act had kicked off the largest public works program in the nation's history. President Dwight Eisenhower considered the interstate freeway network his "favorite by far" of all his domestic programs because it was changing the face of America. Under the Act, the federal government would pay 90 percent of project costs.[20] Cities, counties, and states all over the country would be involved in deciding the routes for these freeways. One such approval, the routing of the north-south Interstate 5 corridor through Portland alongside the east bank of the Willamette River in 1963, drew little opposition at the time but would become, in the 1980s and 1990s, the subject of severe criticism and calls to relocate several miles of I-5 either away from the river or underground.[21] No serious proposals for doing so were on the table by the beginning of the twenty-first century because of the huge costs of such an undertaking.

Thirteen years before the Federal-Aid Highway Act passed, New York's "Master Builder," Robert Moses, had visited the Portland area in 1943 and prepared an ambitious plan for Portland metropolitan freeways.[22] The Oregon State Highway Department (OSHD) had previously chosen several major freeway routes in the Portland area, but the well-known Moses name gave credibility and focus to freeway planning.[23]

In addition to I-5, one or two other north-south freeways were proposed for the east side of the Willamette River; that number was later reduced to one. OSHD conducted numerous studies and held raucous public hearings regarding potential routes along 39th, 52nd, 82nd, 96th, and 109th avenues for a north-south I-205 freeway, with the 96th corridor the ultimate winner. In an effort to stop the I-205 freeway, residents of Maywood Park petitioned the county to incorporate.[24] The City of Maywood Park then kept I-205 from bisecting its neighborhoods by bringing a successful lawsuit against OSHD on procedural grounds.[25]

The Portland City Council vetoed details of the 96th Avenue alignment in order to gain a commitment from OSHD to build Portland's "long-sought" east-west Mt. Hood Freeway through southeast Portland. The Mt. Hood Freeway was to run east-west from the Willamette River to S.E. 122nd Avenue (the other major east-west corridor being I-80, alongside the Columbia River), paralleling S.E. Division Street and S.E. Powell Boulevard, and stopping far short of Mt. Hood itself. The freeway was to proceed almost due east from a new Willamette River bridge to be built south of downtown and across the new north-south "circumferential" I-205, with a possible later extension to the suburban city of Gresham.[26]

Now Multnomah County was in the driver's seat. The entire I-205 corridor would run through unincorporated Multnomah County, with no additional approvals required from the City of Portland except for a Mt. Hood Freeway interchange with I-205. Commissioner Don Clark convinced a majority of his colleagues that I-205 interchange negotiations gave Multnomah County leeway to revisit the Mt. Hood Freeway issue—and perhaps to block its construction permanently.[27] New federal legislation would allow freeway dollars to be used for public transit projects, creating the possibility that the region might be able to retain all the federal freeway dollars earmarked for the Mt. Hood Freeway, even if that project was cancelled.

While various internal county, state, and federal negotiations and hearings were taking place, vigorous protests by groups that had formed to oppose the Mt. Hood Freeway kept the issue in the news.

In May 1972, the Multnomah County Commission formally requested that OSHD delay the final design of I-205 interchanges until an environmental impact statement could be prepared. Six months later, by a four-to-one vote

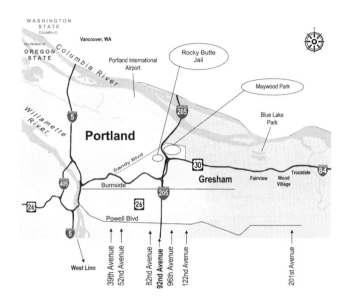

Proposed alternative routes for Interstate Highway I-205 are shown on this map. Street names of various possible routes are printed vertically. (Note: in 2009, 39th Avenue was renamed Cesar E. Chavez Boulevard)

(Chairman Gleason in the minority), and against the advice of the county roadmaster and planning director, Commissioners Don Clark, Mel Gordon, Ben Padrow, and Larry Aylsworth placed a moratorium on construction and condemnation work for the entire Mt. Hood Freeway—this in spite of the fact that the Oregon Department of Transportation (ODOT) had been purchasing and condemning land in the proposed freeway path for some time.[28] In all, the Mt. Hood Freeway plans called for buying up 1,500 houses and 180 businesses to make way for the freeway.[29] County commissioners also insisted that the I-205 route must include bicycle, pedestrian, and mass transit paths along the interstate.[30]

The following year, an environmental impact statement prepared on behalf of ODOT concluded that the Mt. Hood Freeway "would not relieve congestion and would be obsolete by the time it was completed."[31] This statement solidified the positions of Commissioners Clark, Gordon, and Padrow when they voted on February 21, 1974, to withdraw county support for the Mt. Hood Freeway, as detailed in chapter 1. Although Dan Mosee had by now replaced Larry Aylsworth, he stood alone in the three-to-one vote against the new freeway (Chairman Gleason did not attend the meeting).[32]

Five months later, by a contentious four-to-one vote (with Mayor Ivancie in the minority) the Portland City Council joined the Multnomah County Commission and reversed its long-standing support for the Mt. Hood Freeway. The city council voted to divert all freeway funds that had been earmarked for the project to install mass transit and to improve east-west I-84 along the Columbia River. Congress had recently passed legislation to mandate federal reimbursement of local governments for damage that occurred as a result of constructing federal highways.[33]

Supporters of the Mt. Hood Freeway, including Commissioner Dan Mosee, now led an initiative drive to refer the city council's decision to voters. However, a judge ruled that the city council's decision was administrative rather than legislative, and not subject to voter approval, so the measure did not reach the ballot, where it might well have brought the controversial freeway project back to life.[34] That initiative drive was the last hope for its supporters; the Mt. Hood Freeway was now officially dead. Labor unions withheld their support for Don Clark and Mel Gordon in the 1974 elections because the pair had fought the Mt. Hood Freeway.[35] While this union action had little immediate effect, it may well have made Clark's negotiations during a 1980 labor strike more difficult and influenced his unsuccessful race for Oregon governor in 1982.

During the years that the freeway project was on hold, Commissioner Mel Gordon had been globe-trotting, visiting the sites of various successful public transit systems in Europe and elsewhere. He and the county board majority consistently fought to keep light rail as an option in spending federal highway dollars.[36] After first supporting exclusive bus lanes, Portland Mayor Neil Goldschmidt became a light-rail convert. As a key member of a regional transportation planning body, he called for a public transit system "that would be competitive with the freeway network." This paved the way for a 15-mile rapid transit line called MAX (Metropolitan Area Express) that would roughly parallel the east-west I-84 freeway between Portland and Gresham.[37]

Much credit (or blame, depending on one's viewpoint) for the dramatic turn that highway planning took in those years belongs to a group of citizens—educated, articulate, young professionals—who founded STOP, Sensible Transportation Options for People. The first two STOP chairpersons were citizen activist and housewife/mother Betty Merten and lawyer Steve Schell. Others in leadership roles included Ron Buel (Goldschmidt's executive assistant), Jim Howell, Elsa Coleman, and Charles Merten. Buel had written a book, *Dead End,* on the impact of cars and freeways on American cities. In Betty Merten's words, STOP was composed of "young Turks who believed they could overturn a 'done deal.'"[38]

In what was arguably the largest citizen involvement movement ever in Multnomah County, citizens had changed history. The freeway opponents were exhilarated by their influence, later boasting that "nothing shaped Portland so much as the murder of the Mount Hood Freeway . . . [It established] the idea that cities are for people, not just for commerce and cars."[39] On the other hand, no one could deny Mayor Ivancie's argument that southeast Portland remained a "transportation ghetto." Getting to Timberline Lodge on Mt. Hood from almost anyplace in Portland required a circuitous route.[40]

Other proposed freeway corridors fell off planning maps as citizens began to understand the impact on their neighborhoods. Roads that would have gutted Parkrose, Johnson Creek, Rivergate, Laurelhurst, St. Johns, and Rose City quietly disappeared. In its finally approved form, I-405 on the west side of downtown Portland was a four- to six-lane "concrete walled box canyon" dug out between S.W. 13th and 14th in a semi-circle that connected with I-5 at the north and south ends. This "Sunset-Stadium Freeway," today's I-405, cut neighborhoods in half and displaced 1,700 residents, exemplifying the type of damage that was avoided when other proposed routes were eliminated.[41] The existing Harbor Drive Freeway along the Willamette River in downtown Portland was actually dismantled.

Another proposed freeway, I-505, was removed from the drawing board by a "political firestorm from politically conscious northwest Portland neighborhoods," in much the same way that citizen pressure nixed the Mt. Hood Freeway. I-505 would have cut across northwest Portland along Thurman Street to connect with Highway 30 near the former Montgomery Ward store and warehouse, and from there run alongside the Willamette and Columbia rivers via St. Helens Road, presumably continuing as a four-lane freeway to Astoria and the Pacific Ocean. As a result of strong citizen opposition, a long off-ramp from I-405 to the northwest Portland industrial area that was once the site of the 1905 Lewis and Clark Exposition was built instead.[42]

The "reconfiguration" that resulted in closure of Rocky Butte Jail next to I-205 was negotiated by Don Clark and his representatives after Clark became county chair in January 1975. Under a recently passed federal act, the federal government agreed to compensate local governments for the cost of relocations caused by federal highway projects. Multnomah County obtained full functional replacement for both the Rocky Butte Jail and the county maintenance yard.[43] Today's impressive Justice Center in downtown Portland and the Yeon maintenance shops near Gresham were state-of-the-art new structures built at little or no cost to the county.[44]

Looking back, it is interesting to note that "no-build" was never a viable option with regard to I-205, mainly because the Clackamas County portion of I-205 had already been built to the north Clackamas County line before

Multnomah County got serious about limiting freeways, but also because the political will was not there to stop it.[45] In addition, there was general (albeit not universal) agreement that the massive new Glenn Jackson Bridge across the Columbia River at the northern end of I-205 was sorely needed. Fortunately, it was designed and built to accommodate a future light rail line.

Looking forward, what was seen as obstructionist in 1974 would be heralded as visionary in 2009. The far-sighted insistence by the Multnomah County Commission thirty-five years earlier to limit I-205 to six auto lanes, and to include light rail and bike lanes, was to provide a ready-made corridor for the Green Line MAX that opened September 12, 2009. This new east-side mass transit line connected Clackamas County to Portland State University and downtown Portland via Clackamas Town Center and Lloyd Center. By transferring at the Gateway Transit Center, all lines provided access to Portland International Airport.[46]

During Chairman Gleason's final year, Commissioner Don Clark announced his intention to run for chairman. City Commissioner Francis (Frank) Ivancie also stated his interest in the job, which promised a classic race between a progressive liberal (Clark) and a well-financed, glib, campaigner-conservative (Ivancie).[47] But the race never materialized: Ivancie decided his real interest lay in outwaiting Neil Goldschmidt and becoming mayor of Portland.[48] After being coy about running for yet another term, Gleason finally announced that his long career of county electioneering was over.[49] After Ivancie dropped out, Clark won the race easily.

Meanwhile, Gleason limped toward the end of his term in December 1974. He was frequently absent, but that made little difference to the commission's vote tallies. The only vote Gleason could count on was Dan Mosee's, and a three-two vote had no different result than a four to one. Gleason's penurious ways, likely a reflection of his childhood in the Depression, began to cause a stir. He came under fire for using county funds on trips that were perhaps no more than vacations. An *Oregon Journal* report in 1973 listed seven Gleason relatives or in-laws who had been on the county payroll since 1970, plus two more dating back to 1963. Gleason said he showed no favoritism toward his relatives, "but they might be more apt to know whether there's an opening for a job." The report found that county heads were checking with Gleason before making hires. Gleason noted that in one instance he recommended that the county *not* hire a nephew of his, because he wasn't a good worker. "Being a relative of mine isn't an advantage," he said. "It's a disadvantage, because more would be expected

An editorial cartoon suggests that Don Clark found skeletons in the county closet, such as a budget deficit and poor management practices, after he succeeded M. James Gleason as county chairman in 1975. The changing of the guard moved the county into a new era of professional management. (Cartoon by Bruce McGilllivray)

out of you than they would expect out of someone else."[50] Close associates had a nickname for the chairman: "Mike 'Never-Pay-Retail' Gleason."[51]

"Mike Gleason was a superb old-time politician who probably wouldn't make it in today's world of sound bites and television cameras," county administrator Loren Kramer later said. "Gleason was the first commissioner to have a vision for the county, who wanted the county to go beyond what the law required. He didn't go out much, and wasn't particularly good at making speeches, but had a solid reputation of getting things done. He was very much in control of county business."[52]

Reflecting on the downside of Gleason's career, Kramer mentioned his penchant for building roads across vacant fields while providing no infrastructure. Gleason's pay-as-you-go Depression mentality and reluctance to finance new construction through bonding cost the county money in the long run, Kramer said, because opportunities were missed, for example, to replace the aging courthouse and the outdated Sellwood Bridge, and to build a downtown office structure (which would have saved millions of dollars in office rental fees over the years[53]). As noted by the New York Bureau of Municipal Research in 1913,

"To use the tax money of any particular year to construct a building having a life from 25 to 40 years is contrary to all principles of logic and sound finance."

More than three hundred friends, political allies, and Oregon public officials past and present paid tribute to Gleason at the Hilton Hotel in January 1975. The heartiest audience applause came for a speech by Fred Meyer, the retail entrepreneur who had employed Gleason as an electrician many years before. "We used to have some good old days before all these environmental boys and ecologists came along," Meyer said. "We built a store out on Lombard in 58 days, and now it takes two to three years to get a permit . . . The best way you can describe Mike's work is, he used his horse sense. We used to get decisions from Mike. I only pray we get a few more Mike Gleasons around."[54]

U.S. Congressman Bob Duncan told the crowd that he had met Gleason when the two men served in the Oregon House of Representatives together. "He came up to me," Duncan recalled, "and said, 'Bob, we have to quit using the rivers for sewers and the ocean as a septic tank.'" Among others paying tribute to Gleason were Don Clark (Gleason's replacement as county chairman), former U.S. Congresswoman Edith Green, county employees, and labor representatives. Gleason died four years later at age sixty-eight.[55] The M. James Gleason Memorial Boat Ramp, located on the Columbia River near Portland International Airport, was named in his honor.

The waves of change that had swamped city-county consolidation and sunk the Mt. Hood Freeway occurred against a backdrop of national scandals. Revelations regarding the Watergate break-in and the subsequent resignation of President Richard Nixon in August 1974 now placed new emphasis, at least for the time being, on the importance of honesty and integrity at all levels of government.

15

THE DON CLARK ERA, CHARTER UPENDED, NURSING HOME CLOSED, METRO CREATED
(1975–1979)

Energetic Don Clark hit the ground running when he started his term as county chairman in January 1975. No county chair before or since has generated the same degree of *esprit de corps* that motivated Clark's management team. Many of those who were part of Clark's lineup considered his tenure as the chief elected officer to be the county's golden age.[1]

Clark would need abundant energy and drive to deal with the myriad problems facing the county. Two weeks before he was sworn in as chairman, a lengthy front-page article in *Willamette Week*, a crusading weekly newspaper launched only the month before, outlined eight challenges that Clark would have to deal with: a budget shortfall of $7.2 million; loss of federal revenue sharing dollars; unfunded pension liabilities; nonexistent or inadequate inventory/management of county real property and equipment; poor labor relations management that resulted in county workers working seven and a half hours per day but paid for eight; lack of money to renovate the Hoyt Hotel, recently bought by the county for $800,000; tax revenue failing to keep pace with inflation; and layoffs of human services workers who were given severance payments and then in many cases rehired at similar or higher wages.[2]

One of Clark's first hires clearly displayed his willingness to break new ground, namely the appointment of Lee P. Brown as sheriff in January 1975. Brown represented a significant change from any previous sheriff, not only because he was a recent PhD graduate (in criminology) from the University of California, Berkeley, but also because he was the first African-American in the nation to head up a large law-enforcement entity. Clark had met Brown at a police community relations seminar some years before and was so impressed with Brown's potential that he persuaded him to head up a new department of criminal justice at Portland State College in 1968, just one year before PSC

Sheriff Lee Brown (1975-76), shown here being sworn in by Circuit Court Judge Richard Unis, was the first African-American in the nation to head a large law-enforcement entity. (Oregon Historical Society, no. bb009005)

became Portland State University. Then Clark enticed Brown away from PSU to serve as county sheriff.[3]

Lee Brown's tenure coincided with a time when generous federal law enforcement grants were available to local governments. During the short year and a half that he administered the sheriff's office for Multnomah County, he introduced team policing, funded largely by federal Law Enforcement Assistance Administration (LEAA) dollars.

In 1976, Brown resigned to accept the position of public safety commissioner in Atlanta, Georgia. During his tenure there, Brown and his team cracked the infamous Atlanta child murder cases.[4] Brown went on to serve as police chief of Houston, Texas, police commissioner for New York City, and national drug czar under President Clinton before winning election as the first black mayor of Houston. On a Houston television program aired in 2000, Brown praised Don Clark as the mentor most influential in launching his political career.[5]

County commissioners serving with Clark during the early part of his chairmanship were Mel Gordon, Dan Mosee, Alice Corbett (who won Ben Padrow's former seat after Padrow decided not to seek a second term and became the first woman elected to the county commission), and Dennis Buchanan (a former journalist and stockbroker who was appointed to fill Clark's former seat). Gordon, a portly and proud "old-time" politician with the bearing of a wealthy railroad baron, knew how to generate publicity. He had been elected and reelected several times as a Republican but changed his registration to

Democrat in the early 1970s after Republican David Eccles was defeated by Democrat Ben Padrow. Padrow, no longer in office, returned to serve as Clark's executive assistant for a time.[6]

Clark had been county chairman for little more than a month when he announced plans to close Edgefield Manor, a nursing home with 220 patients. He blundered in failing to notify the nursing home patients first; they knew nothing about it until they read it in the newspapers. Thereafter, Clark posted a sign in his office reminding him to communicate with people who would be affected by his decisions.[7] But even without that misstep, the news that Edgefield Manor patients would be moved into private nursing homes raised a storm of protest. Clark argued that the $400,000 cost of bringing the building up to current minimum standards was too high, while at the same time acknowledging that the Manor was "probably the best nursing home in America." The building sat on grounds formerly operated as a poor farm of 345 acres in east Multnomah County near Troutdale.[8] It had opened in 1911 with 211 residents, with the number of "inmates" at the Manor climbing to 554 during the Depression before dropping back down to the 200 range.[9] The farm operation had been shut down in 1969, and the fields were now leased to local farmers.[10]

More than a hundred spectators showed up for a public hearing on the future of Edgefield on April 3, 1975. Two east county state legislators, Representative Glenn Otto of Troutdale and Senator Vern Cook of Gresham, blasted the commissioners who were supporting Edgefield's closure (all of them except Commissioner Dan Mosee), pronouncing them guilty of "gross negligence" and of violating the county home rule charter. Ten days later, Clark announced that he had abandoned his plan to close Edgefield Manor, and Cook and Otto proclaimed victory.[11] It would be seven years before the last Manor patients died or left for smaller homes.

One of Clark's early challenges was to prepare Multnomah County's Comprehensive Land Use Plan in accordance with State Senate Bill 100. Oregon's Land Conservation and Development Commission (LCDC) had been granted broad powers to limit urban growth and control land use.[12] Statewide goals had been set in 1974, with cities and counties directed to adopt local plans during the next two years. Clark's staff negotiated one neighborhood at a time, working toward consensus on details before seeking approval from the county commission and LCDC.

As part of the land-use process, Clark wanted to preserve east Multnomah County east of 82nd Avenue as farmland, but he gave up that idea after staffers warned that they would have to redo the entire planning process, since that region had already been identified for industrial development. Clark's efforts in protecting Sauvie Island from urbanization and the Columbia Gorge from development were more successful.

Commissioner Mel Gordon sometimes struggled with his planning votes, Clark later said, because Gordon's instincts as a small businessman would kick in and he would "get a little nervous because he could visualize being in that guy's shoes." But Gordon had given Clark his word while they were fellow commissioners that he would be a team player, and Clark could almost always count on his vote. "Commissioner Dennis Buchanan would wring his hands and worry and stew and be lobbied by people," Clark said. "Some of those votes were very hard for Dennis."[13] Commissioner Alice Corbett would usually vote with the board majority. The wild card was always Commissioner Dan Mosee, who would often vote according to the views of the last person he talked to before a meeting began. Fortunately for Clark, he seldom needed Mosee's vote.

Occasionally, Commissioner Mosee fell asleep during commission meetings. On one occasion, when planning director Bob Baldwin was presenting a development proposal that included slides and colored maps, Mosee fell off his chair with a thump. The other commissioners helped him up and the hearing continued. At another hearing three weeks later, the same scenario recurred. "I began to wonder if I needed to alter my style," Baldwin later said.[14]

Mosee probably suffered from narcolepsy, a disorder that causes uncontrollable drowsiness. However, he would perk up immediately if he understood that he would be expected to respond to an issue or a question.

A half-year assessment of Clark's performance by *Oregon Journal* reporter Jeff Wohler in late June 1975 described the contrast between Clark's aggressive and energetic approach to the job as "like night and day to the quiet and unobtrusive style of his predecessor, M. James Gleason." In response to critics who claimed that he was isolated and arrogant, Clark responded, "These are not times for timidity in government. There is a desperate need for bold addressing of the issues and solving of the problems."[15]

However, Edgefield advocates had no intention of letting Clark off the hook without retribution. In July, a committee headed by Don Carmichael, director of a Portland senior citizens' center, filed a recall petition against Clark. Petitioners had to collect 32,084 signatures within ninety days to put the measure on the ballot, a goal they failed to reach by "about 2,000 signatures," according to a recall spokesperson.[16] Clark accused Carmichael of using the petition drive to gain

When Donald E. Clark succeeded M. James Gleason as county chairman in 1975, the board was composed of, from left, Dan Mosee, Alice Corbett, Clark, Mel Gordon, and Dennis Buchanan. Buchanan was appointed to succeed Clark as commissioner. Corbett was the first woman elected to the county board. Unlike many women who followed her, she seemed content with a largely silent role during her tenure. (Multnomah County Archives)

name familiarity before running for public office himself, which Carmichael denied. When filing time came around the following March, however, Carmichael was one of six candidates to challenge—unsuccessfully—the recently appointed Commissioner Dennis Buchanan, who was filling the remainder of Clark's commission term.[17]

Never ones to give up easily, Representative Otto and Senator Cook gathered enough signatures by August 1976 to place on the ballot an initiative petition that would dramatically alter county government. By then it had become clear that Clark's attempt to close Edgefield was no longer the main motivating factor; rather, a more generalized dislike for the progressive chairman was involved. Under the terms of the Cook-Otto petition, the elective position of chairman would be eliminated, commission terms reduced from four to two years, and the county divided into five single-member commission districts. In a thinly veiled attempt to dislodge them both from office, under this plan Don Clark and Mel Gordon were assigned to the easternmost commission districts and would have to seek reelection from there.[18]

The Cook-Otto charter amendments approved by voters in November 1976 pitted east county against west county. The *Gresham Outlook*, Gresham Chamber of Commerce, Multnomah County Republican Central Committee, East Multnomah County Democratic Club, AFL-CIO Central Labor Council, and Pomona Grange all came out in favor. Opponents of the measure included both Portland daily newspapers, the City Club of Portland, Portland Chamber of Commerce, Portland League of Women Voters, and the Teamsters.[19] (This was the first of several changes voters would consider—and often approve—affecting county government over the next several years, while Portland's commissioner form of government, instituted in 1913, remained unchanged; see Appendix C.)

By early 1977, more than a hundred county residents had signed on as members of a Citizens for Good Government committee formed to gain repeal of the 1976 charter changes. They hired experienced campaign manager Julie Williamson to oversee collection of the 16,472 valid signatures that were needed by mid-October to place the repeal measure on the November 1977 general election ballot.[20] A big selling point in the measure's successful passage was that it called for a charter review committee to be convened to hold public hearings and propose charter changes. Fortunately for Clark and Gordon, the 1976 measure was rescinded before they were required to run for reelection from the county districts in which they were least popular.

Nevertheless, the Cook-Otto ballot measure ended Don Clark's tenure as the elected county chairman effective January 1977. It was up to the county board to select one of its members to serve as chairman. Don Clark was their unanimous choice.[21]

Numerous hearings were held by the committee appointed in 1977 to review charter provisions and recommend potential changes. "The one issue that members of the committee and persons who testified before us were unanimous in their agreement on," said lawyer Jack Faust, who chaired the review committee, "was that the county chair's power should be reduced." The committee's solution was to adopt the "three branches of government" model used at state and federal levels by creating a county executive position (executive branch) separate from the commission (legislative branch). The five commissioners would elect one of their own as presiding officer at the beginning of each year. All future county elections would be nonpartisan.[22]

The most controversial change the committee proposed was to create the position of an elected executive who was not a member of the board. The introduction of single-member commission districts was also hotly debated. Commissioner Dennis Buchanan argued against single-member districts that pitted one district against another: "The whole board is sitting down here [in the courthouse] making decisions that affect east county, but its residents only get to vote for one [member] if this is approved."[23]

Media representatives were unenthusiastic about the change from a board chairman to an elected county executive. After the provisions went into effect, an *Oregonian* article noted that it was harder to learn what was going on at county departments, now that administrative work was conducted behind doors in closed meetings between county executive Don Clark and his department heads. "In this respect," reporter Kathy Durbin said, "county government is less open than city government because county commissioners serve only in a 'liaison' capacity," rather than as managers, as was the case under Portland's commission form of government.[24]

As "county executive," Don Clark, who lost his seat on the board and the power of the gavel, later declared that he liked the separation of powers structure while it lasted, because not having to sit through board meetings freed him up for other matters. His managers, however, found themselves cut off from access to the board.[25] Residents were unclear as to which commission district they resided in, or who represented their interests on the board.

After fourteen high-profile years as a county commissioner, Mel Gordon, who had played a key role in freeway decisions and the acquisition of Glendoveer Golf Course, was restless. He decided to run for the office of Oregon State Treasurer in the May 1976 Democratic primary, as did county auditor Jewel Lansing. Lansing won a surprise victory over Gordon in the primary, then narrowly lost to Republican Secretary of State Clay Myers in the fall.[26] Gordon retained his county seat, but resigned from the county commission in March 1978 to assume chairmanship of the Pacific Northwest River Basin Commission, a federal water-resource oversight agency.

To fill the remaining nine months of Gordon's term, the board appointed Parkrose School Board member Barbara Roberts.[27] Roberts would go on to win a seat in the Oregon legislature in 1981, be elected Secretary of State in 1984, and serve as Oregon's first (and so far, only) female governor. Gordon resurfaced later in Clark County, Washington, where he morphed back into a Republican and won two terms as a Clark County commissioner starting in 1994.[28]

"Looking back now," Roberts said in 2011, "I realize that my short time as a county commissioner took place at a particularly opportune time with regard to state and local public policy choices." She cast crucial votes for the funding and building of a 15-mile light rail system called MAX (Metropolitan Area Express) between Gresham and downtown Portland, supplied a key vote for adoption of the county's first urban growth boundary, and introduced a successful board resolution to prevent Multnomah County employees from traveling on county business to states that had failed to ratify the national ERA (Equal Rights Amendment) to the U.S. Constitution.[29]

Also in 1978, a young and aggressive state representative from southeast Portland, Earl Blumenauer, defeated Commissioner Alice Corbett and began his first term on the county commission in January 1979. When he moved from the county to a seat on city council, Blumenauer was the first commissioner in seventy-five years to have been elected to both governing bodies. (During the county's first fifty years, nineteen men had served in both jurisdictions.)[30] Blumenauer's side step from the Multnomah County Commission to city council would be replicated by Gretchen Kafoury in 1991, and by Dan Saltzman in 1999. In relocating to city hall, these elected officials gained a broader range of authority and responsibility as well as higher salaries. In addition, county term limits restricted them to eight years of county service, while Portland had no such prohibition. One of Blumenauer's key campaign issues concerned the public library system. The need for library improvements was the subject of one of his television campaign ads.[31]

What many Multnomah County citizens did not realize about their free public library was that, although the county provided a substantial portion of its funding, the libraries were owned and operated by an independent nonprofit organization, the Library Association of Portland (LAP), rather than Multnomah County. In 1976-77, faced with difficult financial times, Multnomah County Chair Don Clark proposed reducing county library funding from $3.6 million to $2 million, which would have forced closure of all but one of ten branch libraries and severely curtailed central library hours. With strong support from community leaders, a three-year $6.6 million library property tax levy passed with 74 percent of the vote. This short-term success did not solve funding and other library problems for long, as will soon be seen.

The idea of consolidating Multnomah, Washington, and Clackamas counties as a super-entity "Willamette County" had been proposed off and on as far back as the 1930s. Future State Representative Richard Neuberger (later U.S. Senator from Oregon) had advocated reducing the number of Oregon counties from thirty-six to twelve. The original reason for having so many counties, he argued, was to make sure all citizens were within a day's trip by wagon of the county seat, a goal long since irrelevant. Subsequently, a proposed merger between Marion and Polk counties had been scuttled because Polk feared domination by Marion.[32] Five small mid-Columbia counties—Morrow, Sherman, Gilliam, Wheeler, and Jefferson—looked seriously at consolidation before a squabble over the location of the county seat ended the discussions.[33] In 1977, Portland metropolitan area state legislators sponsored a bill to create a new county consisting of the urbanized portions of Multnomah, Washington, and Clackamas counties. The bill never got out of committee.[34]

To the surprise of many—if not most—observers, voters in the tri-county Portland area now approved the formation of a new governmental entity—later to be called "Metro"—effective January 1, 1979. The officers of the new metropolitan government were to be elected directly by the people, unlike its predecessor organizations, MSD (Metropolitan Service District) and CRAG (Columbia Region Association of Governments); see chapter 13.[35] The geographic boundaries of the new super-entity included the urban portions of Multnomah, Clackamas, and Washington counties. The new entity was to have jurisdiction over land-use planning, solid waste disposal, transportation planning, and operation of the Washington Park Zoo. It would also be given authority to take over operation of Tri-Met, the regional transportation authority (which had not happened as of 2012).[36]

The measure creating this new entity was aided by a ballot title promising to abolish CRAG, the controversial planning body composed of elected officials from each of several cities and five counties. In actuality, CRAG was merged with the old MSD into this new organization, with none of its basic roles abandoned. The difference was that representatives to this powerful new body would be chosen directly by the voters.[37] In November 1992, a charter change would be approved by the voters to give the organization home rule authority and change its name officially to "Metro."[38] Wags liked to say, "Metro is our name now, and 'service' used to be our middle name."[39]

By 1978, political party registration favored Democrats so strongly that winning the Multnomah County Democratic primary was tantamount to winning in the fall. Thus the ever-resilient Dan Mosee switched parties in time to file as a Democrat in the 1978 partisan primary. (That year, another charter change made all future county races nonpartisan.)

The 1978 election cycle brought more new faces to the county board than just that of State Representative Earl Blumenauer. Gordon Shadburne, an east county resident who taught political science courses at Mt. Hood Community College, was elected to a new commission seat in east county, while Gladys McCoy, a well-known and widely respected African-American woman who had long served as a Portland School Board member, was elected to the Mel Gordon/

Barbara Roberts seat. Both Shadburne and McCoy became notable for their county service in the years ahead—McCoy in generally positive fashion, while the lesser-known Shadburne would flame out ignominiously.

Also in 1978, Don Clark filed to keep his job as county executive, even though his power would be limited to administrative matters. His opponent in the primary was none other than long-time adversary Dan Mosee. The two men differed in both style and substance—Mosee was a talker, Clark a doer; Mosee was a diehard conservative, Clark a diehard liberal; Mosee campaigned against fluoridation,[40] land-use planning, and Project Health, all issues that Clark championed.

Mosee's omnipresent lawn signs were legendary. Not only did he bombard highways and byways from Gresham to the coast with small orange and black wooden signs left up long after election day, but "Mosee Brothers Appliances" signs were nailed to rural fence posts year around. A Doug Baker column in the *Oregon Journal* once reported sighting Dan Mosee signs in rural North Dakota.[41] Interestingly, Mosee's signs included only his name, with no mention of the office he was seeking. That way they could be re-used for any race he decided to enter.

Ten years before their 1978 race for county executive, Clark had successfully challenged Mosee for his commission seat.[42] In its endorsement of Clark at that time, the *Oregon Journal* had credited Clark with imaginative, creative ideas about solving urban problems and praised his genuine contribution to the strengthening of local government as sheriff. Regarding Mosee, the *Journal* had said: "Incumbent Mosee's service has been undistinguished, although he is well-meaning."[43]

Now a *Willamette Week* headline asked: "Will Mosee beat Clark?" Mosee had an astute sense of what the public wanted to hear, the article said, and was shrewd about gauging public sentiment before he voted. For example, Mosee strongly favored construction of the never-built Mt. Hood Freeway, to the delight of east county residents. He was a spokesman for the elderly in opposing closure of Edgefield Manor (an unpopular but budget-wise decision by Don Clark's administration).[44] Mosee attended meetings and gatherings seven days a week, reaching out to shake the hand of every available voter but doing little homework on issue details. He would show up for maybe ten minutes, making sure that people noticed he was there.[45] He was said to be one of the few county commissioners, if not the only one, who actually went around to all county workplaces and talked to employees about their jobs. Line workers often spoke fondly of Mosee's visits.[46]

Commissioner Dan Mosee amazed people with his linguistic skills and sometimes with personal charm, but not with his grasp of county issues. A populist who achieved success selling used appliances and accumulating rental houses, Mosee often made headlines but counted few successes during his terms on the county board. (Multnomah County Archives)

True to his traditional style, Mosee's 1978 campaign against Clark in the race to head Multnomah County government was largely a one-man effort. Mosee put up his well-used orange and black signs and attended meetings: that was it. Clark's loyal political following and strong endorsements from newspapers and unions easily outdistanced Mosee. Then Clark won an easy victory over Republican Clyde Brummell in the fall. This was not to be the end of Mosee's tenure, however; he retained his commission seat for another two years.

When Mosee ran for reelection as a commissioner two years later, Caroline Miller, president of the Portland Federation of Teachers and a Metro councilor, was recruited by Commissioner Earl Blumenauer to challenge Mosee. In its endorsement of Miller, *Willamette Week* said, "With the possible exception of state Rep. Drew Davis, Dan Mosee is the worst public official in local government. His ignorance of the workings of county government is remarkable . . . Almost anyone would be better than Mosee, but Caroline Miller . . . would be enormously better."[47]

After Miller won election, Mosee often called her to advise her how to vote. "As fate would have it," Miller later said, "we were both what might be called populist politicians, and so on some issues Dan and I, both mavericks, weren't far apart. Over time I got to welcome his phone calls, which were never dull."

One day when Miller was running for reelection in 1984, she got lost while walking door-to-door in east county. She was standing on a street corner when who should stop to offer her a ride but Dan Mosee. She climbed into Mosee's passenger seat and was startled to find stacks of her campaign brochures on the floor. Her campaign flyers came from Democratic Party headquarters, Mosee assured her. He was taking the handouts to precinct committee people for distribution. If no one was available to walk a precinct, he said, he planned to hand out those brochures himself. "If I hadn't gotten lost that Saturday," Miller said, "I'd never have known his kindness to me—kindness which helped me win reelection."[48]

16

EMPLOYEES STRIKE, PERS, VOTE-BY-MAIL, AND ROCKY BUTTE JAIL CLOSES

(1980–1982)

Don Clark's second term as the chief county officer—his first term as "chairman" and second as "county executive"—included the longest public employee strike in Oregon history. It placed county government squarely in the media spotlight during the summer of 1980 and Executive Clark in a position he had never wanted. The walkout lasted five weeks and gave union leaders their core economic demands in exchange for eight-hour workdays to replace the seven-and-a-half-hour days that had been the norm for as long as anyone could remember.

The five-column *Oregonian* headline on Saturday, July 18, 1980, told this story: "78% Stay Out in Multnomah County Strike." The following Monday morning, county bridge tenders raised the lifts on the Hawthorne and Steel bridges and then walked away, leaving stranded commuters fuming on both sides of the Willamette. Teamsters jackknifed enough trucks to close the Burnside and Morrison bridges as well. The unions generated constant publicity throughout the strike. For example, in August, county employees repainted "Multnomah County Fair" signs to read "Multnomah County UnFair."[1]

After a dozen carpenters, steelworkers, and laborers refused to cross a picket line at the west end of the Sellwood Bridge, a federally funded $700,000 access improvement project shut down for the entire strike. The Multnomah County Labor Council placed the county on its "unfair list" and personally censured County Executive Clark, who had previously enjoyed labor support in every race he ran, except for the year he voted to kill the Mt. Hood Freeway.[2]

Before the strike began, the county offered an 8.2 percent wage increase. The nurses' union, represented by Burton White, asked for an 11 percent increase.[3] Union Local 88 Business Agent Cecil Tibbetts agreed to accept a fact finder's recommendation of a 9.5 increase plus another increase tied to the cost of living in January. No reference was made to the number of work hours per week. The county rejected the fact finder's opinion.

At the time, the county was experiencing significant budget cuts due to a downturn in the economy and major cutbacks in state and federal grant awards. From the employees' point of view, inflation was growing in double digits and wages were not keeping up. Nevertheless, the county commission had a budget to balance and no hidden pockets from which to pay out additional personnel costs.[4]

The most important management issue at the bargaining table, in addition to holding the line on wages, was to lengthen the regular work week from 37½ hours to 40 hours. The shorter hours dated back to the traditional white collar "9 to 5" working hours for downtown Portland business establishments.[5]

The strike occurred during the second year of a county charter change that created an elected county executive separate from the board of county commissioners. While the entire five-member board—Earl Blumenauer, Dennis Buchanan, Gladys McCoy, Dan Mosee, and Gordon Shadburne—voted to authorize the strike, the actual negotiations fell to County Executive Clark through his labor relations spokesman, Steve Telfer. The five commissioners employed every method possible to avoid crossing picket lines, including ducking in and out of back doors and working from home whenever possible. Commissioner McCoy declined to cross the picket lines altogether, while Commissioner Mosee was unpredictable.[6]

Clark's public information officer, Helen Barney, with Deputy Sheriff Fred Pearce as her field marshal, managed the daunting task of keeping essential services available to the public during the strike. Under the magnifying glass of constant media coverage and picket lines manned by AFSCME Local 88 (American Federation of State, County, and Municipal Employees) and the Oregon Nurses Association, county managers kept county government offices open with skeleton crews and delivered emergency services. As the strike wore on, pressure for a settlement grew while both the county and the unions held fast to their wage positions. Over 1,600 county employees were affected by the strike. The unions estimated that 90 percent of affected workers eventually walked off their jobs.[7]

Toward the strike's end, an *Oregonian* article about Don Clark said: "Normally a witty, gregarious man with great zest and verve, Clark looked wan and tired on the 35th day of the strike . . . Many striking county employees, union officials and members of the public labeled Clark as the 'No. 1 villain' in the strike, the longest of its kind in state history . . . People criticized his 'take-it-or-leave-it' negotiating policies." [8]

The Multnomah County employee strike of 1980 lasted five weeks. This Oregonian *photo taken by Tim Jewell shows Multnomah County Library worker Mary Outlaw (left) and sympathizer Rodney Derrick leading a line of informational pickets outside the downtown Portland library, July 2, 1980.* (The Oregonian)

"My God, I doubt if anyone cares more about the welfare of our county employees than I do," the newspaper quoted Clark as saying. "I was one of them. I came out of their ranks some twenty years ago . . . But I can't give away the store. I have to be sure that any agreement is fair to everyone—not only county employees but the county taxpayers who elected me . . . I never thought we'd come to a strike. And I certainly never expected it to last this long."

"I always knew that Don had great political courage in times of trial," said Commission Chairman Dennis Buchanan. "And I think a lot of other people in government are aware of this now."[9]

In the end, employees won a nonretroactive 10 percent increase for 1980-81 and a 9.1 percent increase for 1981-82, which amounted to a long-term increase in wages of at least 14 percent and as much as 28.8 percent. Strike leader Cecil Tibbetts gloated: "Our people got their double-digit increases. . . . The lower paid people got nearly 30 percent, and the high paid workers got 24 percent over the life of the contract."[10] Left unstated was the fact that employees would now be working an extra two-and-a-half hours per week; virtually the only concession made by the unions was that the regular county workday should henceforth consist of eight hours rather than seven-and-a-half hours.

Some of the overall cost to the county was offset by savings in wages that would otherwise have been paid to employees who stayed off the job during the strike. Elections Clerk Debbie Butzen summarized the end result from her perspective: "Even with the double digit raises slated in the contract, the increase won't make up more than what was lost by workers who stayed out on the strike for the last several weeks."[11] The strike ended Sunday, August 24—thirty-seven days after it began.

County managers such as Billi Odegaard, director of health services at the time, said that the most difficult part of the strike was its aftermath, the deterioration of employee-manager relationships, and internal staff frictions caused by the strike. While at least one member of the union negotiating team felt that the county's failure to treat employees with respect was an underlying cause of the strike,[12] there was no evidence of improved interactions resulting from the strike. On the contrary, hurtful rumors circulated and encounters between strikers and strike-breakers led to wounds that took years to heal.[13]

However, county budget director Felicia Trader noted that unions and management treated each other with courtesy for the most part, particularly in comparison with strikes she had observed while working in other states before she came to Oregon. She also pointed out that the long-term gain in employee hours won as a result of the strike was of significant financial benefit to county taxpayers.[14]

Employee pension funds were *not* negotiated during the 1980 strike, as many people assumed. It was simply a coincidence that a long-range county goal of transferring existing unfunded plans to a funded plan under the state's retirement system, PERS (Public Employee Retirement System), was realized only six months after the strike was settled.[15] By happenstance, the final details of an agreement with PERS to convert the county's underfunded employee pension plans to fully funded plans were being worked out while the 1980 employee strike was in progress. In February 1981, Multnomah County signed a contract to transfer its two inadequate pension plans to PERS. The county planned to amortize its accumulated pension liability of approximately $56 million over a period of thirty years.[16]

Multnomah County, like many public entities that initiated employee retirement systems in the mid-1900s, had started out as "pay-as-you-go," meaning that taxpayers covered only the out-of-pocket cash paid to employees who had retired. Little or nothing was contributed toward *future* retirement costs for *current* employees until the 1970s. Prior to joining PERS, the county had two retirement plans, one for general employees and one for law enforcement. Both plans were only partially funded, although substantial payments were being made to correct this deficiency.[17] By fully funding its retirement systems, accumulated assets would earn interest, dividends, and capital gains, making the plans less costly, in the long run, than pay-as-you-go.[18]

Early in Clark's tenure as county chair, he hired economist Sonny Condor to prepare financial planning reports that would project county capital and maintenance needs for the next fifty years. These reports warned county managers in advance about how much money they needed to earmark in current budgets so that enough money would be available when needed. The distinction between one-time-only (OTO) revenues and continuing revenues, developed by budget director Bruce Harder and administrative services director Denny West, was a key concept of the Clark years.[19]

Years later, in an interview concerning the management team he had assembled, Clark said: "It was absolutely marvelous. I could turn to my staff and ask, 'What are my options here?' and my staff would give me back fifteen different ways to look at that; different approaches and moves I could make. That's the way it ought to be." Unfortunately, however, in Clark's view, much of the money he and his staff had dedicated to county reserves was surrendered to the City of Portland after Clark left the county as part of negotiations regarding Resolution A, a city-county agreement specifying division of functions between the two jurisdictions.[20]

Most onlookers assumed that Commissioner Blumenauer and Clark would be natural allies—both were progressive Democrats who held idealistic views of the importance of public service as a calling. It soon became evident after Blumenauer joined the board, however, that each of these ambitious, goal-driven men was focused on his own agenda. As county executive, Clark had little direct contact with board members, so the competition was less visible to the public than it might otherwise have been. County employees soon found themselves treading carefully to avoid getting caught up in the "Earl-Don" power struggle.

The Earl-Don rivalry strained relationships between the two men "almost to the breaking point" during 1980 county budget hearings. Clark presented the board with a balanced budget, which Blumenauer proceeded to pick apart, sometimes using Commissioner Mosee as his front man.[21] Blumenauer proposed cutting nine positions from the Department of Administrative Services, effectively dismantling the bureau. One position on the chopping block was that of Clark's long-time friend and aide, Don Rocks. County counsel John Leahy advised the board that departmental reorganization proposals required four votes in favor, one more than Blumenauer was able to muster. Additional last minute cuts proposed by Blumenauer engendered "caustic criticisms" from Clark, who said Blumenauer's tactics were causing morale problems among county managers.[22]

In February 1981, in an effort to deal with shrinking federal revenues and increases in state-mandated criminal justice costs, County Executive Clark proposed charging residents of unincorporated Multnomah County a higher property tax rate than that paid by city residents. One day when Clark was giving a speech in Gresham someone stood up and said, "We're not getting our share of county dollars out here in east county." At the same time, Portland residents were convinced that they were subsidizing people living in unincorporated areas and the smaller cities of Gresham, Troutdale, Wood Village, Fairview, and Maywood Park. So Clark contracted with the Portland State University Urban Studies Center to determine whether or not there was a transfer of money for services east of 82nd Avenue to or from west of 82nd. After lengthy study, PSU analysts concluded that there was in fact a transfer of financial support from urban to suburban and rural areas. The biggest subsidy was from Portland residents to unincorporated east county residents for law enforcement and road maintenance.[23]

Clark's rationale for his "zone of benefit" tax was that rural citizens received a higher level of county services than did city residents, so people living in unincorporated areas ought to pay more. In the spirit of Richard Montague's proposal back in 1925, this was another attempt to establish equity of taxes and services between city and unincorporated residents. The difference was that in 1925 the objective was to impose lower taxes on rural residents, whereas in 1981 Clark proposed a surcharge for the now-suburban residents. With little advance publicity or discussion, county voters defeated this "urban subsidy" measure by less than two-tenths of one percent—49.9 percent for the tax to 50.1 percent against.[24]

The May 1981 primary election brought better financial news. Voters narrowly approved a special operating levy for the sheriff's office. The day after the election, Sheriff Ed Martin announced that he would hire twelve new sheriff's deputies immediately to fill slots he had previously left vacant for lack of funds.[25]

Help also was on its way from the state legislature, although its effect would not be felt for another two years. The legislature agreed that the state would assume most of the cost of trial court administration and indigent defense starting in 1983, to be phased in over the five-year period ending in 1987. This was not a matter taken lightly, either by counties or by the state. In the late 1970s, counties "watched with growing alarm the increasing cost of holding court."[26] The Association of Oregon Counties began a campaign to relieve Oregon counties of this onerous burden. In response, the 1979 state legislature convened a Commission on the Judicial Branch to propose improvements in the quality of Oregon's court system. The commission, chaired by Portland attorney Barnes Ellis, chose the financing of court costs as its top priority.

County Executive Clark hired attorney Fred Neal to monitor the commission's deliberations. Clark's goal was to shift circuit and district court administrative costs[27] and indigent defense costs—raised repeatedly in the 1970s through rates set by the state legislature—from counties to the state. Clark and Neal recruited a coalition of thirty-two of Oregon's thirty-six counties, dubbed the State Court Finance Action Committee, to support the effort. Four rural Oregon counties whose traffic fine revenues exceeded their nominal criminal indigent costs chose not to join the coalition.[28]

Two landmark bills were proposed in the 1981 Oregon legislature, one centralizing trial court administration under the chief justice of the state Supreme Court, and the other revamping how court costs were financed. The latter included increased fee and fine schedules and imposed stringent standards for determining the indigence of criminal defendants.[29] Governor Vic Atiyeh supported these court reform measures, as well as a provision that the governor would henceforth appoint the chief justice rather than allowing the Supreme Court justices to continue choosing one of their own as presiding officer. The court measures passed the House as written, but the State Senate, led by Democrats loyal to Supreme Court Justice and former State Senator Berkeley Lent, amended the administration measure to retain collegial appointment of the chief justice. (Lent was next in line for appointment by his colleagues on the Supreme Court.)

The House concurred in the Senate amendments, and the bills were forwarded to the governor for signature. Twenty days after the legislature adjourned, the governor vetoed the bills because the Senate had deleted the provision he sought for a shift in the power to appoint the chief justice.[30]

After much political jockeying, Multnomah County spokesperson Fred Neal proposed that both bills be passed again, with the issue of chief justice appointment to be submitted to a vote of the people as a constitutional "balance of powers" issue. House Speaker Hardy Myers, Senate President Fred Heard, Chief Justice Arno Denecke, and the governor all agreed. Governor Atiyeh then called a special one-day legislative session for October 24, 1981, to deal solely with court reform.[31]

The following May, a ballot measure was referred to statewide voters to have the governor appoint the chief justice. The measure was rejected nearly three to one.[32] To most Oregon voters, leaving the decision to Supreme Court judges sounded less political than allowing a governor who had been elected as a Democrat or Republican to make this choice. Counties, as publicly funded entities, were not allowed to campaign for or against the measure.

State takeover of trial court administration began quickly. By the time state funding had been completely phased in, in 1987, the savings to Multnomah County totaled nearly $10 million per year. A major change in the way state courts were administered and paid for was accomplished, even though counties continued to be responsible for furnishing courtroom space and judges' chambers.[33]

Former county lobbyist Fred Neal later said that the 1983 legislature undermined the intended affordability of the 1981 court reform measures by rescinding new indigent defense qualifying standards. As a result, more accused persons were entitled to free legal representation than was specified in the original 1981 legislation.

A substantive change in long-standing election practices began during the last year of Clark's tenure as county executive: vote-by-mail. This innovation was first tested in September 1982, when the commissioners put a measure on the ballot asking voters to repeal several harsh charter amendments that had passed in May. As passed, the poorly conceived May amendments imposed term limits on all county elected officials, prohibited county officials from hiring a lobbyist, made four offices elective rather than appointive (sheriff, county clerk, district court clerk, and assessor), limited officials' salaries, and required elected officials who sought any other office to resign immediately.

County clerk Bill Radakovich proposed sending the ballots out by mail, an idea he had considered for some time. It would be cheaper, he told the commissioners, than a special election at traditional precinct polling locations. Under Radakovich's proposal, every registered voter would receive a ballot by mail along with two envelopes. The voter would mark the ballot at home, seal it in a secrecy envelope, and enclose that envelope in an outer envelope that the voter would sign and date. The ballot would then be returned to the county clerk's office by mail or at an official drop-off site.[34]

The vote-by-mail experiment won many converts, in spite of the fact that the 1982 charter repeal measure failed; the restrictive provisions all went into effect. Thereafter, the use of vote-by-mail kept expanding year after year, until the time-honored individual voting booth was no more. By law, all Oregon elections are now conducted by mail, to the dismay of citizens who still lament the passing of the red, white, and blue voters' booths.

A strange situation occurred as a result of the May 1982 charter amendment provision that added four elective positions. For the November 1982 ballot, candidates for four-year terms in those offices filed for election through a nominating convention held at the Forestry Center. No one filed against incumbent elections division director Bill Radakovich, so his name appeared on the ballot alone.

The other three successful candidates each beat out one opponent to win their previously appointive positions: Fred Pierce won over John Kerslake as sheriff; assessment and taxation division director Jim Wilcox won over Robert More as assessor; deputy district court administrator Daniel Wood defeated Rosalie Huss as district court clerk. (Wood was actually a state employee because the state had already taken over the courts; for a time he received wages from both the state and county for the same job.)

Newly appointed county clerk Vicki Ervin drew four male opponents in May 1984 for the two years of Radakovich's unexpired term (he had retired in March 1984). Ervin won the election handily, but her election was soon rendered moot by the charter amendments of 1984, which once again made her position an appointive one. She was then named director of elections in a nonelective capacity, serving a record-setting eighteen years. She is the only woman ever to head the county's election division.[35]

Relocations of both Rocky Butte Jail (at a cost of $53.5 million) and the county maintenance facility ($12.5 million) were ongoing construction projects throughout Clark's tenure. They were paid for mainly by state and federal grants and reimbursements resulting from I-205 freeway construction.[36] Dedication of the downtown Justice Center would not take place until October 1983, the year after Clark left office.

The Yeon shops, dedicated on December 14, 1981, were located on top of reclaimed landfill at S.E. 190th Avenue between Stark and Division streets. When it first became clear that the Rocky Butte repair shops would be moved to make way for the I-205 freeway, Clark urged that planning for the new maintenance facility focus on solar energy and energy efficiency. "A Buck Rogers kind of building, a symbol of change from one age to another" was what Clark envisioned, and that is what was built. Huge roof solar collectors resembling the antennae of an interplanetary outpost were projected to generate 45 percent of the building's energy requirements. The site would house 140 employees, 335 pieces of equipment, and all of the county's road maintenance, fleet maintenance, and radio and electric repair divisions; it was mostly underground, another feature expected to provide significant heating and cooling savings. The complex was touted as "one of the most imaginative and energy-efficient public buildings in the United States."[37]

Unfortunately, much of the promised energy generation was never realized because the solar panels had a relatively short life due to the ravages of wind, rain, rock throwers, and gun-toting sharpshooters. New solar panels were installed in early 2009. An annex was added to the Yeon Complex in 1998 to house land use, planning, and other administrative staff. The county's record management and archives division was moved to the underground structure in 2004.[38]

Meanwhile, Rocky Butte Jail was wobbling toward the end of its forty-year life, as construction proceeded on the high-rise Multnomah County Justice Center in downtown Portland. Newspaper headlines provided a quick summary of Rocky Butte's history:

- "Rocky Butte Jail Rated Nation's Best"—*Oregonian*, September 24, 1954

- "Deputies Quell Riot at Rocky Butte; Prisoner Wounded in Melee" —*Oregonian*, August 10, 1960

- "Rocky Butte Conditions Shocked Jury"—*Oregonian*, December 6, 1966

- "Jail at Rocky Butte Labeled Obsolescent"—*Oregon Journal*, April 25, 1967

- "Poor Facilities Blamed for Jail Escape Tries"—*Oregonian*, November 15, 1967

- "Circuit Judge Urges Probe of Alleged Jail Beatings"—*Oregonian*, July 2, 1969

- "Drug Problem at Rocky Butte Plagues Officials"—*Oregonian*, October 8, 1969

- "Prisoners Still Free; 22 Have Fled Jail Here in Past 3 Years"—*Oregonian*, February 4, 1970

"Rocky Butte is perhaps the worst prison in the state of Oregon," said a *Willamette Week* article in November 1978. "Visit B Tank, the jail's maximum-security area where as many as four men are confined to a 10-by-10 foot cell for twenty-three-and-a-half hours a day. It's a place where men have been known to scream all night or defecate and smear their bodies with excrement.... Talk to prisoners and officers alike about a structure that more closely resembles a medieval

The inside of Rocky Butte Jail was not a pretty picture when County Chairman Don Clark visited it in 1977, accompanied by staff assistant Sally Anderson. The jail had a bad reputation for escapes, including a violent one in which a jailer, Irving Burkett, was shot in the head with a tiny pistol that had been smuggled in to inmates. (Sandi Hobbs Morey)

dungeon than a twentieth-century correctional institution. To a man, they will tell you roughly the same thing: Rocky Butte Jail is a brutal dehumanizing place."[39]

An infamous jail break occurred on July 25, 1982, only a year and a half before Rocky Butte Jail was torn down. Inmate Stephen Michael Kessler, a convicted bank robber and head of a Portland heroin distribution ring, shot Deputy Irving Burkett, a 13-year corrections officer, in the head with a tiny .22 caliber single-action handgun. Burkett and Captain James Turney were in the process of moving six prisoners within Rocky Butte Jail when they were taken as hostages and held at gunpoint. All six inmates escaped and were captured a few days later. Burkett was seriously and permanently disabled.[40] County officials tried, without success, to determine how the small gun was smuggled into Rocky Butte.

After 1983, Rocky Butte prisoners were housed downtown in the Multnomah County Justice Center, a towering building across Lownsdale Square from the county courthouse. The new county jail, a high-security institution with 476 beds (later renovated to raise the capacity to 676 beds) occupied five floors in the middle of the building and accounted for 51 percent of the building's total space. The top six floors of the Justice Center became the new Portland Police Bureau headquarters, including a new Oregon State Police Crime Laboratory. The mezzanine level held state courtrooms and judges' chambers, while small

When completion of the Interstate 205 freeway spelled doom for the nearby Rocky Butte Jail, the county used federal, state, city, and county money to build the high-rise Multnomah County Justice Center in downtown Portland. The building technically is a condominium, housing the Central Precinct of the Portland Police Bureau, an Oregon State Police Crime Laboratory, plus four courtrooms, and several floors of the Multnomah County Detention Center. (Multnomah County Archives)

commercial establishments were at street level. The building presented such a unique combination of ownership that the Justice Center was organized as a condominium and was listed as such on the county's real estate records. The $53.5 million cost was paid for by a combination of federal, state, county, and city dollars.[41] The project was supervised from beginning to end by lawyer Lyndon "Tuck" Wilson, who also served as director of the county's justice services department under Clark from 1978 through 1981.

"Marriage of form, function begets beauty for Justice Center," proclaimed a full-page headline in the *Oregonian*. The story notes that the design team, led by the Portland architectural firm of Zimmer, Gunsul, and Frasca, included a domed skylight over the Third Avenue lobby and delicate stained and cut glass along one wall. The result of such design innovations was a building that would "stand out as a gem among Portland's public buildings."[42] Perhaps even more important than the outstanding exterior was the innovative open concept utilized inside the jail to bring prisoners out of their cells most of the day. Outdoor recreational facilities on the tenth floor could be used year around. Dayrooms had showers, bookshelves, and television. Officer work stations were part of the dayrooms rather than separated from the inmates.[43]

In 1982, Clark's last year in Multnomah County, he joined a primary field of seven Democratic candidates seeking the office of Oregon governor. Clark's lack of political finesse and his failure to tout his accomplishments undoubtedly contributed to his loss in the primary to State Senator Ted Kulongoski, as did his loss of labor support following the 1980 employee strike. (Kulongoski was to lose the 1982 fall election to incumbent governor Republican Vic Atiyeh, but returned to claim the governor's seat twenty years later, in 2002, and be reelected in 2006.) Clark never ran again for elective office. He served later as executive director of Central City Concern, a social service program that focused on alcohol and drug rehabilitation and housing, and as executive director of the Housing Authority of Portland, which managed federally funded housing and rent subsidy programs.

Unlike most elected officials, Don Clark was an idea man, a dreamer. Several of his concerns generated innovative policy initiatives that interested insiders and academics, but not the media or citizenry.[44] His more practical innovations included remodeling the county courthouse to eliminate the ugly glass brick windows that had been installed some years earlier, publication of a Multnomah County *Historical Sites Tour Guide and Map* in cooperation with the Oregon Historical Society, and development of a modern logo and seal.[45]

The contemporary county logo that was adopted consisted of a triangular "M" emblazoned in brilliant blue and green hues to represent Mt. Hood, Mt. St. Helens, and the county's many valleys and rivers. "Multnomah County Legend and Logo," a brochure prepared by county employee Don Rocks, was distributed to the public with the compliments of the county commission in 1978 when the logo was adopted.[46]

Clark made little effort to sell himself to the public or the business community, where he had few contacts. He focused instead on what he thought was right, rather than what was politically expedient. His internal management style, largely invisible to the public, was to seek dedicated managers and rely on their judgment. Under his direction, the county developed a disciplined budgeting system and established professional labor relations and personnel departments.

Many of Clark's management employees stayed on to work at the county after Clark left.[47] Other talented employees whom Clark attracted to Multnomah County would go on to distinguished careers in public service elsewhere. One such recruit was Tom Higgins, who headed the county's health and social services department after serving as Deputy Secretary of Health, Education, and Welfare for President Jimmy Carter in Washington, D.C.

The Multnomah County logo adopted in 1978 consists of a triangular "M" emblazoned in brilliant blue and green hues to represent Mt. Hood, Mt. St. Helens, and the county's many valleys and rivers. Today, the logo appears on county buildings, equipment, and stationery, while the county seal continues to be used for official county documents.

Higgins later cited examples of actions by Clark that made Multnomah County a national leader in health care reform and innovation in service delivery: the creation of Project Health, a model for Medicaid reform and care of the indigent; a proposed State Health Plan, which served as a foundation for future health reform; the privatization of county mental health clinics under the control of nonprofit, community-based organizations; the closure of Edgefield Manor and improving conditions for its residents; the opening of the Hooper Detox Center facility and program; and the creation of comprehensive community health centers.[48] (Note that this list includes the closure of Edgefield Manor as a positive achievement, likewise the creation of Project Health. Not everyone agreed with either decision. Patients served by the former hospital and "old folks' home" would henceforth have to rely on mainstream public health programs, with the county as their "last resort." While both actions were sound business decisions, they were not politically popular.)

Ed Martin, who had succeeded Lee Brown as sheriff, resigned during the last year of Don Clark's tenure to pursue a lifelong dream of living in Alaska. He moved to Kodiak as chief of police, then later relocated to Barrow, the northernmost U.S. settlement on the North American mainland.[49]

The year Martin left, a charter proposal on the ballot to make the position of sheriff an elective one once again was heavily favored to pass. So when Martin's chief deputy, Fred Pearce, accepted his appointment as the county's thirty-third sheriff in June 1982, he understood that he would have to run the jails—and that he would probably have to mount a campaign to keep the job.

That fall, the newly appointed Pearce, who had acquired an excellent reputation in his days as a deputy, was elected as sheriff against only token opposition.

After sixteen years during which seven sheriffs were appointed, the pendulum had swung back and future sheriffs were once again chosen at the ballot box.

Looking back on his years as sheriff, county commissioner, and county chair, Clark listed the accomplishments of which he personally felt most proud:

- pioneering community-friendly police service;
- raising educational standards for deputy sheriffs;
- protection of the Columbia Gorge and Sauvie Island from suburban sprawl;
- building of underground public-works shops, an innovative justice center, and a covered bridge;
- establishing Hooper Detox Center;
- creating Project Health;
- reorganizing county health clinics;
- stopping the Mt. Hood Freeway;
- partnering with Portland, Portland State University, and community groups to change transportation priorities, develop land-use plans, and improve metropolitan area governance;
- promoting the Forty-Mile Loop, sidewalks, bike paths, light rail, 911, and court reform;
- advocating for the needy;
- recruiting high-quality managers and staff.[50]

Clark left county elective office at the age of 53—too young, many thought, to end a productive political career. However, he was barred from continuing at the county by a home rule charter provision limiting elected officials to two full four-year terms, and he was not interested in running for Portland mayor or Metro chair.[51] The county's term limits, imposed during the heyday of a national antigovernment movement, probably ousted a few officials who stayed too long, but more often robbed the public of valuable experience and commitment. Proposals to delete term limits from the Multnomah County charter have to date been decisively rejected by the voters.

Not all county employees loved Don Clark. During the employee strike of 1980, *Willamette Week* quoted a former staffer who labeled Clark's management as "inept" and said there was "a whole office of people doing petty busy work." Another former staff member alleged that Clark was too soft in dealing with employees who were his personal friends.[52]

Oregonian reporter John Painter Jr. said of Clark: "His ideals, abilities, and perception of himself are what he projects to others; there is no façade. Clark's strengths are also his failings . . . He is a populist and a liberal. His values are those of the pioneers who settled Oregon—courage, energy, dedication, steadfastness, integrity, creativity, candor and a commitment to the public good . . . . However, nobody considers him a good politician."[53]

Retrospective accolades for Clark's tenure view his accomplishments in broader terms. In 2009, former local government *Oregon Journal* reporter and city editor Jeff Wohler said: "I can't think of another public official besides Don Clark (other than Neil Goldschmidt, regardless of what has transpired in the past few years) who made such a difference in the metropolitan area during the past forty years. Not one. He was very much a forward-thinking official in a time of great change."[54]

While it is true that the availability of federal funds during many of the Don Clark years made certain projects possible, federal funding was only one of the factors that contributed to progress made at the county level during that time. There was an unparalleled spirit of cooperation and citizen involvement throughout Oregon government circles. Governor Tom McCall presided over state government in Salem, while Mayor Neil Goldschmidt was shaking things up at Portland City Hall, Don Clark was pushing for innovations at the Multnomah County Courthouse, and an engaged citizenry was maintaining public pressure. Progress was virtually assured. Betty Merten, a leading opponent of the defunct Mt. Hood Freeway, put it this way: "An energy was sweeping through Portland during the early and mid-'70s that fostered a sea-change in how business got done . . . how we wanted to grow and develop. . . It was an energy for positive change."[55]

17

THE LAUDABLE "RESOLUTION A," CITY OF COLUMBIA RIDGE IS REJECTED, A POWER STRUGGLE AT THE LIBRARY, AND MORE CHARTER CHANGES

(1983–1990)

Dennis Buchanan succeeded Don Clark as county executive in January 1983. Though progressive in attitude, the former newspaper reporter, television journalist, and stockbroker brought a different leadership style to the county executive office. Buchanan was a less visible public figure; he preferred to negotiate quietly behind the scenes, and once described his style as wanting "to clarify problems and rise above the din of political bickering."[1] He was a key figure in negotiating and passing "Resolution A," a document that changed the face of local government without a public vote, a move that succeeded where previous attempts to merge or realign Portland and Multnomah County functions had failed.

Buchanan had been appointed to fill a vacancy on the county board of commissioners in 1975, replacing Don Clark when Clark advanced to county chairman. He was a compromise choice following weeks of deadlock. Two commissioners, Alice Corbett and Dan Mosee, still hoped to reverse the county's decision to scrap the Mt. Hood Freeway. "Each side was determined to get the third vote," Buchanan recalled later. "For weeks they rejected one nominee after another. Finally, perhaps because I was a stockbroker and wore pin stripes, Alice Corbett joined Mel [Gordon] and Don [Clark] and voted for me; she committed her vote to me following a lunch in which she never discussed the freeway."[2] Buchanan's position on the freeway soon became clear; he joined Gordon and Clark in opposing a motion to refer the issue to a county-wide vote. Given his fifteen years as a Portland newspaper and television reporter, Buchanan was familiar with local issues and personalities. Yet the secretive, back-room haggling that led to his appointment prompted voters to pass a charter revision in 1978 stating that future appointed commissioners would be temporary and could not run for a full term in the next election.

As Portland expanded over the years and the needs of its citizens became more complex, so did the needs of unincorporated county residents. Although special fire and water districts fulfilled some requirements, the county was increasingly drawn into providing services such as police patrols, parks, and street mainte-nance (as opposed to rural road maintenance) to residents who did not live in cities. Everyone had a county to turn to, but not every resident had a city. Finding an equitable solution to a problem that became known as "urban subsidy" had presented Multnomah County commissioners with a challenge throughout its 150-year history.

Resolution A, which was the brainchild of running buddies County Commissioner Earl Blumenauer and Portland Director of Finance and Administration Mark Gardiner,[3] focused on specialization of those services to be delivered by the city and those the county would provide, in order to avoid overlap-ping bureaucracies. It was intended to eliminate the so-called urban subsidy that resulted from the fact that the county maintained parks and streets on behalf of unincorporated residents like a city, and patrolled neighborhoods and investigated crimes like a city, but also performed state-mandated duties such as elections, so-cial services, and criminal prosecution. As early as 1977, Chair Don Clark's senior budget analyst, Sonny Condor, had concluded that city residents in Multnomah County (Portland, Gresham, and others) were paying 35 percent of the cost of ser-vices provided to residents of unincorporated areas. In a lengthy analysis released in 1979, the Portland State University Urban Studies Center validated Condor's claim that Multnomah County's city dwellers were paying a hefty urban subsidy.[4]

Several previous attempts had been made to consolidate Multnomah County and its cities, but with little success—the most recent failure being the resounding defeat of a Portland–Multnomah County charter in 1974. In 1981, County Chair Don Clark had proposed a zone-of-benefit tax to eliminate the property tax imbalance between unincorporated areas and city residents, but that measure was also defeated at the polls.

The solution that led to Resolution A was simple in design, yet enormously complicated in its execution. Portland would be the major provider of "city-level services"—police, fire, transportation, parks, water, and sewer service[5]—while Multnomah County would specialize in state-mandated county roles and coun-ty-wide "human and justice services"—corrections, social services, assessment and collection of property taxes, elections, and libraries.[6]

These duties were laid out in Resolution A, adopted in 1983 by Multnomah County, and the complementary Urban Services Policy adopted by Portland city council. The county sheriff would retain responsibility for jail personnel and facilities, as well as limited vehicular patrols in remote areas of the county. The city police department would handle most law enforcement, but the county would still handle river patrol functions on navigable waters and certain special investigations.

Resolution A presupposed that Portland would pressure residents of unincorporated areas to annex themselves to the city. In the meantime, Portland would provide services for these citizens on an interim basis through intergovernmental service agreements. The east county City of Gresham later became a third partner in this allocation of service areas and types of functions.[7]

As Buchanan later explained:

> This left the residents of the unincorporated area with the choice of annexing to Portland or Gresham or doing without the services, primarily police patrols, neighborhood parks, and permits. This area contained about 135,000 people and extended from the Columbia River south to the Clackamas County line and from S.E. 82nd Avenue east to Gresham and Fairview. The plan, accomplished through a coalition which we developed with leaders of the Cities of Portland and Gresham (including Portland mayors Frank Ivancie and Bud Clark, as well as Gresham mayor, Margaret Weil) drove annexation of the area east of 82nd to 165th to the City of Portland and annexation of the area east of 165th to the City of Gresham. In Portland, this doubled the size of the east side and expanded the population by 75,000 to 80,000 thousand people. It jumped Gresham from a modest village to one of the top five largest cities in the state.[8]

Implementation of Resolution A was painful for entrenched bureaucracies that had to downsize or combine missions with an existing agency or organization. "As each agency came under the ax," said County Commissioner Gretchen Kafoury, "the feathers flew; and what was intended to be straightforward division of services often became a battle royal, ending finally in a complex series of compromises."[9] Some highly valued special service districts in the east county area, such as Fire District 10 and the Hazelwood Water District, were absorbed by the City of Portland.[10] Buchanan, who had run for county executive in 1982 on the theme of restructuring local government, often found himself tangled in the thorns of implementing Resolution A. "It's not easy to tell people you are eliminating their police protection," he said at the end of his term.[11]

Likewise, fourteen neighborhood parks in east county were transferred to Portland, and larger regional parks—Blue Lake, Oxbow, Glendoveer Golf Course, and the Expo Center—ultimately were transferred to Metro, the new regional government created in 1978 (see chapters 13 and 15). Major county players who negotiated and implemented this agreement to eliminate city-county duplication of services, in addition to Commissioner Blumenauer, included county executives Dennis Buchanan and Don Clark; County Commissioners Gretchen Kafoury, Pauline Anderson, Gladys McCoy, Caroline Miller, and Arnold Biskar; and Steve Telfer, executive assistant to Buchanan. Commissioner Gordon Shadburne opposed Resolution A on the grounds that it would force unwanted annexations on his constituents.[12]

The most visible result of the 1983 agreement was the transfer of sheriff's deputies from Multnomah County to Portland and Gresham police departments. Sheriff Fred Pearce saw his law enforcement division shrink from 220 to 87 officers. Pearce fought the loss of so many deputies but had to face the reality that a major population shift from rural to urban had occurred in Multnomah County. Annexations to Portland, Gresham, and other east county cities had absorbed most of the available land in what used to be unincorporated Multnomah County.[13] As a result of the changes, the sheriff's primary duty became responsibility for corrections and jails.

The sheriff's deputies who were transferred all had college degrees, and Portland Police Chief Charles Moose undertook to honor this requirement in the future. But although it was written into the joint city-county contract for Resolution A, it was later breached by Portland Police Chief Mark Kroeker (1999-2003), who said such a requirement made it too difficult to recruit new officers.[14]

The county transferred 391 miles of roads and the responsibility for their maintenance to Portland, along with certain county financial reserves that arguably ought to have been retained by the county for bridge maintenance.[15] In subsequent years Portland transferred its youth service centers and its elderly program to Multnomah County.[16]

Future county and city auditor Gary Blackmer (1991-2009) credited Resolution A with effectively addressing many inefficiencies that the failure of prior consolidation attempts had left unaddressed. "There is very little duplication of service between Multnomah County and its cities anymore," Blackmer said in 2009. "The cities and county are focused on different missions, as delineated in Resolution A."[17] (However, only three years later, candidates for mayoral and city council seats were asked whether or not the city ought to assume more responsibility for funding human services, given the county's shrinking financial resources.)[18]

An issue that had arisen before the adoption of Resolution A was the need for sewers in the unincorporated area between Portland and Gresham. The state Department of Environmental Quality (DEQ) had been warning Multnomah County for years that if no local government stepped up voluntarily to build a sewer system in mid-Multnomah County, DEQ would order it done.[19] Several years earlier Portland's Water Bureau, under Mayor Ivancie's guidance, drilled several wells in the unincorporated area to provide a backup water supply for city water users, so Portland had a direct interest in seeing a sewer system installed in the area. The problem was that nobody wanted to shoulder the cost.[20] Under Resolution A, the contruction of sewers was a "city type" of service.

The most highly touted solution was to create a new city that would have been Oregon's second largest, covering fifty square miles and containing 125,000 to 135,000 people, to be called "Columbia Ridge." To the frustration of mid-County activists, both Portland and Gresham lobbied against the creation of this new city. Both jurisdictions instead wanted to annex the areas closest to their boundaries. The state boundary commission rejected the Columbia Ridge application in 1985, on the grounds that it was not financially viable and could not provide needed public services.[21] Thirteen years later, by 1998, sewers had been successfully installed throughout the area under the auspices of the City of Portland's Mid-County Sewer Project.[22]

While Multnomah County retained the obligation of providing libraries under Resolution A, the county's public library system was still legally under the control of a private body, the Library Association of Portland (LAP). This private association dated back to 1864, when use of the library was limited to dues-paying members. The group had been forced to reexamine its purpose and rules in September 1900 after receiving an extraordinary bequest. Merchant John Wilson left 8,000 volumes and $25,000 to the library, stipulating that all books be made available to the public without fee. The collection, too valuable to reject, led to a search for long-term sources of funding.[23]

A bill passed by the 1901 state legislature authorized cities to levy an annual 1/5 mill property tax for library purposes and to contract with private,

The Multnomah County Central Library, completed in 1913 under the supervision of Portland's leading architect of the era, A. E. Doyle, remains one of downtown's most elegant and graceful buildings. Though it was the heart of the library system from the outset, the county government did not obtain full control until 1990, after prolonged battle with the private Library Association of Portland that founded the library. (Multnomah County Archives)

nonsectarian groups to operate their libraries.[24] The Portland city council immediately levied the maximum allowable tax and asked LAP to continue to manage the library. In March 1902, the association opened its doors to the public without charge.[25] The 1903 state legislature broadened the allowable tax base to include levying a 1/5 mill tax on all Multnomah County real property for library purposes. Blessed with public funds, the private association put up a striking main library building on S.W. Tenth Avenue in 1913, designed by leading Portland architect A. E. Doyle. The Central Library is still the crown jewel of the county library system today, while many neighborhood branches have been added over the years.[26]

The relationship between LAP, a private association, and the county that provided most of its operating money became increasingly strained after Earl Blumenauer's election to the county board in 1978. "Imagine my shock and frustration, after being appointed as an 'ex officio' member of the library board," he later said, "to find out how insular it was."

An underlying issue regarding the management of the library system was the exclusive nature of the membership of the 35-person library association board, which was passed down from generation to generation by inheritance. With the help of library advocate Frances McGill, Blumenauer tried various methods to overcome the self-perpetuating nature of the library board. The fact that public tax money was being spent without public involvement or disclosure was troublesome to county officials. "One had the sense," Blumenauer said, "that when the 'ex officio' members were there, the board was more or less going through the motions, and that real decisions were made at other times and other places."[27]

The early 1980s were an especially difficult financial time for the library. The county general fund experienced a sharp decline in revenues, and inflation ate up reserves. In 1982, Montavilla and Lombard branches were closed, thirty staff positions were cut, and the Central Library was closed two days a week. The following year, hours at four branches were reduced to half time, and every library in the system was closed for nine days in March.[28]

At this point, the county commission hired an outside library consultant named Lowell Martin to review the library system and appointed a fifteen-member citizens' commission to follow through on his recommendations. Two May 1984 ballot measures resulted from this "blue-ribbon" committee's deliberations. The first was a property tax levy that would generate $3 million a year for three years, with all proceeds going strictly to libraries. The second measure provided for a nine-member library board appointed by the county to run the library system. The proposal was "understood by almost nobody," according to an article written some twenty years later by the late Tom Stimmel, an *Oregon Journal* reporter. Few people were aware that a private organization had always been in charge of the library system, even though the public's property tax money had paid for its operation for the past eighty-three years. In Stimmel's words:

> The private—very private—Library Association of Portland had become increasingly secretive, elitist, and snobbish [in the view of its critics] and was clearly dominated by one man . . . its domineering president, Portland lawyer Peter Voorhies . . . So county commissioners proposed to replace the LAP with a nine-member board of advisors of its own choosing . . . Under its contract with the county, the LAP owned the library—all the books, the tables and chairs . . . all the branches but Central downtown [and] controlled the endowment fund and art collection."[29]

The tax levy passed with a comfortable 56 percent in favor, but the management reform measure failed by 117 votes out of more than 154,000 cast—it was simply too complicated for the general public to follow.

Interactions between the county and LAP, especially President Voorhies, now became more strained than ever. The year after his election, County Executive Dennis Buchanan visited head librarian James Burkhardt to suggest that LAP board members should henceforth be appointed by the county executive. If LAP was not amenable to that suggestion, Buchanan warned, the county might place another management measure on the ballot in November.[30]

The following month, three county commissioners notified LAP that they would attend the June 26, 1984, LAP directors' meeting, thereby forcing the session into compliance with Oregon's open meetings law. Any time three or more members of a public body were in attendance, meetings had to be open to the public. By their presence at the meeting, county commissioners Arnold Biskar, Gladys McCoy, and Blumenauer attracted a big crowd, including an *Oregonian* reporter.[31]

A grand-niece of library founder and former Portland mayor Henry Failing read a statement lauding past LAP management but supporting two changes advocated by an *Oregonian* editorial. Mrs. Anne Brewster Clarke recommended that LAP meetings and records be public, and that membership in the LAP represent the community. Without waiting for LAP action, the county appointed four citizens to the LAP board in October on the theory that the county was responsible for monitoring expenditure of public funds. It was soon evident, as Blumenauer had noted five years earlier, that most of the organization's policy decisions were made outside of LAP directors' meetings. Rochelle Gray, assistant to the head librarian, said that secret strategy meetings were held at the exclusive Arlington Club. "They'd have a drink and a cigar, decide what they were going to do, then go to the board meeting room in the library and say, 'This is how it's going to be.' Peter [Voorhies] just loved this."[32]

Voorhies continued to engender antagonism throughout his three years as LAP treasurer and four years as its president. Commissioner Blumenauer called him "disdainful, not forthcoming, resistant to change." Commissioner Anderson said Voorhies was belligerent and secretive, that he ran LAP like a personal fiefdom. C. Bruce Ward of LAP called Voorhies "gruff . . . opinionated . . . energetic." However, Ward said that Voorhies believed what he did was good for the library. Ward would later assume the presidency of LAP, after Voorhies left town in late 1990, and would then announce unexpectedly that he thought LAP should relinquish control of both the LAP endowment fund and art.[33]

When head librarian Burkhardt retired in 1984 after twelve years on the job, Sarah Long was hired to replace him, following complicated footwork on the part of Blumenauer and his colleagues on the county board.[34] Long was a

County Commissioner Earl Blumenauer, who served two terms starting in January 1979, was a major player in writing and adopting "Resolution A" in 1983, a document that largely eliminated duplication of services between city and county governments. The resolution substantially quieted long-standing talk of merging the two local jurisdictions. (Multnomah County Archives)

change agent, and she reorganized the library hierarchy, encountering strong resistance as she moved employees around. Resistance so strong, in fact, that library employees went on strike for two days in the summer of 1986. All branches were closed and picket lines appeared in front of the Central Library. Grievances involved benefits, health care, and low wages, especially for employees at the bottom of the scale.

The battle over the library continued, even after Blumenauer left county government at the end of 1986 and Commissioner Gladys McCoy succeeded Buchanan as county chair at the beginning of 1987.

Voters approved a March 1987 library levy, 60 percent voting in favor. The campaign was led by local visionary and businessman Bill Naito. This was only a temporary fix; the need for a permanent tax base was evident.

LAP directors asked the county commission to establish a special library district with a tax base of its own, so they would not in the future have to rely on annual property tax levies and the county general fund. A public opinion poll showed voter support for a special district if the money would go directly to the library system and not to the general fund. However, a state law regarding the establishment of special districts specified that all cities within the district's proposed boundaries must approve any such creation. The City of Portland, suffering its own financial problems at the time, declined to give its approval.[35] (In November 2010, county voters approved a ballot measure recommended by a charter review committee that allowed county commissioners, at a future time, to create a library district without the approval of the county's six cities.)[36]

The extended family of library founder Henry Failing had maintained a presence on the LAP board since its inception. In the late 1980s, his grand-nephew, William (Bill) Failing Jr., emerged as a major player in helping to untangle the situation. He had inherited a position on the LAP and now provided an insider's perspective when he was appointed as an official county representative to LAP by County Chair Gladys McCoy. Failing later said that he recognized that LAP had "lost its way" and was in need of dismantling. "Hardened by old-Portland crust, the old LAP was seriously out of touch vis-à-vis the new wave of emerging civic dynamics," he said. "Until the LAP went away, all was just more of the same."[37]

Librarian Sara Long resigned after five years on the job, leaving a positive legacy of increased circulation and new services and hours, even while she had to contend with the tension and controversy that continued to swirl around LAP president Peter Voorhies. Insiders said Voorhies would stop by Long's office unannounced and start giving her orders. Her departure for the Midwest was undoubtedly influenced by the difficulty she experienced working with him.

In September 1989, the LAP hired former state public utility commissioner Charles Davis as interim library director. Davis immediately set out to determine whether or not the still-private LAP was providing adequate oversight of the $5 million of public tax money it received annually from Multnomah County taxpayers. He hired a certified public accountant to assist him in reviewing LAP records. They concluded that the library association inappropriately diverted fee and fine money, as well as bequests and donations for specific library purposes, into LAP's Endowment Fund.[38] In late October, Davis asked the state attorney general to determine whether or not the LAP and/or its president, Peter Voorhies, had engaged in illegal activities.[39]

Five months after he began his investigation, the state attorney general reported that Voorhies and the LAP had committed "no significant wrongdoing." A spokesman said that $227,000 from twelve funds should have been spent in accordance with donors' wishes instead of being held in an endowment fund made up of personal donations and library fines. In the five months during which the attorney general's inquiry was underway, Davis began negotiations for LAP to turn over the entire library system to Multnomah County. In light of probable management changes, the attorney general decided not to pursue the "minor violations" his investigation had discovered.

Another contentious issue involved the ownership of the library's art and rare books collection, valued at an estimated $2 million to $2.5 million. If county government took over library management, who would inherit the art and rare books? Possible recipients included the Portland Art Museum, Oregon

Where are they now? this photo by Dean Smith, taken at a Multnomah County "old-timers" picnic in September 1989, appeared in the in-house publication County Lines *in October 1989. Former County Counsel George Joseph, identified as person Number 9, in fact served as the chief Oregon Court of Appeals judge, not on the federal bench as the caption states.* (Multnomah County Archives)

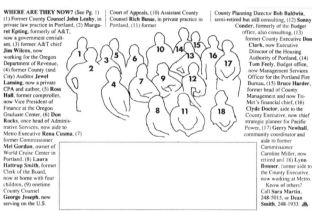

WHERE ARE THEY NOW? (See Pg. 1) (1) Former County Counsel **John Leahy**, in private law practice in Portland, (2) **Margaret Epting**, formerly of A&T, now a government consultant, (3) former A&T chief **Jim Wilcox**, now working for the Oregon Department of Revenue, (4) former County (and City) Auditor **Jewel Lansing**, now a private CPA and author, (5) **Ross Hall**, former comptroller, now Vice President of Finance at the Oregon Graduate Center, (6) **Don Rocks**, once head of Administrative Services, now aide to Metro Executive **Rena Cusma**, (7) former Commissioner **Mel Gordon**, owner of World Cruise Center in Portland, (8) **Laura Hattrup Smith**, former Clerk of the Board, now at home with four children, (9) onetime County Counsel **George Joseph**, now serving on the U.S.

Court of Appeals, (10) Assistant County Counsel **Rich Busse**, in private practice in Portland, (11) former

County Planning Director **Bob Baldwin**, semi-retired but still consulting, (12) **Sonny Conder**, formerly of the Budget office, also consulting, (13) former County Executive **Don Clark**, now Executive Director of the Housing Authority of Portland, (14) **Tom Feely**, Budget office, now Management Services Officer for the Portland Fire Bureau, (15) **Bruce Harder**, former head of County Management and now Tri-Met's financial chief, (16) **Clyde Doctor**, aide to the County Executive, now chief strategic planner for Pacific Power, (17) **Gerry Newhall**, community coordinator and aide to former Commissioner Caroline Miller, now retired and 18) **Lynn Bonner**, former aide to the County Executive, now working at Metro. Know of others? Call Sara Martin, 248-5015, or Dean Smith, 248-1933. 🔎

Historical Society, and the library itself. LAP and the county eventually agreed to let a committee of three—two members appointed by LAP and one by the county—make that decision. Much later, long after a formal contract between LAP and the county was signed, the committee announced that the artworks and rare books would remain with the library.[40]

County Chairman Gladys McCoy assured library contributors that the county would ensure the $227,000 cited in the attorney general's report was used as specified by donors. The $6.8 million LAP Endowment Fund was conveyed to the Oregon Community Foundation (OCF) in late June 1990. By December 2008, OCF had distributed $12 million to the Multnomah County Library and the fund balance had increased to $13.2 million. The fund was structured to continue in perpetuity to provide ongoing support for the county library.[41]

Meanwhile, during the time that library finances were under investigation, the Oregon Supreme Court accepted the Form B resignation (the functional equivalent of disbarment) of Peter Voorhies on December 12, 1989. The *Oregon*

State Bar Bulletin of January 1990 states, "At the time of his resignation, Voorhies was under investigation by the bar for ethics violations stemming from his alleged failure to account for certain fees received while a partner with the law firm of Wood, Tatum, Mosser, Brook and Holden, his alleged mishandling of an estate, and alleged conflicts of interest and improper business transactions with a number of clients."[42]

In March 1990, Ginnie Cooper, head librarian at the Berkeley Public Library in California, was hired to head the Multnomah County library system. She was to serve for thirteen years, overseeing extensive improvement of the entire system, until she left in 2003 to become director of the top-rated Brooklyn Public Library in New York.[43] Library aficionado Bill Failing credits Cooper and an outstanding library board for effecting true integration of the library into the civic cultures of Portland and the county suburbs. "The upgrades of the branches integrated the neighborhoods to the highest levels of participation," he later said, resulting in patrons taking proprietary ownership of their libraries.[44]

On July 1, 1990, Multnomah County government welcomed four hundred new employees—215 full-time and 185 part-time—as permanent transfers from the Library Association of Portland (LAP), which immediately dissolved. To the delight of library personnel, almost all library employees who transferred to Multnomah County received higher wages and benefits, thereby bringing their compensation into line with that of other county personnel.[45]

Integrating library employees into the county's personnel system was not without controversy. The differences in salary levels, health benefits, social security, workers' compensation, and coverage by the Oregon Public Employees retirement plan came with a price tag of $1.7 million to $2.7 million annually.[46] Because there was general agreement on the part of county board members that the library workforce had been woefully underpaid, they declined to create a lower classification scale for these employees. In the end, the battle for control of the Multnomah County Library, from the time Earl Blumenauer first raised the issue, lasted twelve years.

The library was not the county's only long-running saga at the time. Jail management proved another thorny issue. A federal judge held Sheriff Fred Pearce and County Executive Dennis Buchanan in contempt of court for operating the new Justice Center jail beyond its design capacity. The lawsuit, a continuation of one claiming overcrowding and inhumane conditions at the old Rocky Butte Jail, had been expanded to include the new downtown jail.[47]

As the first sheriff to operate under court-imposed limits that specified the maximum number of inmates that could be held in the Justice Center jail, Pearce

Sheriff Fred Pearce (1982-89)
(Multnomah County Archives)

used the media to increase public awareness of the need for more jail beds. A memorable July 10, 1986, front-page *Oregonian* photo showed inmates running out from beneath half-open Justice Center garage doors. Pearce had alerted reporters that he would be releasing sixty-six prisoners because there was no room for them in jail, presenting the media with a ready-made photo opportunity.

Fred Pearce was hired away from Multnomah County as director of the Oregon Department of Corrections in early 1989. County employees interviewed for an *Oregonian* story described him as "determined," "strong," and "aggressive." At six-foot-four, Pearce had the imposing bearing of a championship football player, a formidable public image that had served him well during his seven years as sheriff, the newspaper said.[48] Controversies over jail beds, both in court and out, would continue into the twenty-first century.

On the political front, voters continued with their seemingly incessant changes to the county charter. The 1984 Charter Review Commission proposed returning the county executive and the board to their pre-1978 roles. That meant that the chairman would retain his or her administrative authority, *and* would regain one-fifth of the board's legislative power, thus reducing the number of elective commission districts from five to four. The county chairman and auditor would continue to run county-wide. In the quest for a gender-neutral title for the county's most powerful official, the review commission eschewed "chairman" or "chairperson" in favor of "chair." The county sheriff's job would remain elective, but the county clerk, district court clerk, and assessor would again be appointed, thus ending the nonsensical situation in which Dan Wood, an assistant district court administrator, held two titles.

Wood collected two paychecks for doing one job until the situation became public and District Attorney Michael Schrunk prevailed on Wood to return just over $10,000 he had collected in county pay.[49] While this minor dispute was bubbling, the *Oregonian* ran an editorial titled, "Take the money, Dan, you won it."[50] Perhaps tongue in cheek, the editorial suggested that if the voters were ignorant enough to create the unnecessary county job, its occupant was entitled to keep the pay. The newspaper also said the county commission, aware of the job title without responsibilities, could have set Wood's county salary at $1.

Voters approved the change returning the county executive to a county chair position and making the assessor and two clerks appointive once again, while keeping the sheriff elective. Voters continued to prevent the county from hiring a lobbyist and continued to bar elected officials from having a "free ride" by running for another office in the middle of a term without resigning.

After eight years on the Multnomah County Commission, Earl Blumenauer was elected to the Portland City Council in 1986. During his city council tenure, he made an unsuccessful run for Portland mayor against Vera Katz in 1992. He was elected to the U.S. Congress to represent Oregon's Third District in 1996, becoming the first county official to win a seat in Congress since Rufus Holman served a single term in the U.S. Senate in 1938. Today, Blumenauer's seat in Congress is considered one of the "safest" in the House because of his district's strong Democratic registration, and he continues to work as an effective champion for environmental, civil rights, and livability issues.

Buchanan decided not to seek another term at the helm of Multnomah County, given the uncertainties about the revamped nature of the county chair's job and its salary, and he left county office at the end of 1986. By then, east Multnomah County's representative, the controversial commissioner Gordon Shadburne, would also be gone, but under more disquieting circumstances.

18

EAST COUNTY DISCONTENT, THE FIRST ALL-WOMAN BOARD, AND "WILLAMETTE COUNTY"

(1983–1990)

"MORALITY IN GOVERNMENT: We need moral men in public government; the voter has a right to TRUTH from his representative."—Gordon Shadburne

Twelve years after Gordon Shadburne published the above statement on his page in the 1974 *Oregon Voters' Pamphlet*, the shocking truth came to light that Shadburne's personal life did not equate with his stance as a moral crusader.

Shadburne, a political science teacher at Mt. Hood Community College and an advisor on citizenship for the Boy Scouts, sought the office of Oregon state representative on the Republican ticket in 1974, but lost the fall election to the Democratic incumbent, Glenn Otto, a former mayor of Troutdale.[1]

Four years later, Shadburne, now a boyish-looking 38, faced off against Gresham City Commissioner Paula Bentley in a nonpartisan race to fill a newly created east county seat on the Multnomah County Board of Commissioners. Bentley, as an incumbent office holder, was widely expected to win. Shadburne touted himself as a "born-again Christian" and targeted church groups, senior citizens, and the education community. His supporters wrote letters stressing his strong religious beliefs. He warned voters that Bentley was supported by the Portland Town Council, a gay-rights group. Bentley accused Shadburne of smear tactics.[2] When the votes were counted, Shadburne had won by 4 percent—640 votes out of 15,000 cast.

For the next two years, Shadburne cultivated a visible presence in east county. He gave speeches and attended PTA, Kiwanis, and Rotary Club meetings. "You can't go anywhere around here without running into Gordon Shadburne," commented *Gresham Outlook* editor Lee Irwin.[3]

*Boyish-looking Gordon Shadburne was
popular with conservative East County voters
until news reports indicated that his personal
life differed sharply from the values he espoused
publicly. Shadburne later contended he did not
know that pleading guilty to a misdemeanor
charge would force his removal from the board,
but he was never able to return to prominence
in public life.* (Multnomah County Archives)

The next elections in 1980 brought a rematch between Shadburne and
Paula Bentley, with Shadburne now enjoying the advantages of incumbency. In
its endorsement of Bentley, *Willamette Week* said voters had the opportunity to
exchange "bad representation" from Shadburne—opposition to establishing a
911 emergency number, opposition to hiring of a county economic development
officer, efforts to dismantle the county's Administrative Services Division—with
the "demonstrably good" candidacy of Bentley.[4]

Once again, Shadburne triumphed at the polls. He was so buoyed by his
election and reelection victories that two years later he jumped into the race to
replace County Executive Don Clark, who was prohibited by term limits from
running in 1982. Shadburne's opponent was his colleague on the county commission, Dennis Buchanan, who represented Portland's West Hills.

The primary election result for county chair was close: 44 percent for former newspaper reporter Buchanan versus 41 percent for Shadburne.[5] In the fall
return engagement, however, Buchanan was endorsed by virtually every newspaper in the county and won election handily. Although he lost decisively to his
fellow commissioner, Shadburne was in the middle of a four-year commission
term and retained his board seat.

The four-year terms that Buchanan and his predecessor, Don Clark, each
served as county executive were quite different from those of their predecessors
or successors, because during those years the county executive was not allowed
to set the agenda for board meetings, have a vote, or preside.

A guest editorial that Shadburne wrote for the *Gresham Outlook* the following year reflected his attitude toward his fellow elected officials. "The year 1983 will be recorded by history as the 'year of division' for the county and its board of county commissioners," Shadburne wrote. "From a basically unified board of prior years, 1983 has surfaced a most divisive issue—Resolution A."[6] (As discussed in the preceding chapter, Resolution A was the intergovernmental policy agreement that assigned human services to the county and urban services to the city and presupposed more annexations of unincorporated areas of Multnomah County by Portland and Gresham.) Resolution A was supported by four board members as well as County Executive Buchanan—in other words, by everyone except Commissioner Shadburne. It was his district that had the most to lose in county services such as sheriff's patrols, Fire District 10, and parks.

Shadburne was reflecting the prevailing view of his east county constituents in his opposition to Resolution A (especially the focus on annexations) and easily won another four-year term in 1984. County employees, on the other hand, found Shadburne difficult to work with and considered him a knee-jerk opponent of progressive causes.

In 1985, the year that Shadburne won reelection to a third term, he was joined on the board by former legislator Gretchen Kafoury, a staunch advocate for civil rights (especially for women and gays), and Pauline Anderson, the first female president of the City Club of Portland.[7] The next two years, with a commission composed of Shadburne, Kafoury, Anderson, Caroline Miller, and Earl Blumenauer, would prove even more divisive than they had been for the previous board. Shadburne and Miller occasionally voted together, but more often than not Shadburne was alone on the losing side of issues that came before the board.

Shadburne fostered the belief held by many discontented east county residents that they were "getting the short end of the stick" in dealings with county government. His negative approach may have aided and abetted east county dissidents who later launched antigovernment proposals such as Measure 5, a statewide tax-reduction measure that would seriously restrict local governments.[717]

In early March 1984, Kafoury introduced, and Shadburne opposed, a county ordinance forbidding discrimination in hiring based on sexual orientation. An anti–gay-rights group subsequently filed 14,000 signatures with the county elections division to repeal the ordinance, so Kafoury deleted the term "sexual orientation" from the proposed law and placed the same phrase in a county board resolution that would not be subject to public vote. The commission majority thereby affirmed its support for gay rights but avoided both the

$150,000 cost of a special election and the possibility that the ordinance would be repealed by the electorate.[9]

County citizens got a clear indication in late 1985 that Gordon Shadburne was mixing religion with politics when he sent a letter on county stationery to some fifty churches in east Multnomah County calling homosexuality "the stronghold of Satan." He urged pastors to contact his office if they were interested in forming a "Homosexuals Anonymous" organization to aid gay parishioners in changing their sexual preference to heterosexuality. The letter provoked strong criticism from the media as well as Shadburne's colleagues on the board. Not only had Shadburne used county stationery and government-paid employee time to promote his personal issue, but he had violated the constitutional principle separating church and state.[10]

Shadburne's controversial letter prompted the Metropolitan Human Relations Commission to take a formal public position supporting gay rights. A 13-1 majority declared that homosexuals should have "the same rights as anyone else." The Human Relations Commission chair said Shadburne's letter tended to incite hostility toward gay and lesbian groups.[11]

Commissioner Kafoury told a reporter that Shadburne might have acted in pique over recent county commission support for federal funding of family planning programs. Family planning included information about abortion, which Shadburne opposed, she said. He therefore voted against any government funding that included birth control.[12]

In another dust-up between Kafoury and Shadburne, this one concerning more mundane matters, Kafoury challenged the tradition of assigning county cars to elected officials. Commissioners ought not to use county vehicles for driving to and from work, she said, but should seek reimbursement for miles actually traveled on county business. Shadburne's county car had cost taxpayers $4,436 in 1984, the *Oregonian* reported, an average of 60 miles per day for every workday, more than twice the cost of the next highest user, Commissioner Earl Blumenauer, at $1,900.[13]

The push that started Shadburne's political future rolling downhill began in early 1986, and came from two sources: first, Shadburne aides began talking to the media about internal office difficulties, and then county auditor Anne Feeney and her deputy, Hank Miggins, began examining commissioner expenditures.

In April 1986, five months after the infamous Shadburne letter referring to homosexuality as "the stronghold of Satan," Shadburne fired staffer Richard Levy, a self-professed homosexual whose sexual preference disturbed

Shadburne's "Christian" constituents. Levy's public revelation that he was gay made the working relationship between Levy and his boss "awkward" for both of them, Shadburne said. He claimed it was not a major factor in his decision to ask Levy to clean out his desk and depart.[14]

Three days later, a second Shadburne assistant, his east county constituent liaison, quit. Kay Foetisch cited "significant policy differences" with Shadburne as her reason for leaving after a year and a half on Shadburne's staff. She did not approve of his mixing of personal religious beliefs with his county duties or his "laxness in representing his constituents."[15]

Next, the auditor's office found that Shadburne had made secret payments totaling $4,800 to a longtime friend and political consultant, in apparent violation of county contract regulations. District Attorney Michael Schrunk asked Sheriff Fred Pearce to investigate.[16]

On the same day, the *Oregonian* broke the news that taxpayers had paid the tab for nearly $1,000 in restaurant, hotel, and auto rental bills for Shadburne and two others on a five-day visit to Canada the previous year, a journey described as a "pleasure trip" by Shadburne aides. County expense records also showed that Shadburne billed the county for three trips to California in 1985, but only one of the excursions had a documented business purpose.

Reporters were now hot on Shadburne's trail. Before long, a shocking picture emerged. "Shadburne's private life belies image," declared a May 20, 1986, front-page *Oregonian* headline. The contrast between Shadburne's public side, that of a fiscal conservative and "born-again Christian," the story said, was far different from the Gordon Shadburne who participated in homosexual acts, used cocaine, and charged private business expenses and pleasure trips to his county expense account.

The *Oregonian* obtained affidavits from witnesses alleging that Shadburne participated in a homosexual orgy while on a semi-business trip to Baltimore; that he was seen unclad at a Portland bathhouse having sex with a man on more than one occasion; that he attended two gay bars and a gay bathhouse on specific dates; and that he bought and consumed cocaine.

Rumors of recall efforts began circulating. On June 2, 1986, east county activist Tom Dennehy, who had been active in numerous county initiative campaigns involving charter changes, sent an open letter to Shadburne, pleading with him to answer allegations with facts, not simple denials. Dennehy said he was approached by at least three people about starting a recall campaign, but that he urged patience and restraint until Shadburne's side of the story was heard. He likened Shadburne's responses to date, in which he blamed "sensational" journalism and "unnamed sources," to Richard Nixon's famous "I am not a crook" declaration. Dennehy urged Shadburne to resign if he could not, or refused to, rebut the accusations that had been made against him. "Failure to provide satisfactory answers by next Monday would, I believe, justify a recall drive," Dennehy said.[17]

By mid-July, a recall drive was in full swing. On July 31, Shadburne pleaded guilty in Multnomah County District Court to second-degree official misconduct, a class C misdemeanor, for misuse of county money on his January 1985 trip to Vancouver, British Columbia, and Edmonton, Alberta. On August 6, County Counsel John Leahy told the commission that Shadburne's admission of misconduct constituted forfeiture of his office, and declared the east county commission seat vacant. On August 7, 1986, Gordon Shadburne resigned.[18]

Supporters had urged Shadburne to defend himself publicly, but he declined to do so. His resignation letter said:

> For the past year and a half I have been subjected to an extraordinary degree of public scrutiny and intrusions into all areas of my life. These include not only an unfortunate divorce, a difficult custody battle for my children, but also accusations against my public and private conduct . . . Worst of all, however, is watching what happens to my children as the media reports as fact every rumor, every innuendo and every charge made by disgruntled individuals . . . [This resignation] is best for me and my children.

As the filing deadline approached for the now-vacant east county commission seat, Shadburne surprised enemies and former supporters alike by announcing, 14 minutes before the filing deadline, that he would again be a candidate for the office he had forfeited only two months before. He joined seven other candidates on the ballot. Citizens who were active in his recall movement feared that Shadburne might be elected simply by virtue of name familiarity in such a crowded field.[19]

On an October 3 KPDQ-FM radio program hosted by Lew Davies, Shadburne said he would not have pleaded guilty to a misdemeanor if he had known that he would have to give up his office. He also denied that he was a homosexual or that he had ever used cocaine. He compared his difficulties to those experienced by Job in the Old Testament. His sharpest criticism was aimed at the *Oregonian*. Its coverage was excessive, he said. "They used six different reporters to try to dig things up."[20]

In the November general election, voters turned their backs on Shadburne to elect Polly Casterline, a long-time community activist. Casterline, who had a record of leadership positions in the League of Women Voters and the Mt. Hood Community College board, was sworn in on November 25, 1986, at age sixty-three. Her *Voters' Pamphlet* page noted that she was an active member and past moderator of her church. She pledged to heal divisions plaguing east county, such as annexation and installation of sewers. She pledged to protect "the delicate natural beauty of the recreational environment" of east county and to augment the economic prospects of the region.[21]

Casterline would serve for only two years and two months, until her death from cancer in February 1989. Sharron Kelley, a former Metro councilor, chair of the Multnomah County Parks Commission, and an active member of the League of Women Voters, was elected to take her place.[22]

Shadburne disappeared from public life. In 1988, he moved to Southern California, where he set up a religious missionary organization called Warriors for Christ aimed at trying to convert Native Americans. He later returned to Portland and suffered brain damage in a car crash. In 2004, he told *Willamette Week* that he had never used drugs or engaged in homosexual activity. He said that when he pleaded guilty to the misdemeanor charge over expenses, he thought all he had to do was pay a fine. Although he was represented by a capable lawyer, Shadburne said he did not know that his plea would cost him his county commissioner job. As for his silence at the time: "My lawyer said, 'Don't say anything to anyone.' I would have held a press conference and blasted the *Oregonian*, but I couldn't say anything." [23]

In March 1986, a study committee of the City Club of Portland recommended further study of the idea of a "super county." A proposed "Willamette County" would combine Metro and Tri-Met (the region's transportation authority) with Washington, Clackamas, and Multnomah counties, but would leave the cities as separate entities. The City Club report, entitled "Report on Regional Government in the Portland Metropolitan Area," led to a barrage of media coverage, both positive and negative.[24]

Multnomah County Commissioner Earl Blumenauer (later U.S. Congressman) said he had favored such a plan for fourteen years, declaring that the "super county" idea was long overdue.[25] Washington County's board publicly opposed the idea. A *Washington County News-Times* editorial, titled "'Super County' idea flawed," noted that while consolidation of the three counties would likely reduce administrative costs, payroll costs would soar. Employee unions would no longer come to the bargaining table with comparisons of salary and benefit costs between Washington and Clackamas counties; instead, their comparables would be drawn from huge and wealthy California local governments like San Diego and San Jose.[26]

Clackamas County Commission Chair Dale Harlan said the proposal would likely create a government animal too big for the general public's liking. Nationwide, he said, the track record for consolidation was "dismal, with 52 counties holding 76 elections since World War II, resulting in only 17 successful mergers."[27]

Editorial writers outside the metropolitan area weighed in favorably on the issue. *The Daily Astorian* noted the common interests that linked Multnomah, Washington, and Clackamas counties. "Putting those counties together seems so logical," the editorial says, "that one wonders why it has taken so long."[28]

The City Club of Portland next convened a task force, under the leadership of attorney Cliff Carlson, to examine the "Willamette County" possibilities in more depth, with a specific goal of recommending how and by whom the regional government proposal could be acted upon. After meeting weekly from June through December 1986, the task force recommended the formation of a citizens' commission, to be appointed by the governor, with the authority and commitment to propose a "workable regional government plan for approval by voters of the three counties."[29] The City Club had no authority to proceed further, and no governmental entity stepped forward to move the proposal forward. The report was placed on the shelf along with earlier consolidation studies.

While Gordon Shadburne's political career was collapsing, that of Commissioner Gladys McCoy was headed in the other direction. Political pioneer, state ombudsman, school board member, social worker, college teacher, county commissioner, wife, mother of seven, and finally chair of Multnomah County Board of County Commissioners, McCoy broke so many social and political barriers during her lifetime that she deserves special recognition in Multnomah County history. By winning a county commission seat in 1978, she became the first African-American ever elected to Multnomah County government office (and until 2010 she remained the only one).[30] Not only was McCoy the first woman to serve as chair of the Multnomah County Commission, she also presided over the first all-female county board with dignity and calm.

The all-woman board came about in January 1987 after Polly Casterline had replaced Gordon Shadburne as east Multnomah County's representative

*The first all-woman board of county commissioners took office in 1987 after Polly Casterline filled a seat
vacated by Gordon Shadburne's abrupt departure. The commission members were, from left, Pauline Anderson,
Caroline Miller, Gretchen Kafoury, Casterline, and Chair Gladys McCoy.* (Multnomah County Archives)

and with the election of Gladys McCoy as chair. Casterline and McCoy joined
Gretchen Kafoury, Pauline Anderson, and Caroline Miller. In addition, Anne
Kelly Feeney held the elective position of auditor at the same time that the all-
woman commission served. The six women operated in relative harmony for
two and a half years, until Miller was prohibited from seeking reelection because
of term limits and Rick Bauman won her board seat.

Gladys McCoy was born in Atlanta, Georgia, in 1928. She originally planned to
be a secretary but changed direction after teachers encouraged her to aim higher.
She came to Oregon in 1949 for a one-year job with the YMCA and never left.
In Portland, she met and married Bill McCoy, then spent several years as a stay-
at-home mom raising seven children. After earning a master's degree in social
work from Portland State University, she directed a Head Start program for two
years, was the first African-American elected to the Portland School Board (in

1970, reelected in 1974), and served for three years as state ombudsman under Governor Bob Straub. She resigned that state position to run for the Multnomah County Commission.[31]

The only real setback in Gladys McCoy's political career occurred in 1984, when African-American Charles Jordan resigned his city council seat. Nineteen candidates (sixteen men and three women, including McCoy) filed to succeed him. The race went to a runoff between Herb Cawthorne and former KATU reporter Dick Bogle, both African-Americans, with McCoy a close third. As a result, McCoy lost her county commission seat, because the county charter prohibited an elected official from seeking another elective position without first resigning. Bogle was elected to the Portland City Council in the fall and went on to serve for eight years.[32]

Two years later, when County Executive Dennis Buchanan decided not to seek reelection to the top county position, McCoy jumped into the race. In the 1986 primary, she faced Glenn Otto, a veteran state legislator.[33] Otto, an electrician by trade, was one of the most influential political figures in the area then called east county. He had served on the Troutdale City Council from 1966 to 1972, the final six of those years as mayor. He then moved on to the Oregon House of Representatives from 1973 to 1985, and later to the Oregon Senate from 1986 to 1993. But Otto was no favorite of the county officials. He had been active in the failed attempt to recall Chairman Don Clark and worked in favor of several disruptive county charter amendments.

The *Oregonian* and most other local newspapers endorsed Otto, with the media otherwise paying little attention. The May election count gave Otto 43 percent of the vote, McCoy 40 percent, and the other three candidates together, 17 percent. Since neither Otto nor McCoy won the required 50 percent plus one vote required, their race continued on to a runoff in November. (The commission chair position was actually a new one, replacing the independent executive job that had removed Don Clark and Dennis Buchanan from the board for four years each. Now the county chair would again be entitled to a commission vote as well as acting as the county's chief administrative officer.) The November 1986 contest was so close that absentee ballots had to be counted to determine the result. McCoy squeaked out a win with 50.1 percent of votes cast.[34] The defeat did nothing to damage Otto's career in the eyes of east county voters, but McCoy offered a different take on her one-time opponent, once calling him a "small town, pork-barrel, old-boy network parochial public official."[35]

McCoy was particularly proud of the no-smoking policy that was instituted for county buildings during her tenure as chair, and also that Multnomah

County was the first Oregon governmental entity to provide health-care insurance to domestic partners of county employees, a pioneering policy that was adopted during McCoy's years as chair. The Affidavit of Domestic Partnership developed by Multnomah County later became a model for a number of public and private sector employers.[36]

In February 1988, the Multnomah County Health Division reported that there had been one million visits to county health clinics or community health nurses since 1980. In June 1988, the health division celebrated the twentieth anniversary of its merger with the City of Portland Bureau of Health,[37] one of the few voluntary consolidations implemented without referral to voters.

Other praise for Multnomah County under McCoy's leadership came from the Harvard University Division of Health Policy, which in 1988 credited Oregon as a pioneer in providing adequate health care for children. Multnomah County was cited as a prime example, particularly for its establishment of a school-based, comprehensive teen health clinic with a particular focus on reducing the incidence of teen-aged pregnancy. The pilot school-based project, launched by the county in 1986 at Roosevelt High School, faced considerable opposition when first proposed. The subsequent success of the program was due in large part to sophisticated advocacy by county employees and support from Superintendent of Schools Matthew Prophet and Roosevelt High School Principal George Galati.[38] The Harvard publication said that Oregon had progressed faster and farther than any other state."[39]

Along with health and social issues, McCoy's priorities included ensuring that unincorporated areas in mid-County got the sewers and police services they needed after Resolution A assigned responsibility for providing urban services such as sewers, neighborhood parks, and policing to the cities of Portland and Gresham.[40]

The downside to Gladys McCoy's political career was that she sometimes had difficulty keeping her personal, professional, and political roles separate. She saw nothing wrong, for example, with continuing to sell Amway products and distribute them to customers from her county office. Staff members finally convinced her that this practice was inappropriate, if not illegal. On another occasion, McCoy directed staff to steer a county parking contract to her son, Paul McCoy. Fortunately for Chair McCoy, her staff talked her out of that potential faux pas before the contract became a reality, forestalling any further investigation by the district attorney's office.[41] Credit for keeping McCoy out of these and other potential problems belongs to her chief of staff, Hank Miggins; attorney Fred Neal, and environmental services director Paul Yarborough.[42]

When she ran for reelection in 1989, *Oregonian* columnist Steve Duin opined that McCoy was "frequently caught doing the right thing when the county needs things done right . . . But," he said, "she deserves credit for repairing the Department of Human Services, securing jail space and an additional county prosecutor, hiring some good managers and, in the face of deplorable opposition, promoting in-school teen health clinics."[43]

McCoy won her reelection bid but was unable to serve out her term. After serving as county chair for six and a half years, she died in April 1993 at the age of 65 from an aggressive form of thyroid cancer. When they learned of her passing, elected officials throughout the state eulogized McCoy as a pioneer and praised her devotion to public service. An *Oregonian* editorial credited her leadership with saving Columbia Villa, a North Portland housing project that was being terrorized by criminals day and night. "Bringing diverse peoples together . . . will be [McCoy's] legacy to the community," the editorial said.[44]

Multnomah County voters had approved a charter change six years earlier that required elected officials to designate an alternate who would serve in their stead when a vacancy occurred until an election could be held. Gladys McCoy designated Hank Miggins, her chief of staff and a former deputy county auditor, as her alternate. Miggins was therefore sworn in as the interim county chair in April 1993 and served until mid-August, when former state legislator Beverly Stein was sworn in as the duly-elected chair.[45]

McCoy's years as board chair of an all-female board supported the contention that a social or political barrier, once broken, can quickly become a historic oddity. This was demonstrated in Multnomah County, where voters had elected their first women officials only twelve years before. The first two—Commissioner Alice Corbett and auditor Jewel Lansing—were both elected in 1974.

By contrast, the first three women to serve on the Portland city council reached their positions by appointment, albeit earlier—Dorothy McCullough Lee in 1943, Connie McCready in 1971, and Mildred Schwab in 1973. At city hall, no more than two women had ever served on city council at the same time as of 2009.[46] The main reasons for the difference in the number of women elected county officials compared to the city were that city officials received considerably higher salaries than their county counterparts and (except for the powerful county chair) had considerably more clout.[47] Portland city government had 1,400 more employees than county government, and the city functions of police, fire, and neighborhood street maintenance were closer to the daily lives of its citizens.[48] On the other hand, the county's focus on social, health, and human services was especially attractive to female candidates. Another contributing difference was that city council campaigns were more expensive to run than county races, and were usually won by the candidate with the most campaign funds.[49]

In addition to Gladys McCoy, other African-Americans who deserve recognition for their pioneering candidacies in Multnomah County include District and Circuit Court Judges Aaron Brown and Mercedes Diez; state legislators Margaret Carter, Avel Gordly, and Bill McCoy (Gladys McCoy's husband); and Portland City Council members Charles Jordan and Dick Bogle. At the time of Gladys McCoy's death, three more African-Americans (Herb Cawthorne, Evie Crowell, and Lucius Hicks) had already served on the Portland School Board following McCoy's trailblazing years of service.[50]

Far removed from downtown Portland, residents of the easternmost reaches of Multnomah County had a rather different mix of challenges to deal with than the urban portion of the county. The mid-1980s brought renewed attention to preserving the Columbia Gorge. After years of activism, led largely by a nonprofit group called Friends of Columbia Gorge, Congress in 1986 passed the Columbia River Gorge National Scenic Area Act. A commission of twelve voting members, six each from Washington and Oregon, was established to "develop and implement policies and programs that protect and enhance the scenic, natural, cultural and recreational resources of the Gorge, while encouraging growth within existing urban areas of the Gorge and allowing development outside the urban areas consistent with resource protection." The area covered by the Scenic Act included 292,500 acres on both sides of the Columbia River.[51]

Skamania County, on the Washington side of the Gorge, was so angered by the idea of federal control over its land that, after President Reagan signed the 1986 bill, the courthouse flag hung at half-mast. The county also evicted the staff of a volunteer organization that went by the same name, Columbia River Gorge Commission, and had been renting space in a Skamania county building. The earlier commission had been formed in 1953 by action of the Oregon and Washington legislatures, and its six members—three each from each state—were all Gorge residents who had little more than voluntary persuasion at their disposal in dealing with Gorge development controversies.[52] The new twelve-member commission would have more clout.

As county chair, Gladys McCoy had responsibility for appointing a Multnomah County member to the new commission, and she sought agreement from the county board. Thirteen names were submitted, including that of Nancy

Russell, a southwest Portland woman and longtime chair of the Friends of the Columbia Gorge, who was one of McCoy's nominees. Russell had played the single most important role in winning Congressional approval of the new Scenic Area. Russell drew heavy opposition from east county residents, represented by Commissioner Polly Casterline, who said she could not support Russell's appointment under any circumstances because of her constituents' concerns about Russell's alleged antidevelopment attitudes.[53]

In the end, McCoy and the county board selected Kristine Olson Rogers, a former assistant U.S. attorney who had worked as a consultant to Native American tribes, private agencies, and government entities on the law of cultural resources.[54] Rogers joined former County Executive Don Clark, who was one of the Oregon representatives to the commission appointed by Governor Neil Goldschmidt.[55] In the years ahead, the commission would face difficult challenges in trying to preserve the natural beauty of the Gorge by protecting it from overdevelopment, resolving conflicts between individual property rights and preservation interests, and mediating between the forces of local and federal control.

Faced with court orders limiting inmate populations at the new Multnomah County Justice Center downtown, county voters in July 1987 approved by an almost three-to-one ratio a three-year serial levy to build another new jail.[56] Sheriff Fred Pearce promised that it would be a low-security "no frills" jail for misdemeanor offenders who were serving sentences no longer than one year. He had investigated whether it would be cheaper to convert one or more existing warehouses into a jail, but concluded it would be better to erect a new building. County commissioners chose a site on a dead end road, N.E. Inverness Drive, that terminated at the defunct Inverness Sewage Treatment Plant. The new one-story jail was to house approximately 220 inmates, who would be allowed to leave the jail on work-release projects. Pearce vowed to have the new jail open sometime in 1988—and succeeded in doing so; the first inmates moved in on the first day of November.[57] It remained unclear, though, how jail operations would be funded after the three-year measure expired.[58]

In 1988, at the request of Multnomah County Chair Gladys McCoy, consultant Carol Kirchner examined the level of services provided by Multnomah and Clackamas counties to explore possible areas of consolidation. At the time, Clackamas County's population was 255,000—about half that of Multnomah County's 562,000. More than half of Clackamas County residents lived in unincorporated areas. Clackamas covered an area four times that of Multnomah,

Sheriff Bob Skipper served two separate tenures fourteen years apart: first from 1990 to 1994, then from 2008 to 2009, when he was recruited to fill the position again after the resignation of Sheriff Bernie Giusto. (Multnomah County Archives)

half of it in the Mt. Hood National Forest. Clackamas County was served by forty different water systems compared to Multnomah County's ten.

The officials and employees in both counties whom Kirchner interviewed were "lukewarm" to further consideration of combined activities. The differences between the problems facing an urban population and those of suburban/rural residents were cited as a major impediment to any merging of functions. Clackamas County personnel worried that Multnomah County would dominate any relationship and force a diminution of the services Clackamas was already providing. It was agreed that a combined animal-control function for all three Portland metropolitan area counties was feasible, but no such action was taken,[59] and no further action regarding combined services was proposed by either county at that time.

When Sheriff Pearce resigned in early 1989 to become director of the Oregon Department of Corrections, he named Robert Skipper to fill his sheriff's shoes on an interim basis, in accordance with a new county charter requirement. Armed with solid credentials as Pearce's chief deputy, Skipper was elected by a comfortable margin that fall.[60]

County expenditures for justice services—courtrooms, jails, staffing for the district attorney's and sheriff's offices—continued to spiral as county commissioners struggled to keep budgets in balance while maintaining social and health service levels.

A November 1989 ballot measure asked county voters to approve a special property tax levy to fund the sheriff's operations. In dueling guest editorials in the *Gresham Outlook*, commissioners Gretchen Kafoury and Rick Bauman came down on different sides regarding the proposed levy. Kafoury urged a yes vote, arguing that the sheriff was releasing 300 inmates a month who should be in jail. Bauman declared that the measure was an expensive Band-Aid for "a hemorrhaging criminal justice system that is in need of major surgery." Calling the measure "a half-baked request," Bauman urged the sheriff and others to develop policies, facilities, and programs that would reduce crime.[61]

To the relief of most county officials, the business community, and editorial writers, voters approved the three-year serial levy to cover the cost of operating the existing 220-bed Inverness Jail, adding 210 more beds by expanding the building and providing an additional 120 drug and alcohol treatment beds at two or three locations, as well as paying for two drug-sniffing dogs to assist in narcotics detection.[62]

County law enforcement drew wider attention in the summer of 1989. Fan mail started pouring into the sheriff's office for Sgt. John Bunnell, manager of the county's narcotics team and special investigation unit, who was starring in the syndicated *C.O.P.S.* television series. A typical program showed Bunnell and his team bursting through doors and confronting drug dealers. The county teams took part in fifteen episodes. Bunnell also hosted the first season of ABC's *American Detective*, which featured Multnomah County sheriff's personnel thirteen times.[63] Bunnell himself would hold the sheriff's title briefly after Skipper retired in 1994 but would be defeated by Dan Noelle in a race to keep the job.

Anne Kelly Feeney resigned as auditor in 1988, in the middle of her second term, to take the position of executive director of Loaves and Fishes, a Meals-on-Wheels program for seniors, after voters froze the salaries of county elected officials. A special election was held to replace Feeney. In a field of unknowns who sought the job, the post was won by Dan Ivancie, son of former Portland mayor Frank Ivancie. The Ivancie name had been in politics so long—more than three decades—that it was a household word. When Dan Ivancie filed for reelection as auditor in 1990, he was opposed by Gary Blackmer, a certified internal auditor who ran a sophisticated campaign and made an issue of Ivancie's lack of audit experience and training. Blackmer, a senior management auditor for the City of Portland, won with 55 percent of the vote. He went on to serve with distinction for the maximum allowable eight years as county auditor and for ten years as the elected City of Portland auditor.[64]

As the 1980s drew to a close, the county still had not disposed of the former county farm and nursing home site at Edgefield. The buildings were locked and boarded up, but vandals had nevertheless inflicted damage. County officials gradually decided that the land would be worth more without the old buildings and talked about razing them. The Troutdale Historical Society had other ideas. As early as 1986, the society opposed demolition and followed through with the extensive research required to place Edgefield Manor on the National Register of Historic Places in 1990. The listing would not necessarily prevent demolition, but it could slow the process. For a while, dueling shopping-center developers talked about buying the whole property and building a large mall, but they eventually dropped out. The fate of the old nursing home became the subject of several hearings in Troutdale and before the county board. "Personally, I'd like to see it torn down," Chair McCoy said at a 1988 hearing.[65]

Early in 1990, new bidders arose. Bob and Mike McMenamin, who had pioneered Oregon's brewpub industry in 1974, offered to buy Edgefield Manor, some peripheral buildings, and ten acres of land for $500,000. The McMenamins already had a track record of taking historic but unwanted properties, such as southeast Portland's old Bagdad Theater, and converting them into successful businesses offering beer, movies, and food. After having watched the Edgefield property sit on the real estate market for eight years, county commissioners accepted the McMenamins' offer in March 1990.[66]

Over the next several years, the McMenamins went about planting grapes, building a small winery, converting the manor building to hotel rooms, adding a small golf course, adding several bars in various outbuildings, and turning the Edgefield complex into a thriving business based on beer, wine, food, entertainment, the restoration of quirky old buildings, and a respect for history. The old poor farm had turned into a marvel of entrepreneurial adventure.[67] While nobody congratulated the county commissioners for dragging their feet for eight years, the county's bumbling process saved Edgefield from total destruction until creative minds in private enterprise found an excellent alternative.

19

THE INFAMOUS MEASURE 5, COLUMBIA GORGE BATTLES, AND EAST COUNTY EFFORTS TO SECEDE
(1990–2001)

Just as Resolution A was bringing the county some financial breathing room, a November 1990 statewide ballot measure, Measure 5, significantly changed Oregon's property tax system, affecting school districts and all local governments—including Multnomah County—that relied on property taxes for a sizeable portion of their operating revenues.

Measure 5 restricted most property taxes to 1½ percent of assessed value. Expressed another way, this was a levy of 15 mills, or $15 for each $1,000 of real market value or assessed value, whichever was lower. The only exception was for taxes to repay general obligation bonds approved by voters.[1] A maximum of .05 (½ of 1) percent could be levied for schools and the remaining 1 percent allocated among all other local government operating funds.

Prior to passage of Measure 5, Oregon local governments were allowed to increase property tax bases by 6 percent each year without regard to changes in assessed value. While Measure 5 still allowed this same calculation, depending on the tax rate of all related districts (education or general government), the governmental unit might or might not be able to actually collect all of it. (The automatic 6 percent increase was later reduced by Measure 50—passed in May 1997—to 3 percent plus new construction.[2] Unless inflation remained under 3 percent—an unusual phenomenon—local government property tax revenues would continue to shrink relative to the normal rate of inflation.)

Starting in 1993, a new cast of county leaders faced the funding difficulties exacerbated by Measure 5. State Representative Beverly Stein had planned to run for Multnomah County chair when Gladys McCoy finished her second term, but McCoy's untimely death in April 1993 advanced Stein's timetable by nearly two years. In a special June 1993 mail-in election, Stein won 44 percent of the vote for county chair against eight opponents, an impressive showing but still short of the majority needed to avoid a run-off. In its endorsement of her candidacy, the *Oregonian* called her a "creative, consensus-building ex-legislator." *Willamette Week* said Stein was "that rare visionary who knows how to get things done."[3] In her August 3 face-off against perennial candidate and former state senator Vern Cook, Stein garnered 70 percent of the vote, and was duly elected to complete the remaining sixteen months of McCoy's term. Stein had previously served three terms in the Oregon House of Representatives; she had also been a City of Portland council staff member, and a Legal Aid lawyer.

Two men and two women served with Stein on the board during her first four years—Tanya Collier, Gary Hansen, Sharron Kelley, and Dan Saltzman. In the first budget Stein put forward as county chair, she proposed transferring thirty-three sheriff's deputies to the City of Portland. She argued that July 1 annexations affecting 26,000 people would again shrink the county's unincorporated area, so fewer sheriff's deputies were needed. In spite of vigorous protests by Sheriff Bob Skipper, Stein's fellow commissioners and the *Oregonian* editorial board supported her position. "Stein, Skipper near a face-off over turf and money," said an April 19, 1994, *Oregonian* headline. "Transfer Sheriff's deputies," an *Oregonian* editorial declared. "Unincorporated area is shrinking; so should sheriff's staff and budget."[4]

At the end of negotiations involving the county, City of Portland, and Sheriff Skipper, twenty-three deputies were ultimately transferred to the Portland Police Bureau, which needed the additional police officers to patrol newly annexed city turf. The $2 million in county savings was redirected to help keep social services intact, support programs for curtailing juvenile crime, and enhance data systems.[5] The one downside to the otherwise positive results of a fully implemented Resolution A was the virtual demise of the law enforcement function of the sheriff's office. At one point in its history, the county had hoped that the culture and traditions of the county sheriff's office would prevail over those of the Portland Police Bureau. In the end, it was the larger and more entrenched Portland Police Bureau that won out—another instance of a city-county battle in which the county came out the loser.[6]

As revenues stalled, it became increasingly difficult for the county to sustain its services. A blue ribbon committee that included several downtown Portland business executives convened in the wake of Measure 5. In 1993, the committee released a study titled "Public Safety 2000," calling for delineation between the sheriff's law enforcement and corrections responsibilities. Instead of merging city and county police departments, the committee recommended retaining separate identities but merging functions such as training, gang enforcement teams, and mid-level narcotics investigations.[7]

The Public Safety 2000 review also urged individual evaluations of all correctional facilities overseen by the sheriff, to gauge how cost effectively they were run. The committee suggested "re-appropriating" river patrol funds from the sheriff's budget to "somewhere else." They implied that the sheriff's department was top-heavy with officers and "gave the impression of a sheriff's office jealously guarding its territory and budget," according to researcher David Linn in *A Brief History of Multnomah County Government (1964-2004)*, commissioned by County Chair Diane Linn in 2004.[8]

Sheriff Skipper was "understandably angry," the Linn history notes. Skipper reminded the board and public that he was an elected official and would conduct his department and budget as he saw fit. He argued that Resolution A was not an ordinance but an executive policy directive. Delayed annexations by Portland plus a growing gang problem rendered Resolution A void, he said, "in spirit as well as fact."[9] Nevertheless, implementation of Resolution A moved slowly forward.[10]

Late in 1994, Sheriff Skipper learned that planned changes to the state Public Employee Retirement System would cost him $750 a month in lost pension income if he remained in office after the law went into effect. He resigned "reluctantly" that November to run a 100-acre nursery in eastern Multnomah County. "It was the hardest decision of my life," he later said.[11]

Skipper designated John Bunnell as interim sheriff until the next election. The May 1995 primary saw Bunnell face off against—and lose to—Dan Noelle, a 29-year veteran of the Portland Police Bureau who ran a well-organized campaign. Bunnell therefore served only eight months as sheriff.[12]

As a former street cop frustrated by the lack of adequate jail space, Noelle's main goal was to keep arrested criminals behind bars by increasing available capacity. He found a strong ally in Commissioner Gretchen Kafoury.[13] By the time Noelle left office seven and a half years later, more than 700 beds had been added to the county's jail system. Much of the increase was gained by securing court permission to double-bunk Justice Center cells originally designed as single-bed units. Many observers criticized the concept of double bunking. Former Sheriff Don Clark considered it a "very bad idea"—a corruption of design and a betrayal of inmate safety.[14]

Stein gave high priority to increased cooperation between Multnomah County and other local governments. She and Portland Mayor Vera Katz, who had served together in the Oregon legislature, cofounded the Portland-Multnomah

County Progress Board, which set priorities and standards for improving the area's social and economic health. The two women were honored by the national *Governing Magazine* in December 1994 as "Public Officials of the Year" for bringing "a spirit of teamwork to enterprises where it had been noticeably lacking." Stein and Katz could have survived politically, the magazine said, by "continuing the jurisdictional bickering that typically plagues city-county relationships. They chose, however, to look for new ways to fuse city and county together, and the results have been impressive."[15]

One example of the Katz-Stein cooperation was the Domestic Partners Registry, developed by the county and city, and supported by every Multnomah County commissioner and Portland City Council member. The registry provided public acknowledgment of committed relationships, an opportunity available to heterosexual partners as well as gays and lesbians. Registry promoters hoped that the county registry would gain widespread recognition from employers, hospitals, and other institutions. Stein and Katz signed as witnesses for the first couple who registered when the registry debuted on September 1, 2000. Twenty-seven couples signed notarized certificates that day pledging their commitment to each other.[16]

Stein's style of governance was in sharp contrast to that of former chair Don Clark, who liked to jump into the fray and tackle a challenge head-on. Stein focused more on process and public involvement. The two top county officials who served in the interim between Clark and Stein—Dennis Buchanan and Gladys McCoy—both governed more traditionally than either Clark or Stein.

Stein liked to search out "best practices" to tackle a problem, an abstract methodology that impressed *Governing Magazine*. The team-based management practices that Stein utilized were based on the "Deming" or "Total Quality Management (TQM)" approaches popular in the private sector nationwide at the time. Some county insiders, while admitting they were well intentioned, viewed these techniques as time-consuming processes that talked every problem to death. Even so, the implementation of "quality management techniques in government" resulted in Multnomah County receiving the Oregon Quality Award in 1999 after a year-long assessment process. Stein was also hailed as "an innovative government leader" in the book *You Won—Now What? How Americans Can Make Democracy Work from City Hall to the White House*.[17]

County employees liked Stein's collaborative approach. Her RESULTS program used employee surveys and meetings with workers and employee unions to get new ideas and feedback about management proposals. After Stein had left office, the October 3, 2003, *Northwest Labor Press* said employees felt they were listened to under Stein.[18]

Stein's tenure also saw two bitterly contested private-property rights cases arise in the Columbia Gorge National Scenic Area that had been created by Congress in 1986. One case began in 1996, when Washington State residents Brian and Jody Bea applied to Skamania County for permission to build a home on a bluff above the Columbia River. It was to be a $300,000 "dream house" of 4,000 square feet, located across the river from Multnomah Falls. The land Brian Bea's great-grandfather had homesteaded was now within the federal scenic area. Skamania County followed federal guidelines in approving the Beas' 1997 building permit and specified thirty-three conditions to be met. However, the county neglected to monitor compliance adequately when construction began later that year.

Controversy sparked almost immediately. Critics said the house would be too visible and would ruin scenic vistas. The Columbia River Gorge Commission ruled that the Beas' 35-foot-high house was too high and too close to the bluff. The commissioners ordered the building moved back 200 feet. In July 1998, the commission ruled that Skamania County's approval violated the 1986 Columbia River Gorge National Scenic Area Act. Construction was stopped completely.[19]

The Beas challenged the Gorge Commission decision in court with the help of Pacific Legal Foundation, a nonprofit group that champions private property rights. On June 28, 2001, the Washington Supreme Court ruled unanimously that the Gorge Commission had overstepped its authority in shutting down the project. Construction on the Beas' house could resume.[20]

As finally constructed, the overall building height was reduced by lifting the top floor of the house with heavy equipment, removing the bottom story, and resetting the top floor on the same foundation. The Beas also were required to plant screening vegetation so the house would be hidden from the Oregon side of the river.[21]

While the Bea case was under consideration, Friends of the Columbia Gorge also opposed a land-use permit granted by Multnomah County to the View Point Inn, a nationally known former roadhouse 22 miles east of Portland on the Historic Columbia River Highway—an impressive structure with a massive river-rock fireplace, an elegant dining room, and glass French doors that provided dramatic views of the Columbia Gorge. [22]

At the time the National Scenic Area Act was passed in 1986, the View Point Inn was a private residence. (With the completion of I-84 in 1956, vehicle

Multnomah Falls pictured on the cover of the 1961 edition of the Multnomah County Handbook. *County citizens were justifiably proud that the westernmost portion of the incomparable Columbia River Gorge lay within its boundaries. After Congress passed the Columbia River Gorge National Scenic Area Act of 1986, controversies arose over private versus public property rights.* (Multnomah County Archives)

traffic had shifted to the freeway so dramatically that roadhouses along the old highway went out of business.[23]) The Scenic Act management plan stipulated that no new commercial use of property would be allowed within the Act's boundaries.

In 1997, an entrepreneur named Geoff Thompson purchased the View Point Inn property for $650,000 and applied for a Multnomah County permit to open a vocational school there for the mentally disabled. Thompson planned to earn enough money to support the Portland group home he was operating for physically and mentally disabled adults, including his 36-year-old brother, Matt. In a letter attached to Thompson's application for a conditional-use permit, he said, "We plan to reopen the restaurant on weekends to serve breakfast and lunch and offer two suites for overnight weekend guests." A county hearings officer issued a permit to Thompson and his business partner, Stephen Perkins, in October 1997.[24]

Before the permit was finalized, however, Thompson and Perkins started holding concerts at the Inn and staying open late at night. Neighbors complained that the partners were not abiding by permit restrictions. Multnomah County issued several warning letters and notices of violation, as opponents of the Inn cited excessive noise, increased traffic and inadequate parking.

At one point, relations between County Chair Bev Stein and the entre-preneurs deteriorated so badly that a deputy sheriff started to accompany Thompson when he appeared at county offices. Thompson's "continued verbal abuse, use of profanity, displays of anger and 'physical and verbal' threats" did not sit well with Stein. In July 1999, Circuit Court Judge Jean Maurer issued a preliminary injunction to stop Thompson from operating the View Point Inn as a restaurant and site for weddings and special occasions. The Inn's business permit was revoked and all operations closed.[25]

In November 2005, the Columbia River Gorge Commission changed its po-sition concerning commercial enterprises in the Scenic Area. The commissioners decided that too many historic buildings were deteriorating and that allowing commercial uses would give owners the revenue needed to preserve them.[26]

Four years after leaving Oregon for California, Thompson returned and launched a renewed effort to operate the View Point Inn as a commercial en-terprise. This time, he conducted himself more tactfully. In November 2006, after years of hearings and negotiations, Thompson and his new partner, Angelo Simione, received a new conditional-use permit. The View Point Inn reopened as a 125-guest restaurant and location for weddings and concerts in May 2007.[27] In July 2011, the historic Inn was ravaged by fire that destroyed most of its roof and caused damage to the attic and all three floors. Whether or not the View Point Inn will ever be rebuilt was still an open question in early 2012.[28]

The tightening noose of tax limitations engendered by Oregon Measures 5, 47, and 50 (see Appendix B) prompted Stein and Mayor Katz to revive the possibil-ity of consolidating city and county governments. An eleven-member citizens' "threshold" study group undertook a year-long study, aided by paid consultants and city staff, and issued its conclusions in December 1998. Seven of the eleven task force members favored some kind of future merger or restructuring of city and county governments while four members concluded that no further study or action was warranted.[29] The majority called for convening a "City/County Consolidation Charter Review Committee." This suggestion so alarmed east county officials that they immediately began looking at possible ways to secede from Multnomah County.[30]

East Multnomah County officials first proposed joining Clackamas County, with its more rural population, which they saw as a better fit than a county dominated by the City of Portland. (Nearly 80 percent of Multnomah County's 636,000 residents at the time lived in Portland, while 12 percent lived in east county's largest city, Gresham.) Gresham Mayor Gussie McRobert argued that east county citizens would get better service at a lower price from Clackamas County, citing the unfunded liability in Portland's police and fire pension fund as a major stumbling block to Portland-Multnomah consolidation.[31] At the same time, some Portlanders thought that burgeoning Washington County, with its high-tech industries, would represent a more logical community of interest for Portland than east Multnomah County.[32]

Opposition to the task force's conclusion was so intense that city and county officials backpedaled from the idea of forming a commission shortly after release of the threshold report.[33] This did not satisfy east county officials, who successfully lobbied the state legislature to place a statewide measure on the November 2000 ballot to permit the formation of new counties. The measure failed, but east county citizens had made their point.

Another, albeit indirect, impact of Measure 5 was the county's decision in 1993 to stop funding the Multnomah County Fair. Attendance had been declining since the fair's move to the Expo Center in north Portland in 1970. The decline was probably accelerated by the Expo's more isolated location, but it also reflected the continued decline of agriculture in the metropolitan area. After reaching a high of 170,000 visitors at the old Gresham location, annual attendance had fallen to 35,000. The heyday of the Multnomah County Fairs of the 1950s and 1960s was over. A nonprofit group called Friends of the Fair assumed sponsorship and management of the event after the county commissioners pulled the plug on funding.[34]

From 1997 through 2003, a skeleton Multnomah County Fair was held at Oaks Amusement Park on the Willamette River in southeast Portland. In 2004 and 2005, the Portland Meadows race track hosted the fair, but hot sun and the lack of trees further eroded attendance. The fair then returned to Oaks Park. "True believers make sure the fair goes on," said a May 24, 2007, *Oregonian* headline. The 103rd county fair was held at Oaks Park on Memorial Day weekend 2009, and featured live duck racing and a guitar-playing competition.[35] Today it is difficult to picture the sights and sounds of a rousing country fair where a central Gresham mall, Gresham branch library, and East Hill Foursquare Church are located. The former county fair site is adjacent to a MAX (Metropolitan Area Express) light rail line that runs from downtown Gresham through downtown Portland and westward to downtown Hillsboro.[36]

As for the Expo buildings, Multnomah County relinquished ownership and management of the facility and its appurtenant land in 1996 to Metro, the regional government created by tri-county voters eighteen years earlier.[37] Today, it is the northern terminus of the MAX Yellow Line. Expo hosts over a hundred events a year, attracts more than 500,000 attendees annually, and boasts parking for 2,500 vehicles.[38]

Despite dizzying changes in taxing rules, county voters in May 1996 approved ballot measures that would pay for a sweeping renovation of the county library system as well as for building a major new jail plus enough funding to operate that jail for three years. Newspaper journalists took to calling it the ballot of "books and crooks."[39] Both books and crooks were approved—an operating levy for the library, $29 million in library renovation and electronics, $58 million in jail construction bonds, and a companion levy to the jail bond measure covering three years of operating money.

The "books" part of the "books and crooks" proposals on the ballot produced satisfying results. The biggest chunk of the library levy—approximately $24 million—was devoted to a massive overhaul of the A.E. Doyle-designed Central Library on S.W. Tenth Avenue. While remaining faithful to Doyle's careful design on the outside and in the public spaces, the project "hid" two stories of new administrative offices within the building's original envelope. The money also provided for dozens of computers to provide library patrons with access to the Internet, at Central as well as all the branch libraries. The computers were an instant hit.

While the downtown library project went smoothly (although it took longer than originally planned), the county hit obstacles in building a new Southwest branch library in Hillsdale. After a controversial siting process, the county decided to tear down the former Hillsdale library and build on the same site. Then construction problems forced the county to change contractors in mid-project; in the end, the Hillsdale library was not completed until March 2004—and ran far over budget. Despite those problems, the new library, with its unusual design featuring tree-like steel columns supporting the roof, proved popular with southwest Portland library patrons. The 1996 library measure also paid for new branches in Parkrose and northwest Portland, for replacement library buildings in Hollywood, Hillsdale, and Woodstock, and for substantial renovations to a dozen others. According to the *Oregonian's* architecture critic, it was "the widest roll-out of civic architecture since the creation of Portland's original library system in the 1910s."[40]

The jail measure ended up creating a nightmare for the county board. The goal of the 1996 jail construction measure was to build a 525-bed jail, to be called Wapato, which would take pressure off other county jails and provide more

Modern, sleek—and empty. The Wapato Jail, approved by voters in 1996, wasn't completed until 2004 as a result of land-use hearings and construction delays. And by then the county lacked funds to operate it. Nearly eight years later, the new building remained vacant and was a continuing embarrassment to county government. (Multnomah County Sheriff's Office)

opportunities for rehabilitation—primarily treatment for convicted drug offenders. Delays in winning land-use approval put off the start of construction until 2001, and building problems delayed completion until 2004, by which point the jail operations levy had expired and the county had no money with which to staff the newly finished jail.

In 1999, the county tried to place a Wapato Jail operating levy on the 2000 ballot, but was blocked by Portland, which refused to sign off on the measure. The city cited an agreement by the two governments shortly after passage of Measure 5 that neither jurisdiction would encroach on the other's historical share of the property taxes allowed by Measure 5, in order to avoid reducing the shares of other local government units. County Chair Beverly Stein and budget manager Dave Warren argued that the property tax system had undergone fundamental changes with the passage of Measure 50 and that their earlier agreement should no longer hold sway, but the city council relied on city finance director Tim Grewe's advice and declined to support the county's proposed public safety levy.[41] No jail operating levy appeared on the ballot.

Chief Financial Officer Boyer warned commissioners in November 2004 that there was little hope that the county could operate the 525-bed Wapato Jail, which was standing empty, and also continue to fund social services, the sheriff's office, and maintain state-mandated programs at anywhere near their current levels without a new source of revenue.[42]

Whether or not Measures 5, 47, and 50 were largely to blame for the unopened Wapato Jail is a complicated matter.[43] The limitations imposed by Measure 5 were undoubtedly a major contributing factor. Measure 50, which was passed in 1996, six years after Measure 5, reduced annual increases in operating revenues from an automatic 6 percent to a variable amount based on

3 percent plus new construction and maintained Measure 47's double majority standard.[44]

But a variety of reasons contributed to the county commissioners' inability to find the estimated $14 million per year needed to run Wapato Jail after the operating levy expired without ever being collected. Boyer listed these reasons in analyses presented to the board: [45]

- Required county contributions to PERS (Public Employee Retirement System) increased by $12 million per year between 1999 and 2004.

- Business income taxes decreased by $10 million per year during the same period due to economic slowdowns.

- Motor vehicle taxes and general fund interest earnings together decreased by $4 million per year.

- State funding for state mandates was reduced by millions of dollars.

- "Very optimistic timelines" for jail construction were not met because of land-use appeals and other legal requirements.[46]

An *Oregonian* article of April 2005 implied that Measure 50 was a primary reason that Wapato Jail remained unopened because all county levies had to be folded into a single tax rate. Regarding Wapato Jail construction, the *Oregonian* article says, "County officials could have dropped the plan then [after Measure 50 passed in May 1997]. But they went ahead with locating the jail . . . Paying to run the jail was a far-off concern."[47] According to Dave Boyer, finance director at the time, the county had already sold the general obligation bonds for building the jail when Measure 50 passed. The May 1996 bond measure included $12 million in deferred maintenance and equipment that would have been disallowed had the bonds not been sold before November 1996. That $12 million was used for other public safety needs.[48]

As of 2012, officials were still searching for a solution that would allow Wapato to open. Meanwhile, the county continued to pay $315,000 a year for heat, light, and maintenance of a vacant jail.[49]

Stein's tenure also brought to a conclusion another bricks-and-mortar issue: finding a new home for county government. Just as Don Clark had predicted in the mid-1970s, expansion of the state-run court system gradually took over virtually all the space in the eight-story Multnomah County Courthouse, which

Multnomah County's administrative offices moved out of the Multnomah County Courthouse in 2000 and into the Multnomah Building in southeast Portland. The red brick structure formerly housed administrative offices of a failed savings and loan association. (Jewel Lansing)

dated back to 1914. In the early 1980s, the county commissioners and their staffs relocated their offices temporarily to the top two floors of the new Portland Building (located between the courthouse and city hall) but continued to hold formal commission meetings in the courthouse sixth-floor board room while staff investigated options for a new permanent home.

The search ended in 1999 with the purchase of a former bank building on the east side of the Willamette River near the Hawthorne Bridge. The most innovative and controversial aspect of the renovated building was its roof, where a small windmill and twirling tree were to be installed, an environmentally friendly art project commissioned by the regional arts council. Before the windmill was built, however, so much opposition surfaced that the project was dropped.[50]

The county commissioners moved to the newly remodeled Multnomah County Building at 501 S.E. Hawthorne Boulevard in October 2000.[51] An ecoroof installed in July 2003 (after it was discovered that the existing roof leaked) met with little opposition. Plants rooted in soil were planted over a waterproof membrane to absorb rain and reduce the amount of storm water pouring into Portland's overloaded sewer system. The west-facing ecoroof was made accessible to the public from the fifth floor of the building during county business hours. In addition to providing year-round greenery, the roof incorporated a seating area and interpretive panels.[52]

The year before Stein left the county, she presided over the county's second all-woman board, again in relative harmony. Stein was joined by holdover Sharron Kelley, along with new commissioners Lisa Naito, Diane Linn, and Serena Cruz. Also, for the second time in county history, a woman served

Multnomah County's second all-woman board of commissioners held office near the end of Chair Bev Stein's second term. from left: Lisa Naito, Diane Linn, Stein, Sharron Kelley, and Serena Cruz. This was the last official board photograph taken in the Multnomah County Courthouse, shortly before the move to the Multnomah Building. (Multnomah County website)

concurrently as the elected auditor. Suzanne Flynn held that office from 1999 to 2006, before being elected Metro auditor.

Chair Beverly Stein was midway through her second term in early 2001 when the opportunity arose to seek the office of Oregon governor. She would not be able to run for reelection as county chair, because the county home rule charter limited her to two full terms, so she decided to take the statewide plunge.

The *Oregonian* gave Stein a warm send-off. Summarizing her contributions as the top county official, the editorial said: "Focusing on the details and the flow charts, and on the county's ties with other levels of government, Stein can fairly claim to have given county taxpayers more for their money—and more for their children. Wherever she goes next, Multnomah County residents can be glad Bev Stein was here."[53] Even so, some county observers were critical of her decision to leave the county with nine and a half months still left in her term and no solution in sight for how to open Wapato Jail (although she would not be the only one flummoxed by that problem). Stein later declared her eight years as chair of the Multnomah County Board and as the county's chief executive officer as the "best job she ever had."[54]

Stein finished third in the 2002 Democratic gubernatorial primary, behind Ted Kulongoski and Jim Hill; Kulongoski, an unsuccessful candidate for the office twenty years before, went on to win the general election.[55] Like Frank Shull, Mel Gordon, Jewel Lansing, and Don Clark before her, Stein found that Multnomah County government was no reliable stepping stone to higher office. Stein then joined Public Strategies Group, a national consulting firm headquartered in St. Paul, Minnesota, while continuing to maintain Portland as her home base.[56]

In accordance with county charter provisions, Stein's executive, Bill Farver, served as interim county chair for three months until an election could be held.

20

FROM PIONEERING WOMEN TO "MEAN GIRLS," PLUS A CONTROVERSIAL SHERIFF

(2001–2009)

Money took a back seat to pettiness and minor scandals in Multnomah County government during the first decade of the twenty-first century. Not that the money troubles got any easier. After more a decade there was still no money to open Wapato Jail. It was simply that financial troubles were less prominent in the news than personality issues involving the county's two most high-profile elected officials, Chair Diane Linn and Sheriff Bernie Giusto. Despite putting up strong resistance, Giusto ended up resigning before the end of his electoral term, while Linn, to virtually no one's surprise, saw her elective career end within seconds of the polls closing on primary election night in 2006.

At the start of the decade, no one would have predicted such a downfall for either of them. Linn, who had been elected as a commissioner in 1998, stepped up in 2001 to run for the vacancy created by Bev Stein's resignation as county chair. In its endorsement of her candidacy, the *Oregonian* praised Linn's style of leadership as "tactful, shrewd, balanced." Her credits included her accomplishments as a commissioner in helping redesign the county's mental health system, leading efforts to create more affordable housing, working on library renovation projects, and building stronger partnerships with school districts.[1] "For Linn," said the *Portland Tribune*, "the job is about working with all groups and getting things done, not fighting. She would play the insider, the deal maker. She comes off cool, smart, and well schooled on the issues."[2]

Linn became the third successive woman to hold the county chair job when she defeated Jo Ann Bowman, a former member of Stein's staff. The day after the May 2001 ballots were counted, an *Oregonian* article attributed Linn's victory to the difference in leadership styles of the two candidates. Linn had a reputation "for working cooperatively with others to find compromise and common ground in dealing with issues," while her opponent had a more aggressive style, which she touted during the campaign. Linn outspent her opponent three-to-one, raising $121,000 to win 54 percent of the vote; Bowman raised $40,000.[3]

At the same election, newcomer Maria Rojo de Steffey was elected to complete Linn's unexpired commissioner term. By winning more than 50 percent of the votes tallied, both Steffey and Linn avoided a fall run-off.[4] Cruz and Rojo de Steffey were the first Latinas elected to Multnomah County office.

The board was comprised of four women and one man from 2001 through 2006: Chair Diane Linn; commissioners Lisa Naito and Serena Cruz, elected 1998; commissioner Lonnie Roberts, elected 2000; and commissioner Maria Rojo de Steffey, elected 2001.

As the former director of Portland's Office of Neighborhood Involvement, executive director of a nonprofit organization, and interim manager for Paragon Cable, Linn promised visibility and accountability.[5] She had been elected to represent her southeast/southwest county commission district in 1998, so had two years of experience serving on the board. During her first year as chair, she was widely viewed as charismatic, articulate, photogenic, and a rising star in the Democratic Party, although county elective offices were now nonpartisan.

Meanwhile, nine months before the May 2002 primary, Sheriff Dan Noelle announced that he would not seek reelection, giving potential candidates ample time to plan their campaigns. With typically droll humor, Noelle declared himself an "elder statesman" rather than a "lame duck."[6] He had received high marks for his performance in the job. Two months after announcing his retirement, Noelle had participated in the ground-breaking ceremony for the new Wapato Corrections Facility, slated to open in 2004—the same unopened jail that two *Oregonian* reporters would call "a monument to government waste and dysfunction" in 2008.[7]

The top contenders to replace Sheriff Noelle were a former Gresham police chief, Bernie Giusto, and an African-American sheriff's deputy, Vera Pool. Giusto proved so popular that he garnered 63 percent of the vote—a landslide victory that allowed him to bypass a fall run-off. Vera Pool received 25 percent of the May vote; Kirby Bouillard, 12 percent.[8] Giusto's prior credentials included twenty-eight years in law enforcement, including a stint working for the Oregon State Police on assignment to Governor Neil Goldschmidt's security detail. While his extensive background obviously impressed county voters, his assignment with Goldschmidt would come back to haunt him. Like Linn, Giusto cruised to a second term at the polls before his career started to unravel.

The smiles on the faces of the board members serving with Chair Diane Linn did not survive to the end of her tenure in 2006. from left: Maria Rojo de Steffey, Lisa Naito, Linn, Lonnie Roberts, and Serena Cruz. (Multnomah County website)

Despite her easy win in 2002, trouble was already brewing for Linn in the county's inner circles. Linn appointed John Ball as her chief operating officer and made him an unelected de facto county manager. In mid-2003, the *Northwest Labor Press* reported widespread disgruntlement among county employees because Linn and Ball were "bent on refashioning" the county "to mimic a private sector corporation with a top-down management style and top salaries for managers," which did not please employees.[9] Linn was said to be building an especially close relationship with the city's most powerful business groups via her "boyfriend and ex-chief of staff," John Rakowitz.[10]

Fall 2003 brought public awareness that Linn's honeymoon with fellow commissioners and the media was deteriorating. A two-month public squabble over the salary of the new library director, Molly Raphael, surfaced when board members Naito, Cruz, and Roberts objected to the $138,000 salary Linn had promised, a salary (27 percent more than her predecessor's) that would make Raphael the county's highest-paid employee. The three dissenting board members blocked the promised salary by authorizing only $120,000, $18,000 less than the figure specified in the contract Raphael had signed. "The two month dispute shows a breakdown in Linn's leadership," declared an *Oregonian* editorial, "and reflects very poorly" on the attempt of three commissioners to "micromanage the chairwoman's job." The "tortured solution" that was finally found was to transfer $18,000 from the county's risk management fund to avoid a greater liability for failing to live up to the terms of a contract. Linn's letter to Raphael had neglected to state that her appointment was contingent on the board's approval.[11]

A second public humiliation for Linn came in January 2004, after a heavy winter snowstorm hit the Portland metropolitan area. Linn promised full pay to all Multnomah County employees, whether or not they showed up for work. For those who successfully braved the elements, she offered a day of administrative leave with pay. The resulting public outrage over both these offers was a setback for Linn. Equally embarrassingly, she was forced to rescind the offer of a day's paid leave after it was pointed out that a recently approved ordinance took employee compensation matters out of her hands. That ordinance was itself a direct result of Linn's decision to "settle" a potential breach of contract claim from Raphael by paying her $18,000 per year out of the risk management fund.[12]

The third and most clamorous uproar over Linn's actions involved a question of national scope and interest: same-sex marriage. Only two months after the snowstorm debacle, the four women commissioners—Diane Linn, Lisa Naito, Serena Cruz, and Maria Rojo de Steffey—held a press conference to announce that Multnomah County would henceforth issue marriage licenses to same-sex couples. A county attorney's opinion required them to do so, they said; failure to provide the same rights to same-sex citizens that were bestowed on heterosexual couples would be a violation of the Oregon Constitution.

No Multnomah County issue received more media attention than this marriage license brouhaha. The basic issue of whether same-sex individuals be permitted to marry was controversial enough in itself, but just as controversial was the secretive way in which Linn and her three female colleagues announced their decision without any advance discussion with the public. Furthermore, they did not notify their colleague, Commissioner Lonnie Roberts, or Oregon

cartoon by Jack Ohman, from the Oregonian, *January 17, 2004.*

DIANE LINN STRUGGLES VALIANTLY TO GET INTO WORK DESPITE THE STORM...

Governor Ted Kulongoski about the new policy in advance, a failure that would later cause further falling-out and finger pointing. (The decision and its timing were not well-kept secrets, however, according to then-County Attorney Agnes Sowle. "The emergency management office and sheriff's office were doing crowd control planning for several days prior to the announcement," Sowle said. "The press had word of it at least a day prior to the announcement.")[13]

"Ties that bind and divide," proclaimed a banner headline in the March 4, 2004, *Oregonian*. "Multnomah County recognizes gay marriage amid joy, protest," said a subhead. Newspapers and television stations ran photographs of jubilant couples lined up around the courthouse block waiting their turn to obtain marriage licenses.

Three days later, an *Oregonian* editorial said of Linn: "Politically tone deaf and indifferent to process, the county chair stumbles anew, flouting public trust on same-sex marriage."[14]

Oregonian columnist Steve Duin put it this way: "So much for open government. So much for faith in the people. On Wednesday morning, Chairwoman Diane Linn and three members of Multnomah County's Board of Commissioners—Serena Cruz, Lisa Naito and Maria Rojo de Steffey—finally stepped out from behind closed doors and went public with a shameless crusade designed to make a mockery of open-meetings law and the democratic process."[15]

The surreptitious manner in which Linn and her fellow commissioners dealt with the public's business shocked citizens who were otherwise supportive of gay rights. "The public's business should be done in public" was a time-honored dictum. However, County Attorney Agnes Sowle said she was not aware of any violation of state public meetings law during the process.[16] Any two members of the commission could meet privately, anywhere, anytime. The addition of a third board member would require public notice under the open meetings laws.

A month later, the Oregon Supreme Court ordered Multnomah County to stop issuing such licenses while the court heard arguments on the issue. A year later, the justices ruled that single-sex couples could not legally be married in Oregon. The 3,000 gay and lesbian couples who purchased marriage licenses from Multnomah County now learned that those licenses were invalid. The county had no power to issue such licenses, the court said; that power was vested in the Oregon legislature.[17]

A *Portland Tribune* front-page story about Linn in late March 2003 said, "Wherever county chief Diane Linn goes, controversy follows." A *Tribune* reporter tagged along with Linn for a full day, observing her grinding beans for

Cartoon of Chair
Diane Linn and three
other commissioners
by Jack Ohman, from
the Oregonian, May
10, 2004.

her morning coffee, giving daughter Tess and her fiancé's daughter Ness a ride
to Cleveland High School, attending several county business meetings, making
a trip to the orthodontist for Tess, and ending her day at home with a Papa
Murphy's pizza to be shared with fiancé John Rakowitz and their two daughters.
The *Tribune* article noted that Linn had considered running for Portland mayor,
but that her political prospects now appeared changed. Linn told the reporter
she was not worried about her future. "This is my career," she said. "What you
strive for makes you stronger."[18]

Next, Linn apologized to the public for the mistakes she had made during her tenure as county chief, mistakes that were fueling a potential recall.
Unfortunately, the way in which Linn apologized for how the gay marriage
licenses issue had been handled again put her at odds with her board colleagues. Linn offended Lisa Naito, Serena Cruz, and Maria Rojo de Steffey
by neglecting to consult with them regarding the timing and content of her
apology.[19]

Adding to Linn's problems was the empty Wapato Jail: it had been completed that same year, but there was no money in the county coffers to pay for
staffing it. So the jail sat vacant, racking up an annual bill of $315,000 to cover
the cost of heat, light, and building maintenance,[20] as various media sources
periodically pointed out to the public.

In May 2003, county voters approved a three-year interim income tax as
an emergency measure to keep schools and social services from suffering additional cuts. Opponents feared that once the tax had been imposed, it would

never disappear. However, county commissioners kept their word and let the tax expire as promised. The ITAX raised approximately $90 million each year for county schools and $32 million annually for Multnomah County public safety, health, mental health, and senior services programs.[21] The income tax was relatively easy to collect; taxpayers simply filled out a one-page form using income figures derived from their state and federal tax returns. But it was never popular and did little to bolster Linn's standing with the public.

Linn's internal administration and reorganizations were not faring well, either. She pushed for a management system called Shared Services that was popular in the corporate world to bring control of human services, payroll, purchasing and other internal functions under one roof. When she could not get the four commission votes she needed to create the Department of Shared Services, she made Shared Services a division of an existing department. An April 2004 feature in the *Oregonian* noted that the huge savings Linn promised never materialized, so she "pulled the plug" after two years.[22] To round out a difficult year, *Willamette Week* awarded its "Rogue of the Year" title to Linn in late December 2004 for "her ability to screw up frequently, creatively and in ways that extend far beyond her considerable reach."[23]

Linn's tenure at Multnomah County now took on the derisive title of *Diane Linn versus "the Mean Girls"* after a popular 2004 teen-oriented movie. The phrase referred to a clique of three teenage girls who ostracize a "wide-eyed heroine" in their "reign over their high school." Chair Linn first used the moniker in half-jest to refer to the three women commissioners who served with her—Serena Cruz, Maria Rojo de Steffey, and Lisa Naito. Subsequently, Rojo de Steffey ordered a vanity auto license plate MNGIRL to proclaim her newfound fame, but removed it in the wake of public criticism. Linn later said she regretted using the phrase and apologized to the commissioners, "even as she and her staff maintained its descriptive accuracy."[24]

Linn's troubles continued to escalate. She was criticized for allegedly asking a staff member to doctor her scheduling calendar after a public records request was made for it. Equally damaging was the resignation of Chief Financial Officer Dave Boyer, who left the county in June 2006, a year and a half before his planned retirement date, after twenty-seven years of county employ. Allegedly, his resignation was accelerated because he was asked by Linn's staff to misrepresent financial data to the board and community (which Linn denied), and because he witnessed unequal disciplinary treatment of county managers.[25]

Linn's failure to involve the other four commissioners, to make them feel that they were sharing at least part of her power, contributed to her downfall as leader. Linn supporters said she relied too heavily on staff and wasn't getting good advice. Linn had abandoned a tradition that had begun early in county home-rule days of assigning each board member a liaison role in monitoring part of the county's domain. Under that informal system, board members were expected to become familiar with budgets and operations in the areas they were assigned. Linn and her staff made no such assignments, preferring to keep a tight rein over county operations. The question once again arose: Should taxpayers continue to pay five commissioners when only one, the county chair, had a full-time job?

On the 150th anniversary of the creation of Multnomah County—December 22, 2004—commissioners apparently found no cause for celebration or observance. Unlike the City of Portland's sesquicentennial three years earlier, during which Mayor Vera Katz had dedicated an esplanade along the east bank of the Willamette River and invited the public to a 150th birthday bash at city hall, the county's sesquicentennial elicited no cheers from anyone. The date came and went without notice. *Oregonian* reporter Arthur Gregg Sulzberger later declared that the anniversary came during "an era best known for bickering, controversial policies, and a lousy work ethic."[26]

Despite Linn's difficulties, well-known candidates failed to step forward to challenge her reelection bid in 2006. Was the county chair's job so difficult nobody wanted it? The field was left to a political novice, Ted Wheeler, who was born into a wealthy Portland family, held degrees from upscale universities such as Stanford, Columbia, and Harvard, and had run a wealth management firm founded by his brother before it was sold in 2000. Wheeler was a self-employed small-business consultant when he decided to take on Linn. He started his campaign well in advance, the old-fashioned way. He spent months going to neighborhood meetings and introducing himself. As the news media turned venomously against Linn, Wheeler's reception at meetings was usually warm.

In a campaign article headed, "Why You Should Give a Damn," *Willamette Week* said, "Linn's post is arguably the most powerful in the metro area. She has control over everything from keeping the meth-heads who want to break into your car in jail to making sure the bridges over the Willamette can carry a 10-ton truck. She oversees a budget of $1.2 billion . . ." Noting that no elected chair of Multnomah County had ever lost a reelection campaign, the newspaper pointed

to Linn's most famous blunders. "Linn may well be the most vexed elected official in recent memory. Gay marriage. Library-director salaries. Snow days for
county employees. This is a woman whose good intentions are exceeded only by
a political tone-deafness."[27]

"The current state of dysfunction among Multnomah County commissioners needs to be addressed," said the *Portland Tribune* in its endorsement of
Wheeler. The *Oregonian* endorsement of Linn's opponent said, "Under Linn,
there's no question that Multnomah County has stumbled badly and tumbled in
public esteem."[28]

Commission candidate Jeff Cogen put it bluntly: "Bickering has undermined
people's faith in government . . . It's been clear to me over the last couple of years
that the [Multnomah County] government has really lost its credibility . . . I'm
just stating, frankly, what is the common understanding."[29]

Newspaper articles throughout the campaign itemized the same Linn blunders again and again. The vacant Wapato Jail was mentioned frequently, although it was not a problem of her making.[30] The positive changes Linn made in
restructuring services to the mentally ill and her strong support for libraries and
Schools Uniting Neighborhoods (SUN) were far overshadowed by poor public
relations.

In addition to her public problems, Linn dealt with complications in her personal life throughout her tenure as county chair. She and former State Senator
Dick Springer were divorced. Her father was gravely ill. She became engaged
to a key member of her office staff, who later went to work for the Portland
Business Alliance.[31]

The election itself was a rout. When television newscasts came at 8 p.m. on
election night, ballots collected earlier in the day had been counted and news
anchors announced Linn's defeat just seconds after 8 p.m.[32] Linn tallied a mere
23 percent of the vote, defeated by a more than three-to-one ratio by Wheeler.[33]
Given that Wheeler won well over 50 percent of all votes cast, the election
for county chair was decided in the May primary, eliminating the need for a
November general election race. Linn had entered the race against the advice
of supporters and after her own poll results showed only 20 percent support
from probable voters.[34] Even Linn's previously loyal labor unions turned their
backs on her. AFSCME Local 88 said they switched to Wheeler because he made
commonsense decisions after hearing every view. "We represent the people who
know Linn best," said a Local 88 official. "Multnomah County can't afford four
more years of closed-door decision-making."[35]

In the twenty years between the first all-woman board of 1986 and Linn's final year on the board, relationships between the female colleagues deteriorated dramatically. Because of infighting and bad press, four political careers that once were promising (those of Linn, Naito, Cruz, and Rojo de Steffey) were now derailed, perhaps permanently.[36] Talk of recall movements simmered. [37] In late December 2006, *Willamette Week* awarded the three women commissioners its "Rogues of the Week" award for their "embarrassing display of Roguish hypocrisy" in embracing Linn at her final board meeting rather than making up to her earlier, and for "continuing the petty battles long after Linn lost her election."[38]

By way of contrast, the 1986 all-woman board chaired by Gladys McCoy, nicknamed the "Sob Sisters" by its detractors and "County Mothers" by its supporters, had been perceived positively,[39] as had the year 2000 all-woman board under Chair Bev Stein.

A question frequently asked by former supporters of the three women commissioners who served with Linn was, "Who was most at fault? Was it Linn or her detractors?" District Attorney Michael Schrunk may have put it best: "They're all good people, but together they're a toxic mix."[40]

Former county commissioner Pauline Anderson looked at it a different way when she spoke at a 2008 luncheon observing Women's Equality Day:

> There has been at Multnomah County a plethora of women candidates, undoubtedly because the salary was for a long time so low that men were not as interested. At one time Multnomah County could boast a full complement of women commissioners and a fine, collaborative, effective bunch it was. We were the first county in the nation to enjoy the services of five women commissioners. The latest group of women commissioners proved less collaborative. But I will maintain that until women are granted the same right to be mean that men enjoy—because they are human, not because they are women—we do not have equality.[41]

Meanwhile, difficulties mounted for Sheriff Bernie Giusto. During his first term, criticism arose over Giusto's use of a county vehicle for personal purposes. In 2004, Giusto's name gained negative attention after *Willamette Week* published an article describing former Mayor Neil Goldschmidt's sexual abuse of an underage girl in the 1970s. As an Oregon State police officer, Giusto had served as a driver and bodyguard while Goldschmidt was governor. The question during Giusto's 2006 reelection campaign was what Giusto knew, if

Sheriff Bernie Giusto (2003-8) was elected by wide margins twice before he was pressured into resigning in 2008 after his management of the sheriff's office and personal use of a county vehicle came under heavy criticism. A state agency investigating Governor Neil Goldschmidt concluded that Giusto lied in the early 1990s when he denied having an affair with Goldschmidt's wife while serving as Goldschmidt's driver. (Multnomah County Sheriff's Office)

anything, about the abuse case in the 1990s. In spite of doubts about such questions, Giusto again avoided a run-off and was reelected sheriff in May with 61 percent of the vote.[42]

But the Goldschmidt case wouldn't die. Years later, an Oregon Department of Public Safety Standards and Training Committee investigating Goldschmidt's admission concluded that Giusto lied in the early 1990s when he denied having an affair with Goldschmidt's wife.[43]

Questions about Giusto's management of the sheriff's office increased during his second term. At the request of Commissioner Lisa Naito, former Sheriff Dan Noelle evaluated Giusto's administration and delivered a stinging indictment. Noelle declared that Giusto could save $5.5 million through tighter controls and better management. (The *Oregonian* had previously compared Giusto to Noelle unfavorably. "The reality is that Giusto has abused his office . . . He shouldn't be in charge of anything. . . . What a contrast with former Sheriff Dan Noelle, who wasn't afraid to antagonize union leaders, punish misconduct or fire deputies—dozens of them—in his time. But then, Noelle was a real sheriff.")[44]

Next, District Attorney Michael Schrunk issued a "scathing" report that said Multnomah County's jails had devolved "into violent and costly near-chaos because the elected officials responsible for overseeing them refused to do their jobs." Problems cited included misclassification of inmates and inadequate supervision.[45]

After the November 2006 election of Ted Wheeler as county chair, Wheeler and his fellow commissioners immediately started wrangling with Giusto over his budget. In May 2007, they declared their intention to seize administrative control of the sheriff's office. By the end of the year, Wheeler warned publicly that he might ask voters to make the sheriff's position appointive. In January, Giusto and Wheeler signed an agreement that gave the county commission power over jail spending and employee discipline for a six-month trial period. But it was another private relationship with a woman that finally ended Giusto's sheriff career. In late June 2008, Giusto announced that he would resign and voluntarily surrender his police certification. He settled a separate case with the state ethics commission by paying a $200 fine and admitting that he violated state ethics laws when he drove a government-owned vehicle to Seattle with his girlfriend two years before.[46]

On July 17, 2008, former Sheriff Bob Skipper was sworn in on an interim basis as the county's thirty-eighth sheriff. At the general election that fall, Skipper won a landslide victory to fill the remainder of Giusto's term.[47]

"Skipper presents a striking contrast with the man he's preparing to replace," an *Oregonian* news story said. "Unlike the gregarious and charismatic Giusto, who enjoyed the public spotlight, Skipper is a quiet, serious leader without a showman's streak." Another *Oregonian* article commented: "Skipper's humble, old-fashioned style is in marked contrast to the swagger and tangled personal life of [Giusto] . . . Nearly fifteen years ago . . . Skipper earned praise for bringing stability, integrity and credibility to an agency currently much in need of all those things."[48]

Fourteen months after he assumed the sheriff's duties, Skipper also had to resign because his law enforcement certification was not renewed by the state's Department of Public Safety Standards and Training within the time period allowed. Skipper was unable to pass certification tests demanded by the state. This was a disappointment to a public that held Skipper in high regard. Lt. Dan Staton, a twenty-year sheriff's deputy, was named interim sheriff until an election could be held,[49] and easily won a four-year term in the May 2010 primary election.

In the same 2010 election, Commissioner Jeff Cogen, who had been elected to the county board in 2006, easily won the job of Multnomah County chair to fill the remainder of Ted Wheeler's term after Wheeler accepted appointment as state treasurer. The incumbent treasurer, Ben Westlund, had died unexpectedly in early 2010.[50]

"Is it time for the sheriff's office to get out of law enforcement?" asked a four-page spread in an *Oregonian* supplement on June 28, 2008. Three decades before, the story said, the sheriff's law enforcement division boasted nearly three hundred officers serving Multnomah County's unincorporated population. "The Multnomah County Sheriff's Office was considered, not just in this region or state, but nationally, one of the finest law enforcement agencies," said King City's Police Chief Chuck Fessler, a former Multnomah County undersheriff, noting that the office was one of the first in the nation to use a community policing model and the first to require that deputies have a four-year college degree.[51]

During the thirty-year period from 1978 through 2008, a marked shift had occurred, leaving few county residents living outside an incorporated city. In those thirty years, the sheriff's division experienced a dramatic shift of focus. In 1978, the number of county residents living in unincorporated Multnomah County was 190,000 out of 560,000 total county population. In 2008, only 14,000 out of 670,000 lived in unincorporated Multnomah County.[52] This shift was largely due to aggressive efforts by Portland and Gresham governments to annex the mid-County area between their boundaries.

As of 2009, 98 percent of county residents lived in Portland, Gresham, Troutdale, Fairview, Wood Village, or Maywood Park. The sheriff's 75-person law enforcement division served the remaining 2 percent who resided in the nearly two-thirds of the county's geographical area of 289 square miles, a sizeable portion of which remained federal forest land.[53]

21
QUO VADIS?
(2010)

There may be no better demonstration of the county's role in balancing human and environmental needs than on Sauvie Island, where Europeans first set foot on what would become known as Multnomah County. Today, just as in 1806 when squawking birds irritated explorer William Clark, thousands of geese make noisy migrations along the Pacific Flyway overhead. Ducks, cranes, swans, and bald eagles also inhabit the 24,000-acre island that is the result of silt from the Willamette River building up over more than a million years.

Humans have made little impact on the northern half of the 24,000 acre island, which since 1946 has been a protected wildlife refuge managed by the State of Oregon (it also happens to lie mostly in Columbia County). Whether the southern half, located only minutes from downtown Portland on U.S. Highway 30, can maintain its rural ambience, its rare ecology, and its agricultural economy in the face of momentous urban pressure is one of the challenges facing Multnomah County in the twenty-first century. It is a peculiar paradox, indeed: Will the county that did so little to prepare east Multnomah County neighborhoods for urban density be able to preserve its last bastion of agriculture?

If the ultimate answer is "no," the turning point can be pinpointed easily. A small sign in the Sauvie Island Grange Hall states, "Our quiet, peaceful country life ended on 12-30-50 when the Sauvie Island Bridge was dedicated."

Before then, the island was a small, tight-knit agricultural enclave— agricultural produce and visitors had to cross the Multnomah Channel by ferry. Until dikes were finished in 1941, annual spring floods laid down the best soil in the state. For decades, the unincorporated island resembled a small town without a commercial center. The few hundred residents operated a volunteer fire department and school board; the grange hall and the school were the heart of rural social life.

Oregon's most populous county has always been the smallest in geographic size. As this outline map of the state's thirty-six county boundaries shows, the 465 square miles occupied by Multnomah County (in black) are dwarfed by the 10,228 square miles of Harney County (shown in gray).

However, the new bridge opened the island and its scenic wonders to nearby Portland. The effects were felt quickly, both from forces on and off the island. The county planning commission established in 1953 zoned the island for two-acre house lots. Ralph Walstrom, the county planning commission chairman in 1959, noted that the island was "a unique geographical feature," and added: "The planning commission feels it has tremendous potential for recreation and fine suburban residential development."[1]

One island property owner wanted more than houses. Frances A. Shields wished to sell 138 acres at the island's southern tip to the Alder Creek Lumber Company, but both the planning commission and the board of commissioners rejected her request.[2] She contended the land was too marshy for houses, and filed suit against the county claiming that the zoning was "unreasonable." In a legal claim that would reverberate through state planning laws decades later, her lawyer also contended that the county's land-use rules amounted to "taking land without due process."[3]

A visiting trial judge in July 1959 upheld the constitutionality of the county's ability to zone land, but ordered that the 138 acres in question be rezoned, since it was not appropriate for housing.[4] County officials decided not to appeal and Shields sold the land to the lumber company, which continues to use it.

By the mid 1970s, the idea of suburban development on the island cooled. In response to new state-wide land-use planning laws that included urban growth boundaries, county commissioners adopted land-use regulations requiring a minimum of 38 acres for home sites on Sauvie Island, instead of just two acres. The public hearings were tense. Years later, Commissioner Dennis Buchanan said, "As I recall, before the law went into effect there was actually a petition brought in by farmers on Sauvie Island subdividing their farms into 50 by 100 foot lots. God knows how many homes were to be included in the subdivisions. People were trying to get in under the wire, so they could exploit the land to its absolute maximum. I don't know how many of them really intended to do it, but they wanted to keep their options open." The dilemma was clear: "If you saved the land for the public, it interfered with somebody else's plans," Buchanan said. "People were blinded by dollar signs and refused to see that with land desecrated, paradise is lost."[5]

By 1997, the island that is approximately the same size as Manhattan Island was home to approximately 1,300 residents living in 450 homes and 200 houseboats or sailboats used as permanent residences. County officials updated an extensive rural land-use plan aimed at protecting agriculture and limiting new dwellings.[6] Residents hoping to preserve their way of life and the sensitive island environment fended off proposed plans for a golf course,[7] a major new marina,[8] and expanded tourist facilities at the historic Bybee-Howell House now operated by Metro.[9] But nothing stanched the flow of visitors.

By the late twentieth century, roughly 1.5 million visitors a year crossed the Sauvie Island Bridge for sunbathing and swimming at sandy Willamette River beaches, bicycling, bird watching, private hunting, visiting pumpkin patches, and buying other farm produce. On fall days at the peak of the island's fruit and vegetable harvest, traffic reached gridlock proportions, sometimes requiring residents and visitors to spend literally hours negotiating the few island roads and the narrow bridge across the channel.

``If you took the ratio of island residents to visitors and applied it to Portland, the city would have to accommodate 400 million visitors a year, all without outside help," said Ron Murray, chief of the island's volunteer fire department, at a public hearing about the island's future. "Our visitors come, clog the roads, use the beaches, and leave without having spent anything, and Multnomah County does nothing for us. That's why some people favor a gate or something."[10]

Oregon voters added to pressures on the island in 2004 when they passed an initiative, Ballot Measure 37, aimed at turning back the clock on Oregon's

This historic Multnomah County seal is still used on formal county documents, while the modern logo shown in Chapter 16 appears on county letterhead and property. (Multnomah County Clerk of the Board)

progressive land-use regulations. Echoing the claim filed by Frances Shields in 1959, the measure said property owners who were denied "use" of their land by zoning decisions made after they had purchased their property could seek recompense from the county for the alleged lost value of their land; alternatively, the county would have to permit development that the newer regulations would prohibit.

By early 2007, Multnomah County had received a hundred claims under the new measure, seeking total recompense of $193.7 million.[11] The public face of the campaign for Measure 37 was Dorothy English, a feisty 91-year old grandmother who had hoped to develop 80 houses on 20 steep acres near Forest Park overlooking Sauvie Island. English was the first person at the Multnomah County claims window when Measure 37 took effect on December 2, 2004, seeking $1.15 million in lost value on property she had purchased in 1953.[12] The county agreed to her loss, but then tried to change its position to allow some development. The courts affirmed the original agreement.[13] English died in 2008, before her estate received payment of $1.15 million in July 2010, as well as another $1.15 million to pay for attorney fees.[14]

Roughly a dozen such claims were filed by Sauvie Island property owners. The county allowed permission for the construction of several new residences rather than pay the claims. By 2012, claims that sought more intense development on more than five hundred acres were still in litigation with owners who hoped to subdivide their properties and sell lots and build a new marina. The county contended that creating new lots did not quality as a "use" of land under Measure 37. In 2007, at the recommendation of the Oregon Legislature, voters passed Measure 49, which reduced the scope of new "uses" allowed under Measure 37, adding another layer to the legal complexities.

Meanwhile, county officials took steps indicating they still intended to enforce land-use regulations on Sauvie Island. In one instance, they barred "permanent" residents from living at a recreational-vehicle park where visitors were supposed to stay no longer than thirty days;[15] in another, they concluded that weddings, birthday celebrations, corporate picnics, and bicycle events put on by an entrepreneurial farmer violated agricultural zoning because they were not related to farming.[16]

Still, there was nothing to keep visitors from flocking to Sauvie Island. Far from following Ron Murray's whimsical suggestion and installing a gate, in 2008 Multnomah County opened a new, stronger Sauvie Island Bridge in place of the old one.[17] The east end of the bridge sits not far from a "sunken village"[18] once inhabited by an indigenous Multnomah tribe untold centuries before Europeans arrived. Like most North American tribes, the Multnomahs had no concept of private ownership of property. Their island was for the use of the tribe, just like the air and the rain, the sun and the moon, the rivers and the fish. The question now is whether private property rights will destroy the essence of the million-year-old natural treasure.

When Multnomah County was founded, commissioners met only once a quarter to build roads and bridges, authorize ferries, and reimburse citizens who cared for persons unable to care for themselves. All county laws were made by the state or territorial legislature. Eleven elected officials conducted county business—three commissioners, an assessor, auditor, coroner, district attorney, school superintendent, sheriff, surveyor, and treasurer.

Today, seven elected officials "run" the county—a county chair, four commissioners, a sheriff, and an auditor. A home rule charter passed in 1966 allows Multnomah County commissioners to pass local laws, although that authority was seriously compromised by anti-government charter changes adopted by voters in May 1982. Some, but not all, of those 1982 amendments have now been repealed (see Appendix C).

During the ten-year period from 2000 to 2010, nearly 10,000 African Americans moved from the city's inner north and northeast neighborhoods to the city's eastern edges, displaced by an influx of white residents in a gentrification process tied to rising property values and rents. The Interstate Avenue Urban Renewal Area brought the Yellow Line light rail tracks to north Portland and brought new development to those neighborhoods. Rising rental rates drove out many minority residents who did not own the homes they lived in. This eastward migration from the inner city of Portland cut off these lower-income minority families from amenities such as sidewalks, grocery stores, parks, and access to public transit.[19]

The county's economic base, once heavily oriented toward shipping and wood products, has shifted to metal fabrication, silicone chip manufacturing, food preparation, and the artistic output of a new "creative class" pursuing careers in literature, film, theater, food, music, and other arts and crafts. The county remains a transportation center for water, rail, road, and air transport.[20]

Much of the county's $1.2 billion county budget comes from state and federal money passed through in the form of social services and health assistance. A good deal of social services work is actually performed by private and nonprofit contractors overseen by the county. "Still," notes an *Oregonian* article, "county government is in charge of everything from running libraries to euthanizing unwanted dogs and cats, to maintaining the Willamette River bridges (sometimes barely), and providing services to the mentally ill and the elderly."[21]

The Multnomah County story has been one of adaptation and accommodation to the expectations of its voters, its cities, and the state. Being an urban county has compounded the pressures and made the challenges facing county officials more complex. Only within the past twenty-five years has the county backed away from trying to be all things to all its residents. The state of Oregon continues to sort out its responsibilities in relation to counties, sometimes mandating new county duties without providing funds to cover their costs.

While Multnomah County gained a good deal of local control when voters approved county home rule in 1966, county officials have been hamstrung throughout these years by continual charter changes adopted at the ballot box. The future was foreshadowed when the original charter was repealed at the polls in 1966 before it went into effect, only to be resuscitated by a technical court ruling that allowed the new charter to become law. The first ten years of home rule were amendment-free, because Portland-Multnomah County consolidation on the 1974 ballot was expected to pass, but it did not, and the first crippling changes to the county charter came two years later. Since that time, county government has suffered many reorganizations. For the eight years from 1979 through 1986, the county executive was separated from the rest of the board in a failed experiment modeled on the federal government's three branches.

One of the most restrictive charter changes has been the imposition of term limits on elected officials, mandated by a 1982 amendment that is still in force despite repeated recommendations by citizen charter review boards to repeal the provision. County taxpayers have lost valuable experience and institutional memory because of such frequent turnover. County elected officials often move on even before their eight years are up, because they cannot afford to interrupt their careers for eight years and expect to have a job still waiting for them afterward. Term-limits rules are unbending; they apply no matter how good a job an official is doing.

Frequent charter changes have put Multnomah County at a disadvantage compared to the more stable City of Portland government; city voters have decisively turned down attempts to change its basic structure eight times since a commission form of government was adopted in 1913.

Why have county voters been so willing to constrain their elected officials? Is it fear of domination by Portland on the part of rural residents? Is it simply that county government is so invisible (until trouble arises) that voters are often unaware of its existence? Certainly, county officials are less well-known than their city counterparts. Given that county social service clients are largely poor and unable to stand up for their needs and rights, does county government seem less important to the average voter?

Here's the biggest puzzle: What difference did Multnomah County voters see between having term limits for state legislators and for county commissioners? How does one explain why two-thirds of Multnomah County citizens voted *against* establishing term limits for Oregon legislators in 2006, while only two years before the Multnomah County electorate rejected a repeal of county term limits for elected officials by 54 to 46 percent? And four years after the statewide vote against term limits at state level, why did 52 percent of Multnomah County voters again reject the repeal of term limits imposed on their elected officials?[22]

Today, Multnomah County's role is primarily focused on administrative services and the social, health, and criminal justice needs of its population, while the various city governments within its boundaries provide most of the police, fire, water, sewer, and street repair services. (Not insignificantly, the county still acts in some instances as a city in its unincorporated areas, spending funds on urban services that would traditionally be functions of a city.) Regional government—Metro—now handles land-use planning, transportation planning, solid-waste disposal, and regional facilities management.

In 2011, city auditor LaVonne Griffin-Valade called on city and county officials to revisit the nearly thirty-year-old Resolution A and determine whether to continue, repeal, or amend the agreement. She pointed to "tremendous demographic and economic shifts" that had seriously threatened the county's ability to deliver assistance to needy families. Given the city's relatively comfortable financial situation, the city had quietly slipped into providing some human services. Portland twice led a successful effort to pass a Children's Initiative local option levy that allowed the city to offer programs for children and families—programs in line with services the county had historically provided. Griffin-Valade and others also cited the city's funding of aid to homeless youths and men while the county continued to provide help to homeless families. County mental health services that overlap with city police procedures were also mentioned.[23]

By 2012, the apparent success of Resolution A had quieted talk of city-county consolidation, even though the issue had not died in the minds of previous charter change advocates. In the meantime, Portland critics continued to debate the merits and drawbacks of the city's "five-mayor" commission form of government. At a Town Hall meeting convened by NEMCCA (Northeast Multnomah County

New faces on the board eliminated the animosities of the Linn era. Members in 2009 were, from left, Deborah Kafoury, Jeff Cogen, Ted Wheeler (chair), Judy Shiprack, and Diane McKeel. Cogen succeeded Wheeler as chair after Wheeler was appointed state treasurer by Governor Ted Kulongoski in 2010. (Multnomah County website)

Community Association) on May 8, 1997, several officials presented their ideas for how city-county consolidation could (or could not) work. Of the 78 people who responded to an after-meeting survey, 77 were against city-county consolidation. A few mentioned other options for reconfiguring local government boundaries in the Portland metro area. Only one of the 78 respondents wanted his or her property to remain in Multnomah County. Then the stock market crash of 2008 and its aftermath, a national recession, and the upcoming presidential race of 2012 kept the public's attention focused on the need to create jobs and other economic realities. At the same time, the city auditor's recommendation to reevaluate city and county roles in relation to Resolution A remained on the table.

This is how the $271 million in property tax dollars allocated to Multnomah County annually were spent in 2009-10:

- 43 percent on public safety—jails, prosecution, parole and probation, juvenile crime prevention, rural sheriff patrols;

- 20 percent on community services—animal control, elections, assessment and property tax collection, workforce development, bridges, rainy day fund;

- 19 percent on county libraries;

- 18 percent on health, disability, senior, family, and children's services.[24]

In recent times, county officials have found it increasingly difficult to maintain service levels, because of cutbacks in federal funding of programs and the stringent property-tax limitations imposed in 1990 by statewide Measure 5.

"When Ted Wheeler came to office in 2007," County Attorney Agnes Sowle said two years after the fact, "county employees breathed a sigh of relief. They had felt oppressed and in fear under the last couple of years of Diane Linn's administration."[25]

In spite of the warm welcome incoming Chair Wheeler received when he was sworn in on January 2, 2007, he immediately faced daunting tasks. No solution had yet been found for funding and utilizing the much-needed Wapato Jail, which continued to stand empty. The elected sheriff continued to over-run his budget. The aging county courthouse badly needed replacing, as did the decaying Sellwood Bridge. Social services were cut because otherwise there was not enough money to balance the budget. Employee morale was low. Paying for state-mandated services took precedence over everything else.

"Why is Portland swimming in dough while Multnomah County staggers on Skid Row?" a *Willamette Week* article asked during Wheeler's first year on the job. Newly elected Commissioner Jeff Cogen put the answer this way: "Across the board, the state doesn't give us enough money to perform the services they want us to perform."[26] Federal funding of county programs likewise suffered severe cutbacks, not to mention the continuing short leash imposed by property-tax limitation Measure 5. Portland's urban renewal programs continued to shrink the property tax revenue available to Multnomah County, as did compression (reduction of revenue) caused by Portland's Fire and Police Disability and Retirement Fund (see Appendix B).

Former county and city auditor Gary Blackmer summarized the situation after thirty years of serving both entities: "Multnomah County is in serious financial trouble," Blackmer said. "And it's not their fault. It's the consequence of decisions made in Salem and, to a certain extent, in Portland City Hall . . . The state has delegated more and more responsibilities to the local level without [providing] the funds to pay for it. . . . Mental health got pushed down. Community corrections got pushed down to the local level. . . . Incarceration of felons of less than one year got pushed down to the county level . . . The city has not contributed very kindly to the county situation. Voters approved a levy for Multnomah County to build a jail, but then Portland blocked the county's attempt to put a levy forward to operate that jail [in 1999] . . . Wapato Jail now stands empty and the county has no money to operate it."[27]

In addition to known financial problems dating from 1999, in late 2010 the federal Environmental Protection Agency estimated that it would cost $1 billion to clean up a ten-mile stretch of the Willamette River, and identified Portland's sewer and utility ratepayers, along with hundreds of other property owners, as potentially liable for cleaning up the hazardous waste.[28]

By the time Ted Wheeler left the county to accept the state treasurer's job in March 2010, the Multnomah County Commission had restored a good deal of

The 2012 Multnomah County Commission. from left: Deborah Kafoury, Loretta Smith, Chair Jeff Cogen, Judy Shiprack, and Diane McKeel. (Multnomah County website)

its credibility and vastly improved its public image, thanks in large part to the demeanor and persistence of Chair Wheeler and his successor, Jeff Cogen, and a cooperative board. *Oregonian* columnist Anna Griffin gave Wheeler's stewardship elaborate praise, noting that the county board might well be "the most functional big-time political body in Oregon just a few years [after] the Mean Girls ruled the roost." Griffin also noted that Wheeler, unlike many professional politicians, knew how to respond quickly to mistakes—quickly and honestly.[29]

Although Wheeler did not manage to open Wapato Jail or to finish all the conversations he had started, his three-and-a-half years as county chair produced a record of solid accomplishment. He struggled to minimize cuts in human services, raised important questions about the sheriff's role, reduced sheriff's deputies' use of comp time and sick time, worked to restructure the county's delivery of mental health services, and urged creation of a new bridge authority. At a packed council hearing, he berated Portland city council members for their failure to recognize that city use of urban renewal dollars was diverting money from other local government programs, not to mention the long-term liability packed into the city's Fire and Police Disability and Retirement Plan (FPD&RP). Perhaps most important of all, Wheeler managed to make the county chairmanship "a job serious people actually want again."[30]

Questions whose answers will have a profound effect on the future of Multnomah County include:

• Will the state of Oregon enact meaningful tax reform?

• Will Measure 5 be repealed?

• Will Oregon's urban-rural divide be bridged?

- Will the state help build a new county courthouse?

- Will a regional bridge authority be created?

- Will a regional animal-control authority be created?

- Will Multnomah, Washington, and Clackamas counties combine to form a super-"Willamette County"?

- Will the City of Portland fund the unfunded liability in its Fire and Police Disability and Pension Fund?

- Will Portland help Multnomah County put its finances in order?

- Will Portland's sewer and utility ratepayers be held liable for helping pay the projected $1 billion cost of Willamette harbor cleanup?

- Will Portland and Multnomah County remain committed to Resolution A? If not, will the city and county revert to their previous overlaps of services and duplication of administrative hierarchies?

- Will restrictions on elected county officials—limits on the number of terms and inability to seek another elective office in mid-term without resigning—be removed by voters?

- Will the Multnomah County sheriff's position be made appointive rather than elective?

- Will Wapato Jail open?

Since its inception, Multnomah County has played a key role in providing for the needy, the infirm, the poor. The county has functioned as the heart of our humane society, helping the least among us. Will it continue as that "provider of last resort?" Will the political will be there to clarify this role and fund it adequately? That is an open question.

Barring an unlikely consolidation with the City of Portland or its neighboring counties at some time in the future, Multnomah County will almost certainly retain its position as the smallest of Oregon's counties in geographical size and the largest in population. While county government is often invisible, there is no arguing the importance of its role.

Appendix A
MULTNOMAH COUNTY TIMELINE

1843	Oregon Provisional Government created the original five counties: Clackamas, Yamhill, Tuality (later Washington), and Champoeg (later Marion).
1844-45	(winter) First log cabin built in clearing later to become Portland.
1848	Congress established Territory of Oregon.
1851	City of Portland chartered by territorial legislature.
1854	Multnomah County created from parts of Washington and Clackamas counties.
1859	State of Oregon admitted to the Union.
1864	First Multnomah County Courthouse completed; jail in basement.
1867	Multnomah County contracted with pioneer physician Dr. James C. Hawthorne, to treat indigent medical patients at Hawthorne's clinic.
1868	Portland-Multnomah County consolidation petition ignored by Oregon State Legislature.
1868	Multnomah County bought first "poor farm" for $20 per acre off S.W. Canyon Road.
1876	Indigent medical patients moved to County Poor Farm off S.W. Canyon Road.
1891	Portland, Albina, and East Portland consolidated under the name "Portland."
1899	Portland-Multnomah County consolidation proposed by Mayor William Mason.
1900	Multnomah County opened Kelly Butte Jail.
1902	Statewide initiative and referendum measure (the "Oregon System") adopted by voters.
1903	Citizen-drafted Portland charter adopted, making mayor responsible for administering city affairs and adding other reforms.

1905   City of Gresham chartered.

1906   State constitutional change gave cities and towns the exclusive right
            to enact and amend their own charters.

1906   Kelly Butte Jail opened.

1907   City of Troutdale chartered.

1908   City of Fairview chartered.

1909   First Multnomah County Hospital established in a four-story
            Victorian mansion on S.W. Hooker Street.

1910   Proposals to increase geographic size of Multnomah County
            overwhelmingly rejected by statewide voters.

1911   Multnomah County buys new poor farm on site near Troutdale;
            abandons former "poor farm" off S.W. Canyon Road.

1912   Statewide ballot measure providing method for consolidating cities
            and creating new counties rejected by voters.

1912   Initiative petition to create Cascade County on statewide ballot
            strongly rejected by voters.

1912   Oregon voters approve women's suffrage amendment.

1913   Commission form of government adopted by City of Portland
            voters as an amendment to city's 1903 charter.

1914   Statewide ballot measure proposing identical boundaries for
            Portland and Multnomah County and establishing different
            taxation zones is rejected.

1914   Second Multnomah County Courthouse completed on same block
            where the first one stood.

1917   Interstate Bridge across Columbia River opened, a joint project of
            Multnomah County and Clark County, Washington.

1917   Portland voters decisively rejected repeal of commission form of
            government.

1923   New Multnomah County Hospital opened on Marquam Hill, the
            second building on a campus that included University of Oregon
            Medical School.

1924   Entire three-member Multnomah County Board of Commissioners
            recalled by voters after scandal over bridge contracts for Ross
            Island, Sellwood, and Burnside bridges.

1925   Oregon legislature convened a Government Simplification
            Committee to study Portland's metropolitan government.

1925   Multnomah County completed the Sellwood Bridge.

1926	Portland charter revisions rejected by voters.
1926	Multnomah County completed the Ross Island Bridge and Burnside Bridge.
1927	Statewide ballot measure to enable cities and counties to consolidate was defeated.
1931	Multnomah County completed the St. Johns Bridge.
1934	Future U.S. Congressman Richard Neuberger proposed reducing the number of Oregon counties from 36 to 12.
1941	Construction began on Rocky Butte Jail; Kelly Butte Jail closed.
1950	Multnomah County opened first Sauvie Island Bridge.
1951	City of Wood Village incorporated.
1958	Multnomah County opened new Morrison Bridge.
1958	Portland voters rejected change to a "council-manager" form of government.
1963	Metropolitan Study Commission (MSC) created by Oregon State Legislature.
1963	Multnomah County Correctional Institution, a low security work-release jail, opened on land at the County Poor Farm.
1964	County Poor Farm renamed "Edgefield Acres" to eliminate "poor farm" connotation.
1966	Portland "strong mayor" form of government proposal rejected by voters.
1966	Multnomah County voters adopted a home rule charter giving the county chair powers similar to those of a city "strong mayor."
1966	Columbia Region Association of Governments (CRAG) established to meet federal government requirement for cooperation between local governments.
1967	City of Maywood Park incorporated.
1969	Portland Metropolitan Area Local Government Boundary Commission created by Oregon State Legislature.
1969	Multnomah County halted agricultural operations at Edgefield; dairy cows sold.
1970	Tri-county Metropolitan Service District (MSD) created by Oregon State Legislature to oversee solid waste disposal.
1973	Oregon legislature approved merger of Multnomah County Hospital into University of Oregon Medical School; a surviving portion of the old hospital, now called Multnomah Pavilion, remained in use.

1974   "Portland-Multnomah" charter defeated overwhelmingly by voters.

1978   Voters approved MSD merger with CRAG, thereby creating a
        metropolitan regional government (later called "Metro") with an
        elected governing body and elected executive.

1982   Restrictive Multnomah home rule charter provisions adopted by
        voters (no paid lobbyist allowed; term limits imposed; salaries of
        officials frozen; appointed sheriff, etc.).

1982   Last nursing home patient leaves Edgefield Manor; buildings closed.

1983   Resolution A, a voluntary division of duties between Portland
        and Multnomah County, adopted by county commission and city
        council.

1983   High-rise Multnomah County Justice Center completed downtown,
        containing county jail, Portland police headquarters, and Oregon
        State Crime Lab; Rocky Butte Jail closed and torn down to make
        way for Interstate 205 freeway.

1985   Boundary Commission rejected formation of new City of Columbia
        Ridge in mid-Multnomah County.

1986   Portland City Club committees urged study of a "Willamette
        County" super-county.

1987   County voters approved funds for new low-security jail; Inverness
        Jail completed late 1988.

1990   Statewide Measure 5 passed, limiting most property taxes to 1½
        percent of assessed value.

1990   Multnomah County sold Edgefield Manor and 10 acres of the old
        county farm to the McMenamin brothers for conversion to winery,
        brew pub, restaurant, and inn.

1992   Voters approved home rule charter for Metro.

1996   County voters passed measure calling for major new jail; when new
        Wapato Jail is finally completed in 2004, county had no money to
        operate it.

1997   Mayor Vera Katz and County Chair Beverly Stein convened a
        "consolidation threshold" committee that met with strong east
        county opposition.

1998   Two more studies commissioned regarding east county potential for
        withdrawing from Multnomah County.

2000   Statewide ballot measure to waive county geographic size
        requirement for forming new counties defeated.

2000   Multnomah County moved into new administrative headquarters, called the Multnomah County Building, at 501 S.E. Hawthorne Boulevard.

2001   County "closed" Multnomah County Correctional Institution near Troutdale; it would occasionally be partially reopened until final closure in 2007.

2002   Portland voters rejected change to "strong mayor" form of government by three-to-one ratio.

2007   Portland voters again rejected change to "strong mayor" form of government, again by three-to-one ratio, in the eighth attempt since 1913 to change basic city structure.

2008   County opened new Sauvie Island Bridge.

2010   Regional entity sought to replace aging Sellwood Bridge.

Appendix B
A BRIEF PROPERTY TAX PRIMER: EFFECTS OF MEASURE 5, URBAN RENEWAL, AND FPD&R

In 1990, Oregon voters approved a restrictive property tax proposal, Measure 5, whose ramifications affected every local government entity in Multnomah County. Furthermore, the result of that citizen-sponsored initiative continues to constrict Multnomah County local government tax revenues more tightly every year.

Prior to passage of Measure 5, Oregon local governments were allowed to increase property tax bases by 6 percent each year without regard to changes in assessed value. While Measure 5 still allowed this same calculation, the governmental unit might or might not be able to actually collect all of it, depending on the tax rate of all related districts (education or general government). In addition, the automatic 6 percent increase was later reduced by Measure 50 (passed in May 1997) to 3 percent plus new construction.[1] Unless inflation remains under 3 percent, which is an unusual phenomenon, local government property tax revenues will continue to shrink in relationship to the normal rate of inflation.

Measure 5 restricted most property taxes to 1½ percent of assessed value. Expressed another way, this was a levy of fifteen mills, or $15 for each $1,000 of assessed value. The only exception was for taxes to repay general obligation bonds approved by the voters.[2] A maximum of 0.5 percent could be levied for schools, and the remaining 1 percent was allocated among all other local government entities.

The intent behind Measure 50 was to clarify the confused property tax situation created by Measure 47, which had been passed in November 1996 and attempted to limit increases in assessed property values. Measures 47 and 50 were both attempts to clarify provisions of Measure 5 passed in 1990. Measure 50 reduced each property's assessed value to its 1995 value less 10 percent. Tax bases and temporary operating levies adopted for the fiscal year 1997-98 were reduced by 17 percent. Each governmental unit then had a permanent tax rate, which was calculated using the combined lower levies and lower total assessed value. Existing appraisal inequities were locked into the system permanently, and future increases in property value were limited to 3 percent annually. As was the case with Measure 5, general obligation bond levies were not covered by this.[3]

Local option levies (replacing the old serial levies) were now allowed only when a majority of citizens casting ballots approved the levy *and* a majority of registered voters actually voted—the so-called "double majority" rule. The double majority rule did not apply in November elections in even-numbered years, presumably because voter turnouts were traditionally high in those elections (although voters effectively eliminated the double majority rule in fall 2008).[4] Local option levies provided for in Measure 50 extend for five years, whereas the old serial levies expired after three years.[5]

Every Multnomah County local taxing district suffered a cut in its 1997 operating levy. Portland's Fire and Police Disability and Retirement Fund (FPD&R) was excluded from the Measure 50 cut but was included in the 1.5 percent Measure 5 property tax levy total for local governments, thereby serving to "compress" all other local government levies in the Portland area.

Compression occurs whenever all possible taxes on an individual property combined exceed the allowable 1 percent limit. Total taxes are then reduced by decreasing all taxing district revenues until the needed reduction is reached. However, compression does not reduce all taxing district revenues equally. Local option levies are the first to be reduced and can be reduced to zero, if necessary, to get an individual property's taxes below the limit. For example, the county's local option library levy suffers a much higher percentage loss to compression than the county's permanent rate levy.[6]

Multnomah County lost $1.5 million in property tax revenue in 1997-98 because of compression required by Measure 5, in addition to $23 million lost because of Measure 50 provisions. Since then, a few special local option levies have been approved in Multnomah County, such as the November 2002 county library and city parks levies. However, all jurisdictions have had to be careful not to overload the ballot with local option levies, or compression would occur. (Funding for capital projects backed by general obligation bonds was not subject to the same limitations.)[7]

Between 2001 and 2009, Multnomah County's share of general government property taxes shrank from approximately 36 percent in 2001-2 to 28 percent in 2009-10.[8]

In 2009-10, Multnomah County lost $13.7 million in property tax revenues because of Measure 5 compression, $2 million more than in 2008-9. The county's 2009-10 revenue loss was largely due to the cost of funding the City of Portland's Fire and Police Disability and Retirement Fund (FPD&R) and the loss of property taxes earmarked for Portland urban renewal districts. When general government tax levy rates increase, so do losses due to Measure 5 compression.

In addition to loss of revenue from urban renewal districts as a result of Measure 5 compression, Multnomah County is adversely affected by the removal of property from the property tax roles in those districts. Urban renewal districts have been formed to revitalize "blighted" areas in Portland, Gresham, and Troutdale, with property taxes from those districts frozen for the life of each district. In 2010, Portland had eleven active urban renewal districts and was planning more, on the theory that future increased taxes collected from these districts would more than offset current losses.

Portland representatives of the League of Women Voters frequently testified against the establishment or extension of urban renewal districts because of the negative effect on other taxing districts. "It is absolutely accurate to say Multnomah County is 'losing' money to urban renewal," said Tom Linhares, Multnomah County Tax Supervising and Conservation Commission director, "both for general operations (permanent tax rate limit) and for the library (local option levy). However, it is subjective to say exactly how much." Urban renewal proponents argue that if it were not for urban renewal, property values would not have increased, so taxing districts are not causing any loss of property tax revenues because the higher value would not have been there in the first place. Even so, Mark Campbell, Multnomah County Deputy Chief Financial Officer, estimates that the amount of forgone revenue attributable to urban renewal in the county in 2009-10 was $24.4 million.[9]

By July 2010, Portland's FPD&R unfunded liability had more than doubled within nine years, from $1 billion in 2001 to $2.5 billion.[10] Annual payouts to retired and disabled employees over the same period came close to doubling, from $59 million to $101.5 million per year.[11]

To further compound potential future problems, a 1989 city charter amendment guaranteed that Portland general fund revenues would make up the difference if the FPD&R millage rate failed to cover mandated pension and disability payouts. The hardship that this unfunded liability might cause future Portland generations was downplayed by those backing the amendment.

In 2006, voters approved a reform to require all Portland police officers and firefighters hired after January 1, 2007, to be enrolled in the Oregon Public

Service Retirement Plan (OPSRP) instead of FPD&R. The FPD&R is expected to keep growing until around 2030 to 2035, after which time current fund members will have retired.[12] An annual contribution of $2.3 million is presently being set aside by the FPD&R to cover future retirement benefits for employees who come under the new OPSRP.[13]

In 2009-10, Portland's urban renewal projects and FPD&R combined took up nearly half of the $10 per $1,000 local government limitation allowed by Measure 5 for all units except schools.[14]

Appendix C
HISTORY OF MULTNOMAH COUNTY
HOME RULE CHARTER CHANGES
Adopted 1966; effective January 1, 1967
Amended by the voters in 1976, 1977, 1978, 1980, 1982, 1984, 1986, 1989, 1990, 1998, 2004, 2006, 2010 [1]

A state constitutional amendment passed by voters in 1958 allowed every Oregon county to adopt its own charter to address matters of county concern.[2] Four years later, the Oregon Supreme Court addressed the question of the degree of autonomy that home rule provided to local governments, and came down on the side of local over state control.[3] In 1978, the Supreme Court again addressed the issue of home rule authority. A sharply divided court held that local government powers were limited to matters that did not conflict with state law and mandates. That interpretation remained the controlling law as Oregon entered the twenty-first century.[4]

In 1964, the Multnomah County Board of Commissioners appointed an eleven-member Home Rule Charter Committee to draft a county home rule charter. The proposed charter appeared on the May 1966 county ballot. Under this charter, the county governing body increased from three to five full-time commissioners, who were elected at large for four-year terms. Commission members would be nominated and elected by numbered positions, with Position No. 1 designated as chairman. The board chairman would be the county's chief executive with power to appoint and discharge administrative officers. The board as a whole would retain the authority to approve department heads, adopt the annual budget, fill vacancies in elective offices, and fix the compensation for county offices.

The positions of county auditor and district attorney (whose office was established by the state constitution, not the county charter) would remain elective, but the offices of sheriff, constable, surveyor, treasurer, assessor, county clerk, and district court clerk would be appointive. (An early draft of the charter eliminated the office of auditor as an elected official. However, after incumbent auditor Jack O'Donnell, a former Teamsters' dock worker, threatened to publicly oppose the charter and get his former union colleagues to do likewise, the auditor's position was left elective.)

County Commission Chairman Mike Gleason urged the charter commission to give the county commissioners authority to create special districts. Charter commission member George Birnie represented several water and sewer taxing districts and opposed giving that authority. Birnie's position won by a five-to-four charter commission vote.

Lloyd Anderson, then manager of the local engineering firm CH2M, chaired the charter drafting committee. Other members were George Birnie; William Brunner; Mrs. (Mary) Arnold Damskov, an active member of League of Women Voters; Sylvia Nemer Davidson; Neva Elliott, lawyer; John Elorriaga, then president of U.S. National Bank; Alden Krieg; John Sonderen; and Stanley Swan. Brunner served as vice-chair and Elliott as secretary.

Orval Edder, an attorney with the League of Oregon Cities and the Oregon Bureau of Municipal Research, drafted the charter wording based on substantive decisions made by commission members. Edder copied the ballot title from the Washington County Home Rule measure that had passed four years before.[5]

In May 1966, voters approved the Multnomah County Home Rule Charter by a narrow majority. Perhaps the main reason the county charter passed with so little public debate was because the public's attention was focused on a highly controversial city proposal for a "strong mayor" form of government that was on the Portland ballot at the same time. The Portland measure was rejected by 68,158 votes to 41,848,[6] and allowed the county home rule charter to slip under the radar, so to speak.

November 1966 vote to repeal

Immediately after the May 1966 election, county officials whose elected positions were abolished by the new charter (except the sheriff) circulated a petition to have the vote rescinded. The petitioners obtained enough signatures to put the measure on the November general election ballot before the charter went into effect.

Charter Commission Chair Anderson and others favoring the charter hired attorney Jack Beatty to challenge the petitioners in court, on the grounds that the repeal petition had a misleading ballot title. That court challenge failed. However, Stan Terry, a businessman and frequent (unsuccessful) city council candidate, hired attorney George Joseph to oppose the repeal on different grounds, namely that the petitioners' names were not counted within the time limits set by law.

Before the second court case was heard, the measure to repeal was approved by the voters in the November 1966 election. However, the court subsequently sustained Terry's argument, rendering the November repeal vote null and void. The charter therefore went into effect as originally planned, on January 1, 1967.

Multnomah County was the fourth Oregon county to adopt home rule, after Lane (1962), Washington (1962), and Hood River (1964). Five more counties have adopted home rule charters since 1966: Benton (1972), Jackson (1978), Josephine (1980), Clatsop (1988), and Umatilla (1992). Each charter specifies the organization and, to some extent, the functions and powers of county government.

In 1973 the Oregon legislature created "statutory home rule" via Oregon Revised Statute 203.035, granting all counties legislative authority over matters of county concern, whether or not they have a home rule charter. Twenty-four counties, including the nine with home rule charters, now have a board of commissioners with three to five elected members. The other twelve less-populated counties continue to be governed by a county court with a county judge and two commissioners.[7]

1974 city-county consolidation proposal (rejected)

In the ten years after the Multnomah County Home Rule Charter took effect, not a single proposed amendment appeared on the ballot, probably because a proposal to merge Portland and Multnomah County was being vigorously debated. Polls showed that voters favored the concept of city-county consolidation, so the 1971 state legislature passed a bill enabling the creation of a charter-writing commission. As detailed in chapter 14, a City of Portland–Multnomah County Consolidation Charter that appeared on 1974 ballots was overwhelmingly defeated.

1976 amendments: changing the method of electing the county chair; ending the term of County Chair Don Clark on January 1, 1977; requiring two-year commission terms; establishing five single-member districts (adopted)

Under short-lived provisions proposed by initiative petition and adopted by the voters in 1976, county commissioner terms were reduced from four to two years and all commissioners elected from single-member districts. At-large commission positions were eliminated. Commissioners were to select one of their own members as commission chair. The initial five districts were to be based on the 1970 federal census, with possible new districts to be added as the population grew. Don Clark and Mel Gordon were assigned to represent east county districts. Elected official vacancies were to be filled by election rather than board appointment.

1977 amendments: reversing prior year vote; establishing review committee (adopted)

A measure to reverse the 1976 amendments that had been placed on the ballot by initiative petition was adopted by the voters in November 1977 before elections were held to fill the single-member districts identified. Commission districts were changed back to an at-large format and board terms returned to four years. Vacancies in elected officials' positions were again to be filled by appointment rather than election. A Charter Review Committee composed of sixteen members was to be appointed by the state senator and two representatives from each of the county's four state senate districts.

1978 amendments: separating legislative and executive functions; adding fifth commissioner; requiring nonpartisan elections (adopted); granting authority to issue revenue bonds (rejected)

The Charter Review Committee approved by the electorate in 1977 recommended major changes in governance, most of which were adopted by the electorate in 1978.

The biggest change separated county legislative and executive functions by removing the board chairman from the board and making that person the county executive. The reconstituted board would consist of five commissioners elected by numbered districts for four-year terms. The county executive would have veto power over board actions and would prepare the proposed budget but would not sit on the board. Commissioners would choose one of their number as presiding officer each year. A majority of commissioners present would constitute a quorum, the legal minimum required for a meeting. A commissioner appointed to fill a board vacancy could not run for that office at the next election. All elective county offices would be nonpartisan. The two candidates for an office who received the most votes in the primary would appear on the general election ballot. If there were only one or two candidates for an office, those names would not appear on the primary ballot, only on the general election ballot. The auditor was to reapportion commissioner districts based on population changes. All these provisions were adopted.

The charter change that created the position of an elected executive who was not a member of the board was very controversial. Single-member commission districts were also hotly debated. Commissioner Dennis Buchanan argued against single-member districts that pitted one district against another. "The whole board is sitting down here [in the courthouse] making decisions that affect east county, but its residents only get to vote for one," he said.[8] Most voters were unclear regarding which commission district they resided in or who represented them on the county board.

A measure to allow the county to issue revenue bonds was rejected by voters.

1980 amendments: concerning minor civil service and personnel matters (adopted)

Amendments relating to minor civil service provisions were approved in 1980. The county executive was designated as the county personnel officer. Commission districts were to be reapportioned based on the 1980 decennial census.[9][38]

May 1982 amendments: imposing term limits; making four appointive positions elective; prohibiting a county lobbyist; limiting officials' salaries; restricting officials' filing for another office (adopted)

Charter changes proposed by initiative petition and adopted by the voters in May 1982 reversed several provisions in the original 1966 charter and made basic changes to restrict the authority of county government. Four positions that had been filled by appointment rather than election for the past sixteen years were once again to be elected: sheriff, county clerk, district court clerk, and county assessor. The compensation of all county elected officials was specified, with any future salary increases to be approved by the voters in a primary or general election. The prohibition against hiring a paid county lobbyist was retained. Elective officers were limited to eight years of service, retroactive to 1976. (This provision would be amended in 1984 to specify a limitation of two consecutive, full, four-year terms.) Filing for another office was deemed to constitute a resignation. Charter review committees would meet periodically to recommended charter changes.

September 1982 amendment: repealing May 1982 amendments (rejected)

Multnomah County's first vote-by-mail election (see chapter 16) was a referral by the Board of County Commissioners asking the voters to repeal the potpourri of charter amendments passed in May 1982. The repeal measure failed. (The Oregon Legislature later passed legislation to prohibit all-inclusive charter amendments such as those passed in May 1982.)[10]

A strange situation occurred as a result of the May charter amendment provision adding four elective positions. Candidates for four-year terms in those offices filed for election in November 1982 through a nominating convention held at the Forestry Center. No one filed against incumbent Elections Division Director Bill Radakovich, so his name appeared on the November ballot alone. The other three successful candidates each beat out one opponent: Sheriff and Director of Public Safety Director Fred Pierce won over John Kerslake as sheriff; Assessment and Taxation Division Director Jim Wilcox won over Robert More as assessor; Deputy District Court Administrator Daniel Wood defeated Rosalie Huss as District Court Clerk. (Wood was actually a state employee because the state had already taken over the courts; for a time he received wages from both the state and county for the same job.)

Newly appointed County Clerk Vicki Ervin (Radakovich had retired in March 1984) drew four male opponents in May 1984 for the two years of that unexpired term. Ervin went on to win the election handily, but her election was soon rendered moot by the charter amendments of 1984 (discussed in the following section), which made her position appointive. She went on to be appointed to the position of Director of Elections in a nonelective capacity, serving a record-setting eighteen years. She is the only woman to date to ever serve as County Director of Elections.[11]

1984 amendments: returning county executive to board chair; making three elective positions appointive; allowing issuance of revenue bonds (all adopted); allowing paid lobbyist (rejected); eliminating restrictions against filing for other office (rejected)

After an eight-year trial during which the elected county executive operated separately from the board, the 1984 Charter Review Committee recommended returning the board and executive officer to their pre-1978 roles. The county executive position was eliminated and a board chair position re-created, again reducing the number of the single-member commissioner districts to four. The county sheriff's position remained elective, while the county clerk, district court clerk, and county assessor would again be appointed.

Another charter amendment directed the auditor to convene a five-member salary commission to propose adjustments to the salaries of elected officials. The electorate would approve or reject any increases at a primary election. The auditor's authority was also restated to require internal audits of all county operations and financial affairs, with elected officials directed to respond in writing to audit findings.

The names of all county candidates for elective office would appear on the primary ballot, with any candidate who received a majority of primary votes deemed elected. If no candidate received a majority, the two candidates receiving the most votes would appear on the general election ballot. The office of citizen involvement was created to facilitate communication between citizens and the board. A requirement that voters must approve revenue bonds before they could be issued was eliminated.

The prohibition against hiring a lobbyist or allowing the county to employ a coordinator of intergovernmental relations was retained, as was the prohibition against allowing elected officials to run for another office in midterm without first resigning their current positions.

1986 amendments: making minor adjustments to filing and salary requirements

All three amendments proposed by the Board of County Commissioners on the May 20, 1986, ballot were adopted. County elected officials could henceforth file for another office in the last year of their terms without resigning from office. The compensation of elected officials could be fixed at either a primary or a general election. The new position of county chair, which would be re-created as of January 1, 1987, was to receive the same salary as that previously paid to the county executive.

1989 amendments: setting auditor qualifications and salary; specifying interim replacements for three elected officials (all adopted)

The voters approved all the measures submitted by the Board of County Commissioners for 1989 charter changes. In the future, all county auditor candidates would have to be licensed either as a certified public accountant or a certified internal auditor. The auditor's salary was set at four-fifths of a district court judge's salary. The chair, sheriff, and auditor were to designate an individual to act as an interim replacement in case of a vacancy until an election could take place. If an election were held to fill a vacancy, the top vote-getter would have to receive a majority of votes cast in order to be deemed elected.

1990 amendments: clarifying salary issues (adopted); hiring a county manager (rejected); hiring a lobbyist (rejected); easing filing restrictions (rejected)

The sheriff's salary should not be less than that of any member of the sheriff's office, the 1990 Charter Review Committee said. Voters agreed. Likewise, voters agreed that the board could set commissioner and chair salaries provided that such compensation did not exceed amounts recommended by the county salary commission appointed by the auditor.

Voters rejected a measure to transfer county administrative functions from the chair to an appointed county manager, as recommended by the 1990 Charter Review Committee. The voters also declined to repeal the prohibition against the county hiring a paid lobbyist or an advocate for county interests in state legislative matters. Voters retained the prohibition against elected officials serving more than two consecutive four-year terms in any twelve-year period. Furthermore, the electorate declined to allow any county elected official to file for another office in the last eighteen months of his or her term. This left in place the provision that filing for another office in midterm was considered a resignation.

1998 amendments: requiring recurring charter reviews; specifying interim replacements for all commissioners; mandating performance audits (all adopted); hiring a county lobbyist (rejected); eliminating term limits (rejected)

The 1997 Charter Review Committee proposed, and the voters agreed, that charter review committees should be appointed every six years. No future commission district should have more than 102 percent of the population of any other district. All board members should name designees to act for them in the event of a vacancy in office (to parallel the previously adopted requirement for the chair, sheriff, and auditor). The language of county auditor duties was changed from requiring the auditor to conduct "internal" audits to that of conducting "performance" audits. The auditor was authorized to conduct studies to improve county services.

For the third time, voters rejected a measure that would have repealed the ban against a paid county lobbyist. Likewise, a measure to repeal county term limits was turned down. The charter section that required any elected official who ran for another office in midterm to resign was retained, as were runoff election procedures.

2004 amendments: allowing employment of a county lobbyist (adopted); eliminating term limits (rejected); allowing officials to run in midterm without resigning (rejected)

On the fourth try, voters agreed to allow the county to once again hire a paid county lobbyist. All county elected officials were required to receive a majority of votes to be deemed elected, not just candidates who were seeking to fill a vacancy.

Only the five-member salary commission appointed by the auditor could set future county chair and commissioner salaries. County Civil Service Commission terms were reduced from six to three years.

The repeal of county term limits was again rejected by the voters. A measure to repeal the requirement that elected officials must resign if they run for another office in midterm was defeated. Only in the final year of their terms could officials run for another office without resigning, as provided in a May 1986 amendment.

2006 amendments: housekeeping matters (adopted)

All 2006 amendments were charter housekeeping measures recommended by the 2003 Charter Review Committee. Various charter subsections were moved to clarify previously approved charter changes.

2010 amendments: enabling creation of a county library taxing district; requiring commissioners to continue living in the district they represent; allowing elections to fill vacancies only in May or November; requiring salary commission to set sheriff salary and district attorney supplemental salary (all adopted); eliminating term limits and allowing officials to run in midterm without resigning (both again rejected)

These six measures were placed on the ballot at the recommendation of the 2009-2010 Multnomah County Charter Commission with recommendations that all be adopted. The most significant change was enabling the county board to create a Multnomah County Library District, which in the future, with voter approval, could levy property taxes dedicated exclusively to the county library system.

The unsuccessful proposals to eliminate term limits and to allow elected officials to run for another office in midterm without resigning addressed holdover issues of long standing. The residency requirement was prompted by the fact that Commissioner Lisa Naito moved out of the district from which she was elected while continuing to serve on the commission for the remainder of her term. The salary commission provision and the reduction in the number of dates on which elections could be held to fill vacancies were basically housekeeping measures.

Appendix D
ELECTED MULTNOMAH COUNTY OFFICIALS: A CHRONOLOGICAL LIST
1854-2012

Including officials appointed to fill vacancies. From 1854 to 1917, terms ended in mid-year; from 1918 on, terms began in January.

ASSESSORS

Stansbury, Z. N.	1856		Falloon, Wilbur J.	1948-50
Breck, John M.	1857		Smith, Wiley W.	1951-58
Buckley, W. S.	1858		Hawkins, Joe	1959-66
Breck, John M.	1859		Wilcox, James	1983-84
Frazar, Thomas	1860-62			
Newell, John S.	1863		**COUNTY AUDITORS**	
Dolan, John	1864-67		Norris, Shubrick	1854-56
Costello, John	1868-69		Litchenthaler, D. W.	1857
Dolan, John	1870-73		*[see county clerks]*	1858-1894
Barnard, O. M.	1874-77		Pope, W. H.	1895-1902
Sears, George C.	1878-81		Brandes, C. A.	1903-9
Saunders, I. N.	1882-83		Welch, Hiram U.	1910
Harold, George	1884-91		Martin, Sam B.	1911-24
Sears, George C.	1892-93		Sweeney, Ed	1925-31
Greenleaf, R. S.	1894-1900		Knowles, Roy H.	1932
McDonell, C. E.	1901-4		Gibson, Will E.	1933-36
Sigler, B. D.	1905-12		Rankin, W. C.	1937
Reed, Henry E.	1913-20		Knowles, Roy H.	1937-38
Welch, Hiram U.	1921-36		Brown, Al L.	1939-45
Ringler, Charles	1937-41		Baldwin, George	1945-48
Watson, Tom	1941-48		Barbur, Herbert C.	1949

Kerr, Edwin M.	1949-50	
O'Donnell, John J. "Jack"	1951-74	
Lansing, Jewel	1975-82	
Feeney, Anne Kelly	1983-88	
Ivancie, Dan	1989-90	
Blackmer, Gary	1991-98	
Flynn, Suzanne	1999-2004	
Griffin-Valade, LaVonne	2005-9	
March, Steve	2009-	

COUNTY CLERKS

Litchenthaler, D. W.	1858-59
Norris, Shubrick	1860-61
Breck, John M.	1862-63
Coulson, H. C.	1864-67
Norden, Ben L.	1868-69
Parrish, Charles W.	1870-71
Harris, W. H.	1872-73
Story, George L.	1874-75
Smith, J. A.	1876-79
Borthwick, A. E.	1880-81
Sewall, W. R.	1882-83
Saunders, I. N.	1884-85
Church, William, Jr.	1886-87
Wheeler, E. C.	1888-89
Powell, T. C.	1890-93
Smith, H. C.	1894-97
Holmes, H. H.	1898-99
Swetland, L. O.	1900-1901
Fields, F. S.	1902-12
Coffey, J. B.	1913-16
Beveridge, J. W.	1917-28
Bailey, A. A.	1929-43
Bucktel, A. L.	1944
Brown, Al L.	1945-50
Cohn, Si	1951-66
Radakovich, Bill	1983-84
Ervin, Vicki	1984 (3 mos)

COUNTY COMMISSIONERS

Bybee, James F.	1854
Scott, Emsley R.	1854
Vaughn, George W.	1854
Farman, S.	1855
Walker, Ellis	1855-56
Powell, D.	1855-57
Lucas, M. M.	1856-58
Wilmot, J. F.	1857-58
Lambert, Joseph H.	1858
Ladd, William S.	1859
Ritchey, Caleb	1859
Hamilton, Edward	1859-61
Walker, Ellis	1860-61
White, John S.	1860-61
Marquam, Philip A.	1862-69
Burrell, M. S.	1862-63
Kerns, William	1862-63
Corbett, Henry W.	1864
Shaw, Alva Compton R.	1864-65
Lownsdale, J. P. O.	1865-67
Hanson, Hans	1866-67
Boyd, Hamilton	1868-69
Quimby, E. L.	1868-69
Burton, E. M.	1870-71
Kenulty, John	1870-71
Hamilton, Edward	1870-73
McCormick, S. J.	1872-73
Silver, Clieve S.	1872-73
Hanson, Hans	1874-75
Holman, Charles	1874-75
Woodward, J. H.	1874-77
Kelly, Penumbra	1876-77
Woodward, Tyler	1876-77
Holbrook, Philo	1878-79
Wiberg, W. M.	1878-79
Rice, S. W.	1878-81
Long, George M.	1880-81

Slavin, J. A.	1880-81	Bradley, O. V.	1939-40
Bacon, Charles P.	1882-83	Kreuder, T. J.	1941-42
Giese, E. G.	1882-83	Bradley, Charles C.	1942-43
Stearns, Loyal B.	1882-85	West, Tom H.	1942-48
Corbett, Henry W.	1884-87	Brown, Alan	1944-48
Newell, John S.	1884-87	Rossman, Gene W.	1949-50
Catlin, John	1886-90	Gleason, M. J. "Mike"	1949-66
Smith, B. F.	1888-89	Brown, Al L.	1951-62
Dunne, David M.	1888-91	Bain, Jack	1955-62
Stone, H. S.	1890-97	Aylsworth, Larry W.	1962
Moreland, Julius C.	1891-93	Eccles, David	1963-72
Holbrook, Philo	1892-99	Gordon, Mel	1963-78
Northup, Henry H.	1894-97	Mosee, Dan	1967-68
Steele, W. B.	1898-1900	Aylsworth, Larry W.	1967-72
Cake, W. M.	1898-1901	Clark, Donald E.	1969-74
Mack, J. G.	1900-1902	Padrow, Ben	1971-74
Showers, William	1901-4	Mosee, Dan	1973-80
Webster, L. R.	1902-9	Corbett, Alice	1975-78
Barnes, F. C.	1903-9	Buchanan, Dennis	1975-82
Lightner, William	1905-16	Roberts, Barbara	1978
Hart, D. V.	1910-14	McCoy, Gladys	1979-84
Cleeton, T. J.	1910-16	Blumenauer, Earl	1979-86
Holman, Rufus	1914-22	Shadburne, Gordon	1979-86
Holbrook, P.	1915-18	Miller, Caroline	1981-88
Tazwell, George	1917-18	Biskar, Arnold	1983-84
Muck, A. A.	1917-20	Levy, Richard	1984 (3 mos)
Hoyt, Ralph W.	1919-22	Kafoury, Gretchen	1985-90
Rudeen, Charles	1921-24	Anderson, Pauline	1985-92
Rankin, J. H.	1923-24	Morris, Bonnie	1986 (8 mos)
Walker, Dow V.	1923-24	Casterline, Polly	1986-89
Taft, Erwin	1924-26	Kelley, Sharron	1989-2000
Smith, Amadee	1924-28	Bauman, Rick	1989-92
Phegley, Grant	1924-34	Hansen, Gary	1991-98
Morse, Clay	1927-30	Collier, Tanya	1993-97
German, Fred	1929-32	Saltzman, Dan	1993-98
Shull, Frank	1931-54	Naito, Lisa	1998-2008
Bigelow, Charles	1933-41	Linn, Diane	1998-2001
Taft, Erwin	1935-39	Anderson, Pauline	2001 (3 mos)

Cruz, Serena	1999-2006	Fletcher, O.	1896-97
Roberts, Lonnie	2001-8	Hurlburt, J. A.	1898-1903
Rojo de Steffey, Maria	2001-8	Richmond, A. H.	1904-5
Cogen, Jeff	2007-10	Holbrook, P., Jr.	1906-14
Kafoury, Deborah	2009-	Bonser, R. C.	1915-32
McKeel, Diane	2009-	Marshall, Earl	1933-36
Shiprack, Judy	2009-	Powers, Claude	1937-51
Willer, Barbara	2010 (9 mos)	Welch, Peter W.	1952-55
Smith, Loretta	2011-	Ewing, Donald	1956-62
		Pense, Claire	1962-66

COUNTY COMMISSION CHAIRS

Gleason, M. J. "Mike"	1967-74	**COUNTY TREASURERS**	
Clark, Donald E.	1975-79	Fitch, A. D.	1854-55
McCoy, Gladys	1987-93	Starr, Lewis M.	1856-57
Miggins, Hank	1993 (3 mos)	Stansbury, Z. N.	1858-59
Stein, Beverly	1993-2001	McCracken, John	1860
Farver, Bill	2001 (3 mos)	Doland, W. P.	1861-63
Linn, Diane	2001-6	Steel, George A.	1864-67
Wheeler, Ted	2007-10	Masters, William	1868-69
Cogen, Jeff	2010-	Harbaugh, F.	1870-71
		Showers, William	1878-88
COUNTY EXECUTIVES		Hacheney, Frank	1889-90
Clark, Donald E.	1979-82	Willey, S. B.	1891-92
Buchanan, Dennis	1983-86	Malarkey, C. A.	1893-94
		Lambert, A. W.	1895-96
COUNTY SURVEYORS		Hoyt, Ralph W.	1897-99
Vickers, L. B.	1854	Brooke, T. S.	1900-1901
Hallock, Absalom B.	1855	Lewis, John M.	1902-36
Lownsdale, Daniel H.	1856	Lambert, Francis	1937-48
Mitchell, I.	1857-61	Elder, Iven	1948
Morris, T. W.	1868-69	Dooley, Ray	1949
McCall, A. S.	1870-71	Summerville, J. T.	1949-56
Burrage, Charles W.	1872-81	Campbell, W. W.	1956-66
Austin, R. H.	1882-83		
Marye, W. B.	1884-85	**DISTRICT COURT CLERKS**	
Hurlburt, T. M.	1886-91	Willey, George L.	1913-16
Greenleaf, R. S.	1892-93	Richmond, W. L.	1917-22
Hammond, A. E.	1894-95	Manning, Frank E.	1923

Angell, Fred W.	1924-27
Hoyt, George W.	1928-36
Sophy, J. E.	1937
Conley, Eula I.	1938
Absher, Albert	1939-42
Bennett, Elmer	1943-62
Cawood, Margaret (appt)	1963 (4 mos)
Conley, Eula I.	1963-66
Wood, Daniel	1983-84

DISTRICT ATTORNEYS

Brandon, T. S.	1855-58
Langford, William G.	1858-60
Douthitt, David W.	1860-61
Page, William W.	1861-62
Johnson, William C.	1862-63
Hodkinson, E. W.	1864-66
Mulkey, Marion F.	1866-68
Gibbs, Addison C.	1868-72
Durham, George H.	1872-76
Stott, Raleigh	1876-77
Caples, John F.	1878-84
Gearin, John M.	1885-86
McGinn, Henry E.	1887-89
Stevens, Thomas G.	1890-92
Hume, Wilson T.	1892-95
Lord, Charles F.	1896-97
Sewall, Russell E.	1898-99
Chamberlain, George E.	1900-1902
Manning, John M.	1902-7
Cameron, George J.	1908-12
Evans, Walter Howard	1913-22
Myers, Stanley	1923-30
Langey, Lotus L.	1931-34
Bain, James R.	1935-45
Handley, Thomas B.	1945-46
McCourt, John B.	1946-54
Langley, William M.	1955-57

Smith, F. Leo	1957-58
Raymond, Charles E.	1959-62
Pecore, Chester W.	1962
Van Hoomissen, George	1962-70
Connall, Desmond	1970-72
Haas, Harl	1973-80
Schrunk, Michael D.	1981-2012

COUNTY CONSTABLES

Wagner, Lou	1909-12
Weinberger, Andy	1913-16
Peterson, M. W.	1917-20
Gloss, Ed	1921-32
North, Charles	1933-52
Hensley, Charles L.	1952
Bowerman, Milton W.	1952-56
Bain, John	1956-64
Haggerty, James	1965-66

COUNTY CORONERS

Wilson, R. B.	1854
Powell, J. P.	1855
Davenport, D.	1856
Baker, W. W.	1857
Nelson, Mr.	1858
Baker, W. W.	1859
Elwert, C.	1860
Hawthorne, J. C.	1861
Grooms, William	1862
Elwert, C.	1863
Hiklin, Lewis	1864
Hoffman, A. J.	1865-67
Brown, G. W.	1868-69
Mack, J. M.	1870-71
Dryer, Thomas Jefferson	1872-73
Wetmore, J. A.	1874-75
DeLin, A. P.	1876-77
Cook, H.	1878-79

Garnold, John	1880	Gore, Alice C.	1887
Cook, H.	1881-85	Gore, Charles H.	1888
DeLin, A. P.	1886-89	Wetzell, W. A.	1889-91
River, George H.	1890-91	Ackerman, John Henry	1892-95
Holman, Edward	1892-93	Armstrong, A. P.	1895-99
Cornelius, C. W.	1894-95	Robinson, R. F.	1900-1912
Koehler, George F.	1896-97	Armstrong, A. P.	1913-16
Rand, D. H.	1898-1901	Alderson, W. C.	1917-28
Finley, J. P.	1902-7	Cannon, Roy E.	1929-52
Norden, Ben L.	1908-12	Rees, Errol C.	1953-66
Slocum, Sam	1913-14		
Dammasch, F. H.	1915-17	**SHERIFFS**	
Smith, Earl	1918-32	*(midyear terms)*	
Erwin, R. M.	1933-40	McMillen, William	1854-58
South, F. Foyd	1941-55	Starr, Addison M.	1858-62
O'Toole, Arthur J.	1955-60	Ladd, Robert J.	1862-64
Smith, Earl	1960-64	Stitzel, Jacob	1864-68
Brady, William J.	1964-66	Zieber, Al	1868-70
		Bills, Cincinnati	1870-71

COUNTY SCHOOL SUPERINTENDENTS

		James, George V. (appt)	1871
Limerick, Lamden	1854	Claywood, J. M.	1872-73
Boyakin, W. F.	1855	Jeffery, E. J.	1874-77
Carter, Thomas J.	1856	Norden, Ben L.	1878-79
Carter, William Davis	1857	Buchtel, Joseph	1880-81
Kingsley, C. L.	1858-59	Sears, George C.	1882-84
Pennoyer, Sylvester	1860-61	Jordon, Tom	1885-88
Hoffman, J. J.	1862-63	Kelly, Penumbra	1889-94
Atkinson, George H.	1864	Sears, George C.	1894-95
Frambes, O. S.	1865	Frazier, William	1896-1901
Atkinson, George H.	1866-67	Storey, William A.	1902-4
Wiley, J. R.	1868-69	Word, Tom	1904-6
Anderson, E. C.	1870-71	Stevens, Robert L.	1906-12
Eliot, Thomas Lamb	1872-75	Word, Tom	1913-15
Brown, J. J.	1876-77	Hurlburt, Thomas M.	1915-17
Macrum, J. A.	1878-81	*(calendar year terms, after*	
Paxton, O. F.	1882-85	*1917 state referendum)*	
Gore, Charles H.	1886	Hurlburt, Thomas M.	1918-32
		Pratt, Martin T.	1933-48

Elliott, Marion "Mike"	1949 (10 mos)
Schrunk, Terry D. (appt)	1949-56
Lambert, Francis	1957-62
Clark, Donald E.	1963-66
Shields, "Barney" (appt)	1967 (8 mos)
Holzman, James (appt)	1967-70
Purcell, Bard (appt)	1970-74
Rinehart, Louis (appt)	1974 (8 mos)
Brown, Lee (appt)	1975-76
Martin, "Ed" (appt)	1976-82
Pearce, Frederic "Fred"*	1982-89
Skipper, Robert	1990-94
Bunnell, John (appt)	1995 (6 mos)
Noelle, Dan	1995-2002
Giusto, Bernie	2003-8
Skipper, Robert (appt)	2008-9
Staton, Dan (appt)	2009-

* Fred Pearce appointed early 1982;
position made elective May 1982;
Pearce elected November 1982.

SOURCES

Your Multnomah County Government: A Handbook, published by the Board of County Commissioners, Fourth Edition, January 1965; Past Boards Roster prepared by County Clerk at www.multnomah.lib.or.us/cc/pastboar.html, accessed December 28, 2002, and October 2009; "A History of the Oregon Sheriffs, 1841-1991" at http://gesswhoto.com/sherrif-index.html; various election year newspaper articles.

Appendix E
ELECTED MULTNOMAH COUNTY OFFICIALS: AN ALPHABETICAL LIST
1854-2012

(including officials appointed to fill vacancies)

Absher, Albert	1939-42	District Court Clerk
Ackerman, John Henry	1892-95	Superintendent of Schools
Alderson, W. C.	1917-28	Superintendent of Schools
Anderson, E. C.	1870-71	Superintendent of Schools
Anderson, Pauline	1985-92	Commissioner
Anderson, Pauline	2001*(3 mos)*	Commissioner
Angell, Fred W.	1924-27	District Court Clerk
Armstrong, A. P.	1895-99	Superintendent of Schools
Armstrong, A. P.	1913-16	Superintendent of Schools
Atkinson, George H.	1864	Superintendent of Schools
Atkinson, George H.	1866-67	Superintendent of Schools
Austin, R. H.	1882-83	Surveyor
Aylsworth, Larry W.	1962	Commissioner
Aylsworth, Larry W.	1967-72	Commissioner
Bacon, Charles P.	1882-83	Commissioner
Bailey, A. A.	1929-43	County Clerk
Bain, Jack	1955-62	Commissioner
Bain, James R.	1935-45	District Attorney
Bain, John	1956-64	County Constable
Baker, W. W.	1857	Coroner
Baker, W. W.	1859	Coroner
Baldwin, George	1945-48	Auditor
Barbur, Herbert C.	1949	Auditor
Barnard, O. M.	1874-77	Assessor

Barnes, F. C. . . . . 1903-9 . . . . Commissioner
Bauman, Rick. . . . . 1989-92 . . . . Commissioner
Bennett, Elmer . . . . 1943-63 . . . . District Court Clerk
Beveridge, J. W.. . . . . 1917-28 . . . . County Clerk
Bigelow, Charles. . . . . 1933-41 . . . . Commissioner
Bills, Cincinnati . . . . 1870-71 . . . . Sheriff
Biskar, Arnold . . . . 1983-84 . . . . Commissioner
Blackmer, Gary. . . . . 1991-98 . . . . Auditor
Blumenauer, Earl . . . . 1979-86 . . . . Commissioner
Bonser, R. C.. . . . . 1915-32 . . . . Surveyor
Borthwick, A. E.. . . . . 1880-81 . . . . County Clerk
Bowerman, Milton W. . . . . . . 1952-56 . . . . County Constable
Boyakin, W. F.. . . . . 1855. . . . . Superintendent of Schools
Boyd, Hamilton . . . . 1868-69 . . . . Commissioner
Bradley, Charles C.. . . . . 1942-43 . . . . Commissioner
Bradley, O. V. . . . . 1939-40 . . . . Commissioner
Brady, William J. . . . . 1964-66 . . . . Coroner
Brandes, C. A. . . . . 1903-9 . . . . Auditor
Brandon, T. S.. . . . . 1855-58 . . . . District Attorney
Breck, John M.. . . . . 1857. . . . . Assessor
Breck, John M.. . . . . 1859. . . . . Assessor
Breck, John M.. . . . . 1862-63 . . . . County Clerk
Brooke, T. S.. . . . . 1900-1901 . . . . . . Treasurer
Brown, Al L.. . . . . 1939-45 . . . . Auditor
Brown, Al L.. . . . . 1945-50 . . . . County Clerk
Brown, Al L.. . . . . 1951-62 . . . . Commissioner
Brown, Alan . . . . 1944-48 . . . . Commissioner
Brown, G. W. . . . . 1868-69 . . . . Coroner
Brown, J. J.. . . . . 1876-77 . . . . Superintendent of Schools
Brown, Lee. . . . . 1975-76 . . . . Sheriff
Buchanan, Dennis . . . . 1975-82 . . . . Commissioner
Buchanan, Dennis . . . . 1983-86 . . . . County Executive
Buchtel, Joseph. . . . . 1880-81 . . . . Sheriff
Buckley, W. S.. . . . . 1858. . . . . Assessor
Bucktel, A. L. . . . . 1944. . . . . County Clerk
Bunnell, John . . . . 1995 *(6 mos)* . . . . Sheriff
Burrage, Charles W. . . . . 1872-81 . . . . Surveyor
Burrell, M. S. . . . . 1862-63 . . . . Commissioner
Burton, E. M.. . . . . 1870-71 . . . . Commissioner
Bybee, James F.. . . . . 1854. . . . . Commissioner

Cake, W. M. . . . . 1898-1901 . . . . . . Commissioner
Cameron, George J. . . . . 1908-12 . . . . District Attorney
Campbell, W. W.. . . . . 1956-66 . . . . Treasurer
Cannon, Roy E. . . . . 1929-52 . . . . Superintendent of Schools
Caples, John F. . . . . 1878-84 . . . . District Attorney
Carter, Thomas J. . . . . 1856. . . . . Superintendent of Schools
Carter, William Davis. . . . . . . 1857. . . . . Superintendent of Schools
Casterline, Polly . . . . 1986-89 . . . . Commissioner
Catlin, John . . . . 1886-90 . . . . Commissioner
Cawood, Margaret. . . . . 1963 *(appt)*. . . . . . District Court Clerk
Chamberlain, George . . . . . . 1900-1902 . . . . . . District Attorney
Church, William, Jr. . . . . 1886-87 . . . . County Clerk
Clark, Donald E. . . . . 1963-66 . . . . Sheriff
Clark, Donald E. . . . . 1969-74 . . . . Commissioner
Clark, Donald E. . . . . 1975-79 . . . . County Chair
Clark, Donald E. . . . . 1979-82 . . . . County Executive
Claywood, J. M.. . . . . 1872-73 . . . . Sheriff
Cleeton, T. J.. . . . . 1910-16 . . . . Commissioner
Coffey, J. B. . . . . 1913-16 . . . . County Clerk
Cogen, Jeff . . . . 2007-10 . . . . Commissioner
Cogen, Jeff . . . . 2010- . . . . County Chair
Cohn, Si . . . . 1951-66 . . . . County Clerk
Collier, Tanya . . . . 1993-97 . . . . Commissioner
Conley, Eula I. . . . . 1938. . . . . District Court Clerk
Conley, Eula I. . . . . 1963. . . . . District Court Clerk
Connall, Desmond . . . . 1970-72 . . . . District Attorney
Cook, H. . . . . 1878-79 . . . . Coroner
Cook, H. . . . . 1881-85 . . . . Coroner
Corbett, Alice. . . . . 1975-78 . . . . Commissioner
Corbett, Henry W. . . . . 1864. . . . . Commissioner
Corbett, Henry W. . . . . 1884-87 . . . . Commissioner
Cornelius, C. W.. . . . . 1894-95 . . . . Coroner
Costello, John . . . . 1868-69 . . . . Assessor
Coulson, H. C.. . . . . 1864-67 . . . . County Clerk
Cruz, Serena. . . . . 1999-2006 . . . . . . Commissioner
Dammasch, F. H. . . . . 1915-17 . . . . Coroner
Davenport, D.. . . . . 1856. . . . . Coroner
DeLin, A. P. . . . . 1876-77 . . . . Coroner
DeLin, A. P. . . . . 1886-89 . . . . Coroner
Dolan, John . . . . 1864-67 . . . . Assessor

Dolan, John . . . . 1870-73 . . . . Assessor
Doland, W. P. . . . . 1861-63 . . . . Treasurer
Dooley, Ray . . . . 1949 . . . . Treasurer
Douthitt, David W.. . . . . 1860-61 . . . . District Attorney
Dryer, T. J. . . . . 1872-73 . . . . Coroner
Dunne, David M.. . . . . 1888-91 . . . . Commissioner
Durham, George H. . . . . 1872-76 . . . . District Attorney
Eccles, David . . . . 1963-72 . . . . Commissioner
Elder, Iven . . . . 1948 . . . . Treasurer
Eliot, Thomas Lamb. . . . . 1872-75 . . . . Superintendent of Schools
Elliott, Marion "Mike". . . . . . 1949 . . . . Sheriff
Elwert, C.. . . . . 1860 . . . . Coroner
Elwert, C.. . . . . 1863 . . . . Coroner
Ervin, Vicki . . . . 1984 *(3 mos)* . . . . County Clerk
Erwin, R. M. . . . . 1933-40 . . . . Coroner
Evans, Walter Howard. . . . . . 1913-22 . . . . District Attorney
Ewing, Donald . . . . 1956-62 . . . . Surveyor
Falloon, Wilbur J.. . . . . 1948-50 . . . . Assessor
Farman, S. . . . . 1855 . . . . Commissioner
Farver, Bill . . . . 2001 *(3 mos)* . . . . County Chair
Feeney, Anne Kelly . . . . 1983-88 . . . . Auditor
Fields, F. S. . . . . 1902-12 . . . . County Clerk
Finley, J. P. . . . . 1902-7 . . . . Coroner
Fitch, A. D.. . . . . 1854-55 . . . . Treasurer
Fletcher, O.. . . . . 1896-97 . . . . Surveyor
Flynn, Suzanne . . . . 1999-2004 . . . . . . Auditor
Frambes, O. S. . . . . 1865 . . . . Superintendent of Schools
Frazar, Thomas. . . . . 1860-62 . . . . Assessor
Frazier, William . . . . 1896-1901 . . . . . . Sheriff
Garnold, John . . . . 1880 . . . . Coroner
Gearin, John M.. . . . . 1885-86 . . . . District Attorney
German, Fred . . . . 1929-32 . . . . Commissioner
Gibbs, Addison C. . . . . 1868-72 . . . . District Attorney
Gibson, Will E.. . . . . 1933-36 . . . . Auditor
Giese, E. G.. . . . . 1882-83 . . . . Commissioner
Giusto, Bernie . . . . 2003-08 . . . . Sheriff
Gleason, M. J. "Mike" . . . . . . 1949-66 . . . . Commissioner
Gleason, M. J. "Mike" . . . . . . 1967-74 . . . . County Chair
Gloss, Ed . . . . 1921-32 . . . . County Constable
Gordon, Mel . . . . 1963-78 . . . . Commissioner

Gore, Alice C............1887...........Superintendent of Schools
Gore, Charles H. ....1886...........Superintendent of Schools
Gore, Charles H. ....1888...........Superintendent of Schools
Greenleaf, R. S.............1892-93 ....Surveyor
Greenleaf, R. S.............1894-1900 ......Assessor
Griffin-Valade, LaVonne .....2005-9 ....Auditor
Grooms, William ....1862...........Coroner
Haas, Harl ....1973-80 ....District Attorney
Hacheney, Frank ....1889-90 ....Treasurer
Haggerty, James ....1965-66 ....County Constable
Hallock, Absalom B.........1855...........Surveyor
Hamilton, Edward ....1859-61 ....Commissioner
Hamilton, Edward ....1870-73 ....Commissioner
Hammond, A. E. ....1894-95 ....Surveyor
Handley, Thomas B.........1945-46 ....District Attorney
Hansen, Gary.............1991-98 ....Commissioner
Hanson, Hans ....1866-67 ....Commissioner
Hanson, Hans ....1874-75 ....Commissioner
Harbaugh, F. ....1870-71 ....Treasurer
Harold, George ....1884-91 ....Assessor
Harris, W. H. ....1872-73 ....County Clerk
Hart, D. V. ....1910-14 ....Commissioner
Hawkins, Joe ....1959-66 ....Assessor
Hawthorne, J. C. ....1861...........Coroner
Hensley, Charles L.........1952...........County Constable
Hiklin, Lewis ....1864...........Coroner
Hodkinson, E. W...........1864-66 ....District Attorney
Hoffman, A. J. ....1865-67 ....Coroner
Hoffman, J. J.............1862-63 ....Superintendent of Schools
Holbrook, P. (Philo?) ....1915-18 ....Commissioner
Holbrook, P., Jr. ....1906-14 ....Surveyor
Holbrook, Philo...........1878-79 ....Commissioner
Holbrook, Philo...........1892-99 ....Commissioner
Holman, Charles ....1874-75 ....Commissioner
Holman, Edward ....1892-93 ....Coroner
Holman, Rufus............1914-22 ....Commissioner
Holmes, H. H. ....1898-99 ....County Clerk
Holzman, James C..........1967-70 ....Sheriff
Hoyt, George W............1928-36 ....District Court Clerk
Hoyt, Ralph W. ....1897-99 ....Treasurer

Hoyt, Ralph W. . . . . .1919-22 . . . . .Commissioner
Hume, Wilson T.. . . . . .1892-95 . . . . .District Attorney
Hurlburt, J. A. . . . . .1898-1903 . . . . . .Surveyor
Hurlburt, T. M. . . . . .1886-91 . . . . .Surveyor
Hurlburt, T. M. . . . . .1915-32 . . . . .Sheriff
Ivancie, Dan . . . . .1989-90 . . . . .Auditor
James, George V. . . . . .1871 . . . . .Sheriff
Jeffery, E. J.. . . . . .1874-77 . . . . .Sheriff
Johnson, William C.. . . . . . . .1862-63 . . . . .District Attorney
Jordon, Tom. . . . . .1885-88 . . . . .Sheriff
Kafoury, Deborah. . . . . .2009- . . . . .Commissioner
Kafoury, Gretchen . . . . .1985-90 . . . . .Commissioner
Kelley, Sharron. . . . . .1989-2000 . . . . . .Commissioner
Kelly, Penumbra . . . . .1876-77 . . . . .Commissioner
Kelly, Penumbra . . . . .1889-94 . . . . .Sheriff
Kenulty, John . . . . .1870-71 . . . . .Commissioner
Kerns, William . . . . .1862-63 . . . . .Commissioner
Kerr, Edwin M.. . . . . .1949-50 . . . . .Auditor
Kingsley, C. L. . . . . .1858-59 . . . . .Superintendent of Schools
Knowles, Roy H. . . . . .1932 . . . . .Auditor
Knowles, Roy H. . . . . .1937-38 . . . . .Auditor
Koehler, George F. . . . . .1896-97 . . . . .Coroner
Kreuder, T. J.. . . . . .1941-42 . . . . .Commissioner
Ladd, R. J. . . . . .1862-63 . . . . .Sheriff
Ladd, William S.. . . . . .1859 . . . . .Commissioner
Lambert, A. W.. . . . . .1895-96 . . . . .Treasurer
Lambert, Francis . . . . .1937-48 . . . . .Treasurer
Lambert, Francis . . . . .1957-62 . . . . .Sheriff
Lambert, Joseph H. . . . . .1858 . . . . .Commissioner
Langey, Lotus L.. . . . . .1931-34 . . . . .District Attorney
Langford, William G.. . . . . . .1858-60 . . . . .District Attorney
Langley, William M.. . . . . . . .1955-57 . . . . .District Attorney
Lansing, Jewel . . . . .1975-82 . . . . .Auditor
Levy, Richard . . . . .1984 *(3 mos)* . . . .Commissioner
Lewis, John M.. . . . . .1902-36 . . . . .Treasurer
Lightner, William . . . . .1905-16 . . . . .Commissioner
Limerick, Lamden . . . . .1854 . . . . .Superintendent of Schools
Linn, Diane . . . . .1998-2001 . . . . . .Commissioner
Linn, Diane . . . . .2001-6 . . . . .County Chair
Litchenthaler, D. W. . . . . .1857 . . . . .Auditor

Litchenthaler, D. W. . . . . 1858-59 . . . . County Clerk
Long, George M. . . . . 1880-81 . . . . Commissioner
Lord, Charles F. . . . . 1896-97 . . . . District Attorney
Lownsdale, Daniel H.. . . . . . . 1856. . . . . Surveyor
Lownsdale, J. P. O. . . . . 1865-67 . . . . Commissioner
Lucas, M. M. . . . . 1856-58 . . . . Commissioner
Mack, J. G.. . . . . 1900-1902 . . . . . . Commissioner
Mack, J. M. . . . . 1870-71 . . . . Coroner
Macrum, J. A.. . . . . 1878-81 . . . . Superintendent of Schools
Malarkey, C. A. . . . . 1893-94 . . . . Treasurer
Manning, Frank E.. . . . . 1923. . . . . District Court Clerk
Manning, John M.. . . . . 1902-7 . . . . District Attorney
March, Steve . . . . 2009- . . . . Auditor
Marquam, Philip A.. . . . . 1862-69 . . . . Commissioner
Marshall, Earl . . . . 1933-36 . . . . Surveyor
Martin, Edgar "Ed" . . . . 1976-82 . . . . Sheriff
Martin, Sam B.. . . . . 1911-24 . . . . Auditor
Marye, W. B.. . . . . 1884-85 . . . . Surveyor
Masters, William . . . . 1868-69 . . . . Treasurer
McCall, A. S. . . . . 1870-71 . . . . Surveyor
McCormick, S. J. . . . . 1872-73 . . . . Commissioner
McCourt, John B.. . . . . 1946-54 . . . . District Attorney
McCoy, Gladys. . . . . 1979-84 . . . . Commissioner
McCoy, Gladys. . . . . 1987-93 . . . . County Chair
McCracken, John . . . . 1860. . . . . Treasurer
McDonell, C. E. . . . . 1901-4 . . . . Assessor
McGinn, Henry E. . . . . 1887-89 . . . . District Attorney
McKeel, Diane . . . . 2009- . . . . Commissioner
McMillen, William. . . . . 1854-57 . . . . Sheriff
Miggins, Hank . . . . 1993 *(3 mos)* . . . . County Chair
Miller, Caroline . . . . 1981-88 . . . . Commissioner
Mitchell, I. . . . . 1857-61 . . . . Surveyor
Moreland, Julius C. . . . . 1891-93 . . . . Commissioner
Morris, Bonnie. . . . . 1986 *(8 mos)* . . . . Commissioner
Morris, T. W. . . . . 1868-69 . . . . Surveyor
Morse, Clay . . . . 1927-30 . . . . Commissioner
Mosee, Dan . . . . 1967-68 . . . . Commissioner
Mosee, Dan . . . . 1973-80 . . . . Commissioner
Muck, A. A. . . . . 1917-20 . . . . Commissioner
Mulkey, Marion F. . . . . 1866-68 . . . . District Attorney

Myers, Stanley . . . . 1923-30 . . . . District Attorney
Naito, Lisa . . . . 1998-2004 . . . . . . Commissioner
Nelson, Mr. . . . . 1858 . . . . Coroner
Newell, John S.. . . . . 1863 . . . . Assessor
Newell, John S.. . . . . 1884-87 . . . . Commissioner
Noelle, Dan . . . . 1995-2002 . . . . . . Sheriff
Norden, Ben L.. . . . . 1868-69 . . . . County Clerk
Norden, Ben L.. . . . . 1878-79 . . . . Sheriff
Norden, Ben L.. . . . . 1908-12 . . . . Coroner
Norris, Shubrick. . . . . 1854-56 . . . . Auditor
Norris, Shubrick. . . . . 1860-61 . . . . County Clerk
North, Charles . . . . 1933-52 . . . . County Constable
Northup, Henry H. . . . . 1894-97 . . . . Commissioner
O'Donnell, "Jack" . . . . 1951-74 . . . . Auditor
O'Toole, Arthur J. . . . . 1955-60 . . . . Coroner
Padrow, Ben . . . . 1971-74 . . . . Commissioner
Page, William W. . . . . 1861-62 . . . . District Attorney
Parrish, Charles W.. . . . . 1870-71 . . . . County Clerk
Paxton, O. F.. . . . . 1882-85 . . . . Superintendent of Schools
Pearce, Frederic "Fred". . . . . 1982-89 . . . . Sheriff
Pecore, Chester W. . . . . 1962 . . . . District Attorney
Pennoyer, Sylvester . . . . 1860-61 . . . . Superintendent of Schools
Pense, Claire. . . . . 1962-66 . . . . Surveyor
Peterson, M. W. . . . . 1917-20 . . . . County Constable
Phegley, Grant . . . . 1924-34 . . . . Commissioner
Pope, W. H. . . . . 1895-1902 . . . . . . Auditor
Powell, D.. . . . . 1855-57 . . . . Commissioner
Powell, J. P.. . . . . 1855 . . . . Coroner
Powell, T. C.. . . . . 1890-93 . . . . County Clerk
Powers, Claude . . . . 1937-51 . . . . Surveyor
Pratt, M. T.. . . . . 1933-48 . . . . Sheriff
Purcell, Bard. . . . . 1970-74 . . . . Sheriff
Quimby, E. L.. . . . . 1868-69 . . . . Commissioner
Radakovich, Bill. . . . . 1983-84 . . . . County Clerk
Rand, D. H. . . . . 1898-1901 . . . . . . Coroner
Rankin, J. H. . . . . 1923-24 . . . . Commissioner
Rankin, W. C.. . . . . 1937 . . . . Auditor
Raymond, Charles E.. . . . . . 1959-62 . . . . District Attorney
Reed, Henry E.. . . . . 1913-20 . . . . Assessor
Rees, Errol C.. . . . . 1953-66 . . . . Superintendent of Schools

Rice, S. W. . . . . 1878-81 . . . . Commissioner
Richmond, A. H. . . . . 1904-5 . . . . Surveyor
Richmond, W. L.. . . . . 1917-22 . . . . District Court Clerk
Rinehart, Louis . . . . 1974 *(8 mos)* . . . . Sheriff
Ringler, Charles . . . . 1937-41 . . . . Assessor
Ritchey, Caleb . . . . 1859 . . . . Commissioner
River, George H.. . . . . 1890-91 . . . . Coroner
Roberts, Barbara . . . . 1978 . . . . Commissioner
Roberts, Lonnie . . . . 2001-8 . . . . Commissioner
Robinson, R. F.. . . . . 1900-1912 . . . . . . Superintendent of Schools
Rojo de Steffey, Maria . . . . . . 2001-8 . . . . Commissioner
Rossman, Gene W. . . . . 1949-50 . . . . Commissioner
Rudeen, Charles. . . . . 1921-24 . . . . Commissioner
Saltzman, Dan . . . . 1993-98 . . . . Commissioner
Saunders, I. N. . . . . 1882-83 . . . . Assessor
Saunders, I. N. . . . . 1884-85 . . . . County Clerk
Schrunk, Michael D.. . . . . 1981-2012 . . . . . . District Attorney
Schrunk, Terry D.. . . . . 1949-56 . . . . Sheriff
Scott, Emsley R. . . . . 1854. . . . . Commissioner
Sears, George C.. . . . . 1878-81 . . . . Assessor
Sears, George C.. . . . . 1882-84 . . . . Sheriff
Sears, George C.. . . . . 1892-93 . . . . Assessor
Sears, George C.. . . . . 1894-95 . . . . Sheriff
Sewall, Russell E. . . . . 1898-99 . . . . District Attorney
Sewall, W. R. . . . . 1882-83 . . . . County Clerk
Shadburne, Gordon . . . . 1979-86 . . . . Commissioner
Shaw, Alva Compton R. . . . . 1864-65 . . . . Commissioner
Shields, Bryon . . . . 1967 *(8 mos)* . . . . Sheriff
Shiprack, Judy . . . . 2009- . . . . Commissioner
Showers, William . . . . 1878-88 . . . . Treasurer
Showers, William . . . . 1901-4 . . . . Commissioner
Shull, Frank . . . . 1931-54 . . . . Commissioner
Sigler, B. D.. . . . . 1905-12 . . . . Assessor
Silver, Clieve S.. . . . . 1872-73 . . . . Commissioner
Skipper, Robert . . . . 1990-94 . . . . Sheriff
Skipper, Robert *(appt)* . . . . . . 2008-9 . . . . Sheriff
Slavin, J. A.. . . . . 1880-81 . . . . Commissioner
Slocum, Sam. . . . . 1913-14 . . . . Coroner
Smith, Amadee. . . . . 1924-28 . . . . Commissioner
Smith, B. F.. . . . . 1888-89 . . . . Commissioner

Smith, Earl . . . . 1918-32 . . . . Coroner
Smith, Earl . . . . 1960-64 . . . . Coroner
Smith, F. Leo . . . . 1957-58 . . . . District Attorney
Smith, H. C. . . . . 1894-97 . . . . County Clerk
Smith, J. A. . . . . 1876-79 . . . . County Clerk
Smith, Loretta . . . . 2011- . . . . Commissioner
Smith, Wiley W. . . . . 1951-58 . . . . Assessor
Sophy, J. E. . . . . 1937. . . . . District Court Clerk
South, F. Foyd . . . . 1941-55 . . . . Coroner
Stansbury, Z. N. . . . . 1856. . . . . Assessor
Stansbury, Z. N. . . . . 1858-59 . . . . Treasurer
Starr, Addison M. . . . . 1858-62 . . . . Sheriff
Starr, Lewis M. . . . . 1856-57 . . . . Treasurer
Staton, Dan *(appt)* . . . . 2009- . . . . Sheriff
Stearns, Loyal B. . . . . 1882-85 . . . . Commissioner
Steel, George A. . . . . 1864-67 . . . . Treasurer
Steele, W. B. . . . . 1898-1900 . . . . . Commissioner
Stein, Beverly . . . . 1993-2001 . . . . . County Chair
Stevens, R. L. . . . . 1906-12 . . . . Sheriff
Stevens, Thomas G. . . . . 1890-92 . . . . District Attorney
Stitzel, Jacob . . . . 1864-67 . . . . Sheriff
Stone, H. S. . . . . 1890-97 . . . . Commissioner
Storey, William A. . . . . 1902-4 . . . . Sheriff
Story, George L. . . . . 1874-75 . . . . County Clerk
Stott, Raleigh . . . . 1876-77 . . . . District Attorney
Summerville, J. T. . . . . 1949-56 . . . . Treasurer
Sweeney, Ed . . . . 1925-31 . . . . Auditor
Swetland, L. O. . . . . 1900-1 . . . . County Clerk
Taft, Erwin . . . . 1924-26 . . . . Commissioner
Taft, Erwin . . . . 1935-39 . . . . Commissioner
Tazwell, George . . . . 1917-18 . . . . Commissioner
Van Hoomissen, George . . . . . 1962-70 . . . . District Attorney
Van Schuyver, W. . . . . 1855. . . . . Assessor
Vaughn, George W. . . . . 1854-55 . . . . Commissioner
Vickers, L. B. . . . . 1854. . . . . Surveyor
Wagner, Lou . . . . 1909-12 . . . . County Constable
Walker, Dow V. . . . . 1923-24 . . . . Commissioner
Walker, Ellis . . . . 1855-56 . . . . Commissioner
Walker, Ellis . . . . 1860-61 . . . . Commissioner
Watson, Tom . . . . 1941-48 . . . . Assessor

Webster, L. R.. . . . . .1902-9 . . . . Commissioner
Wheeler, E. C.. . . . . .1888-89 . . . . County Clerk
Wheeler, Ted. . . . . .2007-10 . . . . County Chair
Weinberger, Andy. . . . . .1913-16 . . . . County Constable
Welch, Hiram U. . . . . .1910. . . . . Auditor
Welch, Hiram U. . . . . .1921-36 . . . . Assessor
Welch, Peter W. . . . . .1952-55 . . . . Surveyor
West, Tom H.. . . . . .1942-48 . . . . Commissioner
Wetmore, J. A. . . . . .1874-75 . . . . Coroner
Wetzell, W. A.. . . . . .1889-91 . . . . Superintendent of Schools
White, John S. . . . . .1860-61 . . . . Commissioner
Wiberg, W. M. . . . . .1878-79 . . . . Commissioner
Wilcox, James . . . . .1983-84 . . . . Assessor
Wiley, J. R.. . . . . .1868-69 . . . . Superintendent of Schools
Willer, Barbara *(appt)*. . . . . . .2010 *(9 mos)* . . . . Commissioner
Willey, George L. . . . . .1913-16 . . . . District Court Clerk
Willey, S. B. . . . . .1891-92 . . . . Treasurer
Wilmot, J. F.. . . . . .1857-58 . . . . Commissioner
Wilson, R. B. . . . . .1854. . . . . Coroner
Wood, Daniel. . . . . .1983-84 . . . . District Court Clerk
Woodward, J. H. . . . . .1874-77 . . . . Commissioner
Woodward, Tyler . . . . .1876-77 . . . . Commissioner
Word, Tom. . . . . .1904-06 . . . . Sheriff
Word, Tom. . . . . .1913-15 . . . . Sheriff
Zieber, Al . . . . .1868-69 . . . . Sheriff

NOTES

CHAPTER 1

1   *Oregon Journal*, Feb. 21, 1974, 1.

2   "East Portland Review," Portland Planning Bureau, 2007.

3   See Gregory Thompson, *Oregon Journal*, "How Portland's Power Brokers Accommodated the Anti-Highway Movement of the Early 1970s: The Decision to Build Light Rail," in Business and Economic History On-Line, Vol.3, 2005, archived at www.h-net.org/~business/bhcweb/publications/BEHonline/beh.html.

4   *Oregonian*, July 26, 1974, 1.

5   Comment by City Commissioner Francis Ivancie to author Leeson, 1973.

6   *Oregonian*, Dec. 26, 1994, B1.

7   See "Recollections of David Hupp" at www.pdx.edu/usp/planpdxorg-home.

8   Don Clark, interview with Ernie Bonner at www.pdx.edu/usp/plandpdxorg-home.

9   *Oregonian*, Jan. 6, 1972, Sec. 2, 14.

10 Clark, interview with Bonner.

11 *Oregonian*, Nov. 22, 1972, 1.

12 Ibid., July 25, 1974, 27.

13 Ibid., Feb. 9, 1986, B1.

14 Ibid., Jan. 8, 1974, 12.

15 Ibid.

16 *Oregon Journal*, Feb. 21, 1974.1.

17 *Oregonian*, Feb. 22, 1974, 1.

CHAPTER 2

1   Journals of Lewis and Clark, Nov. 5, 1805; http://lewisandclarkjournals.unl.edu/index.html.

2   McArthur, 528. Other authors variously spelled the name as Multonomah and Multenomough. Holman, 42-48; *WPA Inventory, Vol. I*, 3. On the Lewis and Clark return trip homeward in 1806, they used the present-day spelling of Multnomah. McArthur, 528; McCarthy, 172; Corning, 53; *Historical Sites Tour Guide, Multnomah County*, Item #8.

3   McArthur, 528, 652-53. The name Wapato is today preserved as the name of a 525-bed county corrections facility in North Portland, completed in 2004 but still unoccupied as of 2012.

4   Beckham, 38; Zucker, inside front cover; McArthur, 652-53; *Oregon Blue Book*, 2007-2008, 257.

5   Chilton, 38.

6   Nearly 25 miles of the Sandy River are included in the Wild and Scenic Rivers system. www.rivers.gov/; accessed Nov. 17, 2008.

7   Zucker, 60; Corning, 80-81, 173. At the time Multnomah County was created, the northernmost part of the island was assigned to Columbia County.

8   Robbins, 58-59; *WPA Inventory, Vol. I*, 4; Holman, 42. Also see *Oregon Historical Quarterly*, June 1928, 152-57.

9   1930 Census data, as reported in "Historical Sketch of Multnomah County," INV-1, 42; 2000 data from U.S. Census Bureau, Census 2000.

10 http://quickfacts.census.gov/qfd/states/41000.html; accessed April 12, 2006; U.S. Census Bureau, Census 2000; accessed June 19, 2000. The federal 2000 census counted 39,000 multiracial Native Americans in the Portland Metropolitan Service Area. Of the Multnomah County total, 40 percent were under the age of twenty-five. Half of the total were 200 percent under the poverty level.

11 "Portland Oregon Urban Native DATA Sheet," Native American Youth and Family Center (NAYA), Feb 2009, and 2004 study by the Northwest Area Foundation; U.S. Census Bureau; Census 2000.

12 Overall Bureau of Indian Affairs policy of the 1950s was also a factor in moving Native Americans off reservations and into cities. Jaimes, 15-16; Native American Youth and Family Center (NAYA) fact sheet, Feb. 2009.

13 *Oregon Blue Book*, 2007-2008, 223. Smaller reservation populations included The Confederated Tribes of the Warm Springs, 4,306; Siletz, 4,294; Klamaths, 3,572; Umatilla, 2,557; Cow Creek, 1,397; Coquille, 848; Coos, Lower Umpqua, and Siuslaw, 831; and Burns Paiute, 349.

14 *Oregon*, Federal Writers' Project, 208; Maddux, 11.

15 Lansing, 20-21.

16 MacColl, *Shaping*, 66, 70.

17 *Oregonian*, Dec. 21, 1854, 1.

18 Washington County provided 440 of the 869 votes cast against calling a constitutional convention. The total tally was 3,210 for to 4,079 against. *Oregonian*, July 15, 1854; Scott, vol. 2, 77-78.

18 Voters had resisted the call for a constitutional convention for several years. Republican *Oregonian* editor Dryer argued that taxes would rise, that the Democratic Party would benefit, and that the territory lacked sufficient men of quality to fill state offices. *Oregonian*, Feb. 15, 2009, B6; Maddux, 33.

20 *WPA Inventory, Vol. I*, 3. The weather was mild, with ample annual rainfall of around 44 inches. Annual rainfall for the years 1971-2000 ranged from 37 to 43 inches at Portland stations, 45 inches at Troutdale, and 78 inches at Bonneville Dam. www.ocs.orst.edu/county_climate/Multnomah_files/Multnomah.html; accessed Oct. 22, 2007.

21 In 1950, the population of Multnomah County was 471,537, while the entire state had reached 1,521,341. In 2010, the U.S. Census Bureau estimated the population of Multnomah County

as 726,855; Washington County as 537,318; Clackamas as 396,143; and the State of Oregon as 3,825,657. www.census.gov/population/cencounts/or190090.txt; "Population of Oregon Cities, Counties, and Metropolitan Areas, 1850-1957," Bureau of Municipal Research and Service, University of Oregon, Information Bulletin no. 106, April 1958. In the twenty-five year period of 1960 through 1985, Portland's population of approximately 375,000 would have decreased by 11 percent without substantial mid-county annexations. This population shift was part of a nationwide trend toward smaller household sizes in general and more specifically to larger numbers of families with children moving out of cities to suburbia. "City of Portland Annexation Impacts from 1960 to 1985," Portland Office of Fiscal Administration, Nov. 25, 1985.

22 Mount Sylvania in the far southwest corner of the county, bordering both Washington and Clackamas counties, is 970 feet. Other "tall hills" in today's City of Portland include Mt. Tabor at 645 feet; Rocky Butte, 607 feet; and Kelly Butte, 577 feet. "There's a Story Behind Sylvania," *Oregonian*, Apr. 14, 1963, 29; www.mountainzone.com/mountains/detail.aspfid=2249856; accessed Nov 28, 2009.

23 Informational sign at Willamette Stone Park, viewed by author Lansing in Sept. 2009. The park is along Skyline Boulevard just south of West Burnside Road and provides parking for half a dozen vehicles. *Oregon Blue Book*, 2007-2008, 348; Corning, 268; *Oregonian*, Apr. 14, 2009, C1. Multnomah County has more than 2,000 survey markers of concrete or steel columns topped by brass medallions scattered throughout the county. "Mult Co Transportation Newsletter," Fall 2000.

24 An *Oregonian* article commenting on the county's 100th birthday puts the annual lease cost at $300 but gives no source for this figure. *Oregonian*, Dec. 21, 1954, 1.

25 Portland City Council minutes of May 9, 1853. Lansing, 65.

26 *WPA Inventory, Vol. I*, 27-28, Board
    minutes of April 2, 1855.

27 *WPA Inventory, Vol. I*, 16.

28 Board minutes of April 2, 1855. The
    Oregonian of Jan. 19, 1955, page 14,
    quotes former Commissioner Frank
    Shull as saying that the rates were six
    cents per person, eleven cents for a team
    of horses, and twelve cents for a team of
    oxen.

29 David Powell drew the three-year term,
    Ellis Walker the two-year, and Samuel
    Farman, the newly elected chairman, the
    one-year. *WPA Inventory, Vol. I*, 13.

30 Lansing, 64, 68, 76, 448.

31 Communication by author Lansing
    with Michael Powell, owner of Powell's
    Books, June 2007; McArthur, 191;
    Snyder, *Names*, 191.

32 MacColl, *Merchants*, 52-53; Lansing,
    47.

CHAPTER 3

1 *Oregon Blue Book*, 2007-2008, 255,
   353. *New York Bureau of Municipal
   Research Multnomah County Survey*, 1.

2 Leeson, 21. After statehood, the three
   Oregon Supreme Court judges served as
   the state's trial judges.

3 Communication from former county
   and city auditor Gary Blackmer to
   author Lansing, Sept. 27, 2009.

4 See Chapter 4 concerning Sheriff J. M.
   Caywood.

5 Portland was now operating under its
   third charter, testing the proposition that
   the mayor should operate as a separate
   branch of government from the council.
   The first council member chosen to
   serve as city council president, James
   Field, resigned after only three months.
   McMillan was elected to succeed Field
   in June 1854. Lansing, 70.

6 King, 7-9; McMillan won 57 percent
   of the 578 votes cast in his first election
   challenge. King, 95. Sheriffs' duties
   were spelled out in detail by the Oregon
   Territorial Legislature and reaffirmed
   after 1859 by the Oregon State
   Legislature.

7 Addison Starr had bested former
   Portland mayor George Vaughn for
   the mayor's job in 1858. Vaughn had

previously edged out Starr in an 1855
bid for the mayoralty. Lansing, 74, 90.

8 *Oregonian*, June 16, 1855; June 6 and
   12, 1858, as quoted in King, 52-53.

9 Ibid., June 5, 1858, 3.

10 Ibid., June 12, 1858, 3.

11 Two other sheriffs also served as
    Portland mayors: William Storey
    became sheriff in 1902, three years after
    his short term as mayor, while Terry
    Schrunk, elected mayor in 1957, served
    six years as sheriff before assuming the
    mayor's chair.

12 *Oregonian*, May 1, 1891, 8; Lansing,
    90-91.

13 For complete details of the Mortimer
    Stump murder and its aftermath, see
    Snyder, *We Claimed*, 9-15.

14 In his mayoral message, Stephen
    McCormick declared that the city
    needed better police protection and said
    council needed to appropriate more
    money if the newly completed city jail
    was to be put into usable condition.
    Oregon Historical Quarterly, Summer
    1979, 29, 134-36.

15 Snyder, *We Claimed*, 11-12; *Oregon
    Historical Quarterly*, Spring 1979,
    28-29.

16 *Oregonian*, Aug. 20, 27, and Oct. 22,
    1859; *Oregon Historical Quarterly*,
    Summer 1981, 180; Lansing, 175-76.
    (The city jail was then at Second and
    Taylor.)

17 Goeres-Gardner, xvii, 33.

18 Snyder, *We Claimed*, 13-14.

19 Goeres-Gardner, xxii, 250.

20 One entry to the Wildwood Trail starts
    near the Danford Balch home site, a
    trail that began as a route from the
    Forestry Building, which was built
    during the 1905 World's Fair, to Upper
    Macleay Park. Draft *Portland Parks and
    Recreation, A Chronological History*,
    Dec. 1998, 5-6.

21 *Oregonian*, Mar. 24, 1860, 2.

22 Ibid., Mar. 24, 1860, 2; Scott, *Portland*,
    134; Gaston, vol. 1, 225; Lansing, 105,
    133.

23 For further details regarding levee
    ownership, see Lansing, 53-54, 91,
    105-6.

24 *Oregonian*, May 2, 1892; *Oregon Historical Quarterly*, Summer 1979, 141-42.

25 Lansing, 90-93.

26 *Oregon Journal*, Nov. 6, 1949.

27 Ibid., Nov. 6, 1932, 5.

28 *Oregonian*, Nov. 22, 1912, 1.

29 *Oregonian*, May 9 and 10, 1912; Corning, 157.

30 *Oregonian*, Sept. 24, 1966, 13.

31 http://www.portlandonline.com/parks/finder/index.cfm?action=ViewPark&PropertyID=251.

32 Lansing, 108, 196.

33 The 19 elected officials who served on both the Multnomah County Commission and Portland City Council during the county's first fifty years included Charles Bigelow, Hamilton Boyd, E. M. Burton, John Catlin, Edward Hamilton, Charles Holman, William S. Ladd, J. P. O. Lownsdale, M. M. Lucas, Philip Marquam, Stephen McCormick, Julius Moreland, Emsley R. Scott, Alva C. R. Shaw, William Showers, Clieve S. Silver, George Vaughn, John S. White, and Tyler Woodward. Between 1986 and 2012, three county commissioners moved from the county to city hall: Earl Blumenauer, Gretchen Kafoury, and Dan Saltzman. See Appendixes D and E.

CHAPTER 4

1 Other notable buildings designed by Piper and Burton included Portland's New Market Theater in 1872 (still standing), the Marion County Courthouse (now demolished) of 1873, and Deady Hall at the University of Oregon, also 1873 (still standing).

2 National Historic Landmark Nomination, Skidmore-Old Town Historic District, U.S. Department of Interior, National Park Service.

3 *Oregon Journal*, Nov. 6, 1949; Wiederhold, 85. Prior to construction of the first Multnomah County Courthouse, the county rented a building at the northwest corner of Front and Salmon for court trials. That building would later become the Metropolitan Hotel; it was destroyed in the devastating city fire of 1873. *Oregon Journal*, Nov. 5, 1911, Sec. 6, 5; *1882 City Directory*, 55.

4 Hawkins, 36.

5 *Oregonian*, ca. Aug. 1866, as quoted in Hawkins, 36; Clark, *Pharisee, vol. 1*, 2976; *Your Multnomah County Government*, 1961, 7; Leeson, 24-25.

6 Goeres-Gardner, viii; Leeson, 24-25.

7 *Portland, the Rose City*, S.J. Clarke Publishing Co., 1911, 77.

8 In addition to his Multnomah County contract, Dr. Hawthorne provided treatment for insane patients under contract with the State of Oregon until his death in 1881. The state government subsequently built a state hospital for mental patients in Salem. www.salemhistory.net/places/state_hospital.htm.

9 *Oregon Journal*, Feb. 23, 1939, 12.

10 *Proposal to merge Multnomah County Hospital into University of Oregon Medical School*, Oregon Executive Department, Oct. 1972.

11 Courtney Smith, *History of the Origin and Growth of the Multnomah County Hospital*, University of Oregon Medical School Medical History Club, 1933.

12 Ibid.

13 Petition filed in papers of 5th Regular Session of the Oregon House of Representatives, 1868.

14 *Oregonian*, Sept. 3, 1868, 2.

15 Ibid.

16 Carey, *Oregon Constitution*, 415-16.

17 The only exceptions granted to counties for incurring debt over $5,000 were to suppress insurrection or repel invasion. Carey, *Oregon Constitution*, 424.

18 In 1919, the Oregon legislature gave Multnomah County authority to borrow money to construct and reconstruct bridges across the Willamette by issuing bonds. Bridges constructed under this act were the Sellwood Bridge, the Ross Island Bridge, the replacement Burnside Bridge, and the St. Johns Bridge. "Historical Sketch of Multnomah County," *Inventory of the County Archives of Oregon (WPA), vol. 1*, 21.

19 Carey, *Oregon Constitution*, 428.

20 The Oregon House of Representatives Journal for Wednesday, September 23, 1868, says, "Mr. (W. W.) Chapman

offered the petition of the citizens of Portland to amend the corporate law of the city of Portland, by consolidating the city government with that of the county of Multnomah. On motion of Mr. Chapman, the petition was referred to the Multnomah members of the house." No tracking number was assigned to the petition, and the petition back simply says, "Referred to the members from Portland."

21 *Oregonian*, Aug. 29 and 30, 1867; *Oregon Historical Quarterly*, Summer 1979, 140-41. Anti-Chinese sentiment had dissipated considerably by the time the federal Chinese Exclusion Act of 1882 was repealed during World War II. Lansing, 146-47, 171.

22 See Gregory Nokes, *Massacred for Gold* (Corvallis, Oregon State University Press, 2009), 76-79.

23 Clark, *Pharisee, vol. 1*, 39.

24 *Oregonian*, June 10, June 25, and July 10, 1874, as quoted in King, 48-49, 57.

25 *Oregon Historical Society Scrap Book No. 77*, 22, 172, as quoted in King, 57-59.

26 By 1954, the sheriff's salary had increased to $8,400, and by 1963 to $14,750. King, 50-51. After home rule took effect in Multnomah County in 1967, the state legislature no longer set Multnomah County salaries.

27 The three young men were Archie Brown, 25; James Johnson, 25; and Joseph Swords, 18. Brown was an alias for Eugene Avery; Johnson an alias for Frank Taylor. Brown later claimed to be the ringleader of California bank robbers. Johnson used a pseudonym because he didn't want his family on the East Coast to know about his record, which included incarceration at San Quentin.

28 Goeres-Gardner, xvii.

29 "A Hanging in Old Portland," *Oregon Journal*, Jan. 16, 1949; Goeres-Gardner, xx, 84-90.

30 Goeres-Gardner, 89.

31 Maddux, 86-87; Goeres-Gardner, 98.

32 Goeres-Gardner, 96-101; Lansing, 146-47; Maddux, 77-94.

CHAPTER 5

1 Gaston, vol. 1, 515; MacColl, *Shaping*, 100-8, 195; MacColl, *Merchants*, 308-9.

2 MacColl, *Merchants*, 307-9; *Shaping*, 101-4.

3 *An Illustrated History of the State of Oregon* (Chicago: The Lewis Publishing Company, 1893), 1122, as quoted in King, 60, 62; MacColl, *Shaping*, 104; *Historical Sites Tour Guide, Multnomah County*, #27.

4 MacColl, *Merchants*, 309-10.

5 Portland's city council then consisted of 11 council members, elected by wards. Councilman Eugene Shelby was acting as mayor in the absence of Mayor William Mason when the Coxey's Army contingent reached Portland in early April 1894. Lansing, 214, 484; Herman C. Voeltz, "Coxey's Army in Oregon, 1894," *Oregon Historical Quarterly*, Sept. 1964, 272-74; MacColl, *Merchants*, 309-10.

6 MacColl, *Merchants*, 309-10; *Oregon Historical Quarterly*, Sept. 1964, 272-91.

7 *Oregon Historical Quarterly*, Sept. 1964, 279.

8 Clark, *Pharisee, vol. 1*, xxvi.

9 *Oregon Historical Quarterly*, Sept 1964, 281-82; King, 64.

10 "Veterans Bonus March," *Oregonian*, July 21, 1963, 23; *Oregon Historical Quarterly*, Fall 1964, 295; Paul Dickson and Thomas B. Allen, *The Bonus Army: An American Epic* (New York: Walker & Co., 2004; DePastino, 95-105.

11 County Facilities and Property Management website accessed Nov. 10, 2007 and July 25, 2010; *Oregonian* Nov. 19, 2011, E2.

12 Lansing, 214, 484; King, 98.

13 *Oregonian*, June 9, 1894, 8; King, 98.

14 King, 61-62.

15 Ibid., 62, 98.

16 McCarthy, 173.

17 Hardin was hired by Multnomah County in 1897. "150-Year Pictorial History of the Multnomah County Sheriff's Office," July 2005, compiled by Steve Wright, Fiscal Unit, Sheriff's Office; "Portland Police Historical

Society List of Significant Events and Dates," compiled circa 1989.

18 Goeres-Gardner, 245-50.

19 Ibid., 245-51.

20 Ibid., xxii, 250.

21 Lansing, 227.

22 Annual message from Mayor Mason to council, Administrative folder, 1899, Portland City Council Documents file.

23 Mayor Mason died at his home following a six-week bout with liver complications and grippe. Maddux, 142; MacColl, *Shaping*, 214-15.

24 Letter from W. H. Pope, Multnomah County auditor, to A. L. Mills, president of the board of public works, July 14, 1900. Finances folder, 1900, City Council Documents file.

25 Wiederhold, 47.

26 "150 Year Pictorial History of the Multnomah County Sheriff's Office," July 2005, compiled by Steve Wright, Fiscal Unit, Sheriff's Office.

27 *Oregon Journal*, Oct. 29, 1914, 12.

28 "A History of the Office of the Multnomah County Sheriff, Multnomah County, Oregon," thesis by John Gordon King, Lewis and Clark College, 1965.

29 *Oregon Journal*, Sept. 13, 1918. Lionel Webster was a Connecticut native who migrated to Oregon in the 1880s and served as a circuit court judge for Klamath and Jackson Counties before he arrived in Portland in 1895.

30 The new courthouse was finished in 1914.

31 Lansing, 230-31, 237, 479, 482; King, 99.

32 Goeres-Gardner, 257-61.

33 Ibid.

34 Ibid., 268-73.

35 Ibid., xxii, 289-90.

36 www.oregon.gov/DOC/PUBAFF/cap_punishment/history.shtml; accessed Dec. 14, 2007. Aggravated murder is defined at ORS 163.095 by seven specified circumstances, one of which is that the murder was related to the victim's performance of official duties in the justice system. Crime Victims United website accessed Oct. 1, 2009.

37 *Oregonian*, Dec. 21, 2007, D5. The last person executed in Oregon was Harry Charles Moore, by lethal injection, in May 1997. Moore declined to appeal his death sentence. Authorities argue that life imprisonment is considerably cheaper than execution. *Oregonian*, Mar. 8, 2009, A5.

CHAPTER 6

1 *2007-2008 Oregon Blue Book*, 362-63; Lansing, 245.

2 Lansing, 86.

3 Ibid., 246-61.

4 Monihan, 211-12.

5 King, 99.

6 Dean Collins, in Aikman, 187-88.

7 King, 67.

8 Ibid., 68.

9 *Oregonian*, July 27, 1904, 14, as quoted in King, 68.

10 Dean Collins, in Aikman, 187-88.

11 *Oregonian*, Jan. 5 and 8, 1905, 1, as referenced by Sidney Teiser in "Life of George H. Williams: Almost Chief Justice," *Oregon Historical Quarterly*, Dec. 1946, 439.

12 Maddux, 157-58.

13 MacColl, *Merchants*, 366.

14 Pendleton newspaperman Charles S. "Sam" Jackson founded the *Oregon Journal* on July 23, 1902. Turnbull, *Newspapers*, 187-89; Maddux, 164; MacColl, *Shaping*, 251; Corning, 126.

15 "Law Enforcement in Portland and Multnomah County," *Portland City Club Bulletin*, Feb. 20, 1948, 141; Lansing, 258-60; 264-66.

16 Maddux, 189; Scott, *Oregon*, v III, 113; MacColl, *Shaping*, 324, 467-72; *Oregonian*, Aug. 19, 1979; Abbott, *Extravaganza*, 64; Lansing, 258-60, 264-66.

17 King, 69, 99.

18 *Oregonian*, June 22-30, 1906, as quoted in King, 70.

19 *2007-2008 Oregon Blue Book*, 291; *Oregonian*, June 23, 1907, 13; King, 70-71.

20 "150-Year Pictorial History of the Multnomah County Sheriff's Office," July 2005.

21 Myers, 1-50; "Portland Police Historical Society History," 4; *Oregonian*, Dec. 4, 2000, B10.

22 Chilton, 166; 1968 *Your Multnomah County Government*, 49-51; www.co.multnomah.or.us/County_Managements/FREDS/Records/archival; accessed Mar. 27, 2009.

23 *2007-2008 Oregon Blue Book*, 292.

24 *2007-2008 Oregon Blue Book*, 293; *Oregonian*, June 2, 1912, 8.

25 *2007-2008 Oregon Blue Book*, 293

26 Statement by Harvey G. Starkweather of Oak Grove, Chairman, Clackamas County Division Committee, *Oregon Voter*, Jan. 1, 1921, 48.

27 Ibid., Feb. 21, 1921, 4-5.

28 *Oregonian*, Oct. 10, 1914, 9.

29 Ibid.

30 Ibid., Oct. 11, 1914, 6.

31 *1995-96 Oregon Blue Book*, 337.

32 The equal suffrage vote was 61,265 yes to 57,104 no, a margin of 4,161 votes. *2007-2008 Oregon Blue Book*, 292.

33 *Historical Sites Tour Guide*, items 15 and 20.

34 *2007-2008 Oregon Blue Book*, 291; King, 99.

35 O'Donnell and Vaughan, 58; MacColl, *Shaping*, 402-8.

36 Dean Collins, in Aikman, 191; *Oregon Historical Quarterly*, Summer 1999, 163; MacColl, *Shaping*, 404-10.

37 Dean Collins, in Aikman, 192.

38 MacColl, *Shaping*, 404; O'Donnell and Vaughan, 58.

39 Maddux, 164; MacColl, *Shaping*, 251; Corning, 126.

40 *Oregon Journal*, Nov 4, 1912.

41 Ibid.

42 Ibid., Sept. 17, 1913, 8.

43 Ibid., Sept. 27, 1913, 5.

44 Munk, 57.

45 *Oregon Journal*, Feb. 17 and 18, 1914.

46 Ibid., Apr. 15 and 17, 1914.

47 *Proposal to Merge Multnomah County Hospital into University of Oregon Medical School*, Oregon Executive Department, 1972, 41.

48 Smith, *History of the Origin and Growth of the Multnomah County Hospital*, 1933, Oregon Health and Science University archives.

49 *Oregonian*, Jan. 20, 1909, 8.

50 Lansing, 312.

51 Smith, *History of the Origins and Growth of the Multnomah County Hospital*, 1933.

52 *Oregonian*, Oct. 30, 1945, 6.

53 Nesbit, 8-10.

54 *Oregonian*, Oct. 30, 1945, 6.

CHAPTER 7

1   Rabin, Bartley and Miller, *Handbook of Public Administration*, CRC Press, 2006, 827.

2   New York Bureau of Municipal Research (NYBOMR): Administrative Methods of Multnomah County, Oregon, Report of a General Survey, Sept. 1913, prepared by the New York Bureau of Municipal Research.

3   New York Bureau of Municipal Research (NYBOMR), "Organization and Business Methods of the City Government of Portland, Oregon," 1913; MacColl, *Shaping*, 438; Lansing, 289-91; *Oregonian*, May 3, 1913, 1.

4   *Oregonian*, May 21, 1913, 18.

5   *New York Bureau of Municipal Research Multnomah County Survey*, 4-13, 47-50.

6   Ibid., 17.

7   Ibid., 37-43.

8   Ibid., 23.

9   Ibid., 33-35.

10 *1961 Your Multnomah County Government*, 26; *2007-2008 Oregon Blue Book*, 175.

11 *New York Bureau of Municipal Research Multnomah County Survey*, 14-15.

12 Ibid., 19-22.

13 Ibid., 3-4, 32.

14 Ibid., 37, 45-47.

15 Janet M. Kelly and William C. Rivenbark, *Performance Budgeting for State and Local Governments*, M.E. Sharpe Inc., 2003, 23-24.

16 *Oregon Journal*, Dec. 17, 1913, 2.

17 *1961 Your Multnomah County Government*, 55.

18 Ibid., 50.

19 The state legislature created the vacancy when it elevated Thomas Cleeton from presiding county judge to a seat on the Multnomah County Circuit Court.

20 *Oregon Journal,* June 4, 1913, 2.

21 Ibid., March 22, 1914, 4.

22 Ibid.

23 *2007-2008 Oregon Blue Book,* 316, 328.

24 *Time,* May 24, 1944.

25 Columbia River Highway, National Register of Historic Places Registration Form, U.S. Department of Interior, National Park Service, Feb. 4, 2000; 47.

26 Ibid., 48.

27 Ibid., 60.

28 "Historic Columbia River Highway, Multnomah Falls Footbridge," Historic American Engineering Record, no. OR-36-I, National Park Service, U.S. Department of Interior, 1995, 6.

29 Columbia River Highway, National Register of Historic Places Registration Form, U.S. Department of Interior, National Park Service; Feb. 4, 2000, 61.

30 Ibid., 62.

31 Abbott, *Gateway,* 106; King, 17; Multnomah County Sheriff's 1939 Annual Report, 21; *Oregonian,* Sept. 20, 1935.

32 Pintarich, 224.

33 King, 17; Multnomah County Sheriff's 1939 Annual Report, 21; *Oregonian,* Sept. 20, 1935.

34 *Oregonian,* June 29, 1947, as quoted at King, 74-75.

35 Ibid., Oct. 13, 1905, B9, citing Oregon Dept. of Transportation, History Committee, *A Chronological History of the Oregon Department of Transportation, 1899 to August 1993* (Support Services Branch, Business Services Section, Records Management, ODOT History Committee, 1993).

36 Correspondence to author Lansing from Judy Davis, Columbia Gorge Commission member, Feb. 14, 2010.

37 www.odot.state.or.us/hcrh/trail/trail. htm, accessed July 23, 2000; correspondence to author Lansing from Jeanette Kloos, former Scenic Area Coordinator for Oregon Dept. of Transportation,

now president of Friends of the Historic Columbia River Highway, May 26, 2010.

38 *Oregon Voter,* Feb. 22, 1922, 10.

39 *Vancouver Columbian,* Feb. 14, 1917, 1.

40 Ibid.

41 *Oregon Voter,* Feb. 4, 1922, 10.

42 Wortman, 2006, 109.

43 *Oregon Journal,* Oct. 29, 1914, 12.

44 Ibid., Dec 17 and 27, 1914; Jan. 24, 1915, 6.

45 Ibid., Aug. 8, 1925, 4.

46 Ibid., Sept. 3, 1925, 10.

47 *Oregon Journal,* Feb. 6 and 7, 1929; *Oregonian,* Feb. 6, 1929, 19.

48 Leeson, 87-88.

49 Wiederhold, 85.

50 Communication from Don Clark to author Lansing, June 9, 2009; Wiederhold, 83; Leeson, 88-89; *Historical Sites Tour Guide,* #5.

CHAPTER 8

1 The county's population had grown from 103,167 in 1900 to 275,898 in 1920; U.S. Bureau of Census, Population by Counties by Decennial Census, 1900-1990.

2 *Proposal to Merge Multnomah County Hospital into University of Oregon Medical School,* Oregon Executive Department, Oct. 1972, 41.

3 Smith, "History of the Origin and Growth of the Multnomah County Hospital," 1933, 9.

4 For 1914, *Oregonian,* Dec. 4, 1914, 12; for 1915, *Portland Telegram,* Oct. 2, 1915.

5 *Proposal to Merge Multnomah County Hospital into University of Oregon Medical School,* Oregon Executive Department, Oct. 1972, 41.

6 *Oregon Journal,* Nov. 29, 1915, 2.

7 Ibid.

8 Ibid.

9 *Ellis Lawrence Building Survey,* letter dated July 9, 1919, University of Oregon.

10 *Proposal to Merge Multnomah County Hospital into University of Oregon*

Medical School, Oregon Executive Department, Oct. 1972, 41.

11 *Portland Telegram*, Nov. 17, 1917, 2.

12 Ibid.

13 Ibid., 4.

14 *Oregon Journal*, Sept. 2, 1921.

15 *Oregon Voter*, May 20, 1922, 34.

16 MacColl, *Growth*, 260-66.

17 Ibid., 168, 262.

18 Ibid., 261-62.

19 *Oregon Voter*, March 4, 1922, 22.

20 268 U.S. 510 (1925).

21 MacColl, *Growth*, 259-60.

22 *Oregon Journal*, April 2, 1924, 1.

23 *Portland Telegram*, April 4, 1924, 6.

24 MacColl, *Growth*, 264.

25 *Portland Telegram*, April 2, 1924, 1.

26 Ibid., May 6, 1924, 1.

27 *Oregon Journal*, April 13, 1924, 1.

28 *Oregonian*, April 22, 1924, 9.

29 *Portland Telegram*, May 28, 1924, 1.

30 Official results, May 24, 1924, election, Multnomah County Archives.

31 *Portland Telegram*, May 26, 1924, 1.

32 Wortman, 2006, 84.

33 *Oregonian*, June 25, 2004.

34 Ibid., Jan. 26, 2011.

35 *Portland Telegram*, June 11, 1924, 1.

36 MacColl, *Growth*, 266.

37 Montague was a member of the 1913 Portland charter commission that resulted in adoption of the commission form of government. *History of the Bench and Bar*, 188.

38 *Oregon Journal*, June 19, 1927, Sec. 1, 1, 4, and June 26, 1927, Sec. 1, 1, 5. www.ci.portland.or.us/auditor/Elecarchives2/GEN26.htm & SPEC27.htm; accessed July 28, 2000.

39 Paper dated June 20, 1927, by Richard W. Montague, Commission Chairman, titled "Arguments on Consolidation Amendment." An attached note page explained the Government Simplification Commission history.

40 *Oregonian*, June 28, 1927, 7.

41 *2007-2008 Oregon Blue Book*, 296.

CHAPTER 9

1 Multnomah County Archives, May 1928 primary election final count.

2 As a young engineer, David Steinman had worked in the office of Gustav Lindenthal, who had been hired by the county in 1924 to complete the Burnside, Ross Island, and Sellwood bridge projects stalled by the alleged bribery scandal. Steinman was now a leading figure in American bridge design.

3 *Portland Telegram*, April 15, 1929, 1.

4 Ibid., April 13, 1929, 1.

5 www.oregon.gov/ODOT/HWY/REGION1/StJohns/index.shtml

6 *Oregonian*, June 14, 1931, 1.

7 www.oregon.gov/ODOT/HWY/GEOENVIRONMENTAL/historic_bridges_Portland1.shtml, accessed June 26, 2010.

8 Wortman, 2006, 5.

9 Leeson, 122.

10 Ibid., 122-23. Royal fish, such as sturgeons, porpoises, and whales, when brought ashore, were always the property of the king.

11 Oregon Constitution, Article VI, Sec. 6; *2007-2008 Oregon Blue Book*, 397; King, 44, 72; McCarthy, 174.

12 *Oregonian*, May 25, 1954.

13 Multnomah County Sheriff's 1939 Annual Report, 21; Don Clark interview by author Lansing, Apr. 11, 2006; *Gresham Outlook*, Mar. 11, 1978.

14 *Oregon Journal*, Apr. 5, 1960, 26.

15 *Oregonian*, Aug. 5, 1927, 14.

16 *Oregon Journal*, Sept. 16, 1932.

17 Ibid., Apr. 2, 1960, 1.

18 See list of county commissioners who also served on Portland City Council in Chapter 3 endnotes. Prior to 1913, the city council was composed of eleven part-time council members elected by wards. After 1913, a mayor, four council members, and a city auditor were elected for four-year terms comparable to terms served on the Multnomah County Commission.

19 Lansing, 318.

20 *Oregonian*, Jan. 19, 1941, 8.

21 www.u-s-history.com/pages/h1792.html.

22 "Historical Sketch of Multnomah County," *WPA Inventory-1*, 28-29.

23 Bowman, 306; Roe, 149, 170.

24 MacColl, *Growth*, 570.

25 Gunther, 129.

26 Lucia, *Conscience*, 19.

27 Abbott, 118; MacColl, *Growth*, 437-38, 445, 450, 452; Lansing 333.

28 http://www.bpa.gov/corporate/ pubs/70_proud_moments_history.pdf; accessed June 28, 2010.

29 *Portland Tribune*, July 30, 2009, 1.

30 Author Leeson interview with Bill Murlin, Aug. 22, 2010.

31 Lansing, 341.

32 *Oregonian*, Sept. 20, 1935; *Willamette Week*, July 13, 1994.

33 *Oregonian*, Sept. 20, 1936.

34 Emails to author Lansing from Tina L. Breiten, Multnomah County Sheriff's Office work release unit, and Steve Wright, Multnomah County Sheriff's Office fiscal unit. Aug. 24, 2010.

35 *Oregonian*, Jan. 12, 1941, 16.

36 *Historical Sites Tour Guide* Item, #10, says the cost was $682,000.

37 *Oregonian*, Jan. 12, 1941, 16.

38 Ibid., Nov. 2, 1943, Sec. 3, 2.

39 King, 40; undated, unidentified newspaper story, circa early 1941.

40 Lansing, 337-47.

41 *Oregonian*, June 12, 1943; Maben, 96-97, 104; Lansing, 351; conversation and correspondence between author Lansing and Don Clark, Oct. 8 and Dec. 3, 2008.

42 Doris Kearns Goodwin, *No Ordinary Time*, 416-18, 622.

43 By 2000, Kaiser Permanente had eight million members in eleven states and the District of Columbia. Lansing, 342.

44 See *Gresham, Stories of Our Past*, Gresham Historical Society, chapter 20.

45 Kessler, 154-205.

46 Ibid., 154-73, 204-5.

47 Kessler, 162, 166; www.expocenter.org; accessed Apr. 13, 2009.

48 *Oregonian*, Aug. 4, 1990, D5.

49 Ibid., July 30, 2010.

CHAPTER 10

1 Bylaws of Mult Co Sheriff's Aero Squadron adopted Oct. 19, 1948; 1950 Sheriff's Annual Report.

2 *Oregonian*, Feb. 18, 2001, A23; Dec. 4, 1950, B14.

3 Maben, 92-93. 102-3.

4 MacColl, *Growth*, 593-95. Robert Moses had noted during his visit two years before that many community leaders believed it was neither "possible nor desirable" for Portland "to keep all of the war workers attracted from other parts of the country," with the term "war workers" understood to mean Negroes. "Portland Improvement," by Robert Moses, 1943, as quoted in O'Donnell and Vaughan, 66.

5 Maben, 74-80, 102-3.

6 *Oregonian*, May 29, 2011, B2.

7 Maben, 105-6.

8 *Oregonian*, May 29, 2011, B2.

9 Maben, 106.

10 Ibid., 110-11.

11 Ibid., 113, 116-17.

12 Ibid., 104, 120-22.

13 MacColl, *Growth*, 652-3; *Oregonian*, May 31, 1948; Maben, 105-8, 121, 124-26.

14 Conversation by author Lansing with Mike Howlett, Portland Mapping Div, July 9, 2009.

15 *Oregonian*, Jan. 15, 1948; *Portland City Club Bulletin*, Feb. 20, 1948, 132-48; MacColl, *Growth*, 610-11, 613-14, 647-48; Pitzer, *Oregon Historical Quarterly*, Spring 1990, 13.

16 MacColl, *Growth*, 614, 647-48; Pitzer, *Oregon Historical Quarterly*. Spring 1990, 13.

17 King, 101; *Oregonian*, May 25, 1954; *Oregon Historical Quarterly*, Spring 1990.

18 MacColl, *Growth*, 653.

19 Pitzer, *Oregon Historical Quarterly*, Spring 1990, 23; MacColl, *Growth*, 652-53.

20 Stanford, 94.

21 The recall against Elliott passed by 57 percent to 43 percent. King, 101; MacColl, *Growth*, 652-3; Maddux, 204;

Pitzer, *Oregon Historical Quarterly*, Spring 1990, 25.

22 Some fifty years later, a rumor circulated that the Teamsters Union had made a $10,000 payoff to the county commissioners (Frank Shull, Tom West, and Alan Brown) in return for the appointment of Schrunk as sheriff. The only source given for this allegation by reporter Phil Stanford in his 2004 *Portland Confidential* was an unnamed police informant. Stanford, 95.

23 Lansing, 355-57.

24 *Oregonian*, Aug. 5, 1950.

25 *Oregonian*, Oct. 9, 1950; King, 101.

26 *Oregon Journal*, Oct. 18, 1954; King, 101.

27 King, 101; *Oregon Journal*, Oct. 14, 1954; *Oregonian*, July 25 and Oct. 18, 1954.

28 "The Rise and Fall of Big Jim Elkins," by Phil Stanford, in Pintarich, 335. Stanford also alleges that "when he finally left office in 1972, [Terry Schrunk] was a serious drunk." Pintarich, 345.

29 *Gresham Outlook*, Mar. 11, 1978.

30 *Oregonian*, May 25, 1954.

31 Correspondence from Don Clark to author Lansing, Dec. 3, 2008.

32 Uris, 202.

33 *Oregonian*, Apr. 19, 1956, 1; Uris, 92; King, 81-82.

34 Schrunk was known to be a heavy drinker. Rumors circulated after the bribery allegation became public that Schrunk had been drunk at the time and had leaned over to vomit. Correspondence from Dick Feeney to author Lansing, Oct. 14, 2009.

35 Schrunk offered to take a lie detector test, then refused to answer some questions put to him. *Oregonian*, March 13, 1957; Uris, 138-41, 186-92.

36 Leeson, 150-53; *Oregon Journal*, Apr. 13 and 23, 1958.

37 *Oregonian*, Aug. 11, 1956, as quoted in Leeson, 151-52.

38 *Oregonian*, Sept. 16, 1956, 1.

39 Ibid., June 27, 1957, 1.

40 *Oregon Journal*, Mar. 4, 1975.

41 Telephone conversation with Don Clark by author Lansing, Nov. 1, 2000.

CHAPTER 11

1 *Oregonian*, Oct. 28, 1979.

2 Ibid., Dec. 6, 1950.

3 MacColl, *Growth*, 455-57; Abbott, *Gateway*, 108; Draft *Portland Parks and Recreation, A Chronological History*, Dec. 1998, 1932 section; *1968 Your Multnomah County Government*, 94.

4 Houle, 12-13.

5 Ibid., xi.

6 O'Donnell and Vaughan, 184.

7 *1961 Your Multnomah County Government*, 19-20.

8 The east-west township gridlines included Fremont, Halsey, Stark, Division, Holgate, each one mile distant from the other. There is a surveyor's township marker at the corner of S.E. 82nd and Stark streets and another six miles further east near S.E. Stark and 220th streets. Communication to author Lansing from Robert Hovden, county surveyor, Aug. 21 and 24, 2009.

9 Author Lansing interview with Bud Kramer, former Gleason executive, July 17, 1997.

10 Ibid.; Correspondence to author Lansing from Ken Upton, former county labor relations manager, June 28, 2009.

11 *1968 Your Multnomah County Government*, 95.

12 Correspondence to author Lansing from Bob Baldwin, Jan. 16, 2007.

13 Abbott, *Portland*, 236-37.

14 Ibid.; Ernie Bonner interviews with Lloyd Anderson (Feb. 27, 1995) and Bob Baldwin (Dec. 1994); memo from former county planning director, Bob Baldwin, to author Lansing, Jan. 16, 2007.

15 *Comparison of City of Portland Population Growth and Suburban Population Trends*, www.library.oregonmetro.gov.

16 *Oregon Journal*, Jan. 6, 1958; *Oregonian*, Jan. 3, 1958.

17 *Oregon Journal*, Jan. 6, 1958; www.we-stegg.com/inflation; accessed February 9, 2011.

18 *Oregonian*, Jan. 8, 1958.

19 Ibid., Jan. 3, 1958.

20 *Oregon Journal*, May 27, 1958; *Oregonian*, June 2, 1958.

21 *Oregon Journal*, Jan. 6, 1958.

22 *Oregon Journal*, Apr. 28, 1960; *Oregonian*, Apr. 29, 1960.

23 *1961 Your Multnomah County Government*, 46.

24 Intergovernmental agreement transferring ownership of eighteen natural areas and regional facilities and fourteen pioneer cemeteries from Multnomah County to Metro, signed March 21, 1996, by County Chair Beverly Stein and Metro Executive Officer Mike Burton.

25 Portland Bureau of Planning, *East Portland Review*, 2007, 45.

26 Wortman, 2006, 57.

27 Ibid.

28 *Oregon Journal*, Feb. 27, 1946, sec. 2, 2.

29 Wortman, 2006, 56.

30 *Oregon Journal*, Nov. 8, 1955, 1.

31 Ibid., May 25, 1958, 2.

32 *Oregon Journal*, July 6 and 8, 1958; *The Enterprise*, July 9, 1958.

33 *Oregon Journal*, Sept. 3, 1958.

34 *Oregon Journal*, Dec. 10, 17, 18, 25, and 26, 1958; *Oregonian*, Jan. 4, 1959.

35 *Oregonian*, Jan. 4, 1959.

36 Ibid., Oct. 19, 1959.

37 *Oregonian*, Mar. 3, 2009, B2; correspondence to author Lansing from Capt. Monte Reiser, Investigations Division, Multnomah County Sheriff's office, Aug. 23, 2008.

38 *Oregonian*, Sept. 27, 1966; Mar. 29, 1967; Oct. 29, Nov. 4 and 15, 1969; Dec 7, 1969; *Oregon Journal*, June 16, 1965; Aug. 19 and 20, 1968; Mar. 17, 1970. McCarthy, 176; *Portland Tribune*, July 10, 2007.

39 McCarthy, 176.

40 *Portland Tribune*, July 10, 2007, A2; Stanford, *Peyton-Allan Files*, 13-7.

41 *Oregon Journal*, Oct. 29, 1969.

42 Stanford, *Peyton-Allan Files*, 192; *Portland Tribune*, July 10, 2007, A2.

43 *Oregon Journal*, Dec. 31, 1981. Son had recently contracted prostate cancer. He died of a gunshot wound and was believed to have taken his own life. However, nearly fifty years after the Peyton-Allan murders, *Tribune* columnist Phil Stanford reported that former DA Des Connall "now believes that [Detective] Son was murdered." *Portland Tribune*, Feb. 16, 2007. See also Stanford, *Peyton-Allan Files*, 85-86, and *Oregon Journal* Sept. 27, 1966.

44 Stanford, *Peyton-Allan Files*, 134, 146.

45 McCarthy, 176; Stanford, *Peyton-Allan Files*, 151.

46 Stanford, *Peyton-Allan Files*, 176; *Portland Tribune*, July 10, 2007, A2; McCarthy, 176.

47 Ibid., 178.

48 Ibid., 187.

CHAPTER 12

1 Author Lansing interview with Bud Kramer, July 17, 1997.

2 Memo from former county planning director Bob Baldwin to author Lansing, Jan. 16, 2007.

3 *Oregonian*, Jan. 10, 1960.

4 *Oregon Journal*, Feb. 26 and 29, 1964; July 1 and Sept. 29, 1965.

5 Ibid., Apr. 25, 1962, 1.

6 Ibid., July 7, 1962, 8.

7 Ibid., Aug. 9, 1962, 2.

8 *Oregonian*, Jan. 27, 2006, B1.

9 Ibid., Aug. 11, 1989, D10.

10 *Gresham Outlook*, Jan. 16, 1964.

11 *Portland Reporter*, Jan. 2, 1964.

12 *Oregon Journal*, Nov. 23, 1963, 12.

13 *Oregonian*, Jan. 3, 1958; Intergovernmental Agreement between Multnomah County and Metro, Mar. 21, 1996, Sec. 3N; phone call to Heather Kent at Metro, Dec. 3, 2008.

14 *Historical Sites Tour Guide*, Item #7; *County Lines*, Mar. 1979, 9; *Oregonian*, Aug. 21, 2011, B2.

15 *Oregonian*, June 12, 2010, B2.

16 *Portland Reporter*, Dec. 30, 1963; *Oregonian*, Aug. 18, 1967.

17 *1968 Your Multnomah County Government*, 41-42.

18 *Oregonian*, Nov. 4, 1964, May 8, 1965; *Oregon Journal*, Oct. 25, 1964, May 10, 1965; *Portland Reporter*, Dec. 30, 1963.

19 *Oregon Journal*, May 10, 1965.

20 *Portland Reporter*, Aug. 27, 1964;
    Nesbit, 11; http://en.wikipedia.org/wiki/
    Frankie_and_Johnny_(song), accessed
    Mar 3, 2009. Various versions of the
    ballad have appeared as folk songs, at
    least as far back as 1904.

21 *Portland Reporter*, Aug. 27, 1964.

22 *Oregonian*, Apr. 15, 1964, 11.

23 Nesbit, 13; *Portland Reporter*, Apr.
    14 and Aug. 27, 1964; *1968 Your
    Multnomah County Government*, 94.

24 *1961 Your Multnomah County
    Government*, 44.

25 *Oregon Journal*, July 16, 1969.

26 McCarthy, 174.

27 *Oregon Journal*, May 7, 1964;
    Northwest Magazine, Feb. 19, 1967;
    King, 102; Ernie Bonner interview with
    Clark, Mar. 8, 2002, 3. One of the sher-
    iff candidates on the Republican side
    was Captain Peter Rexford, "a nice old
    fellow" who had first suggested painting
    lines down the middle of highways as a
    safety measure. Correspondence from
    Clark to author Lansing, Dec. 3, 2008.

28 Ernie Bonner interview with Clark, Mar.
    8, 2002, 3.

29 Ibid., 3.

30 *Oregonian*, Dec. 13 and 20, 1962, as
    quoted in King, 87-89. King was a his-
    tory student at Lewis and Clark College
    in June 1965 when he wrote his thesis.

31 *Oregon Journal*, Jan. 13, 1966;
    Oregonian, May 10, 1967.

32 In December 2007, County Chair Ted
    Wheeler announced that he might ask
    voters to once again make the office of
    sheriff appointive, but no formal pro-
    posal was put on the ballot. *Oregonian*,
    Jan. 31, 2008, A4.

33 From 1856 to 1864 and from 1913 to
    1915, the county treasurer served as
    tax collector. The sheriff served in that
    capacity all other years through 1966.
    King, 28-29.

34 Correspondence from Don Clark to
    author Lansing, Dec. 3, 2008.

CHAPTER 13

1   Correspondence to author Lansing from
    Dan Ellis, administrative assistant to
    Mel Gordon, May 28, 2009.

2   Names from Multnomah County
    Home Rule Charter pamphlet printed
    and distributed to citizens after charter
    passage in 1966. Other information
    related to the author by Lloyd Anderson
    in 2006 and 2007.

3   Communications between the author
    and Lloyd Anderson, December 2006.

4   www.ci.portland.or.us/auditor/
    Elecarchives2/PRIM66.htm; accessed
    Sept. 12, 2000. The City of Portland
    measure was proposed by a City Club
    of Portland study committee.

5   *Oregon Journal*, May 21, 1966.

6   Lansing, 380-82.

7   *Oregon Journal*, Nov. 9, 1966.

8   Correspondence from Bob Baldwin to
    author Lansing, Jan. 10, 2007.

9   Author Lansing interview with Bud
    Kramer, July 17, 1997.

10 *Oregonian*, June 26, 1967.

11 Ibid., July 2, 1967.

12 Ibid., July 3, 1967.

13 Ibid., Sept. 23, 1967.

14 McCarthy, 174.

15 *Oregonian*, Aug. 9, 1967

16 Ibid., Dec. 30, 1967.

17 Holzman was also facing difficulties
    at home. Two years after he arrived
    in Portland, both his wife and that
    of former sheriff Don Clark were
    granted divorce decrees on the same day.
    Oregonian, Nov. 20, 1969.

18 *Oregonian*, Feb. 5, 1970; *Oregon
    Journal* , Feb. 18, 1970; McCarthy, 174.

19 *Oregon Journal*, July 31, 1980.

20 Ibid.

21 Ibid.

22 Nesbit, 14, 17, 20.

23 By 1972, his last year on the board,
    David Eccles, a "gentleman of the old
    school," was said to be dealing with a
    significant drinking problem.

24 Phone call from Clark to author
    Lansing, Oct. 8, 2007; correspondence
    to author Lansing from Easton Cross,
    former Gleason staffer, Sept. 28, 2008.

25 Each of the thirty-eight legislators in the
    four counties appointed one member of
    MSC. Letter from McKay Rich, former
    MSD executive director, to author
    Lansing, Dec. 12, 2000.

26 CRAG included Columbia County, Oregon, and Clark County, Washington, as well as Multnomah, Washington, and Clackamas counties. Abbott, *Portland*, 242, 262.

27 Correspondence from Dick Feeney to author Lansing, Nov. 16, 2009.

28 Abbott, *Portland*, 254.

29 *Oregonian*, May 25, 1978, C1; conversation with McKay Rich, by author Lansing, Nov. 30, 2000.

30 Correspondence from Bob Baldwin to author Lansing, Jan. 10, 2007; http://library.oregonmetro.gov/files//abbott-a_history_of_metro_may_1991.pdf/.

31 The Local Government Boundary Commission charter specifically excluded elected officials from its membership. For the first twenty years of its existence, its commissioners were appointed by the governor. The organization was to become "a major force in implementing land use planning by testing boundary changes against plans for land development and the provision of public services," in the words of historian Carl Abbott. http://library.oregonmetro.gov/files//abbott-a_history_of_metro_may_1991.pdf/.

32 Author Lansing, interview with Don Clark, Oct. 17, 2006.

CHAPTER 14

1 *Proposal to Merge Multnomah County Hospital into University of Oregon Medical School*, State Executive Department, 1972, 5.

2 Ibid., 171.

3 www.ohsu.edu/xd/about/facts/history.cfm.

4 Sheriff Purcell's chief deputy, Louis Rinehart, served as sheriff for nine months, April through December 1974.

5 Other influential Multnomah County employees during the Mike Gleason years included chief legal counsel Willis West, road department director Paul Northrup, elections director John Weldon, Bill Radakovich, Lansing Stout, John Rice, Jerry Justice, Ross Hall, Easton Cross, Dan Ellis, Jerry Frey, and Dick Engstrom.

6 Congresswoman Green had been instrumental in amending the 1967 poverty bill to require involvement of local governments in Community Action programs. Correspondence from Dick Feeney to author Lansing, Oct. 14 and Nov. 16, 2009.

7 Correspondence from former county and city auditor Gary Blackmer to author Lansing, Sept. 27, 2009.

8 *Oregonian*, Sept. 10, 2008; Don Clark interview by Ernie Bonner, Mar. 8, 2004, 12.

9 *Oregonian*, Sept. 10, 2008, D5.

10 Members of the 1973 City-County Charter Commission were lawyer George Joseph, chair; Gresham newspaperman Lee Irwin, vice-chair; citizen activist Ruth Hagenstein, secretary; William E. Bradley, Polly Casterline, Joseph M. Edgar, Joseph A. Labadie, Loyal Lang, Glen Otto, Frank Roberts, and Morton A. Winkel. Members who resigned early in the process were Richard Bogle, Sylvia Davidson, R. W. deWeese, and Earl Klapstein. "Proposed Charter, City-County of Portland-Multnomah, Oregon, 1973."

11 *Oregon Journal*, May 28, 1974, 1; Abbott, *Portland*, 260-61.

12 ORS 199.730(6), Proposed Charter, City-County of Portland—Multnomah, Nov. 1, 1973; Lansing, 402-3.

13 Four-page color tabloid published by "Vote No on 7 Committee," John H. Wilson, chairman, printed May 11, 1974; *Oregon Journal*, May 28, 1974, 1.

14 *Oregon Voters' Pamphlet*, May 1974, 200.

15 *Oregon Journal*, May 29, 1974, 1.

16 Conversation by author Lansing with the late George Joseph, Chair of the 1974 City-County Charter Commission, on Nov. 27, 2000; *Consolidation Study Task Force, Final Report*, Sept. 1998, 7; author Lansing interview with Bud Kramer, July 17, 1997.

17 The consultant firms were Booz, Allen & Hamilton, and the Arthur Young CPA firm. Multnomah County Audit #5-77, "Payroll Function: Internal Control and Reporting Systems," Nov. 1977.

18 Letter from former city accounting manager Marino Bual to author Lansing, Dec. 15, 2000; letter from PDC controller and former city accountant Bill Blauvelt to author Lansing, Dec. 12, 2000; "Portland of Years Past," 1975 Section, *Oregonian*, March 16, 2000, E3; *Oregonian*, Jan. 6, 2000, E7.

19 The CPA hired by O'Donnell was Rod Sauer. Certified Public Accountant Jewel Lansing, the coauthor of this book, was recruited by Kramer and incoming chair Don Clark to run for the county auditor's job. Lansing won the 1974 Democratic primary with a mere 23 percent of the vote against five opponents and was the only candidate to run an organized, albeit shoestring, campaign. In the fall she easily defeated her Republican opponent, computer specialist Newton Wang. Lansing was to leave her mark on Multnomah County by making it the first governmental jurisdiction in Oregon to institute performance auditing. She also pushed for a home rule charter provision that would require all future auditor candidates after 1992 to have professional audit certification. Lansing and Commissioner Alice Corbett, by winning their fall 1974 elections, became the first women ever elected to Multnomah County government office.

20 U.S. Dept. of Transportation, Federal Highway Administration web site, accessed July 14, 2009; Lansing, 258, 366, 532 n14; Federal-Aid Highway Act of 1956.

21 Lansing, 463, 549 n91.

22 Abbott, *Portland*, 207; Lansing, 344-45.

23 MacColl, *Growth*, 589.

24 Letter from Bob Baldwin to author Lansing, Sept. 1, 2006; Dennis Buchanan interview by Ernie Bonner, June 2001; Don Clark interview, Feb. 2000. Maywood Park residents first requested incorporation in May 1967. Former county planner David Hupp interview by Ernie Bonner, Mar. 2001, 2.

25 "A Summary History of I-205," Oregon Department of Transportation, 1973, 4; 23-24. Another lawsuit was filed in July 1972 by the Southeast Freeway Defense Fund (Al and Kayda Clark et al.) against ODOT and the Federal Highway Department. The court ruled in February 1974 that ODOT had selected the Mt. Hood Freeway route before it held the required public hearing. Letter from attorney Charles Merten to author Lansing, Oct. 11, 2006.

26 S.E. 96th Avenue to West Linn was the approved I-205 route. "A Summary History of I-205," Oregon Department of Transportation, 1973, 1-2, 4-5, 26; Abbott, *Portland*, 197, 239, 255; *Willamette Week*, Nov. 10, 1999, 9.

27 Don Clark interview by Ernie Bonner, Mar. 8, 2002, 12; "A Summary History of I-205," Oregon Department of Transportation, 1973.

28 David Hupp interview by Ernie Bonner, Mar. 2001, 4; Abbott, *Portland*, 256; "A Summary History of I-205," Oregon Dept of Transportation, 1973, 1-5, 26.

29 *Oregonian*, Nov. 22, 1972, 1.

30 "A Summary History of I-205," Oregon Department of Transportation, 1973, 4-5.

31 *Willamette Week*, Nov. 10, 1999, 9-10.

32 *Oregon Journal*, Feb. 21, 1974, 1.

33 Leeson, 185; Abbott, *Portland*, 197, 255-57; Price, 83, 139; letter to author Lansing from Dick Feeney, former Clark executive, July 4, 2009.

34 Leeson, 185; Abbott, *Portland*, 197; Price, 83, 139.

35 *Oregon Labor Press*, Jan. 24, 1975.

36 Bob Baldwin interview by Ernie Bonner, Dec. 1994, 8; author Lansing communications with Dennis Buchanan, Don Clark, and Fred Neal, Aug. and Sept., 2009.

37 Abbott, *Portland*, 256-57: Lansing, 383-85, 405-6.

38 Betty Merten interview by Ernie Bonner, Dec. 9, 2001, 3; Merten correspondence to author Lansing, Feb. 23, 2011.

39 *Willamette Week*, Nov. 10, 1999, 9-10.

40 Correspondence to author Lansing from Ken Upton, former county labor relations manager, June 28, 2009.

41 Abbott, *Portland*, 212: "The Stadium Freeway . . . razed and paved over 282 houses and 131 apartment houses, and displaced 1,700 persons along with many small shops, cafes and hotels."

McCormack and Pintarich, 156; Arrieta-Walden, 102.

42 Former county planner David Hupp interview by Ernie Bonner, Mar. 2001; Bonner interview with Arnold Cogan, March 10, 1999; Lansing, 383-85, 405-6; correspondence to author Lansing from Cogan, June 18, 2009; correspondence from Dick Feeney to author Lansing, Oct. 14, 2009.

43 "The Justice Center, Portland, Oregon" booklet prepared 1983; correspondence to author Lansing from Dick Feeney, former Clark executive, July 4, 2009; correspondence to author Lansing from Tuck Wilson, July 2009.

44 *Oregonian*, Oct. 16, 1983; Leeson, 220-21; www.mcso.us/public/facilities. htm, accessed Aug. 12, 2008.

45 Bob Baldwin interview by Ernie Bonner, Dec. 1994, 7; David Hupp interview by Ernie Bonner, Mar. 2001, 1-2; Dennis Buchanan interview by Ernie Bonner, June 2001, 4; communication from Don Clark to author Lansing, Sept. 5, 2009; "A Summary History of I-205," Oregon Department of Transportation, 1973.

46 *Portland Tribune*, Sept. 10, 2009, A1-2; *Oregonian*, Sept. 12, A1, 4.

47 *Oregon Journal*, Feb. 2, 1974, 3.

48 *Oregonian*, Mar. 5, 1974, 1.

49 *Oregon Journal*, Feb. 2, 3, 1973.

50 Ibid., June 5, 1973, 2.

51 Anecdote related to author Leeson by Mel Gordon.

52 Author Lansing interview with Bud Kramer, July 17, 1997.

53 Email from Dave Boyer to author Lansing, Dec. 28, 2011.

54 *Oregon Journal*, Jan. 13, 1975; Abbott, 197-98.

55 *County Lines*, June 1982, 8.

CHAPTER 15

1 The roster of Don Clark staffers included at various times Ken Gervais, McKay Rich, Ben Padrow, Dick Feeney, and Clyde Doctor, as Clark's executive; Felicia Trader, Helen Barney, Fred Pearce, Ed Martin, Andy Thaler, Don Rocks, Sonny Condor, Martin Crampton, Bob Baldwin, Dan Ellis,

Dean Smith, Sandi Hobbs Morey, Suzi McKeen, Wanda Waldren, Donna Dunbar, Alma Hill, Maggie Pendleton Silverstein, Dave Fredricksen, Mary Fellows, Sally Anderson, Jerry Haggin, Dave Warren, Jim Wilcox, Tanya Collier, Kathy Busse, Steve Telfer, Billi Odegaard, Dave Boyer, Martin Marglowski, Ken Upton, Wayne George, Bruce Lawson, Ed Pritchard, Lynn Bonner, Betsy Bergstein, Bill Radakovich, Diane Trudo, Easton Cross, Fred Neal, Myra Lee, Al Rivers, Peggy Ecton, Tom Rocks, Margaret Epting, Kim Duncan, Gerry Newhall, Michelle Williams, Jerry Frey, Rena Cusma, Denny West, Dick Engstrom, Bruce Harder, Leon Johnson, Berna Plummer, Kurt Englestad, Ed Capen, Jim Sullivan, Beth Gilson, Golden Dillabah Riley, Charles Schade, John Johnston, Dick Hancock, Roger Olson, Bob Johnson, Becky Belangy, Tor Lyshaug, Oliver Domeries, Gary Newbore, Carl Mason; Justice Services directors Tuck Wilson, Jake Tanzer, Lee Brown, Larry Craig; county council staffers George Joseph, John Leahy, Larry Kressel, Jack Hoffman, Rich Busse, Gary Zimmer; Human Services directors Hugh Tilson, David Lawrence, Tom Higgins, Jewel Goddard, Duane Lemley. Correspondence from Don Clark to author Lansing, Mar. 27, 2009.

2 Front-page *Willamette Week* article by Editor Ron Buel, Dec. 16, 1974.

3 Ernie Bonner interview with Don Clark, Mar 8, 2002, 8.

4 Ibid., 7.

5 Debra's Channel 13 TV show, Dec. 7, 2000, "I Never Said Thank You" (ABC).

6 Correspondence from Don Clark to author Lansing, Dec. 8, 2009.

7 Seen by author Leeson, Apr. 1975.

8 *Oregon Journal*, Feb. 6, 24, 27, 1975; Nesbit, 6-19; *1961 Your Multnomah Government*, 26; Lansing, 312, 510.

9 Superintendent O.A. Johnson told the Multnomah County Tax Supervising and Conservation Commission in 1934 that, given the value of food produced at the farm, each meal was costing 6.9 cents. An inventory at the poor farm in July 1935 broke down this way: total population (including county

employees) 614; men, 535; women, 63; hospitalized, 65; infirmary ambulatory, 135; horses, 5; cows, 65; pigs, 225; chickens, 2000. Nesbit, 2002, 11.

10 Auditor Will Gibson told the oversight commission that a double-entry book-keeping system had been adopted in all county departments to keep closer track of cash. *Oregon Journal*, Sept. 19, 1934, 22.

11 *Oregon Journal*, Apr. 14, 1975.

12 Walth, 356-61, 403, 591; Department of Land Conservation and Development, www.lcd.state.or.us/history.html; accessed Nov. 22, 2000.

13 Don Clark interview by Ernie Bonner, Mar. 8, 2002.

14 Letter from Bob Baldwin to author Lansing, Jan 16, 2007.

15 *Oregon Journal*, June 27, 1975.

16 *Oregonian*, July 18, 1975; *Oregon Journal*, Aug. 28, Oct. 13, and Dec. 31, 1975.

17 *Oregon Journal*, Mar. 17, 1976.

18 *Oregon Journal*, Mar. 23, Aug. 18 and 21, 1976; *Oregonian*, Oct. 17, 1976.

19 *Oregonian*, Oct. 17, 1976; *Oregon Journal*, Nov. 3, 1976.

20 *Oregon Journal*, July 19, 1977.

21 Ibid., Oct. 25, Nov. 3, Dec. 29, 1976.

22 *Oregonian*, June 1, 1978.

23 Ibid., Jan. 14, 1980.

24 Ibid.

25 Conversation with Don Clark by author Lansing, Aug. 31, 2005.

26 Salem *Capitol Journal*, Nov. 7, 1976. Jewel Lansing is coauthor of this book. Also at the state level, Republican Norma Paulus was elected in fall 1976 as Oregon Secretary of State, the first woman to hold statewide state office.

27 *County Lines*, May 1978.

28 *Oregonian*, Dec. 26, 1994, B1.

29 Roberts, 77-79.

30 Three county auditors were to follow county auditor Will Gibson's 1939 lead from county to city—Jewel Lansing (the coauthor of this book) in 1982, Gary Blackmer in 1999, and LaVonne Griffin-Valade in 2009. Terry Schrunk vaulted from county sheriff to Portland mayor in 1956.

31 Correspondence from Earl Blumenauer to author Lansing, Sept. 30, 2009.

32 *Statesman-Journal*, Mar. 20, 1986.

33 *Daily Astorian*, Mar. 31, 1986.

34 HB 3284, 1977 Regular Assembly, Oregon State Legislature.

35 CRAG included Columbia County, Oregon, and Clark County, Washington, as well as Multnomah, Washington, and Clackamas counties. Abbott, *Portland*, 242, 254, 262.

36 "A History of Metro," Carl Abbott, May 1991, www.oregonmetro/gov, accessed April 4, 2009.

37 *Oregonian*, May 25, 1978, C1; Price, 138; Abbott, *Portland*, 242, 249, 254, 256-57, 262; communication to author Lansing from McKay Rich, former zoo director for seventeen years, Nov. 30 and Dec. 22, 2000. The margin of voter approval in 1978 was 110,600 yes and 91,090 no. *2007-2008 Oregon Blue Book*, 303.

38 Preamble to 1992 Metro charter and Metro time line; accessed at www.oregonmetro/gov, June 10, 2009.

39 Correspondence to author Lansing from former county and city auditor Gary Blackmer, Sept. 27, 2009.

40 Only 20 percent of Oregon's drinking water was fluoridated as of Aug. 2007, compared to 67 percent nationwide. No Multnomah County city fluoridated its water as of 2009. *Oregonian*, Aug. 1, 2007; correspondence from Jeanne Burget, Portland Water Bureau, to author Lansing, Oct. 20, 2008.

41 Ernie Bonner interview of Don Clark, Mar. 8, 2002, 9.

42 In 1968, Mosee filed a lawsuit against Clark, claiming that Clark had implied that he was still the incumbent sheriff, thereby misrepresenting his credentials. The *Mosee v. Clark* case went to the Oregon Supreme Court, where it was decided in Clark's favor after the election. Don Clark interview by Ernie Bonner, Mar. 8, 2002, 10; *Willamette Week*, Apr. 24, 1978.

43 *Oregon Journal*, Oct. 30, 1968.

44 *Willamette Week*, Apr. 24, 1978.

45 Ibid.

46 Letter to author Lansing from Ken Upton, former labor relations manager, June 28, 2009.

47 *Willamette Week,* Aug. 12 and Nov. 28, 1980.

48 Letter from Caroline Miller to author Lansing, Oct. 21, 2006.

CHAPTER 16

1 Phone call by author Lansing to Joe Devlaeminck, a member of the union bargaining team, Nov. 27, 2007; letter from Devlaeminck to author Lansing, Feb. 26, 2008.

2 *Oregonian,* July 15 and 22, 1980, B1.

3 Ibid., July 2, 15, and 23, 1980, E1, B1, and C1, respectively.

4 Letter to author Lansing from former finance officer Dave Boyer, Nov. 14, 2007.

5 *Oregon Journal,* May 26, 1950.

6 Tape of Don Clark reunion roast, Nov. 5, 2003.

7 *Oregonian,* Aug. 25, 1980, A1; Oct. 1, 1980, D6. Three unions were not part of this strike: Local 117, an AFL-CIO affiliate established in 1959 to represent deputy sheriffs; a corrections officers' union; and District Court personnel. Public safety personnel were prohibited by state law from striking. Letter from former labor relations manager Ken Upton to author Lansing, Aug. 9, 2008; King, 36.

8 *Oregonian,* Aug. 24, 1980, B1.

9 Ibid.

10 Ibid., Aug. 25, 1980, A1; Oct. 1, 1980, D6.

11 Ibid., Aug. 25, 1980, A1.

12 Phone call by author Lansing to Joe Devlaeminck, Nov. 27, 2007.

13 Letters to Ken Upton from Billi Odegaard, Nov. 23, 2007, and to author Lansing, Mar. 1, 2008.

14 Correspondence to author Lansing from Felicia Trader, Mar. 2008 and May 18, 2009.

15 Letters to author Lansing from former budget director Dave Warren, Nov. 10; Ken Upton, Nov. 21; and county strike manager Helen Barney, Nov. 17, all 2007.

16 The county's unfunded pension liability as of Dec. 31, 1982, was $56,395,720. Multnomah County Comprehensive Annual Financial Report (CAFR), June 30, 1983, 20. The county finance office and PERS took two years after 1981 to finalize the pension transfer and verify that all county employee records were correct.

17 Communications from former finance officer Dave Boyer and former labor relations manager Ken Upton, Feb. 2008 and Dec. 2009.

18 Lansing, 352.

19 Harder later was to utilize the same concept at transportation agency Tri-Met for nearly twenty years. Correspondence from Dick Feeney to author Lansing, Oct. 14 and Nov. 16, 2009.

20 Don Clark interview by Ernie Bonner, Mar. 8, 2002.

21 Clark would later characterize Blumenauer, at that period of his life, as "manipulative, power-grabbing, and mean-spirited." Taped interview with Don Clark by author Lansing, Apr. 11, 2006.

22 *Oregonian,* May 2, 1980.

23 "Multnomah County Municipal Services Reexamined," by the Center for Urban Studies, School of Urban Affairs, Portland State University, Mar. 1979; Nohad Toulan, project director; Judy Barmack, principal investigator; correspondence from former County Auditor Gary Blackmer to author Lansing, Sept. 27, 2009.

24 *Gresham Outlook,* Feb. 19, 1981. Only 58,000 votes were cast in this election.

25 *Oregonian,* Oct. 16, 1980; June 2, 1981.

26 *Oregon Journal,* July 27, 1981.

27 On Jan. 15, 1998, Oregon's district courts were merged into circuit courts. There are no longer any district courts in Oregon. www.ojd.state.or.us/courts/circuit; accessed Aug. 15, 2009.

28 Correspondence from Fred Neal to author Lansing, Jan. 28, 2009.

29 *Oregonian,* Aug. 7 and 21, 1981.

30 *Oregon Journal,* July 7 and 27, 1981; *Oregonian,* July 22, 1981.

31 *Oregonian,* Oct. 25, 1981.

32 The vote tally was 453,415 no votes; 159, 811 yes votes. *2007-2008 Oregon Blue Book*, 304.

33 *Oregonian*, July 22 and Oct. 25, 1981.

34 *Oregon Journal*, Aug. 30, 1982; *Oregonian*, Aug. 31, 1982.

35 1982 and 1984 sample ballots and *Oregon Voters' Pamphlet*s; communications between the author and former county elections director Vicki Ervin Paulk in Mar., Sept., and Oct. 2007.

36 *Oregonian*, Aug. 3, 1981, and Oct. 16, 1983; Leeson, 220-21.

37 Dedication ceremony program, Dec. 14, 1981.

38 Email to author Lansing from Terry Baxter, Aug. 17, 2009; conversation by author Lansing with Tom Guiney, former FREDS division manager, and archivists Dwight Wallis and Terry Baxter, June 14, 2007.

39 *Willamette Week*, Nov. 27, 1978.

40 *Oregonian*, Sept. 1, 1982; Sept. 5, 1987; Nov. 20, 1987; Aug. 27, 2003.

41 *Oregonian*, Oct. 16, 1983; Leeson, 220-21; www.mcso.us/public/facilities. htm, accessed Aug. 12, 2008.

42 *Oregonian*, Oct. 16, 1983.

43 "The Justice Center, Portland, Oregon" booklet prepared 1983; letter from Ken Upton to author Lansing, June 28, 2009.

44 Letter from Clyde Doctor to author Lansing, Jan. 26, 2007.

45 *County Lines*, Mar. 1979.

46 *Oregonian*, June 4, 1975; pamphlet "Multnomah County Legend and Logo," 1978. Board members in 1978 were County Chairman Don Clark and Commissioners Dennis Buchanan, Alice Corbett, Dan Mosee, and Barbara Roberts.

47 Testimony at a taped reunion roast for Clark, Nov. 5, 2003; correspondence from Ken Upton, former labor relations manager, to author Lansing, June 28, 2009.

48 Letter from Thomas J. Higgins to author Lansing, Mar. 22, 2007.

49 Don Clark conversation with author Lansing, Aug. 9, 2008.

50 Letter from Don Clark to author Lansing, Apr. 11, 2006.

51 Clark interview with author Lansing, Apr. 11, 2006.

52 *Willamette Week*, Aug. 12, 1980.

53 *Oregonian*, Dec. 12, 1982.

54 Correspondence from Jeff Wohler to author Lansing, Nov. 9 and 11, 2009. The Neil Goldschmidt reference was to information that became public in 2004 that Goldschmidt had sexually abused a teenage girl while he served as Portland mayor (1973-79). Lansing, 2005, 410-11.

55 Betty Merten interview by Ernie Bonner, Dec. 9, 2001.

CHAPTER 17

1 *Oregonian*, Jan. 16, 1986, B1.

2 Dennis Buchanan interview with Ernie Bonner, June, 2001.

3 Communication to author Lansing from Gary Blackmer, former county and city auditor, Sept. 27, 2009.

4 "Multnomah County Municipal Services Reexamined," by the Center for Urban Studies, School of Urban Affairs, Portland State University, Mar. 1979; Nohad Toulan, project director; Judy Barmack, principal investigator; correspondence from former county auditor Gary Blackmer to author Lansing, Sept. 27, 2009.

5 City Council Resolution #33327, adopted Feb. 23, 1983, as cited in "Urban Services Report IAR #3-86," City Auditor's Office, Sept. 1986, 1, 111, 113; Yeates, 23.

6 "City at a Crossroad, Creating a Framework for Change," a paper prepared by Mark Gardiner, former City of Portland fiscal administrator, June 9, 1989.

7 Ibid.

8 Buchanan interview with Ernie Bonner, June 2001.

9 Yeates, 23. *Oregon Journal*, Mar. 16, 1977.

10 *Oregonian,* Aug. 24, 1995, B4.

11 Ibid., Jan. 2, 1987, D2.

12 *Gresham Outlook*, Jan. 18, 1984. City officials taking part in Resolution A negotiations and implementation, in addition to financial administrator Mark

Gardiner, included mayors Frank Ivancie and Bud Clark and council members Charles Jordan, Mike Lindberg, Mildred Schwab, Margaret Strachan, and Dick Bogle.

13 *Oregonian*, July 13, 1986; Jan. 24, 1988; Mar. 7, 1989.

14 County Commissioner Tanya Collier, a member of the county's negotiating team, insisted that the college degree requirement be part of the transfer agreement. Correspondence from Don Clark to author Lansing, Dec 3, 2008, and from Tanya Collier to author Lansing, Jan. 14, 2009; "150-Year Pictorial History of the Multnomah County Sheriff's Office," July 2005, compiled by Steve Wright, Fiscal Unit, Sheriff's Office.

15 *Consolidation Threshold Study, Final Report*, Sept. 1998, 8; communication from Don Clark to author Lansing, Jan. 2009.

16 Communication to author Lansing from Gary Blackmer, former county and city auditor, Sept. 27, 2009.

17 Ibid.

18 Author Lansing conversation with Eileen Brady, 2012 mayoral candidate, Aug. 15, 2011.

19 "Portland Mid County Sewer Project," Talbot, Korvola & Warwick, and Suzanne Crane Engineering, Dec. 1993, 5.

20 Correspondence to the author from former county and city auditor Gary Blackmer, Sept. 27, 2009.

21 *Oregonian*, Mar. 3 and 4, 1985; *Gresham Outlook*, Feb. 13, 1985.

22 "Portland Mid County Sewer Project," Talbot, Korvola & Warwick, and Suzanne Crane Engineering, Dec. 1993; Dan Vizzini, customer services manager, Mid-C Sewer Project, letter to author Lansing, Oct. 6, 2006; *Oregonian*, Oct. 28, 1983.

23 *Oregon Historical Quarterly*, Fall 2002, 331, 337; Anderson, 5-8, 13-15; Lansing, 243-44, 472-73.

24 *Oregonian*, Dec. 9, 1901; *General Laws of Oregon, 1901*, 19-22, approved Feb. 13, 1901.

25 Lansing, 243-44; Anderson, 5, 7-8, 13, 15; *General Laws of Oregon, 1901*, 19-22, approved Feb. 13, 1901.

26 Ritz, 1. By 2010, the county library system included eighteen branches. *Oregonian*, Aug. 13, 2010, B1.

27 Correspondence from Earl Blumenauer to author Lansing, Sept. 30, 2009.

28 "Liberating the Library," an unpublished, 29-page article written in 2002 by former *Oregon Journal* reporter Tom Stimmel and made available to author Lansing courtesy Eleanor Davis and Fred Neal, 8.

29 Stimmel, 1-2.

30 Ibid., 9-11.

31 Ibid., 10-12.

32 Ibid., 13.

33 Ibid., 12-13, 24.

34 Earl Blumenauer made a fact-finding trip to the East Coast to check out the qualifications of the person nominated as library director by the library board. He found the nominee "underwhelming" at best and was successful in opening up the hiring process. The library board then hired Sarah Long, "who helped break the mold and move it forward." Correspondence from Earl Blumenauer to author Lansing, Sept. 30, 2009.

35 Stimmel, 17.

36 *Oregonian*, Nov. 6, 2010, E2.

37 Correspondence from Bill Failing to author Lansing, Dec. 3, 2009.

38 Linn, 33.

39 *Oregonian*, May 11 and Oct. 6, 1989; Jan. 2, 1990.

40 Stimmel, 26-27.

41 Correspondence from Nancy Wilson, OCF Vice-President for Fund Services, June 22, 2009.

42 *Oregon State Bar Bulletin*, Jan 1989, 31. Conversation with OSB investigator Kateri Walsh by author Lansing, Oct. 20, 2009; *Oregonian*, Mar. 15, 1990. Information obtained through a public records request to the Oregon State Bar in Dec. 2009 shows that, among other illegal actions, Voorhies mishandled the $5 million estate of Mary Malarky Baker; improperly pocketed cash of more than $110,000; improperly

represented both parties in legal transactions; neglected to file required legal documents and IRS fiduciary returns; and failed or refused to turn over documents and records to successor personal representatives. Voorhies moved to Texas and declared bankruptcy there. When he and his wife Molly divorced, she was awarded most of his assets. The couple then came back together, spending summers on Bainbridge Island in Washington State's Puget Sound and wintering in Palm Springs, California. Correspondence to author Lansing in Oct. and Dec. 2009 from Connie Morgan, widow of Don Morgan, the managing partner of the Wood Tatum law firm at the time.

43 *Oregonian*, Aug. 8, 2003. Head-hunter Paul Milius recruited Ginnie Cooper for the Multnomah County job. Correspondence from Bill Failing to author Lansing, Dec. 3, 2009.

44 Correspondence from Bill Failing to author Lansing, Nov. 13, 2009.

45 *County Lines*, June 1990.

46 Stimmel, 24, 27.

47 Leeson, 220-21; letter from county auditor Suzanne Flynn to author Lansing, Sept. 4, 2006; *Oregonian*, Oct. 6, 1983.

48 *Oregonian*, Mar. 17, 1989.

49 Ibid., May 11, 1983, A1

50 Ibid., May 12, 1983, B10

CHAPTER 18

1 *November/ 1974 Voters' Pamphlet*, 129-30.

2 *Oregon Journal*, May 13, 1980.

3 *Oregonian*, Jan. 14, 1980.

4 *Willamette Week*, Aug. 12, 1980; *Gresham Outlook*, May 8, 1980.

5 *County Lines*, June 1982.

6 *Gresham Outlook*, Jan. 18, 1984.

7 Prior to Anderson's election as District 1 commissioner, Arnold Biskar was appointed to fill the remainder of Dennis Buchanan's term when Buchanan was elected county executive. Biskar was prohibited from seeking election to the position by the county charter. Buchanan and Bill Vandever correspondence to author Lansing, Sept. 2008.

8 Lansing, 455.

9 *Oregonian*, Mar. 1, 5, and 8, 1985.

10 Ibid., Nov. 28, 1985.

11 Ibid., Dec. 18, 1985.

12 Ibid., Nov. 28, 1985.

13 Ibid., Jan. 12, 1986.

14 Ibid., Apr. 14, 1986.

15 Ibid.

16 Ibid., May 15, 1986.

17 Open letter from Tom Dennehy to Commissioner Gordon Shadburne, June 2, 1986.

18 *Oregonian*, Aug. 6, 1986; Shadburne resignation letter, Aug. 7, 1986.

19 *Oregonian*, Oct. 2, 1986.

20 Ibid., Oct. 3, 1986.

21 *Voters' Pamphlet*, Nov. 1986; *Oregonian*, Nov. 26, 2008.

22 Letter to author Lansing from Sharron Kelley, Oct. 1, 2008.

23 *Willamette Week*, Nov. 10, 2004.

24 March 1986 City Club committee was chaired by Judge Stephen Herrell.

25 *Gresham Outlook*, Mar. 19, 1986.

26 *News-Times*, Apr. 3 and 9, 1986.

27 *Oregonian*, Mar. 15, 1986.

28 "Dick Neuberger's Dream," *The Daily Astorian*, Mar. 31, 1986.

29 The City Club report was titled "Formation of a Tri-County Commission on Regional Services." Task force members were Cliff Carlson, Richard Ares, Ilo Bonyhadi, Chuck Clemans, Mark Gardiner, E. Andrew Jordan, Jewel Lansing (coauthor of this book), and Ned Look, plus advisors Tom Higgins, Norm Smith, Stephen Herrell, and Paul Carlson. City Club staffing was provided by Nina Johnson and Mark Fritzler.

30 In a fall 2010 runoff for Chair Jeff Cogen's former commission seat, two African-American women faced each other as the two top vote-getters in the primary. In the fall, Loretta Smith was elected over Karol Collymore. *Oregonian*, Nov. 3, 2010.

31 *Oregonian,* Apr. 13, 1993; *Voters' Pamphlet*, May 1978; Portland Women's History blog, accessed Mar. 15, 2007.

32 *Oregonian*, Nov 8, 1984.

33 *Voters' Pamphlets*, 1978 and 1986.

34 McCoy bested Otto by 1,800 votes. KPTV news, Nov. 6, 1986.

35 *Oregonian*, Apr. 26, 1994, B4.

36 *Oregonian*, Nov. 25, 1987, and Sept. 2, 1988; correspondence between author Lansing and former county employees Dave Boyer, Ken Upton, Merrie Ziady, and Darrell Murray, Sept. 18, 2008.

37 "Promise & Progress History Book, The Development of Health Care in Multnomah County from 1774 to 1988," published by the Multnomah County Dept. of Human Services, Health Division, June 1988.

38 "Healthy Children, Oregon," Harvard University Division of Health Policy, ca 1988, 8. County employees involved included Multnomah County Health Division Director Billie Odegaard, Mary Lou Heinrich, Anne Cathey, and Public Health Nurse Susan Imbrie. State Representative Rick Bauman also assisted.

39 Preface to "Healthy Children, Oregon," Harvard University Division of Health Policy, ca. 1988; copy obtained from Billie Odegaard, former director, Multnomah County Health Division.

40 KPTV news, Nov. 6, 1986; *Oregonian*, Dec. 2, 1986, and Mar. 1, 1990.

41 *Oregonian*, Apr. 13, 1993, A12; Interview by author Lansing with Fred Neal, former advisor to McCoy, Mar. 11, 2007.

42 Conversation between Hank Miggins and author Lansing, Aug 13, 2007; correspondence to author Lansing from former labor relations manager Ken Upton, Aug. 12, 2009.

43 *Oregonian*, Oct. 5, 1989.

44 Ibid., Apr. 13, 1993.

45 Ibid., Apr. 19, 1994.

46 City council members Connie McCready and Mildred Schwab served concurrently from 1973 through 1980; Schwab and Margaret Strachan from 1981 to 1986; Mayor Vera Katz and Commissioner Gretchen Kafoury from 1993 to 1998. Jewel Lansing served as the elected city auditor with Schwab and Strachan from 1983 though 1986. For the first four years of Barbara Clark's

eight-year tenure as city auditor, she was the only female elected official in city hall. She then served eight years concurrently with Gretchen Kafoury and six years with Vera Katz. No woman served as a City of Portland elected official from 2005 until 2008. Amanda Fritz won a council seat in 2008 with financial assistance from Portland's experimental "Voter-Owned" elections program. LaVonne Griffin-Valade began her tenure as city auditor in 2009. See also Lansing, 343, 477-78, 483.

47 In 2009, county commissioner salaries were 16 percent lower than city council member salaries ($88,000 compared to $102,294). The county chair for many years was the highest paid local official in the Portland Metro area, but Chair Ted Wheeler declined pay raises and took a pay cut so that his salary declined to 6 percent lower than the Portland mayor ($113,933 compared to $121,451), and virtually the same as the Metro Council president ($114,468). Author Lansing communication with Portland city auditor's office, Metro Auditor Suzanne Flynn, and Elizabeth Nunes, interim director, Multnomah County Human Services Dept., Aug. 18, 2009; *Oregonian*, Jan. 15, 2009.

48 According to June 30, 2008, city and county financial statements, there were 4,528 county employees compared to 5,955 city employees.

49 In 2006 and 2008, Portland city government conducted an experimental "voter-owned" taxpayer-paid campaign funding program that went down to defeat by the slim margin of 50.4 percent to 49.6 percent, a difference of only 1,574 votes, when placed on the ballot in November 2010. *Oregonian*, Nov. 4, 2010, A6, and Nov. 6, 2010, E2.

50 *Oregonian*, Apr. 13, 1993.

51 www.gorgecommission.org; accessed May 5, 2009.

52 *Oregonian*, Jan. 17, 1979, 11.

53 Ibid., June 9, 1987, Metro East, B4.

54 Ibid., June 24, 1987, B5.

55 Ibid., June 9, 1987, Metro East, B4.

56 Ibid., July 2, 1987, C5.

57 Ibid., Dec. 3, 1988, D2.

58 Ibid., Dec. 10, 1987, D2.

59 Multnomah-Clackamas Comparison Study, Carol Kirchner, Oct. 25, 1988.

60 *Oregonian*, Feb. 5, 1970; *Oregon Journal*, June 4, 1975 and Jan. 28, 1980; McCarthy, 174; www.co.multnomah.or.us/sheriff/history.htm, accessed Oct. 26, 2005.

61 *Gresham Outlook*, Oct. 27 and 28, 1989.

62 1989 Sheriff's annual report, 1; *Oregonian*, Oct. 27, 1989.

63 *Oregonian*, Oct. 5, 1989; www.co.multnomah.or.us/sheriff/history.htm, accessed Oct 26, 2005.

64 *Oregonian*, May 7, 11, 17, 1990; Jan. 1, 2009.

65 Ibid., Oct. 6, 1988, G10.

66 Ibid., Mar. 30, 1990, F4.

67 Nesbit, 32-41.

CHAPTER 19

1   Measure 50 changed the value used to test Measure 5 limits to real market value only. Insert to November 1997 Multnomah County property tax statements; Arrieta-Walden, 133-34; "The Ballot Measure That Ate Oregon," by Patty Wentz, *Willamette Week*, Nov. 10, 1999, 1990 section.

2   *Oregonian*, Feb. 3, 2008, B4; correspondence to author Lansing from Linhares, Sept. 17, 2009.

3   *Willamette Week*, June 10, 1993; *Oregonian*, June 3 and Aug 6, 1993; *Jewish Review*, Aug. 15, 1993.

4   *Oregonian*, Apr. 19, 1994.

5   *Governing Magazine*, Dec. 1994; letter from Stein to author Lansing, Aug. 21, 2008.

6   Correspondence from Dick Feeney to author Lansing, Oct. 14, 2009.

7   *Oregonian*, Sept. 9, 2005.

8   Linn, 19-20; *Oregonian*, Mar. 30, 1990, and Apr. 16, 1990.

9   Memo from Sheriff Skipper to County Chair Gladys McCoy, Nov. 3, 1992.

10 According to then-county auditor Gary Blackmer, the underlying sheriff's budget issue was, and is, that all sheriffs have protected their law enforcement function by offering up only cuts in corrections division personnel at budget time. "The inefficiencies of the patrol and investigation functions are costly," Blackmer later said, "but no one has ever been able to convince a sheriff that he needed to get out of his law enforcement duties." Correspondence from Blackmer to author Lansing, Oct. 2009. (Blackmer began his thirty-year government career as a six-year sheriff's office analyst under Public Safety Director Ed Martin and Sheriff Fred Pearce, 1979-85. In 1985, Blackmer was hired as a performance auditor for the City of Portland. After five years at the city, he was elected Multnomah County auditor for two full terms, and as City of Portland auditor from 1999 until his resignation in May 2009. He then accepted the position of Oregon Audit Division Director under Secretary of State Kate Brown. No other individual has held a longer or more opportune catbird seat for observing the six most recent Multnomah County sheriffs.)

11 *Oregonian*, July 18, 2008.

12 County elections web site, 1995 summary, accessed Aug. 13, 2008.

13 The *Oregonian* endorsed Kafoury for election to Portland city council in part because of her crucial role in the doubling of jail beds in Multnomah County. *Oregonian*, Apr. 27, 1995.

14 Correspondence from Don Clark to author Lansing, Dec. 3, 2008.

15 *Oregonian*, Apr. 19, 1994; *Governing Magazine*, Dec. 1994; letter from Stein to author Lansing, Aug. 21, 2008.

16 *Oregonian*, July 7 and Sept. 2, 2000.

17 *Business Journal*, Dec. 24, 1999; *Oregonian*, Jan. 13, 2000; *Skanner*, May 1998.

18 *Northwest Labor Press*, Oct. 3, 2003, 4.

19 *Seattle Times*, May 20, 1993.

20 *Seattle Post-Intelligencer*, June 29, 2001.

21 Correspondence to author Lansing from Friends of the Columbia Gorge staff attorney Nathan Baker and land use law clerk Rick Till, June 9, 2009.

22 *Willamette Week*, Sept. 29, 1999, 2.

23 *Oregonian*, Nov. 23, 2006; *Willamette Week*, Sept. 29, 1999, 2-3.

24 *Willamette Week*, Sept. 29, 1999, 1-2.

25 Ibid., Sept. 29, 1999; Feb. 8, 2006.

26 *Willamette Week*, Feb. 8, 2006;
    Oregonian, Nov. 23, 2006; correspon-
    dence to author Lansing from Judy
    Davis, Columbia Gorge Commission
    member, May 26, 2010.

27 *Oregonian*, Nov. 23, 2006; Dec. 16,
    2008, B7.

28 Ibid., July 11, A6 and July 12, 2011, B1.

29 *Consolidation Study Task Force, Final
    Report*, Sept. 1998, xv-xvii. Author
    Lansing was a member of that task
    force. She concluded that no further
    study or action of consolidation was
    warranted. The seven-member-majority
    was unable to reach agreement as to
    which of three options for overall frame-
    work put forward would be preferable.

30 "Bills provide Gresham option to quit
    county," *Oregonian*, May 15, 1999;
    Task Force report, xv.

31 *Oregonian*, Sept. 29, 1998, B1 and B5;
    Oct. 2, 1998, Portland page.

32 "A tug of war of two cities," *Oregonian*,
    Oct. 20, 1990; conversation by author
    Lansing with George Joseph, chair
    of the 1974 City-County Charter
    Commission, on Nov. 27, 2000. Joseph
    said he would not vote for Portland-
    Multnomah County consolidation if it
    were on the ballot that day.

33 *Oregonian*, Sept. 29, 1998, B1 and B5;
    Oct. 2, 1998, Portland page; *2007-2008
    Oregon Blue Book*, 309.

34 *Portland Tribune*, May 23, 2006, A2.

35 www.neighborhoodlink.com/org/mult-
    cofair/, accessed June 3, 2009.

36 *Gresham Outlook*, Apr. 29, 2009.

37 Intergovernmental Agreement,
    Multnomah County and Metro, Mar.
    21, 1996.

38 www.expocenter.org, accessed Apr. 13,
    2009.

39 *Oregonian,* May 22, 1996, C2.

40 Ibid., March 7, 2004, E1.

41 Chair Beverly Stein memo to city
    council, Oct. 7, 1999; budget manager
    Dave Warren memo to Multnomah
    County Board, Oct. 6, 1999; city finance
    director Tim Grewe memo to Dave
    Warren, Oct. 5, 1999; joint city and
    county resolution 93-19, Jan. 21, 1993.

42 "History of 1996 Public Safety & G. O.
    Bond Levies and SB 1145 Capital," by
    David Boyer, Chief County Financial
    Officer, Nov. 29, 2004; *Oregonian*, "In
    Portland" section, Apr. 14, 2005.

43 Measure 47, passed in 1996, was
    completely eliminated by Measure 50.

44 Correspondence to author Lansing from
    Tom Linhares, Sept. 17, 2009.

45 Passage of SB 1145 by the 1995 Oregon
    legislature brought responsibility to the
    county for supervising felons sentenced
    to less than one year. The state assumed
    the burden of providing facilities in
    which to house those felons. The
    construction funds authorized by SB
    1145 applied chiefly to Inverness Jail,
    and had nothing to do with the county's
    failure to open Wapato Jail, according to
    then-Chief Finance Officer David Boyer.
    In Boyer's opinion, the sheriff's office
    did not negotiate sufficient operation
    funds for those prisoners, which
    continues to be a problem. "History of
    1996 Public Safety & G. O. Bond Levies
    and SB 1145 Capital" by Boyer, Nov.
    29, 2004; letter from Boyer to author
    Lansing, Nov. 25, 2008.

46 Regarding Measure 50's effect on future
    revenue, analysis conducted by Tom
    Linhares, director of the Multnomah
    County Tax Supervising and
    Conservation Commission, concluded
    that, except for the two years of 1997-
    98 and 1998-99, the county actually
    received more property tax revenue
    than it would have under the old
    pre-Measure 50 system (although not
    pre-Measure 5) because two special
    levies would have expired. It was county
    revenue other than property taxes
    that had substantially declined. Memo
    "Comparison of County's Tax Base
    with Measure 50 Taxes" dated Sept. 29,
    2008, by Linhares; correspondence to
    author Lansing from Linhares, Nov. 10
    and 14, 2008.

47 *Oregonian*, "In Portland" section, Apr.
    14, 2005.

48 Correspondence from David Boyer to
    author Lansing, Nov. 20, 2008.

49 *Oregonian*, Mar. 6, 2008.

50 *Willamette Week*, May 23 and June
    27, 2001; correspondence from former

Chair Bev Stein to author Lansing, Oct. 20, 2009.

51 Conversation by author Lansing with county clerk Deborah Bogstad, May 4, 2009.

52 *Oregonian,* "In Portland," Oct. 27, 2005, 19.

53 *Oregonian,* Mar. 18, 2001.

54 www.psg.us/team/teambios/bevbio.html; accessed Mar 3, 2008; correspondence from Stein to author Lansing, Mar. 16, 2009.

55 www.sos.state.or.us/elections/may212002/abstracts/gov.him; accessed Mar. 3, 2008.

56 www.psg.us/team/teambios/bevbio.html; accessed Mar. 3, 2008.

CHAPTER 20

1 *Oregonian,* Apr. 27, 2001, C8.

2 *Portland Tribune,* Apr. 27, 2001, A1, 4.

3 *Oregonian,* May 16, 2001, C1, 10.

4 www.co.multnomah.or.us/dbcs/elections/2001-05/results.shtml, accessed Mar. 3, 2008.

5 *Oregonian,* Oct. 24, 2005, D6.

6 Ibid., Aug. 21, 2001.

7 Ibid., Mar. 6, 2008.

8 County elections website, May 2002 election, accessed Aug. 13, 2008.

9 *Northwest Labor News,* Oct. 3, 2003, 1.

10 *Oregonian,* May 2, 2003.

11 *Oregonian,* Aug. 21, Sept. 8 and 19, Oct. 7 and 8, 2003; correspondence to author Lansing from county attorney Agnes Sowle, Oct 7, 2009.

12 *Oregonian,* Jan. 15, 2004, D1, and Jan. 5, 2005; correspondence to author Lansing from county attorney Agnes Sowle, Oct. 7, 2009.

13 Correspondence to author Lansing from county attorney Agnes Sowle, Oct 7, 2009.

14 *Oregonian,* Mar. 3, 4, and 7, 2004.

15 Ibid., Mar. 4, 2004, D1.

16 Correspondence to author Lansing from county attorney Agnes Sowle, Oct. 7, 2009. State Public Meetings law prohibits a board quorum from meeting without advance notice to the public. For Multnomah County, that meant that no more than two commissioners could meet in private at the same time.

17 *Oregonian,* Apr. 15, 2005, B6-7, May 1, 2008.

18 *Portland Tribune,* Mar. 23, 2004, A1-3.

19 *Oregonian,* May 6, 2004, A1 and B6.

20 Ibid., Mar. 6, 2008, and Mar. 18, 2009.

21 "History of 1996 Public Safety & G. O. Bond Levies and SB 1145 Capital" by David Boyer, Chief Financial Officer, November 29, 2004.

22 *Oregonian,* "In Portland," Apr. 13, 2006, 18; *Northwest Labor Press,* Oct. 3, 2003, 2.

23 *Willamette Week,* Dec. 29, 2004.

24 *Oregonian,* Oct. 26, 2006; June 28, 2009.

25 Letter from David Boyer to Chair Diane Linn, Mar. 10, 2006; *Oregonian,* June 23, 2006, B2: *Oregonian,* Jan. 15, 2004; D1; *Oregonian,* May 16, 2004, B12; *Northwest Labor Press,* Oct. 3, 2003.

26 *Oregonian,* Oct. 16, 2008.

27 *Willamette Week,* Jan. 18, 2008.

28 *Portland Tribune,* Apr. 7, 2006; *Oregonian,* Apr. 9, 2006.

29 *Oregonian,* Oct. 19, 2006.

30 Ibid., Mar. 21, 2006.

31 *Oregonian,* Mar. 23, 2003; *Northwest Labor Press,* Oct. 3, 2003.

32 *Oregonian,* May 17, 2006, 1.

33 Wheeler's more than three-to-one victory over an incumbent head official was paralleled only by the 1948 victory of Dorothy McCullough Lee, who defeated incumbent Portland Mayor Earl Riley after a grisly murder had occurred and revelations of widespread corruption and vice.

34 *Oregonian,* "In Portland," Jan. 4, 2007, 14.

35 Online Voters' Guide, Multnomah County Chair – May 2006 Primary Election, accessed Aug. 10, 2008.

36 Then county auditor LaVonne Griffin-Valade notes that Serena Cruz Walsh was extremely bright and able to think and act like a real leader much of the time, but that it was unfortunate that in the end Cruz Walsh's apparent disdain for Linn and her policy decisions became the primary focus of the press

and the public. Of Naito's ten years on the board, Griffin-Valade says: "Naito was a smart, staunch, and studied advocate for mental health clients and children, and she was a capable and progressive public safety activist. Sadly, those qualities may have gotten lost because of her participation in the gay marriage decision and her reputation as one of the supposed mean girls."

37 No recall movements made it to the voters. As of this writing, all four women county officials had left public office; Linn had been hired as the executive director of the Ritter Center in Marin County, Calif., an organization dedicated to helping homeless people. *Oregonian*, Feb. 26, 2008, B1.

38 *Willamette Week*, Dec. 20, 2006.

39 Yeates, 25.

40 *Oregonian*, "In Portland" section, Jan. 4, 2007, 1.

41 Anderson speech delivered Aug. 26, 2008, at a lunch observing Women's Equality Day.

42 County elections web site, May 2006 election, accessed Aug. 13, 2008.

43 *Oregonian*, July 9, 2008; *Willamette Week*, May 2004; Lansing, 410-11.

44 *Oregonian*, Jan. 31, 2008.

45 Ibid., Nov. 2, 2006.

46 Ibid., Dec. 2, 2005; Jan. 31, July 9, 15, and 18, 2008.

47 Ibid., Nov. 5, 2008.

48 Ibid., June 4 and July 18, 2008.

49 Ibid., Sept. 9, 2009, A1; Sept. 10, 2009, B4.

50 *Oregonian*, Mar. 10, 2010, A1, B6; *Willamette Week*, Mar. 17, 2010, 8.

51 *Oregonian*, "In Portland" section, 12-15, June 28, 2008.

52 By 2009, 85 percent of the sheriff's budget was dedicated to the 450-person corrections division that ran the jails.

53 *Oregonian*, "In Portland" section, 15, June 28, 2008; www.uscensus.quick-facts.gov, accessed Aug. 20, 2008.

CHAPTER 21

1 *Oregonian*, May 3, 1959, 28.

2 Ibid.

3 Ibid.

4 Ibid., July 16, 1959, 30.

5 Dennis Buchanan interview with Ernie Bonner, June 2001.

6 Sauvie Island/Multnomah Channel Rural Area Plan, 1997, 3.

7 *Oregonian*, June 7, 1989, B1.

8 Ibid., Feb. 5, 1992, C2.

9 Ibid., Feb. 8, 2002, C3.

10 Ibid., March 3, 1997, B1.

11 "Summary of Measure 37 Claims as of Jan. 11, 2007," memo from Derrick Tokos, senior planner, to Karen Shilling, planning director, Multnomah County Department of Planning and Transportation, accessed at http://www2.co.multnomah.or.us/Community_Services/LUT-Planning/Measure37/M37_status.PDF, July 2010.

12 *State ex rel English v. Multnomah County*, Oregon Supreme Court, June 10, 2010.

13 Ibid.

14 *Oregonian*, July 19, 2010.

15 Ibid., Nov. 20, 2009.

16 Ibid., July 30, 2009.

17 Ibid., June 23, 2008, B1.

18 Sauvie Island/Multnomah Channel Rural Area Plan, 1997, 32.

19 *Oregonian*, May 1, 2011, A1.

20 Engeman, 260; *Oregonian,* July 5 and 27, 2009.

21 *Oregonian*, Mar. 21, 2006.

22 The 2006 term limits measure targeting state legislators failed in Multnomah County by 167,205 (66%) to 84,024 (33%). The 2004 vote against repealing county term limits was 163,454 (54%) to 140,209 (46%). In 2010, the county charter amendment count was 128,958 (52%) against repeal to 118,416 (48%) voting yes. The 2006 statewide ballot measure failed by 788,895 against to 555,016 for. Sources: Multnomah County Elections Division, Aug. 24, 2011: *2007-2008 Oregon Blue Book*, 312.

23 *Portland Tribune*, May 19 and 26, 2011; correspondence to author Lansing from Griffin-Valade, Aug. 7 and 12, 2011.

24 2009-10 Multnomah County Property Tax Statement, November 2009; correspondence from Julie Neburka,

Multnomah County Principal Budget Analyst, to author Lansing, Nov. 6, 2009.

25 Correspondence to author Lansing from county attorney Agnes Sowle, Oct. 7, 2009.

26 *Willamette Week*, Apr. 25, 2007.

27 Gary Blackmer testimony to Portland City Council on March 19, 2009, after he announced his resignation as city auditor to serve as Oregon state audit division director in Salem.

28 *Oregonian*, Nov. 5, 2010, A1.

29 Ibid., Aug. 12, 2009.

30 Ibid., Mar. 10, 2010, B1 and B6

APPENDIX B

1 *Oregonian*, Feb. 3, 2008, B4; correspondence to author Lansing from Tom Linhares, Multnomah County Tax Supervising and Conservation Commission Director, Sept. 17, 2009.

2 Measure 50 changed the value used to test Measure 5 limits to real market value only. Insert to November 1997 Multnomah County property tax statements; Arrieta-Walden, 133-34; "The Ballot Measure That Ate Oregon," by Patty Wentz, *Willamette Week*, Nov. 10, 1999, 1990 section; correspondence to author Lansing from Mark Campbell, Deputy Chief Financial Officer, Apr. 4, 2011.

3 Arrieta-Walden, 141.

4 Measure 56 exempted elections in May and November from the double majority standard, but it still applies to any March or September election. Correspondence from Tom Linhares to author Lansing, Dec. 8, 2009; *Oregonian*, Nov. 5, 2008.

5 Correspondence to author Lansing from Mark Campbell, Deputy Chief Financial Officer, Mar 1, 2011.

6 Ibid.

7 Synopsis prepared by author Lansing based on information from Multnomah and Washington County property tax statements, the 1997-98 Summary of Assessments and Taxes prepared by the Multnomah County Dept. of Assessment and Taxation, through correspondence between author Lansing

and Tom Linhares, Sept. 10 and Nov. 10, 2008; *Oregonian*, Nov. 9, 2008.

8 In 2001-2 the tax levy for FPD&R was $62,969,651 with a tax rate of $1.8892 per $1,000 of assessed value. This represented 15.8 percent of the total tax rate for general governments of $11.9552 per $1,000. In 2009-10 the levy had jumped to $114,980,456 and the tax rate, calculated using the lower assessed values under Measure 50, was $2.6259. The FPD&R levy tax rate made up 14.6 percent of the total tax rate of $14.2048 that year. Correspondence from Tom Linhares to author Lansing, Oct. 22, 2009.

9 Correspondence to author Lansing from Mark Campbell, Deputy Chief Financial Officer, Mar. 1, 2011; conversations by author Lansing with League members Debbie Aiona and Shelley Lorenzen, Dec. 6, 2010; Correspondence to author Lansing from Tom Linhares, Dec. 7, 2010; Lansing, 458-59.

10 Portland financial statement for 1999-2000, Note 17, Fire and Police Disability and Retirement Plan, 52-56.

11 City of Portland FPD&R Actuarial Valuation Report 2008, 1; correspondence to author Lansing from Tom Linhares, Oct. 28, 2010.

12 *Oregonian*, Oct. 27, 2010, B1.

13 Correspondence to author Lansing from Tom Linhares, Oct. 28, 2010; *Oregonian*, Oct. 27, 2010, B1.

14 Correspondence to author Lansing from Tom Linhares, Sept. 21, Oct. 12, and Oct. 22, 2009.

APPENDIX C

1 http://www.co.multnomah.or.us/counsel/ charter.shtml, accessed Sept. 22, 2006, and Sept. 29, 2010; edited and condensed by author Lansing. Home rule charter amendments originally compiled in Jan. 1988 by then county counsel Tom Sponzler.

2 Oregon Constitution, Art. VI, Sec. 10, as printed in *2007-2008 Oregon Blue Book*, 397.

3 *State ex rel. Heinig v. City of Milwaukie*, 231 Or. 473, 373 P.2d 680 (1962).

4   *City of La Grande v. Public Employees Retirement Bd*, 281 Or. 137, 576 P.2d 1204 (1978). An article by Sarah Burgundy in *University of Oregon Law Review* 85 (2007): 829-33, provides a good overview of court findings.

5   Names from the Multnomah County Home Rule Charter pamphlet printed and distributed to citizens after charter passage in 1966. Other information related to author Lansing by Lloyd Anderson in 2006 and 2007.

6   www.ci.portland.or.us/auditor/Elecarchives2/PRIM66.htm, accessed Sept. 12, 2000.

7   www.co.multnomah.or.us/counsel/charter.shtml; accessed Sept. 22, 2006; edited and condensed by author Lansing. Home rule charter history originally compiled in January 1988 by then county counsel Tom Sponzler.

8   *Oregonian*, Jan. 14, 1980.

9   Commissioner district boundaries specified in the charter were revised in Aug. 1991 and Aug. 2001 in accordance with this 1980 charter requirement.

10   Letter to author Lansing from former County Director of Elections Vicki Ervin Paulk, Mar. 24, 2007; *County Lines* newsletter, June 1982, 1-3.

11   1982 and 1984 sample ballots and editions of the *Voters' Pamphlet*; communications between author Lansing and former County Director of Elections Vicki Ervin Paulk in Mar., Sept., and Oct. 2007.

BIBLIOGRAPHY

Abbott, Carl. *Greater Portland: Urban Life and Landscape in the Pacific Northwest.* Philadelphia: University of Pennsylvania Press, 2001.

———. *Portland: Planning, Politics, and Growth in a Twentieth-Century City.* Lincoln, NE: University of Nebraska Press, 1983.

———. *Portland in Three Centuries,* Corvallis, OR: Oregon State University Press, 2011.

Aikman, Duncan, ed. *The Taming of the Frontier.* Freeport, NY: Books for Libraries Press, Inc., 1967. First printed in 1925.

Anderson, Katherine E. *Historical Sketch of the Library Association of Portland.* Portland: Library Association of Portland, 1964.

Arrieta-Walden, Michael, ed. *The Oregon Story, 1850-2000.* Portland: Graphic Arts Center Publishing, 2000.

Beckham, Stephen Dow. *The Indians of Western Oregon: This Land Was Theirs.* Coos Bay, OR: Arago Books, 1977.

Bingham, Mason L. *A Short History of the Tax Supervising and Conservation Commission, County of Multnomah.* (10-page paper, 1956.)

Bourke, Paul, and Donald DeBats. *Washington County: Politics and Community in Antebellum America.* Baltimore and London: The Johns Hopkins University Press, 1995.

Bowman, John S., ed. *The World Almanac of the American West.* New York: Pharos Books, 1986.

Carey, Charles Henry. *A General History of Oregon Prior to 1861, vol. 2.* Portland: Metropolitan Press, 1936.

———. *History of Oregon, vol. 1.* Chicago and Portland: The Pioneer Historical Publishing Co., 1922.

———, ed. *The Oregon Constitution and Proceedings and Debates of the Constitutional Convention of 1857.* Salem, OR: State Printing Department, 1926.

Chilton, W. R., ed. *Gresham: Stories of Our Past, Campground to City.* Gresham, OR: Gresham Historical Society, David and Fox Printing, Inc., 1993.

Clark, Malcolm H., Jr. *Eden Seekers, The Settlement of Oregon, 1818-1862* Boston: Houghton Mifflin Company, 1981.

———, ed. *Pharisee among Philistines: The Diary of Judge Matthew P. Deady, 1871-1892, 2 vols.* Portland: Oregon Historical Society, 1975.

Comprehensive Annual Financial Report, Multnomah County, Oregon (CAFR). Portland: Board of Multnomah County Commissioners, 2005.

Consolidation Threshold Study, Final Report of the Consolidation Study Task Force. Portland, 1998.

Corning, Howard McKinley, ed. *Dictionary of Oregon History.* Portland: Binfords & Mort, 1956.

DePastino, Todd. *Citizen Hobo: How a Century of Homelessness Shaped America.* Chicago: University of Chicago Press, 2003.

Duncombe, Herbert Sydney. *County Government in America.* Washington, DC: National Association of Counties, 1966.

———. *Modern County Government.* Washington, DC: National Association of Counties, 1977.

Edwards, Cecil L., comp. *Alphabetical List of Oregon's Legislators.* Salem: State of Oregon Legislative Administration Committee, 1993.

Engeman, Richard H. *The Oregon Companion: An Historical Gazetteer of the Useful, the Curious, and the Arcane.* Portland: Timber Press, 2009.

53 Years of Property Tax Relief in Oregon. Salem, OR: State of Oregon Department of Revenue, Research and Special Services Division, April 1975.

Gaston, Joseph. *Portland, Oregon: Its History and Builders.* Vols. 1, 2 & 3. Chicago: The S. J. Clarke Publishing Co., 1911.

Goeres-Gardner, Diane L. *Necktie Parties: Legal Executions in Oregon, 1851-1905.* Caldwell, ID: Caxton Press, 2005.

Gordly, Avel, and Patricia Schechter. *Remembering the Power of Words.* Corvallis, OR: Oregon State University Press, 2011.

Guide to the Manuscript Collections of the Oregon Historical Society. Portland: Federal Works Agency, Work Projects Administration Official Historical Records Project No. 65-1-94-25, August 1940.

Hamilton, Nanci. *Portland's Multnomah Village: Images of America.* San Francisco: Arcadia Publishing, 2007.

Hawkins, William John III. *The Grand Era of Cast Iron Architecture in Portland.* Portland: Binford & Mort, 1976.

Hayes, J. W. *Looking Backward at Portland.* Portland: Kilham Stationery & Printing Co., 1911.

Historical Sites Tour Guide and Map, Multnomah County, Oregon (brochure). Portland: Multnomah County in cooperation with Oregon Historical Society, 1979.

History of the Bench and Bar of Oregon. Portland: Historical Publishing Co., 1910.

Holman, Frederick V. "Oregon Counties: Their Creations and the Origins of Their Names." *Oregon Historical Society Quarterly* (Portland), March 1910.

Inventory of the County Archives of Oregon, No. 26, Multnomah County, Vol. I. "Historical Sketch of Multnomah County," Survey Project No. 65-1-94-25 (Work Projects Administration, 1940).

Inventory of the County Archives of Oregon, No. 26, Multnomah County, Vol. II. Survey Project No. 65-1-94-25 (Work Projects Administration, 1940).

Jaimes, M. Annette. *The State of Native America.* Cambridge, MA: South End Press, 1992.

Kessler, Lauren. *The Stubborn Twig.* Corvallis, OR: Oregon State University Press, 2005.

King, John Gordon. *A History of the Office of Multnomah County Sheriff.* Bachelor's degree thesis, Lewis and Clark College, Portland: 1965.

Labbe, John T. *Fares, Please! Those Portland Trolley Years.* Caldwell, ID: The Caxton Printers, Ltd., 1980.

Lansing, Jewel. *Portland: People, Politics, and Power, 1851-2001.* Corvallis, OR: Oregon State University Press, 2003, 2005.

Leeson, Fred. *Rose City Justice: A Legal History of Portland, Oregon.* Portland: Oregon Historical Society Press, 1998.

Linhares, Tom. *Recent History of Oregon's Property Tax System, with an Emphasis on Its Impact on Multnomah County Residents*. Portland: Multnomah County Tax Supervising and Conservation Commission, 2011.

Linn, David. *A Brief History of Multnomah County Government (1964-2004)*. Portland: Office of the Multnomah County Chair, 2004.

Lockley, Fred. *History of the Columbia River Valley, from The Dalles to the Sea*, Vols. 1, 2, & 3. Chicago: The S. J. Clarke Publishing Co., 1928.

Lucia, Ellis. *The Conscience of a City, Fifty Years of City Club Service in Portland*. Portland: The City Club of Portland, 1966.

Maben, Manly. *Vanport*. Portland: Oregon Historical Society Press, 1987.

MacColl, E. Kimbark. *The Shaping of a City: Business and Politics in Portland, Oregon, 1885 to 1915*. Portland: The Georgian Press, 1976.

———. *The Growth of a City: Power and Politics in Portland, Oregon, 1915 to 1950*. Portland: The Georgian Press, 1979.

MacColl, E. Kimbark, with Harry H. Stein. *Merchants, Money, and Power: The Portland Establishment, 1843-1913*. Portland: The Georgian Press, 1988.

Maddux, Percy. *City of the Willamette: The Story of Portland, Oregon*. Portland: Binfords & Mort, 1952.

McArthur, Lewis A. *Oregon Geographic Names*. Fifth Edition. Portland: Western Imprints, 1982.

McCarthy, Linda. *A History of the Oregon Sheriffs, 1841-1991*. Oregon State Sheriffs' Association, Taylor Publishing Company, 1992.

McKay, Floyd J. *An Editor for Oregon: Charles A. Sprague and the Politics of Change*. Corvallis, OR: Oregon State University Press, 1998.

McLagan, Elizabeth. *A Peculiar Paradise: A History of Blacks in Oregon*. Portland: The Georgian Press, 1980.

Monihan, Ruth Barnes. *Rebel for Rights: Abigail Scott Duniway*. New Haven, CT: Yale University Press, 1983.

Munk, Michael. *The Portland Red Guide: Sites and Stories of Our Radical Past*. Portland: Ooligan Press, 2007.

Myers, Gloria E. *A Municipal Mother: Portland's Lola Greene Baldwin, America's First Policewoman*. Corvallis, OR: Oregon State University Press, 1995.

Nesbit, Sharon, and Tim Hills. *Vintage Edgefield: A History of the Multnomah County Poor Farm and McMenamins Edgefield*. Portland: McMenamins, Inc., 2002.

O'Donnell, Terence and Thomas Vaughan. *Portland: An Informal History and Guide*. Portland: Western Imprints, 1984.

Oregon: End of the Trail. American Guide Series. Federal Writers' Project, Oregon. Work Projects Administration. Portland: Binfords & Mort, 1940.

Oregon Blue Book, 2007-2008. Salem: Oregon Secretary of State, 2007.

The Oregon Judiciary, Part II: Challenges for the 21st Century. Salem: League of Women Voters of Oregon Education Fund, 2007.

The Oregon Law Index: An Index to Oregon Territorial and State Laws up to 1886. Portland: Stevens-Ness Law Publishing Co., 1937.

Peterson del Mar, David. *Oregon's Promise: An Interpretive History*. Corvallis, OR: Oregon State University Press, 2003.

Pintarich, Dick, ed. *Great and Minor Moments in Oregon History*. Portland: New Oregon Publishers, Inc., 2003.

Price, Larry W., ed. *Portland's Changing Landscape*. Portland: Geography Dept., Portland State University and Association of American Geographers, 1987.

Purdy, Ruby Fay. *The Rose City of the World*. Portland: Binfords & Mort, 1947.

Ritz, Richard E. *An Architect Looks at Downtown Portland*. Portland: The Greenhills Press, 1991.

———. *Central Library, Portland's Crown Jewel*. Portland: The Library Foundation, Inc., 2000.

Robbins, William G. *Landscapes of Promise: The Oregon Story, 1800-1940*. Seattle: University of Washington Press, 1997.

Roberts, Barbara. *Up the Capitol Steps: A Woman's March to the Governorship*. Corvallis, OR: Oregon State University Press, 2011.

Roe, JoAnn. *The Columbia River: A Historical Travel Guide*. Golden, CO: Fulcrum Publishing, 1992.

Scott, Harvey W. *History of the Oregon Country*. 6 vols. Compiled by Leslie M. Scott. Cambridge, MA: The Riverside Press, 1924.

———, ed. *History of Portland, Oregon*. Syracuse, NY: D. Mason & Co., 1890.

Snyder, Eugene E. *Early Portland: Stump-Town Triumphant*. Portland: Binfords & Mort, 1970.

———. *Portland Names and Neighborhoods*. Portland: Binford & Mort, 1979.

———. *We Claimed This Land: Portland's Pioneer Settlers*. Portland: Binford & Mort, 1989.

Sponsler, Thomas [Multnomah County legal counsel]. "History of Multnomah County Home Rule Charter." Unpublished article dated Jan. 6, 1998.

Stanford, Phil. *Portland Confidential*. Portland: WestWinds Press, 2004.

———. *The Peyton-Allan Files*. Portland: ptown books, 2010.

Stone, Stephen A. *Oregon Memorabilia: Stories from the Files of an Oregon Newsman*. Eugene, OR: Parkstone Company, 1967.

Turnbull, George S. *Governors of Oregon*. Portland: Binfords & Mort, 1959.

———. *History of Oregon Newspapers*. Portland: Binfords & Mort, 1939.

Uris, Joseph Samuel. *Trouble in River City: An Analysis of an Urban Vice Probe*. PhD thesis for Urban Studies Department, Portland State University, 1981.

Walth, Brent. *Fire at Eden's Gate: Tom McCall and the Oregon Story*. Portland: Oregon Historical Society Press, 1994.

White, Victor H. *The Story of Lige Coalman*. Sandy, OR: St. Paul's Press, 1972.

Wiederhold, Kathleen M. *Exploring Oregon's Historic Courthouses*. Corvallis, OR: Oregon State University Press, 1998.

Wortman, Sharon Wood. *The Portland Bridge Book*. Portland: Oregon Historical Society Press, 2001; Urban Adventure Press, 2006.

Yeates, Marian. *The Story of Gretchen Miller Kafoury*. Salt Lake City: Marian Yeates, Publisher, 1998.

Your Multnomah County Government: A Handbook. Third edition. Portland: Board of Multnomah County Commissioners, 1961.

Your Multnomah County Government: A Handbook. Fourth edition. Portland: Board of Multnomah County Commissioners, 1965.

Your Multnomah County Government: A Handbook. Fifth edition. Portland: Board of Multnomah County Commissioners, 1968.

Zucker, Jeff, Kay Hummel, and Bob Høgfoss. *Oregon Indians: Culture, History, and Current Affairs. An Atlas and Introduction*. Portland: Western Imprints, The Press of the Oregon Historical Society, 1983.

INDEX

Note: Page numbers in italics refer to photographs or illustrations. Most names listed in the appendixes, acknowledgments, bibliography, and end notes are not included herein.

Abbott, Carl, 106
African Americans, 74, 93, 203, 222; current county board member Loretta Smith, *143*; first county commissioner, 157, 198, *199*; first Portland council member; first school board members, 157, 198, 203; first sheriff, 149; migration to East County, 238. *See also* minorities
agriculture: county fair, 122-124; land-use planning, 151-152; Poor Farm, 133-134. *See also* Expo Center; Oregon Agricultural College; Sauvie Island
alcohol and drugs: allegations about usage, 195; treatment beds, 206. *See also* Hooper Detox Center
Allan, Beverly, 111, *112*,113
American Red Cross, 95
Anderson, Lloyd, 106, 127, 129, 132
Anderson, Pauline, 180, 184, 193, *199*, 230
Anderson, Sally, *171*
animal control, 205; shelter, 122, 238-239. *See also* Edgefield Complex
animals: fair exhibits, 123; livestock, 122; whale, 83; wildlife refuge, 234
annexations, 105, 179-180, 193, 209-210, 233
Army Corps of Engineers, 94, 96
assessor, 127, 169, 238

Association of Oregon Counties (AOC), 138, 166-167
Atiyeh, Gov. Vic, 157-168, 173
auditor, 115, 127-128, 189, 194, 202, 206-207, 238, 241
automobiles, use by elected officials, 194, 230, 232
Aylsworth, Larry, 117, 130-132, 134, 143
Bain, Jack, 106, 115-118
Baker, Doug, 123, 158
Baker, Frankie, 121
Baker, George, 72, 73
Balch, Anna, 20
Balch, Danford, 20-22
Baldwin, Bob, 106, 152, *187*
Baldwin, Lola Green, 46
Ball, John, 223
Barney, Helen, 162
Bauman, Rick, 199, 206
Bea, Brian and Jody, 212-213
Beatty, Jack, 129
Belding, A.H., 39
Bennett, Clifford O., 100
Bentley, Paula, 191-192
bicycles, paths for, 143, 146, 175, 64, 236-237
Bigelow, Charles, 85
Bills, Cincinnati, 29
Bird, Nathan, 43
Birnie, George, 127-128
Biskar, Arnold, 180, 184
Blackmer, Gary, 180-181, 206-207, 242
Blumenauer, Earl, 156, 162, 193-194; library focus; 178, 180, 182-184; *185*, 186-188; "Earl-Don rivalry," 165; in later years, 190, 197

Boat Ramp, M. James Gleason Memorial, 148
Bogle, Dick, 200, 203
Bonner, Lynn, *187*
Bonneville Dam, 85-86
Bonneville Power Administration, 86
Bouillard, Kirby, 222
Bowman, Jo Ann, 221-222
Boyer, David, 217-218, 227
Bradley, Charles, 95
bribery: accusations of, Al Brown, 115; Jack Bain, 115; Terry Schrunk, 101
bridges, 229; bidding scandal, 74-78; Burnside, 74-75, 77, 161; first interstate; 64-65; first Sauvie Island, 234; Glenn Jackson, 146; Hawthorne, 26, 161, 219; maintenance of, 180; Marquam, 24; Morrison, 26, 108-109, 161; Mt. Hood Freeway, proposed, 142; Ross Island, 74; Sellwood, 147, 161, 242; St. Johns, *80*, 81-83; second Sauvie Island, 237; Steel, 161
Brom, Robert, 114
Broughton, Lt. William, 9
Brown, Aaron, 203
Brown, Alan, 104
Brown, Albert "Al," 106, 109, 115-116
Brown, Archie, 30-31
Brown, Lee, 149, *150*, 174
Brummell, Clyde, 159
Buchanan, Dennis, 150, 152, *153*, 154, 162-163, 177, 179-180, 184, 188, 190, 192-193, 200, 211, 235-236
Buchtel, Joseph, 32
Buel, Ron, 144
buildings: Hansen, ix; Inverness, 204; Multnomah County Building, *219*; need for maintenance of, 149, 218; Penumbra Kelly, 140; Yeon maintenance shops, 169-170. *See also* jails; Justice Center; libraries; MAX; Multnomah County Courthouse; Wapato Jail
Bunnell, John, 206, 210
Burkette, Irving, 171
Burkhardt, James, 184
Burnett, Peter, 12

Busse, Rich, *187*
Butzen, Debbie, 164
Bybee, James F., 14, 16
Bybee-Howell House, 119
Campbell, Judge J.U., 78
Carlson, Cliff, 198
Carmichael, Don, 152-153
Carson, Joseph Jr., 85
Carter, Margaret, 203
cartoons, 140, 147, 224, 226
Caruthers, John, 16
Casterline, Polly, 197-198, *199*, 204
Cawthorne, Herb, 200, 203
Caywood, James M., 29
Central City Concern, 139, 173
Chamber of Commerce, Gresham, 153; Portland, 140, 154
Chamberlain, George, 37, 40
Chapman, William W., 12
charter. *See* home rule charter
child care center, WWII, 89-90
Chinese Exclusion Act, 29
citizen involvement, 144-145, 154, 176
City Club of Portland, 154, 197-198
civil service, 56, 59, 124
Clackamas County, 13, 135, 145-146, 156-157, 179, 197-198, 204-205, 214-215
Clark County, Washington, 5, 64, 103, 110, 155
Clark, Donald E. "Don," 117, *123*, 124-126, 128-129, 133-135; 137-138, 142-146, *147*, 148-152, *153*, 154-159; 161-163, 165-169, *171*, 172-78, 180, *187*, 192, 200, 204, 210-211, 218, 220; accomplishments, personal list of, 175; as commissioner, 2, 4-7, 134; as county chair, 103, 149; as deputy sheriff, 99, 103; as sheriff, 113, 117, 124; "Earl-Don rivalry," 165; employee strike of 1980, 161-164; in later years, 175-176; petition to recall, 152
Clark, Jon Elwood "Bud," 179
Clarke, Anne Brewster, 184
Cleeton, Thomas J., 54
Coffee, J.B., 57
Cogen, Jeff, 229, 232, *241*, 242, *243*

Coleman, Elsa, 144
Collier, Tanya, 209
Columbia County, 234
Columbia Ridge, City of, creation rejected, 181
Columbia River, 119, 122, 144-145, 148, 179
Columbia River Gorge, 152, 175; Columbia Gorge Commission, 203-204, 212; Friends of Columbia Gorge, 203-204, 212, 215; Highway, vii; 61-62, *63*, 124; National Scenic Act, 203, 212-213. *See also* Crown Point, planning and zoning, View Point Inn
Columbia Valley Authority, proposed, 86
Columbia Villa, 202
Committee of Fifty, 104
Comprehensive Land-Use Plan. *See* planning and zoning
computers, 216; computerized accounting systems, 140-141
Condor, Sunny, 165, 178, *187*
Connall, Des, 113
consolidation: boundary commission authority, 135; city-county proposals for, 55-56, 139, 178, 197-198, 240-241; Clackamas County study, 204-205; failure of voluntary efforts, 140-141, 180; FPD&R as impediment, 215; 1974 charter rejected, 140, 148, 239; other proposals for, 1, 7, 27-28, 38, 78-79, 156; statewide vote, 48; threshold study, 214; voluntary health departments merger, 201. *See also* home rule charter; "Resolution A"
constable, 30, 56, 59, 127
Cook, Vern, 151, 153-154, 209
Cooper, Ginny, 188
Corbett, Alice, 130, 149, 152, *153,* 156, 177, 202
Corbett, Henry, 24
coroner, 16, 24, *57,* 59, 95-96, 238
Couch, John, 12
counties, Oregon: border changes proposed, 47-48; proposal to permit formation of new, 215; proposal to reduce number of, 156-157
county clerk, 115, 127, 189-190
county counsel, 165, 224-225
county court, as forerunner of county commission, 18
county fair: at Gresham, 46, 47, 122, 161; at "PI," 122-123; 4-H and FFA exhibits, 122; in later years, 124, 215
county judge, 14, 18
county logo and seal, 173, *174, 236*
county seat, move to Portland from Hillsboro, 13
Coxey's Army, 34-35; as forerunner to Bonus Army, 36
CRAG (Columbia Region Association of Governments), 134-135; merger with MSD, 157; proposed abolishment of, 157
Crawford, Judge James, 83
Crowell, Evie, 203
Crown Point Vista House, 62
Cruz, Serena, 219, *220,* 222, *223,* 224-227, 230
Cusma, Rena, 138, *187*
Dalton, B.H., 37, 40
Davis, Charles, 186
Davis, Drew, 159
Deaderick, Kelly, 99
Deady, Matthew, 22, 29, 35
Delta Dome Stadium, proposed, 120-121
Dennehy, Tom, 195-196
Department of Environmental Quality, (DEQ) Oregon, 181
Depression, the Great, 82, 146, 151
Derrick, Rodney, *163*
detoxification centers, 126, 139, 175
Diez, Mercedes, 203
disasters, natural: Columbus Day storm, 115; Vanport flood, 94-96
district attorneys, 127, 205, 238. *See also* Schrunk, Michael
district court: clerk of, 127, 169, 189-190; judges, 127, 138; state assumption of trial court costs, 167-168
Doctor, Clyde, *187*

Domestic Partners Registry, 201, 211

Dow, Polly, 124

Doyle, A. E., 182, 216

Dryer, Thomas; "T, J." 13, 19-20, 28

Duin, Steve, 202, 225

Duncan, Bob, 148

Duniway, Abigail Scott, 49

Durbin, Kathy, 155

Eccles, David, 118-120, 122, 128, 130-132, 134

economy: affect of world's fair, 44, 45; Great Depression, 151; shift to high tech from wood products and shipping industries, 215, 238

Edder, Orval, 128

Edgefield: Lodge, 122; Manor (nursing home), closure of, 133-134, 151-153, 158, 174, 207; McMenimum brothers' enterprises, 207. See also Poor Farm; MCCI

Edmundson, S.A., 49

Eisenhower, Dwight, 141

elections: Corrupt Practices Act, 42; demise of voters' booths, 168; nominating convention required, 169; non-partisan, 154, 157; partisan, 190; political parties; 129-130, 157; state-mandated duty, 178; Vote-by-mail 168; "voter-owned" (Portland's public campaign finance experiment), 302n. 46. See also home rule charter; recall threats

Elliott, Jack, 113

Elliott, Marion Leroy "Mike," 97, 98, 103

Ellis, Barnes, 167

emergency phone number, 911 system, 126, 175

employees: benefits, 188, 197-198; felt listened-to under Stein, 211-212; layoffs, 149; low moral of, 242; personnel department established, 173; 7 ½ hour days, 149; strike of 1980, 161-164. See also unions

English, Dorothy, 237

environment: ecoroof, 219; energy-efficient public buildings, 169-170, 219; first county land-use plan, 151;

no-smoking policy, 200; solar roofs, 169-170; state land-use act (LCDC), 151

Environmental Protection Agency (EPA) See Willamette River cleanup

Epting, Margaret, 187

Ervin, Vicki, 169

Essex, Nikki, 113

executions: by hanging, 21, 30-32, 37, 39, 41; by lethal gas, 41; death penalty, 41; moved to Salem, 37-38

Expo Center, 96, 124, 180, 215-216

Failing, Bill, 186, 188

Failing, Henry, 184, 186

fair. See county fair

Fairview, City of, 117, 166, 179, 233

farm. See Poor Farm

Farver, Bill, 220-221

Faust, Jack, 154

federal versus local control, 203-204

Feely, Tom, 187

Feeney, Anne Kelly, 194-195, 199, 206

Ferguson, Eugene, 124

ferries: Sauvie Island, 234; St. Johns, 81; Stark Street, 20-21; Switzler, 16

Fessler, Chuck, 233

Fiedler, George, 87

finances, 162, 164, 180-181, 218, 238, 242; adoption of modern budgeting, 165, 173; debt limitation, 28; financial status, 176; property tax dollars, allocation of; 241; responsibility to furnish courtroom space, 168; state-mandated duties, funding of, 166, 172, 178, 217-218, 242, tracking systems, 140; use of bonding to build infrastructure, 57, 146. See also pension plans, unfunded liabilities of; revenues

First National Bank, 20, 23, 124

Fitzgerald, W.H., 50

Flynn, Suzanne, 220

Foetisch, Kay, 195

folk songs: "Roll on Columbia," 87; "Frankie and Johnny," 121

form of government: commissioner form, 78, 154, 240-241; elected executive versus elected board chair,

154, 239; strong mayor, 128-129, 131-132, 139-140; three branches of government model, 154-155, 239

FPD&R (Fire and Police Disability and Retirement), Portland, negative affects of unfunded liability, 251-253. *See also* property taxes

Frank, George P., 36

Frazier, Charles, 37

Frazier, William, 37

freeways, 141-142, *143*; Columbia River Gorge, 124, 212-213; Harbor Drive, 145; interstate network; I-5, 141, 145; I-80N/I-84, 64, 144; I-205, 2, 142-146; I-405, 145, 158; ODOT (Oregon Department of Transportation), 80, 143; Oregon State Highway Department (OSHD), 142, proposed "Sunset-Stadium" I-505 through NW Portland, 145. *See also* Mt. Hood proposed freeway; MAX; roads

Friends of the Columbia Gorge, 203-204, 212, 215

functions, city versus county. *See* services; "Resolution A"

Galati, George, 201

gambling. *See* vice.

garbage. *See* Metro; MSD

Gardiner, Mark, 178

gay-rights. *See* sexual orientation.

General Land Office section lines, 105

geographical features, vii, 235

German, Fred, 81

Gifford, Frederick L., 74

Giusto, Bernie, 205, 221-222, 230, *231*, 232

Gleason, M. James "Mike;" 5-6, 115-117, *118*, 119-120, 127-138, 143, 146, *147*, 148, 152; background, 103; charges of nepotism; 133, 146; failure to build infrastructure, 5, 105, 147; health, 137; longevity of; 2, 103; support for planning and zoning, 106

Glendoveer Golf Course, 137, 155, 180

Goldschmidt, Neil, 4, 138-139, 144, 146, 176, 204, 222, 230-231

Gordly, Avel, 203

Gordon, Mel, 2, 4-7, 118-120, 127, 130-131, 134, 136-137, 143-144, 150, 152, *153*, 155-157, 177, *187*, 220

Government Simplification Committee, 78-79

Grand Ronde tribes, 11

Grant, Ulysses, S., 42

Gray, Rochelle, 184

Green, Edith, 118-119, 138, 148

Gresham, 106, 117, 120, 140, 145, 151, 153, 155, 158, 214-215, 233; fairgrounds, 122-124, 166, 178-181, 215; Grange, 153; *Gresham Outlook* editor, 191

Grewe, Tim, 217

Griffin, Anna, 243

Griffin-Valade, LaVonne, 240

Guthrie, Woody, 86-87

Hall, Ross, *187*

hangings. *See* executions

Hansen, Gary, 209

Harder, Bruce, 165, *187*

Hardin, George, 37

Harlan, Dale, 198

Hart, D.V., 54, 60

Hatfield, Mark, 124

Hawthorne, Dr. James S., 26

Hays, Jeff, 37

health issues, 135, 238-240; as "provider of last resort," 136, 174, 244; birth control, 194; cancer, 197, 202; community health centers, 174, 201; diseases contacted by Native Americans, 10; fluoridation, 158; health departments, 95, 201; narcolepsy, 152; no-smoking policy, 200; Project Health, 158, 174; teen clinics, 201-202; venereal diseases, 29, 50, 71. *See also* Edgefield Manor; mental health clinics; Multnomah County Hospital; OHSU; Poor Farm

Hicks, Lucius, 203

Higgins, Tom, 173

Hill, Jim, 220

Hill, Samuel, 61

Hillsboro, 13

Holman, Rufus: Columbia Gorge Highway, 61; county commissioner, appointment as, 60; county hospital, 70; defeat as commissioner, 73; dispute with George Baker, 72; early years, 61; Interstate Bridge, 64-65; Poor Farm management, 73; U.S. Senator, 61, 72, 190;

Holzman, James C., 113, 125, 132-133

home rule charter, 5-6, 119, 125, 127, 238-239; City-County Charter Commission, 1, 139; county executive position eliminated, 189; effective date, 129-130; efforts to abolish, 128; form of government, 154; gender-neutral language adopted, 189; hiring of lobbyist prohibited, 168, 190; organization charts, 130, 131; proposed restrictive charter provisions, 128, 153-154, 156; review committee established, 154; single-member versus at-large commission districts, 154; vacancies to be filled by election, 177-178. See also Appendix C; consolidation, city-county; Multnomah County chairs; Multnomah County Commission; term limits

Hood River County, 127

Hooper Detox Center, 139, 175

Hospital, Portland Adventist, 137. See also Multnomah County Hospital

Housing Authority of Portland (HAP), 94, 96, 173

Howell, Jim, 144

human services, 242; department of, 202; responsibility for, 181, 193, 240. See also services; "Resolution A"

Hunt, Charles, 35

Hurlburt, Thomas, 65-66, 68, 72, 83-84

Indian John Island, 10

indigent care, 4, 26, 51, 136, 174; Board of Relief, 56

indigent defense, 166-168

Irvington, 44

Irwin, Lee, 191

ITAX on income, 226-227

Ivancie, Dan, 206-207

Ivancie, Frank, 140, 143, 146, 181, 206

Iwakoshi, Miyo, 90-91

Jackson, Charles S. "Sam," 50

Jackson, Glenn, 146

jails, 116-118, 178-179, 205; alternatives to, 139; city jail, 21, 139; county courthouse basement, 25; courthouse eighth floor, 68, 88; Donald E. Long Juvenile Home, vii; double-bunking, 211; inmate escape attempts, 89, 117, 133, 170-171; Inverness, 204, 206; Kelly Butte, 39, 72, 88; law suit re overcrowding, 188, 210; mismanagement accusations, 231; more humane treatment of prisoners, 121, 172; Multnomah County Corrections Institute (MCCI), vii, 116-118, 122. See also buildings; Justice Center; Rocky Butte Jail; Wapato Jail

Japanese internment, 90-92; Japanese-American Historical Plaza, 92

Jeffrey, Edward J., 30, 31

Jewell, Tim, 163

Johnson, James, 30

Jones, Emma, 69, 71

Jordan, Charles, 200, 203

Jorgensen, Carl, 114

Jorgensen, Edward, 113

Joseph, George, 129, 187

Justice Center, 145, 169-171, 172, 188, 204, 210. See also jails.

Kafoury, Deborah, 241, 243

Kafoury, Gretchen, 156, 179, 193-194, 199, 206, 210

Kaiser Permanente, 90

Kaiser shipyards, 89, 94

Kaiser, Edgar, 89

Katz, Vera, 190; eastside esplanade, 228; Katz-Stein cooperation, 210-211, 214

Kelley, Sharron, 197, 209, 219, 220

Kelly, Penumbra, 33, 34, 35-36

Kessler, Lauren, 92

Kessler, Stephen Michael, 171

Kimberling, Mrs., 15, 17

King, John Gordon, 37, 125

Kirchner, Carol, 204-205
Kramer, Loren "Bud," 137, *138,* 140-141, 147
Kremers, Robert E., 76-77
Kroeker, Mark, 180
Ku Klux Klan, 74, *75*
Kulongoski, Ted, 173, 220, 205
Ladd Carriage House, 24
Ladd, William S., 24
Lambert, Francis, 124
Lambert, William, 100
Lancaster, Samuel, 61-62, 65
land-use, 137, 157-158, 218; ballot measure #37 (2004), 236-237; Measure #49 (2007), 237; compensation claims, 2004 to 2012, 237; county's Comprehensive Land-Use Plan, 151; planning; 116, 135. *See also* planning and zoning
Lane County, 127
Lane, Dr. Harry, 40
Langley, William, 100-101
Lansing, Jewel, viii, 155, *187,* 202, 220
Lappeus, James, 21, 22
Larsson, Clara, 49
Latourell, Joseph, 49
Lauritz, Phyllis, 88
lawn signs, 134, 158-159
Lawrence, Ellis, 70
Lazarus, Edgar, 62
LCDC (Land Conservation and Development Commission) of Oregon, 151
LEAA (Law Enforcement Assistance Administration), 150
League of Women Voters, 154, 197, 252
Leahy, John, *187,* 196
Lee, Ah, 31
Lee, Dorothy McCullough, 45, 96-97, 103, 202
Lent, Berkeley, 167
Lessard, Delmore and Edward, 83
Levy, Richard, 194-195
Lewis and Clark Centennial Exposition, 44, 47
Lewis and Clark Expedition, 9

libraries, 156, 163; Central Library, *182,* 183, 185; Central Library renovation, 216; funding of system, 178-179, 181-183, 185; Gresham branch, 215; Hillsdale branch; 216; internet access by patrons, 216; Library Association of Portland (LAP), 156, 181-188; library district proposed, 185; misuse of endowment funds, 186; public access mandated by bequest, 181; salary dispute, 223; transfer of library employees to county payroll, 188
Lightner, William, 73
Lindenthal, Gustav, 77
Linhares, Tom, 252
Linn, David, 210
Linn, Diane, *220,* 221-222, *223, 224, 226,* 227-230, 241; "Mean Girls," 227
Linnton, 12, 81
Lloyd Center, 112, 146
lobbyist, charter prohibition against hiring, 168, 190
local versus federal control. *See* Columbia River Gorge
Loll, Ernest, (sheriff's deputy) memorial, 87-88
Lonergan, Judge Frank, 100
Long, Sarah, 184, 186
Love, Lewis, 16
MacColl, E. Kimbark "Kim," 34, 36, 74, 78, 97
MacKenzie, Dr. R.A.J., 70
MacKinnon, Andrew, 91
Manning, John, 43, 44
maps and surveys: comparative county sizes, *235;* county commission districts, *3;* earliest proposed roads, *12,* Historic Sites Tour Guide and Map, 173; "immoral places;" *50;* proposed freeways and interstate highways, *143*
Marion County, 13
Markle, George, 33
Marquam, Philip A.; as county judge, 23; bridge named for, 24; Grand Opera House, 23; Nature Park, 24

marriage, same-sex, 224-226, 229
Marshall, Henry, 16
Martin, Ed, 133, 166, 174
Martin, Kenneth and Barbara;
    daughters Barbara, Virginia, Susan,
    110, *111*
Martin, Lowell, 183
Martin, S.B, 55, 59, 73
Maryhill, Washington State, 61
Mason, William, 38
mass transit, 146; proposed corridors,
    144. *See also* freeways; MAX
Matson, Dr. Ralph, 52
Maurer, Judge Jean, 214
MAX (Metropolitan Area Express) light
    rail, 4, 8, 144, 155, 215; Blue Line,
    4; Green Line, 146; Yellow Line,
    215-216, 238. *See also* mass transit
Mayo, Dr. Charles, 70-71
Maywood Park, City of, 140, 142; 166,
    233
McCall, Tom, 114, 136, 176
McCormick, Stephen, 22
McCoy, Bill, 203
McCoy, Gladys, 157-158, 162, 180,
    184-187, 198, *199*, 200-204, 207-
    209, 211, 230
McCoy, Paul, 201
McCready, Connie, 202
McGill, Frances, 183
McKeel, Diane, *241, 243*
McLaughlin, John, 49
McMenamin, Bob and Mike, 207
McMillan, William, 16, 19
McRobert, Gussie, 214-215
"Mean Girls," 227, 243
Measure 5: *See* property taxes.
Meier, Gov. Julius, 83
mental health, 240, 242; clinics,
    privatization of, 174
Merten, Betty, 144, 176
Merten, Charles, 144
Metro regional government, 107, 135,
    137, 157, 175, 180, 197, 240; solid
    waste disposal, 135, 157
Metropolitan Area Local Government
    Boundary Commission, 135, 181

Metropolitan Human Relations
    Commission, 194
Metropolitan Planning Commission
    (MPC), 135
Metropolitan Service District (MSD),
    136, 157
Metropolitan Study Commission
    (MSC), 135
Meves Restaurant, 51
Meyer, Fred, 148
Miggins, Hank, 194-195, 201-202
Miller, Caroline, 159-160, 180, 187,
    193, *199*
minorities: Chinese; Latinas, 222. *See
    also* African American; Chinese
    Exclusion Act; jails; Japanese
    internment; Native American
Minto, John W., 36-37
Montague, Richard, 78-79, 166
Moore, Chester, 94
Moose, Charles, 180
Morrow, James Barkley, 37
Morrow, Judge William, 78
Morse, Clay, 82
Morse, Wayne, 7, 60, 72
Mosee, Dan, 2, 5-7, 130, 132, 134, 143-
    144, 146, 150-152, *153*, 157-158;
    159, 160, 162, 165
Moses, Robert "Master Builder,"
    141-142
Mowry, George, 77
Mt. Hood Freeway, proposed, 2, 4, 6-8,
    143-145, 161, 176-177
Mt. Hood, 145, 173-174; Community
    College, 157, 191, 197; National
    Forest, 205
Mt. St. Helens, 173-74
Multnomah Athletic Club, 74
Multnomah County Bar Association, 48
Multnomah County: boundaries
    of, 235; county seat, 156;
    creation of, 3, 13; logo, 173, *174*;
    mountains, 14; number of elected
    officials; 150th birthday ignored;
    organization charts, 130-131;
    population, 13, 106; seal, 173, 236;
    sesquicentennial observance, lack of,
    228; size of, comparative, *235-236*;

unincorporated areas of, 180. *See also* annexations; bridges; buildings; county fair; Multnomah County Hospital; courthouse; freeways; health issues; home rule charter; Poor Farm; roads

Multnomah County chairs, 127; 238; elected executive experiment, 154-155, 177, 189-190, 192, 200, 239; leadership style, 134, 211, 221-223; most powerful local government official, 132, 228; salary of, 190; title of, 189, 192; title of commission chair, 161

Multnomah County Commission, 238; administrative authority, 132, 156, 239-240; as Board of Relief, 56; dysfunction, 228-229; election of presiding officer, 154; elective executive, 131; first all-woman board, 198-199; liaison roles for commissioners, 134, 228; media coverage, 155, 170-172, 223-224, 227, 229; number of members, 127; organization charts, *130, 131;* power block of three votes, 134. 137; reorganization of county departments, 166, 227; second all-woman board, 219-220; work load of commissioners, 132, 134, 228. *See also* home rule charter; Multnomah county chairs; rivalries

Multnomah County Commission districts, 154; map, *3;* single member versus at-large, 154

Multnomah County Courthouse, 138, 141, 147, 171, 218-219, 242; inadequate space, 25, 38, 218-219; original, *25, 27;* remodeling of; 100; responsibility for providing, 218, 226; second, *67, 68*

Multnomah County Hospital, vii; *52, 53, 58, 69, 71;* merger with University of Oregon Medical School, 136; Multnomah Pavilion wing, *71,* 137

Multnomah Falls, *213*

Multnomah Indian Tribe, 9-10

Multnomah Village, 119

Murase, Robert, 92

murders, 21, 87; Peyton-Allan, 111-115. *See also* executions

Murlin, Bill, 87

Murray, Ron, 236-237

Myers, Clay, 155

Myers, Hardy, 167

Myers, Stanley, 77

NACO (National Association of County Officials), 119

Naito, Bill, 185, 192

Naito, Lisa, *220, 222-223, 224-227,* 230-231, 262

National Register of Historic Places, 62, 207

Native Americans, 9-11, 49, 204, 237-238; Youth and Family Center, 11

Neal, Fred, 167-168, 201

Neuberger, Richard, 156

New York Bureau of Municipal Research (NYBMR), 54-60, 69, 118, 147-148

Newhall, Gerry, *187*

Noelle, Dan, 206, 210, 222, 231

Norden, Ben, 30, 31

Norris, Schulbrick, 16

Northrup, Paul, 109

Nyberg, Clayton, 116

O'Donnell, Jack, 128, 141

O'Shea, Walter, 30

Oaks Amusement Park, 215

Odegaard, Billi, 164

Olcott, Gov. Ben, 74

Oregon: admitted to union, 13; constitution, 18; court reform, 166-168; judicial system, viii; legislature, 136-137, 139, 166, 181; provisional government, 11; state-mandated duties, 178, 217-218, 239; supreme court, 18, 187, 225; territorial legislature, 12, 19; transfer of municipal judges to district court, 138

Oregon Agricultural College, 73

Oregon City, 12

Oregon Commission on the Judicial Branch, 167-168

Oregon Community Foundation (OCF), 187

Oregon gubernatorial candidates, unsuccessful, 173, 220
Oregon Health and Science University (OHSU), 136-137, 173; medical school, 69-70
Oregon Historical Society, 119
Oregon Journal, founding of, 42; 44, 50
Oregon National Guard, 95
Oregon Public Employee Retirement System (PERS), 164, 188, 210, 218; Oregon Public Service Retirement Plan (OPSRP), 253. *See also* pension plans.
Oregonian, first editor, 13, 19-20, 28
organization charts, county, *130, 131*
Otto, Glenn, 151, 153-154, 191, 200
Ough, Grace, 49
Outlaw, Margaret, *163*
Ownbey, Clarence and Ruth, 121-122
Pacific International Livestock Exposition, "PI." *See* Expo Center
Pacific Legal Foundation, 212
Packwood, Bob, 7
Padrow, Ben, 2,4, 6-7, 134, 137, 143, 150
Painter, John Jr., 176
parks, 119, 137; Blue Lake, *107,* 108, 180; Forest, 21, 82, 104-105, 111-112, 237; Gleason Boat Ramp, 148; improvements during Great Depression, 104; Oaks amusement park, 215; Oxbow, 120, 180; Rooster Rock, 107; transfer of county ownerships to Metro, 137, 180; Wood Memorial Natural Area, 103-104. *See also* Glendoveer Golf Course
party politics, Salem Democratic "Clique," 19. *See also* elections
Patterson, Ferd, 22- 23
Pearce, Fred, 162, 169, 180, 188, *189,* 195, 204-205
Pennoyer, Sylvester, 35
pension plans: amortization of county unfunded liabilities, 149; county unfunded liability transfer to PERS, 164-165; law enforcement employees, 164; "pay-as-you-go"

plans, 164-165. *See also* Portland FPD&R
performance auditing, viii, 295n. 19
PERS. *See* Oregon PERS
Perkins, Stephen, 213-214
Peterson, Fred, 98, 100-102
Peyton, Larry, 111-113
Peyton-Allan murders, 111-115
pheasants, ringneck, 119-120
Phegley, Grant, 77
Pierce v. Society of Sisters, 74
Pierce, Gov. Walter, 66, 74
Piper, W. and Burton, Elwood, architects, 25
planning and zoning; 106, 116, 155; code adopted, 106; constitutionality of zoning upheld, 235. *See also* land-use, comprehensive plan; Sauvie Island
polling, first use of to determine voter support, 121
pollution, 119
Pool, Vera, 222
Poor Farm, 117, 121, 133; Baker, Frankie, 121; closure of, 51-52, 134, 151; first location, 26; management by Oregon Agricultural College, 73; name change to Edgefield Acres, 121-122; Troutdale location, 52, 57, 73; use of patients for labor. *See also* agriculture; Edgefield
Pope, W.H., 38
population, growth, 1950-60, 178-179, 233
Portland Building, 219
Portland Club, 43
Portland Heights, 44
Portland International Airport, 146, 148
Portland International Raceway, 96
Portland Rose Festival, 47, 82, 96
"Portland-Multnomah" proposed entity, 140
Portland State University (PSU), 93, 129, 138, 146, 149, 166, 178
Portland *Telegram,* 43, 44
Portland Traction Co., 94
Portland, City of: adopts commission form of government, 154-155,

239; as county seat, 13; "city-type" services versus "county-type" services, provision of, 177-181; council actions, 143-144, 176; council rejects county library levy, 185; council rejects county jail levy, 217; electorate rejects "strong mayor" form of government, 128, 139-140; first women elected officials, 202; freeway votes by council, 142; new city hall, 38; police, 140, 171, 178-179; population, 178-179; Urban Services Policy, 179; women elected officials. *See also* annexations; boundaries; Portland FPD&R; "Resolution A;" urban renewal districts

Portland-Multnomah Progress Board, 210-211

Potella, "Kansas," 40

Powell Boulevard, 142; Valley Road, 17

Powell, David, 16

Pratt, Ard, *90, 110*

Pratt, Birdie, 89, *90*

Pratt, Martin, 63, 84, 88-89, *90*, 93-97, 99

private versus public property rights, 212-213, 236-238

property taxes: collection of, 125, 178; compression effect of Measure #5, 242, 251-252; double majority requirement, 218; early levy, 17; effect of Portland's FPD&R, unfunded liability of, 251-252; foreclosures, 104; inequitable appraisal of property values, 55-56, 251; ITAX, 226-227; library levies, 183; local governments' shares of, 208, 217; Oregon statewide limitation measures, #5, 17, 68, 193, 208, 215, 217, 241-243; #47, 214, 217-218; #50, 208-209, 214, 217-218; urban renewal districts, effect of, 242, 252-253; urban subsidy, 166, 178. *See also* zone-of-benefit tax, proposed.

Prophet, Matthew, 201

public power, utility districts, 86

Public Safety 2000 study, 209-210

Purcell, Bard, 137

purchasing function, 140

qualifications for elective offices: professional certification for auditor, 260; fitness tests for sheriff, 232

Radakovich, Bill, 169

Rakowitz, John, 223, 226, 229

Rankin, John H., 73-74, 76-78

Raphael, Molly, 223

recall threats, against: Bigelow, Charles, 85; Clark, Don, 152; Linn, Diane, 226; "Mean Girls," 230; Shadburne, Gordon, 195-196

recalls, successful: Elliott, Mike, 101; Rankin, J. H., 77; Rudeen, Charles, 77; Walker, Dow, 77

religion as a political issue, 191, 194-195

"Resolution A.," 165, 177-181, 193, 201, 208-210, 240-241,244, 240. *See also* services; consolidation, proposals for

revenues: federal revenue sharing, loss of, 149; one-time "OTO," 65. *Also see* finances; LEAA

Rexford, sheriff's deputy Peter, 63, *64*

Riley, Earl, 94, 96

rivalries: between east and west Multnomah County, 153, 193, 214-215; "Diane-Lisa/Serena/Maria," 223-230; "Earl-Don;" 165-166; "Mike-Mel," 118-119

roads, 58, 236; highway center stripe experiment, 63; Portland and Tualatin Plains Plank Road, 17; post World War II development, 105; siting of, 15; transfer of reserves to Portland, 180; transfer of roads to Portland, 180; U.S. Highway #30, 83, 145, 234. *See also* freeways.

Roberts, Barbara, 155-156, 158

Roberts, Lonnie, 222, *223, 224*

Rocks, Don, 165, 173, *187*

Rocky Butte Jail, 68, 88, 89, 116-117, 133, 145, 169-172, 188.

Rogers, Kristine Olson, 204

Rojo de Steffey, Maria, 222, *223, 224*-227, 230

Roosevelt, Eleanor, 89
Roosevelt, Franklin, 86
Roosevelt, Theodore, 42
Rossman, Gene, 99
Rowlands, Jack, 114
Rudeen, Charles, 73, 76, 77
Russell, Nancy, 203-204
S.S. Multnomah, 90
Sakamoto, Henry, 92
salaries: comparison of county to city,
    156, 202; of library director, 223; of
    library staff, 188
Salzman, Dan, 156, 209
Sandy River, 10, 15, 110, 120
Sauvé, Laurent, 9
Sauvie Island, 9, 10, 14, 119, 152, 175,
    234-237; Bybee-Howell House,
    119; first known as Wapato Island,
    14. *See also* agriculture; bridges;
    planning and zoning
Schell, Steve, 144
Schools Uniting Neighborhoods (SUN),
    229
Schrunk, Michael, 114, 190, 195, 230
Schrunk, Terry, 98-100, *101*, 102, 118,
    124, 138
Schwab, Mildred, 202
Schwager-Wood Company, 116
Scott, Harvey, 17, 43
Scott, John Emsley, 14, 16
Sears, George, 36- 37
secession, threats of, 48; by east
    Multnomah County officials,
    214-215
services: allocation of "city-type"
    services versus "county-type"
    services, provision of, 177-179;
    differences between city and
    county, 202-203, 240; proposed
    co-location of functions, 140. *See
    also* "Resolution A;" special services
    districts.
sewers, 219, 204, 219, 242; financing of
    east county network, 181; mandated
    by state DEQ, 181
sexual orientation, 192, 195; anti-
    discrimination board policy, 193-194

Shadburne, Gordon, 157-158, 162, 180,
    190-191, *192*, 193-199. *See also*
    sexual orientation.
Shelby, Eugene, 34
sheriff, 238; administration of office,
    125; aero squadron, 93; elected
    versus appointed, 125, 127-128, 174-
    175, 190, 232; funding of, 205-206;
    motorcycle unit, 64; river patrol,
    210. *See also* sheriff's deputies
sheriff's deputies: college degree
    requirements, 125, 132-133; 180,
    233; crowd control, 225; history of,
    125; in unincorporated Multnomah
    County, 209, 233; law enforcement
    function, loss of, 209, 233; team
    policing, 150, 233; transfers to
    Portland and Gresham Police
    departments, 180, 209
Shields, "Barney," 132
Shields, Frances A., 235
Shiprack, Judy, *241, 243*
Shull, Frank, 84-85, 96, 104, 109, 220
Signal Fireworks & Specialty Co., 109
Simione, Angelo, 214
Skamania County, Washington, 203,
    212
Skipper, Robert "Bob," 111, *205*, 206,
    209-210, 232
Smith, Amadee, 73
Smith, Annie, 40-41
Smith, George, 39, 41
Smith, Laura Hattrup, *187*
Smith, Loretta, *243*
Smith, U.G., 73
snow days, controversial closure policy,
    224
social services, 178, 217, 238. *See also*
    "Resolution A"
Socialist Labor Party, 51
Son, Earl, 113
Sowle, Agnes, 225, *241*
special service districts, county, 128,
    178, 255; Fire District #10, 179, 193
sports: Blue Heron Golf Course;
    Edgefield Golf Course, 207; Forty-
    Mile Loop Trail, 175; Glendoveer
    Golf Course, 137; proposed Delta

Dome Stadium, 120-121; Portland Meadows Racetrack, 122, 215; Multnomah Stadium, 121

Springer, Dick, 229

St. Johns, 12, 47, 81-82, 145

Stanford, Phil, 99, 113, 114

Staples, G.W., 22

Starr, Addison, 19-20, *21*, 22-23

Staton, Dan, 232

Stein, Beverly, 208-212, 214, 217-219, *220*, 221; Katz-Stein cooperation, 210-211; Oregon Quality Award, 211; second all-woman board, 219, 230

Steinman, David B., 81-82

Stevens, Robert, 45-46, 49-50

Stimmel, Tom, 183

Stitzel, Joseph, 29

Stone, H.S., 23

STOP (Sensible Options for People), 144

Storey, William, 39, 40, 42

Stott, James, 43

Stump, Mortimer, 21

Sulzberger, Arthur Gregg, 228

surveyor, 127, 238

Sutton, Albert, and Whitney, Harrison, architects, 70

Svendrup & Parcel, 109

Swan Island Child Care Cener, 89

Taft, Erwin, 77

Tax Supervising and Conservation Commission (TSCC), 252

Taxpayers League of Portland, 53, 55

television shows: *American Detective* and *C.O.P.S.*, 206

Telfer, Steve, 162, 180

term limits: imposition of, 168, 175, 239; rejected statewide, 240. *See also* home rule charter

Terry, Stan, 129

Thompson, Geoff, 213-214

Tibbetts, Cecil, 161-164

Timberline Lodge, 86, 145

Trader, Felicia, 164

transportation, 238; planning, 145. *See also* freeways.

treasurer, 59, 104, 127, 238

Tri-Met, regional transportation body, 157, 197. *See also* MAX

Troutdale, City of, 35, 49, 57, 106, 116-117, 119, 121, 151, 166, 191, 200; historical society, 207. *See also* Edgefield

Truman, Harry, 95

Tuality County, 12

Turner, Wallace, 98, 100

Turney, James, 171

Unis, Judge Richard, *150*

U.S. Coast Guard, 95

U.S. Supreme Court, 91

U'Ren, William S., 42

unincorporated area, Multnomah County, 178, 233; lack of amenities, 238

unions, 132, 140, 144, 148, 153-154, 159, 173, 229; Industrial Workers of the World (IWW), 36, 50-51; law enforcement personnel, 164-165; Local 88 AFSCME (American Federal, State, County, and Municipal Employees) strike of 1980, 161-162, *163*, 164, 173, 176; nurses, 161-162; restaurant "eat-in," 51; teamsters, 100. *See also* employees; pensions

urban renewal districts, effect of, 238, 242, 252-253

urban subsidy, 166, 178. *See also* property taxes

urban-rural divide, vii, 48, 214-215, 243. *See also* rivalries.

Van Winkle, Isaac, 76

Vancouver, Capt. George, 9

Vancouver, Washington, 22, 49, 64, 83, 89

Vanport: as WWII housing project, 89; devastating flood, 94, *95*, 96, 120; Extension Center, 93; unincorporated status, 89;

Vaughn, George W., 14, 22

vice: brothels, owners of, 50; gambling, 42-44, 49, 66, 96-101; kick-backs, 76; prostitution, 44, 50

View Point Inn, 213-214

Vollmer, August, 96
Voorhies, Peter, 183-184, 186-188
Wade, John, 37, 40
Wagner, Richard, 109-110
Walker, Dow V., 73-74, 76-78
Walstrom, Ralph, 235
Wapato Island, 9, 10, 14
Wapato Jail, vii, 216, *217*, 218, 220-
    222, 229, 242-244; maintenance
    cost, 226
Ward, C. Bruce, 184
Warren, Dave, 217
wars: nuclear war fears, 98; World War
    I, 36, 71; World War II, 84, 87-93;
    Vietnam, 115
Washington County, 116, 127-128, 133,
    135, 156-157, 197, 215; Hillsboro as
    county seat, 13; Portland as part of,
    13; zoning disputes, 116
Washington State Supreme Court, 212
water systems,135, 178-179, 181, 205,
    219, 238
Weatherby, George W., 119
Webster, Lionel, 39
weddings, catered, proposed sites:
    Sauvie Island, 237; View Point Inn,
    214
Weil, Margaret, 179
Welsh, N.B., 107
West Linn, 12
West, Denny, 165
West, Oswald, 49, 75
West, Tom, 96, 104
Westlund, Ben, 232
Weston, Ferdinand, 87
whale, baby, *83*
Wheeler, Jacob, 16-17
Wheeler, Ted, 228-229, 232, *241*, 242;
    accomplishments of, 243
Whidden, William, and Lewis, Ion,
    architects, 66, 100
White, Burton, 161
Wilcox, Jim, 169, *187*
wildlife refuge, 195, 234
"Willamette County," proposed,
    156-157

Willamette River, 119, 141-142, 145,
    219, 234, 236; cleanup of hazardous
    waste, 242. *See also* bridges; ferries
Willamette Stone, 14
Willamette Week, founding of, 149
Williams, George H., 42-43
Williamson, Julie, 154
Wilson, John, 181
Wilson, Lyndon Jr."Tuck," 172
Wohler, Jeff, 152
women's issues: early women's rights
    advocate, 193; first all-woman
    county board, 198-199, 202, 230;
    first female county board staff
    member, 138; first female sheriff's
    deputy, 124; first woman Portland
    City Club president, 193; first
    women county elected officials,
    202; first Portland elected women
    officials, 202; second all-woman
    board, 219-220, 230; suffrage, 58-59
Wood Village, 106, 140, 166, 233
Wood, C.E.S., 60
Wood, Daniel, 169, 189-190
Wood, Tatum, Mosser, Brook and
    Holden, law firm, 188
Woods Memorial Natural Area,
    103-104
Woods, Hosea, 103
Word, Tom, 43, *45,* 46, 49-51, 65-66
Works Progress Administration (WPA),
    86, 88
Wyeth, Nathaniel, 10
Yarborough, Paul, 201
Yasui, Min, 91
Yeon Maintenance Shops, vii, 145
Yeon, John B., 62
Zimmer, Gunsul, and Frasca, architects,
    171-172
zone-of-benefit property tax, proposed,
    166, 178
zoning, 151. *See also* planning and
    zoning; land-use.
zoo, 10, 52. 157